Money
Unequal World

Keith Hart and His
Memory Bank

Keith Hart

TEXERE

New York • London

Published by

TEXERE
55 East 52nd Street
New York, NY 10055

Tel: 212.317.5106
Fax: 212.317.5178
www.etexere.com

In the UK:

TEXERE Publishing Limited
71-77 Leadenhall Street
London EC3A 3DE

Tel: 44 20 7204 3644
Fax: 44 20 7208 6701
www.etexere.co.uk

This book was originally published in the UK in 2000 by Profile Books, Ltd.

Library of Congress Cataloging-in-Publication Data has been applied for.

ISBN 1-58799-097-0

Printed in the United States of America.

This book is printed on acid-free paper.

10   9   8   7   6   5   4   3   2   1

This book is dedicated to the memory
of
Janice Hart
and
Skip Rappaport

CONTENTS

LIST OF TABLES AND FIGURES

ALVIN

The sun was already high when I drove my new Japanese car round the last bend onto the straight stretch before the junction. It looked as if a pile of rags had been left in the road. Rather than run over them, I stopped. It was a very thin man, a beggar with tangled dreadlocks, apparently asleep. I got out and tried to rouse him. It wasn't easy.

"Hey! Get to the side of the road. You'll be run over here."

"It's warmer in the middle than the side."

(In desperation) "What's your name?"

A beautiful smile lit up his face. "Alvin. No one has asked me my name for twenty years."

"OK, Alvin. How about moving to the side?"

He moved.

"Have you had anything to eat today?"

"No."

"Here, take this and get some patties down at Liguanea."

I gave him a small banknote, which he put straight in his mouth. He began to eat it pensively. I ran to the car and drove away as fast as I could.

As Dr. Johnson says: "Smile with the wise, eat with the rich."

Jamaica
1987

INTRODUCTION

Chapter 1
Money in the Making of Humanity

Ours is an age of money. Half the world worships money and the other half thinks of it as the root of all evil. In either case, money makes the world go round. If human society has any unity at this time, it is as a world "market." There is nothing wrong with people exchanging goods and services as equals. The problem is that markets use money: Some people have lots of it, and most people have much less than enough. The unequal face of the age of money is capitalism; and the principal source of that inequality has been a machine revolution whose uneven development is only two centuries old. The combination of money and machines is the engine pushing humanity from the village to the city as our normal habitat. But, although we generally think of ourselves as a modern people, our institutions still look backwards to the previous phase of agrarian civilization. The economic forms we live by are themselves archaic. Indeed, capitalism could be said to be a sort of feudal economy matched to a machine revolution whose potential we barely understand. The lethal result is a polarized world society that resembles nothing so much as the old regime of eighteenth-century France, with an isolated elite controlling the destiny of powerless human masses to whose fate they are largely indifferent.

Something must be done or life on this planet will soon be ruined. This book's main premise is that the latest stage of the machine revolution could support a more democratic economic agenda. The convergence of telephones, television and computers in a global communications network, which we know as the Internet, is very much a phenomenon of the 1990s. As yet, a minute proportion of humanity participates fully in it, although half the world occasionally watches major sporting events on television. This communications revolution is both the means of improved social connection on a planetary scale and the main source of escalating economic inequality at all levels of world society. The dominant institutions of the twentieth century, that alliance of government bureaucracy and big business that I call "state capitalism," also dominate the Internet. Those who are "wired" are still a Western, largely American minority. Yet, just as Marx and Engels found in a few Manchester factories in the 1840s both the seeds of a new world economy and its revolutionary antithesis, this book explores how the potential of the Internet might serve the interests of economic democracy.

Money is the problem, but it is also the solution. We have to find ways of organizing markets as equal exchange and that means detaching the forms of money from the capitalist institutions that currently define them. I believe that, instead of taking money to be something scarce beyond our control, we could begin to make it ourselves as a means of accounting for those exchanges whose outcomes we wish to calculate. Money would then become multiple sources of personal credit, building on the technology that has already given us plastic cards. The key to repersonalization of the economy is cheap information. Money was previously impersonal because objects exchanged at distance needed to be detached from the parties involved. Now, growing amounts of information can be attached to transactions involving people anywhere in the world. This provides the opportunity for us to make circuits of exchange employing money forms that reflect our individuality, so that money may be more meaningful to each of us as a means of participating in the multiple associations we choose to enter. All of this stands in stark contrast to state-made money in the twentieth century, where citizens belonged to one national economy whose currency was monopolized by a political class claiming the authority of representation to manage its volume, price and allocation.

This book started off life as *The Memory Bank*.[1] Memory banks are, of course, found in computers, but banks are, for most people, places to store money. Money today takes the principal form of electronic digits travelling at the speed of light over telephone wires. Capitalism itself has gone virtual, being concerned with exchanging money for money in forms increasingly separated from the concerns of real production and trade. The line between the exchange of objects by means of money (markets) and the exchange of meanings through words and signs (language) is becoming blurred. Money is becoming information and information money. This provides us with an opportunity to reassess the positive relationship of money to culture and civilization. For "the memory bank" is money itself. I argue that money's chief function is as a means of remembering. Indeed the origins of the institution in Europe drew a firm association between money and collective memory. And today money remains one of the main infrastructures of communication and shared memory, with its power now amplified by the widespread use of machines.

I have drawn on my own memory banks in writing this book, since the book was written from memory, a memory formed by my lifelong preoccupation with money and all the connections it makes. *Money in an UnequalWorl* is itself a memory bank, both for its author and hopefully for his readers too. And in this age of communication revolution, the print version takes on a more dynamic form of memory bank as a Web site (see www. thememorybank.co.uk). In this and many other ways, the worlds of money and language converge.

My aim throughout this book is to present the case for thinking of the present age of money as a possible prelude to the formation of a world society fit for humanity as a whole, one in which the administration of justice for all could be a realistic goal, and money and markets would become the instruments of economic democracy that they are falsely represented to be today. We need to face the machine revolution and harness its potential to the purposes of our common well-being, instead of leaving its benefits to be monopolized, as hitherto, by businessmen, bureaucrats and politicians. If we are to take steps in this direction, we must begin to see how the institutions we live by are made by us, the people in general, and can be remade by us. This is my true objective. I wish to articulate a vision of human agency in history that enables my readers rather than disabling them, as much of modern education and culture does. The formation of world society as a single interactive network is a means toward this end; for only when each of us can make a meaningful connection between our individual purposes and the collective predicament of humanity will we have any hope of addressing the problems with which the age of money confronts us.

On money, machines and the market

We experience society these days in two principal forms: states and markets. The former are clearly less inclusive than the latter. The world market

expresses our new sense of constituting a single social network and its principles of organization (or disorganization) are those of networks.[2] As such,
markets subvert the pretension of territorial states to be the exclusive, centralized referent of their citizens' idea of society. In any case that claim once
depended on the dominance of national markets in economic life, a condition that is being rapidly eroded. It follows that our civilization conceives of
itself as an economy rather than as a means of political association. The step
I want to take here is to conceive of social order as an economy serving the
interests of all humanity, as the human economy. And that economy will operate with money at its heart, since buying and selling are indispensable to
complex social life.

The word "economy," as used by Greek writers such as Xenophon and
Aristotle, originally meant household management, budgeting for domestic
self-sufficiency.[3] As late as the early nineteenth century Jane Austen could use
the word "economist" for a woman who knew how to handle the servants.[4] In
the course of the nineteenth century, however, a new science, "political economy," arose to address the organizing principles of a public sphere dominated
by markets of infinite scope.[5] Largely through the synthesizing efforts of
Adam Smith, the new idea took hold that markets were a vehicle for the expression of rational order; and modern economics was born. Later still, in
our century, it was recognized that states had the power to organize their national economies (Keynes's "macro-economics"). And now we face the necessity of constructing economic order at the global level. The force bringing us
to this point has been state capitalism, the system of money-making in which
nation-states preside over the social hierarchy; but I will argue that its grip is
weakening, not least as a consequence of the communications revolution.[6]

The original condition of life on this planet was to produce and reproduce alone. The discovery of sex and society vastly increased the scale and
complexity of both operations, making interdependence a necessity, especially for ours, the most social of species. The development of humanity thus
consists significantly in devising ways of working for and with others. When
production and consumption are separated, mechanisms must be found to
restore the linkage between them. Exchange in its various forms is the most
prominent of these, but it is by no means the only one. Money and markets
allow for a widening of the social range of exchange relations, so that people

can produce for ultimate consumers with whom they have no personal ties. The world market of our day is just the latest stage of a process that is pulling the whole of humanity into an increasingly integrated economy. This world market is young. Leaving aside the small quantities of booty plundered by Europeans in the centuries after they first discovered the rest of humanity, it began in earnest under a century and a half ago, when a transport revolution (railways, steamships and the telegraph) gave a decisive boost to the integration of global trade.[7] Since then we have ventured into space to see the earth from the outside. And lately the communications revolution of the 1990s is bringing us even closer together in practical terms.

The means of engaging in complex, long-distance transactions, however, has been impersonal coins and latterly banknotes—detachable means of payment carrying no information about the persons involved—so that the price of economic integration has seemed to be the alienation and objectification of human work. And this has been confirmed by our experience of state capitalism in this century, an alliance of centralized bureaucracy, financial interests and scientific experts, all of them dedicated to the hegemony of impersonal processes in social life. Seen in this light, the communications revolution looks like yet another stage in the progressive abstraction of labor through commodity exchange, with goods and services now being registered as nothing more than numbers on a computer screen. The modern world economy is thus to a growing extent virtual. It would not be surprising if most of us concluded that these developments are more about removing people from the economic picture than about restoring them to an active place in it. Yet the latter is precisely the claim I am making.

It is true that impersonal abstraction is indispensable to economic integration and that our world is becoming more abstract, not less. We depend on the use of quantification to make social calculations of money, time and energy, for example; and few of us would rather be ruled by powerful personalities than by impersonal law justly administered. The idea that the communications revolution contains some potentially redeeming features rests on one overwhelming fact: That large amounts of information concerning the persons involved in economic transactions at any distance can now be processed cheaply, thereby making possible the repersonalization of complex economic life. I cannot imagine a future civilization in which calculation of the value of many transactions would not be a central part of everyday life. Rather than be overwhelmed by money as an external object of unknown provenance, however, people may come to express themselves subjectively through it. Money would then be seen not as the preserve of either states or anonymous markets, but as the ongoing invention of people seeking to measure the consequences of some of their interactions.

A secondary, but in some ways more immediately strategic point is that electronic commerce undermines territorial monopoly—the land—as a basis for coercive economic extraction (tax and rent). This means that the Internet may be finally what the democratic revolution of the seventeenth and eighteenth centuries was waiting for before it was diverted into the reactionary project of nation-building. The Internet offers for the first time a technical means of expressing the possibilities for communication, democracy and humanity that have always been present in markets and money. After a century and a half when machine production favored centralization, the trend may now be in the opposite direction, with the widespread diffusion of miniaturized technologies such as mobile phones, digital TV and personal computers. The transfer of cheap information concerning particular individuals is becoming a routine feature of exchange. If overcoming distance was the chief function of impersonal money, people can now participate in markets of infinite complexity and size as carriers of digitalized personal identities. This has already begun with the development of plastic money, electronic payment systems and customized markets. Virtual shopping is in its infancy, but the profiles of individual consumers can be accommodated, even at this early stage, in more sophisticated ways than was ever envisaged in the days when we picked uniform products off a shelf.

If one general aim of humanity is to make society, as opposed to just having to take it as it comes, part of the failure of twentieth-century experiments in democracy is that they have often concentrated on political rights while leaving the economic system as unfair as ever. Democratizing access to money is indispensable to progress. Although developments involving the Internet are as yet in their infancy, some promising tendencies are discernible. I have already mentioned the rapid rise of digitalized personal credit since the introduction of plastic cards a few decades ago. The emergence of new forms of electronic money, interest-free savings and loan schemes, closed circuits of labor exchange and the like point in the same direction. The communications revolution makes customized marketing, personal banking and other manifestations of individual consumer power more feasible. Active participation in capital markets by individuals and groups seeking to protect their own pensions and life insurance is facilitated by the new system.[8] It seems likely that, before long, we will look on money as one of many instruments invented by people to record some features of their interactions and associations.

"Economy" has as its twin term "ecology," the science of living at home, the systematic study of habitats. The evolution described briefly above, in bringing humanity to confront the problem of order at its most inclusive level, requires us to take life as a whole on this planet as the ultimate frame of reference for human civilization. My aim here, however, is to consider the leap involved when the idea of economy, having moved via markets from being at home in the house to being at home in the state, might now move via markets to being at home in the world. There are those who would consider money and markets themselves to be inimical to human survival. I do not. But I recognize that, in order to be persuasive, I must begin to separate the two faces of money, capitalism and markets, the institutions that express the unequal reality and the potential equality of money. In this way perhaps we will discover some of the principles of social order and disorder underlying human attempts to make money more amenable to their will.

Not long ago I attended a meeting of old Trotskyites. It was principally a celebration of an author who was in his nineties. The atmosphere was warm and mutually supportive. At the end, a man stood up and said, "Comrades, tea is now available. Unfortunately, because we live in a capitalist society, we will have to charge you thirty pence a cup." I almost wept, for the confusion between markets and capitalism is as deeply rooted on the left as it is in right-wing ideology. Markets require money, and people with lots of money exercise disproportionate power in them. Capitalism may be said to be that variant of market economy in which the owners of big money control, for example, the right of most people to work for a living. But when a few friends make a service available to those who choose it and seek to recover their costs by charging a price below the public norm, that is not capitalism. The rejection of market civilization that led to some fairly disastrous experiments in state socialism was based on this confusion.

Accordingly, I have built the argument around a fundamental distinction between "making money with money," the sparsest definition of capitalism, and "buying and selling with money," the timeless formula for the market. The first half of the book (Chapters 2–4) examines that conjuncture of money and machines that makes our phase of economic history capitalist. The second half (Chapters 5–7) is devoted to an exploration of money and markets from a humanist point of view. The sequence of chapters is as follows: the machine revolution; money in the institutional form first of capitalism (two chapters) and then of the market; the history of money considered as itself; and finally the relationship between all of these in our common future.

Although I have emphasized common human interests at the expense of the usual social divisions, one thread of the book's argument concerns the political economy of the Internet. The increased mobility of people, goods, money and information is having a cumulative impact on landed systems of association, states in other words. The "wired" (or, as the French prefer, the "internauts") are in the vanguard of a broad movement to escape state control. This movement, which amounts to a tax revolt, already includes the extremely wealthy, criminal mafias and nomads of all kinds. There is no guarantee that the weakening of state structures will do anything to promote greater economic democracy; indeed, evidence to date points at least as strongly in the other direction. Even so, fractions of the middle class have been a powerful force for general social reform in the past; and the new experience of global community afforded by the Internet might just be the stimulus needed to launch a campaign in the honorable tradition of international struggles against slavery, colonialism and other institutions of entrenched inequality. But this book is only indirectly a call to use the resources of the Internet for collective mobilization; it is mainly an exploration of the potential for more of us to feel at home in the world economy.

At home in the world

The method[9] of this book is anthropology, but of a rather different kind from what is vaguely known by the term these days. Immanuel Kant coined the expression in its modern sense when he published a set of lectures he had given regularly on anthropology for thirty years.[10] Kant lived in the Baltic port of

Königsberg (now Kaliningrad) over two centuries ago. At a time when large states were becoming dominant, he speculated on the possibility of a world society whose principle he called "cosmopolitan." The Portuguese sailors he met in the docks made society in the open seas, on the edges of states and between the laws of states. He wondered what might be the basis for people all over the world to live peacefully together without coercion; and he found the answers in human nature, perhaps in universal practices of early education. But he also drew on the best comparative evidence of his day, accounts of the indigenous social arrangements found in North America and the South Pacific. Kant believed that human co-operation required us to rely on personal judgement moderated by common sense, the latter coming from shared social experience and taste (good food and good talk, good company).

Toward the end of his life, he wrote the essay "Idea for a Universal History with Cosmopolitan Intent" (1784),[11] which included the following propositions:

1. In man (as the only rational creature on earth) those natural faculties that aim at the use of reason shall be fully developed in the species, not in the individual.

2. The means that nature employs to accomplish the development of all faculties is the antagonism of men in society, since this antagonism becomes, in the end, the cause of a lawful order of this society.

3. The latest problem for mankind, the solution of which nature forces us to seek, is the achievement of a civil society that is capable of administering law universally.

4. This problem is both the most difficult and the last to be solved by mankind.

5. A philosophical attempt to write a universal world history according to a plan of nature that aims at perfect civic association of mankind must be considered to be possible and even capable of furthering nature's purpose.

The world is much more socially integrated today than two centuries ago, and its economy is palpably unjust. We have barely survived three world wars (two hot, one cold), and brutality provokes fear everywhere. Moreover, the natural (we would say "ecological") consequences of human actions are likely to be severely disruptive, if left unchecked. Histories of the universe we inhabit do seem to be indispensable to the construction of institutions capable of administering justice worldwide. When Roy Rappaport wrote recently that "Humanity . . . is that part of the world through which the world as a whole can think about itself,"[12] he was repeating the central idea of Kant's prescient essay. The task of building a global civil society for the twenty-first century is an urgent one, and anthropological visions must play their part in that.

The last two hundred years of mechanization have brought about a deterioration in the global vision of the Western middle class's intellectual representatives. The nineteenth century put the spirit of democratic revolution firmly behind and addressed a world brought into being by imperialism, an imperialism powered by machines. The question Victorians asked was how they were able to conquer the planet with so little resistance. They concluded that their culture was superior, being based on reason rather than on superstition, and that this superiority was owed to nature, to the biology of racial difference. The object of Victorian anthropology was thus to explain the origin of the racial hierarchy they found in the world; and its method was evolutionary history.[13] The assumption of human psychic unity supported the notion that "they" could eventually become like "us," once they submitted to an appropriate form of government and education by us.

The prevailing ideology of anthropologists since the First World War has been one of cultural relativism, the notion that every place has a right to its own customs, however barbaric. This reflects a dominant worldview that has the whole of humanity pigeon-holed as separate tribes, each the owner (or would-be owner) of a hybrid entity, the *nation-state.* Nationalism was an escape from modern history, from the realities of urban commercial life, into the timeless rural past of the *Volk,* the people conceived of as a homogeneous peasantry, living in villages near to nature, unspoiled by social division, the very archetype of a community bound together by kinship. Before we began to think of ourselves as nations, Western intellectuals compared their societies with the city-states of the ancient world. Now they fabricated myths of their own illiterate ethnic origins in primeval forests.[14] The Polish adventurer Malinowski[15] reinvented romantic nationalism in the form of vivid narratives about the everyday life of South Sea islanders whose autonomous, "primitive" culture mirrored the self-image of contemporary nationalities. If the nation-state is a living contradiction, the anthropology of our century has done its best to convince Western readers that society everywhere, even the most "primitive" and microscopic, is constructed along similar lines.

The peoples who were forcefully incorporated into world society by Western imperialism in the nineteenth century have not been outside modern history during the twentieth; they have been making it. If we are looking for continuing evidence of the cosmopolitan tradition in anthropology, we would be better off with the intellectuals of the anti-colonial movement; and none of these was greater than Mohandas K. Gandhi. Gandhi's critique of the modern state was devastating.[16] He believed that it disabled its citizens, subjecting mind and body to the control of professional experts when the purpose of a civilization should be to enhance its members' sense of their own self-reliance. He proposed instead an anthropology based on two universal postulates: That every human being is a unique personality; and as such participates with the rest of humanity in an encompassing whole (the individual and the species of Kant's essay). Between these extremes lie proliferating associations of great variety. As an Indian who had absorbed much that the West had to teach, Gandhi settled on the village and therefore on agricultural society as the most appropriate social vehicle for human development.

This backward-looking solution to the problem of the modern world makes Gandhi a typical twentieth-century figure. But the problem he confronted has been largely ignored by social theorists. It is this. If the world of society and nature is devoid of meaning, being governed by remote impersonal forces known only to specially trained experts, that leaves each of us feeling small, isolated and vulnerable. Yet modern cultures tell us that we are personalities with significance. How do we bridge the gap between a vast, unknowable world, which we experience as an external object, and a puny self endowed with the subjective capacity to act alone or with others? The answer is to scale down the world, to scale up the self, or a combination of both, so that a meaningful relationship might be established between the two. Gandhi chose the village as the site of India's renaissance because it was where most Indians lived, but more importantly because it had a social scale appropriate to self-respecting members of an agrarian civilization. Moreover, he devoted a large part of his philosophy to building up the personal resources of individuals. Our task is to bring this project up to date.

We now have virtual means of constructing subject–object relations on more favorable terms. The popularity of novels and films is based on this relationship between actual and possible worlds: They bring history down in scale to a familiar frame, the paperback or the screen, and they allow their audiences to enter into that history subjectively on any inflated terms that their imagination permits. Once men and women prayed to God with a similar effect. What human beings need is to feel *at home in the world*. The sources of our alienation are too commonplace to be repeated here, even if they will have to come under closer scrutiny later. What interests me is resistance to alienation, whether this takes the form of religion, spectator sports, outdoor recreation, craft production or domesticity. Home has been described as a "haven in a heartless world,"[17] where the self is stabilized by an environment we have chosen and reshaped. But what does it take for us to feel at home out there, in the restless turbulence of the modern world?

The communications revolution may be understood in part as a response to this universal human problem. We feel at home in intimate, face-to-face relations, but we must engage in remote, often impersonal exchanges at distance. Improvements in telecommunications have this evolutionary imperative, that they cannot stop until we replicate at distance the experience of face-to-face interaction. For the drive to overcome alienation is even more powerful than alienation itself. We will not settle for being objects manipulated by remote control. Humanity is a quality, a collective noun and a historical project. We have just reached the point when we have established universal communications; now we must make world society in our own best self-image, the image of our humanity. It is hard to grasp how far we have come and how quickly.[18]

Anthropology, Kant's brainchild, represents the aspiration to place knowledge of humanity as a whole on a rigorous footing. As such it is part of the effort to co-ordinate human intelligence at a species level for common ends. It occupies the space vacated by religion after the latter was driven from the governance of society by science.[19] Perhaps it prepares the ground for another religion, but it is not itself religion. This book is a contribution to anthropology. In it I seek to make a bridge between a realistic awareness of the world we live in and our hope for a better future. That is why I have entitled this chapter "Money in the making of humanity."

Reading this memory bank

A "bank" is a place where things of value, usually money, are stored for safe-keeping, to be withdrawn for use when needed.[20] A memory bank is a store from which past experiences may be recalled. In computing this refers to files containing stored information such as operational software and more transient data. For present purposes, "the memory bank" is money, but it is also this book itself, which was written from memory and is intended to function as a memory bank for readers. Money provides a useful starting point and central focus for gaining some perspective on our moment in history. C.L.R. James once wrote, "Time would pass, old empires would fall and new ones take their place . . . before I discovered that it is not the quality of goods and utility that matter, but movement; not where you are or what you have, but where you have come from, where you are going and the rate at which you are getting there."[21] This idea of life as a trajectory, at once individual and collective, would be impossible without memory; and its sources lie equally in shared traditions and our own unique experiences. Even as we swim in the river of life, we need to draw on the more stable sources of memory accumulating slowly at its edges. There are good reasons for approaching money as a memory bank in this sense.

To begin with, the word "money" itself comes from the Roman mint at the temple of Juno Moneta.[22] Moneta is the Latin equivalent of Mnemosyne, the Greek goddess of memory and mother of the Muses, custodians of the principal arts and sciences. The verb *moneo* means to remind and, like Muse (as in museum, music, etc.), is derived from the root *men-*, mind.[23] Thus, for the Romans and implicitly for all those European cultures that take their word for coinage from them, money was at first a store of collective memory linked to the reproduction of the arts as living tradition. The religious origin of banking is attested by the fact that people once put their wealth in temples for safekeeping.

The idea of money as a source of social memory was also crucial for John Locke, who figures prominently in our story as the philosopher who inaugurated the modern age of democratic revolutions. Locke was obsessed with money's role both in establishing a progressive social order and in subverting it as its criminal antithesis. Indeed, he believed that money launched humanity from the state of nature onto the road to civil government. As long as men's possessions were limited to perishable products, the scope for property was restricted. Money, by offering a durable store of value convertible against all useful things, unleashed the potential for property accumulation and for the intergenerational transmission of inequality. For Locke, then, money was indispensable to that development of cultural memory on which civilization depends.

In our own day, we have seen money transformed from metallic objects to paper notes and now to electronic digits. These "bits" travel at the speed of light via satellite and cable, to be captured in the memory banks of computers whose operations know no territorial frontiers. In the recent film *Entrapment*, Sean Connery plays an ageing master burglar who claims not to enjoy robbing banks any more. The money "stuff" has all gone, he says: There used to be gold and deposit boxes full of jewelry to steal, now there are only computers and digitalized information.[24] Money in this form is little more than traces of memory, and the banks that keep it are mechanized minds.

If, for some centuries now, society has been dominated by the owners of money, "capitalists," today the form of that domination has moved on to what I call *virtual capitalism*. This is a phase of "making money with money" in which the money circuit is increasingly detached from real production and even from trade in anything but itself. The principal markets are for information services rather than for objects; and long-distance exchange is mainly of money for money in a bewildering variety of derivative forms. Although this phase of capitalism has been building for over twenty years, the emergence of the Internet as a vehicle for commerce makes it very much a phenomenon of the 1990s. The rapid convergence of financial markets and the communications revolution provides the most compelling reason for locating money in the memory banks of computers at this time.

In the later chapters of this book I suggest that money will eventually take as many forms as the plurality of associations we enter. I take this to be a likely consequence of the reduced power of states to control the economic activities of their citizens (not least as a result of Internet commerce). To an increasing degree we will be able to *make* money for our personal and shared purposes. In the context of more democratic access to money, it will become clearer that its main function is to help us keep track of those exchanges with others that we choose to calculate. We will make money in many different ways as a means of *remembering*.

Seen in this light, money and language are the chief cultural infrastructures that allow us to communicate. And rediscovery of this ancient truth comes precisely when humanity has formed world society as a single interactive network for the first time. The memory bank to whose formation this book points, through its discourse on money, machines and the market, is thus the human conversation that might inform the construction of a better global society. This conversation is already many millennia old and has sources everywhere that people have been. Each of us lives off that accumulation and contributes to it in our own way. I have written the book self-consciously with that relationship in mind; and I end this introductory chapter with some reflections on how I imagine readers might enter into the spirit as well as the content of my arguments. For "the memory bank" of the title refers also to the exchange of meanings (communication) made possible by writing and reading the book.

The first version of this book was a textbook, *Anthropology and the Modern Economy*.[25] Its scope was limited to what student readers could follow up in readily accessible publications. Many of these texts were classic and would have appeared in any similar book, but others were more idiosyncratic. Their selection was based on their place in my memory. Every chapter was written initially from memory, as if it were an improvised lecture (my preferred style of teaching). Only later did I return to the texts to check whether I had got them right. In the process of checking, I added new items that seemed apt even though they were not initially part of my stock repertoire. This too is how memory works, a continuous process of loss and addition built around the elements that last.[26]

I decided not to publish the textbook, mainly because I felt myself to be excluded by its impersonality. It failed to express those parts of my knowledge that are not to be found in books, since I could hardly represent my own informal experience as the common tradition. Yet I relied on personal anecdotes to enliven my lectures and make them accessible to audiences at various levels. In these, by improvising a line of general argument mixed with stories taken from life, I hoped to bring together analytical reason and narrative through the continuous rhythms of oral performance. Apart from demonstrating to audiences that ideas and life need not be opposed, I discovered that improvisation gave me access to previously unconscious patterns of memory. I often learned something new from spontaneous connections made while telling a story already familiar to me in outline. The textbook form blocked off most of that possibility; and I turned to other ways of bringing my experience as a teacher to the task of writing a book. For a time I worked on a fictional dialogue with an African woman student; but then I found this form too contrived, as well as being limited to an academic setting.

About two years ago I hit upon the idea of writing a general book about money, drawing on all my experience, both professional and otherwise. There were numerous precedents for choosing such a theme. When I was offered the chance to give a public lecture to my peers in British social anthropology, I had chosen the topic of money.[27] My own lifelong interest in money had taken many forms inside and outside the academy, such as gambling, business enterprise, ethnographic research and a general obsession with prices and quantification. Money provided a common thread linking me to the Manchester of my roots, to its history as the first industrial economy and beyond.[28] This time the book took shape from my memory as a whole. I was anxious to show the intellectual sources of my thinking, since they occupy so much of my adult life; but I devised a method of writing that crossed the boundaries of scholarship into the personal experiences that have shaped my own responses to that tradition. The result documents an unfinished journey that I hope my readers will be able to share in their own way.

As modern people, we tend to live from day to day in a world of private busy-ness, preoccupied with our own immediate concerns: getting out of bed, having a cup of coffee, cleaning our teeth, catching a bus to work, making some phone calls, meeting a friend for lunch, getting in a report to deadline, withdrawing cash from the bank, shopping at the supermarket, trying to relax with a drink, watching the TV news, going to bed again. We rarely take time to ask what makes this daily routine possible. If we do, the images we sustain of society are usually quite restricted, formed by ideas about what we are not, as much as by what we share with others. In this century we have taken refuge in the myopic notion that the world is divided into tribes each owning or aspiring to own a nation-state, a source of security to its inmates and a means of excluding all the rest. Within these states, society is often conceived of in terms of class divisions based on wealth, occupation, race or gender. The intellectuals have tended to mirror such a worldview, offering visions of society that are themselves stuck in the rut of what is familiar.

For all the above reasons, the style of what follows will probably seem odd or even presumptuous to many readers. I believe that humanity stands on the threshold of a new era in which there will be a pressing need to develop, conceptually and in practice, an awareness of the common problems facing world society as a whole. In a sense, to be explored below, such a society already exists; but we have scarcely begun to contemplate how to establish and maintain the social, technological and cultural infrastructures we will need to survive the twenty-first century. Obviously, the divisions of kind and interest that now constitute our world present many obstacles to such a project. No one book could claim to overcome them. But it is still possible to make a start. I have, therefore, chosen to write as if the world were already one and humanity an inclusive "we." I offer a vision of world history, an anthropology, in which readers may or may not be able to place their own personal trajectories. Above all, I have put myself inside the processes of which I write, not outside them; and I offer readers anecdotal evidence of the person who chooses to write in this way, rather than hide behind a mask of objectivity.

This strategy inevitably may seem to cloak my particular experience with the pretension of universality. The habit of doing this is more common than we may think, but not usually in a book written by a modern intellectual. I have been reinforced in my ambition from two sources. One is the philosophers of the democratic revolution (especially Locke, Rousseau, Kant, Marx and Gandhi), who sought to express themselves in language addressing humanity as a whole and largely succeeded. The other is my mentor, C.L.R. James, a West Indian revolutionary and writer, who managed to make his audiences feel that they lived inside the movement of history he described in his speeches and who had the courage to write about "the world we live in."[29] There is something magical about the way human beings reach agreement, especially since, in my view, we all carry around in our heads a private language based on experiences that are unique to us as individuals.[30] Communication depends on our suspending incomprehension and disbelief long enough to sustain the illusion that we know what someone else means when they say something. But, of course, we can never know the full context of historical associations (i.e., memory) that lie behind each person's use of specific words.

The twentieth century's greatest economist, Maynard Keynes, was unusually open to the artistic and subjective dimensions of economics (he married a Russian ballerina). He said, more than once, that a writer depends heavily on the sympathy of his readers, on their willingness to collaborate in the act of communication involved. Reading (or listening) is as creative a process as writing (or speaking). All communication is two-sided, an exchange of meanings in which the "we" formed by the interaction is constructed out of the irreducible separateness of "you" and "me." If I seem to presume too much, it is because my rhetoric is designed to overcome a very pessimistic view of what human beings can actually share at this time. We really are primitives, locked in our private worlds, dipping our toes gingerly in the ocean of human possibility. The most we can hope for is to co-operate as equals in this limited context. Given that I have written the book with this in mind, I do not expect readers to follow my line of thought slavishly (the textbook model). For reading is also a spontaneous outcome of the interplay between the objective contents of the text and the subjective interests and experience of the reader. My aim is to stimulate further inquiry, and I expect readers to react differently and selectively both to my text and to those I have referred to. Do not be surprised if my interpretations are not yours; and cherish the moments when we appear to agree.

Marcel Mauss is acknowledged to be the most brilliant writer in the field of economic anthropology (almost entirely for his celebrated essay *The Gift*).[31] He used to lecture in Paris's Institute of Ethnology during the 1930s to audiences drawn from that city's intellectuals in general. The lectures were well received, but people could not agree on what they were about. Three members of the surrealist movement, among them Georges Bataille, decided to conduct an experiment by separately writing down their versions of his lectures. Sure enough, they turned out to be entirely different. When consulted on the matter, the great man said that it was no part of his intention to impose his own thoughts on the audience, but rather to allow each listener to discover their own. Abstract ideas must be made personally relevant in order to live. Our education system discourages awareness of this fact, with its hose-and-bucket approach to the acquisition of knowledge. Any single act of reading or listening takes its meaning from the accumulated memory of the recipient. The experience of revelation, whenever it occurs, is invariably a process of self-discovery, when a passage of a book or lecture triggers off conscious recognition of something we half understood already. We are conditioned to attribute this process to the author or lecturer; but the relationship of this sense of enlightenment to the immediate experience is often at best contingent. The intellectuals would like us to believe that ideas govern life and that the rest of humanity consequently should take our lead from them; but it is the other way round, on both counts.

Like most other books, this one has a linear organization. There is a definite logic to the order in which I have chosen to place each section and chapter. This sense of forward movement is intrinsic to the writing of each chapter, and it favors a conventional reading style (from the beginning to the end). I do not recommend, however, that the book be approached initially in this way. Have a look at the table of contents, the index, the concluding paragraphs of a section. Dip into the argument at random, allowing your eye to rest where it finds fertile ground (and to move on if it does not). Later you will return to particular bits of the argument for more prolonged reflection. If you find yourself sticking on a specific page, pass on and return to it later or give it a miss altogether. This too is how the mind works when you are sitting through a lecture or watching television, fastening on items here and there, trying to keep up with the thread or not, as the mood takes you. And the great advantage of a book is that you don't have to sit through a unique performance while it happens. Being in control yourself was not invented with the VCR; books got there first.

Finally, we come to the really difficult bit. Who are you, my readers? I have assumed that the frame of reference here is universal, taking in a global comparative perspective. Yet both my biography and my subject have their roots in the history of the English-speaking peoples; and my profession, anthropology, has been dominated in the twentieth century by the three major Western imperial powers—America, Britain and France. While I have tried to reflect the diversity of my own global experience in what I have written, there is no denying where I have come from, nor that most of humanity will be excluded from reading the book, for reasons of education, class, language or whatever. This tension between universal generalization and particular cultural background is intrinsic to the anthropological project. It is self-evident to me that the Western capitalism of our day is not the endpoint of human evolution that its apologists sometimes claim;[32] and that the voices of the non-Western masses must still be heard on their own terms. But, equally, the most general processes always start out somewhere in particular, and the leaders in the machine age that is transforming humanity's relationship to the planet have been Britain, America and a few other Western societies.

This is something of a minefield, and I urge readers to defer judgement concerning my own relationship to the contradictions involved until they have read more of the book. I hope to diffuse the charge of ethnocentric bias, first by admitting it and second by asking readers to approach the text as individuals before leaping to grand classifications as an explanation for our personal differences. This too is a reason for including myself in this story: We can reach out for the universal together, but each of us comes from somewhere in particular and we must never lose sight of that. My hope for human society is that this principle will come to be more widely accepted than at present.

Finally, I do not claim that this book is a work of scholarship. Its scope is too broad for that. But I have tried to enable readers to trace my most specific citations and, where relevant, the direct sources for some of my more general remarks. These references to published texts are contained in numbered notes at the end of each chapter. I have added in the same place a short guide to further reading in essay form. The Index of Names at the end of the text may also be used to follow up literary sources. A few endnotes offer points of interest that I felt would clutter up the flow of the main text. In general, however, I have tried to capture the style of my lectures, improvisations that draw on my working memory. Many of the statements I make can no longer be traced to an objective source. They are just stuck in my memory, and I can only hope that they are not wrong. I could have spent an extra year or so establishing the veracity of my account in minute detail and leaving behind a compendious system of notes. But that would be to make the book more like a late-twentieth-century academic text than I would like. I have relied, more than anything, on the classical canon of modern social thought, and it occurred to me that most authors whose books have lasting value were not so concerned with extensive annotation of their arguments. That may not be an adequate defense, but it calms my anxieties a little.

Guide to further reading

I am a classicist. I like to read the writers whose books made a big difference. I have picked up a personal intellectual genealogy over the years, but not in the order of their historical occurrence or with any fixed ranking of their importance to me. When I started out as an anthropologist, I was attracted to the French founders of the modern discipline, Emile Durkheim and Marcel Mauss. Then, as a research student, I leaned heavily on Max Weber, whose *General Economic History* is his single most accessible text.[33] Soon afterwards, I underwent a Marxist conversion and for many years I depended most on Karl Marx and his followers; but it took me many years to get a handle on *Capital*.[34] Then I discovered how much Marx, Weber and Durkheim all owed to Hegel and particularly to his *The Philosophy of Right* (1821).[35] With the help of C.L.R. James's *Notes on Dialectics* (1948) and Shlomo Avineri's *Hegel's Theory of the Modern State*,[36] I began to see how dialectic might be applied to an understanding of modern history and Hegel's central place in that history better recognized.

My next revelation was the cosmopolitan political philosophy of the late Kant and especially his anthropology. I also began to grasp his way of knowing. At the same time I drew inspiration from Jean-Jacques Rousseau's amazing output in the mid-eighteenth century, especially his *Discourse on the Origins and Foundations of Inequality among Men* (1754), which I take to be, with Kant's lectures, the source of modern anthropology, and *Emile: or, On Education* (1762), which is simply the most subversive book ever written.[37] By now it became clear that I was heading for Locke, and, true enough, I found him in the course of writing this book, particularly the *Two Treatises of Government;* but with the immense assistance of George Caffentzis's *Clipped Coins, Abused Words and Civil Government: John Locke's Philosophy of Money.*[38]

Apart from Locke and Marx, who between them set the intellectual agenda for a constructive debate on the principles of modern economy, I have drawn extensively on the examples of two later writers on money, Georg Simmel and Maynard Keynes.[39] The latter, in particular, has been a constant source of inspiration. Otherwise, I get my economics mainly from the eighteenth-century Scottish political economists, with a slight preference for the Jacobite Sir James Steuart over the better-known Adam Smith.[40] Roy Rappaport's great *Ritual and Religion in the Making of Humanity,* published posthumously in 1999, showed me that anthropologists can transcend our twentieth-century limitations. If all of this is taken exclusively from the Western tradition, I have also been much influenced by several writers from the twentieth-century colonial world, notably Mohandas K. Gandhi[41] and C.L.R. James.[42] This, then, is my all-time greats batting line-up. There is no telling which of these might be a trigger to your own greater self-knowledge, as they all have been to mine.

The book shows its origins in academic life. Readers would not guess from the references that I do actually read and learn from works of literature. To some extent, this is because I have written the text from memory and my functioning memory has been formed by thirty years in the classroom. I never learned to quote poetry or literary aphorisms. Which is a pity. But if this book persuades a few people that the classical heritage of social theory may be accessible to them, I will be content with that.

Notes

1. Keith Hart, *The Memory Bank: Money in an Unequal World* (London, Profile Books, 2000).
2. M. Castells, *The Information Age: Economy, Society and Culture,* especially *Volume 1: The Rise of the Network Society* (3 vols, Blackwell, Oxford, 1996).
3. *Oikos* meant house and the root *nem-* referred to imposing order.
4. J. Austen, *Mansfield Park* (Oxford University Press, Oxford, 1975; first pub. 1814).
5. The term *political economy* was introduced from the French by the Jacobite exile Sir James Steuart. His mercantilist *Principles of Political Oeconomy* (1767) was soon superseded by Adam Smith's work *The Wealth of Nations,* which was published in 1776, but it is in many ways more relevant for us today.

6. This has two sides: The technology of information-processing and transfer, and the social relations people enter by this means. It is because I wish to address both sides that I prefer the term "communications revolution" to "information revolution."

7. W.A. Lewis, *The Evolution of the International Economic Order* (Princeton University Press, Princeton, 1978).

8. R. Blackburn, "Grey Capitalism," *New Left Review* (forthcoming).

9. The word *method* comes from the Greek *meta-hodos,* meaning before or after the road; preparation for a journey, the end of a journey.

10. I. Kant, *Anthropology from a Pragmatic Point of View* (Southern Illinois Press, Carbondale, 1978).

11. I. Kant, "Idea for a Universal History with Cosmopolitan Intent" in C. Friedrich, ed., *The Philosophy of Kant* (The Modern Library, New York, 1993; first pub. 1784).

12. R. Rappaport, *Ritual and Religion in the Making of Humanity* (Cambridge University Press, Cambridge, 1999), p. 461.

13. G. Stocking, *Victorian Anthropology* (Free Press, New York, 1987).

14. M. Thom, *Republics, Nations and Tribes* (Verso, London, 1995).

15. B. Malinowski, *Argonauts of the Western Pacific: An Account of Native Enterprise and Adventure in the Archipelagos of Melanesian New Guinea* (Dutton, New York, 1961; first pub. 1922). Bronislaw Malinowski, founder of the modern school of British social anthropology and author of prototypical ethnographies, especially *Argonauts of the Western Pacific* (1922).

16. B. Parekh, *Gandhi's Political Philosophy: A Critical Examination* (University of Notre Dame Press, Indiana, 1989).

17. C. Lasch, *Haven in a Heartless World: The Family Besieged* (Norton, New York, 1995).

18. In 1998 nearly half of the world's population watched a football match on television, the same number of people as existed on earth in 1960 (3 bn). Think about it. I could say more about the potential of games to overcome the contradiction between self and society; but the point has been made sufficiently at this stage.

19. E. Durkheim, The *Elementary Forms of the Religious Life* (Free Press, Glencoe, Ill., 1965; first pub. 1912); K. Hart, foreword to R. Rappaport, *Ritual and Religion in the Making of Humanity* (see note 12).

20. *American Heritage Dictionary* (third edition, 1993). The *American Heritage Dictionary* lists three separate words under "bank": 1. A piled up mass, as of snow or clouds, a collection of things lying one on top of the other; also the slope of land at the edge of water 2. A business establishment in which money is kept 3. A set of similar things arranged in a row, such as keys on a keyboard and oarsmen in a galley. It lists the first as Middle

English of Scandinavian origin, the second as coming from Late Latin *banca,* a bench, in particular a moneychanger's table, and the third from a Germanic variant of the same. Between them these meanings suggest a slow natural accumulation and an imposed cultural order, both sources of security like a memory bank, a place to stand on the edge of the river of time. But the place we stand on is itself moving.

21. C.L.R. James, *Beyond a Boundary* (Hutchinson, London, 1963), p. 116.

22. C. Lewis and C. Short, *A Latin Dictionary* (Oxford University Press, London, 1933).

23. Ibid.

24. K. Marx, *Grundrisse* (Vintage Books, New York, 1973; first pub. 1857–8), p. 98. As Marx once put it, in order to demonstrate the priority of production over distribution, "A stock-jobbing nation cannot be pillaged in the same manner as a nation of cow-herds."

25. Commissioned by Polity Press, for whose confidence in the project I am grateful. Unfortunately I lost confidence in the project.

26. S. Rushdie, *Imaginary Homelands: Essays and Criticism 1981–1991* (Penguin, Harmondsworth, 1992).

26. K. Hart, "Heads or Tails? Two Sides of the Coin," *Man,* December 1986. My 1986 Malinowski lecture at the London School of Economics was "Heads or Tails? Two Sides of the Coin."

28. D. Haslam, *Manchester England* (Fourth Estate, London, 1999).

29. C.L.R. James, *Mariners, Renegades and Castaways: The Story of Herman Melville and the World We Live In* (Allison & Busby, London, 1984; first pub. 1953); *American Civilization* (A. Grimshaw and K. Hart, eds, Blackwell, Oxford, 1993). I was fortunate to work with James for a couple of years before he died in 1989. See C.L.R. James, *American Civilization,* edited by A. Grimshaw and K. Hart (1993).

30. I share this opinion with John Locke, who, along with Jean-Jacques Rousseau, held that language developed in human evolution before society proper. Almost all subsequent modern thinkers have held the opposite view, namely that language is inseparable from our experience of society. It is as a necessary corrective to this that I entertain the notion of each of us as the bearer of a unique set of meanings in our heads (our personal memory) drawn from a bewildering variety of sources that can never be assumed to be shared with others. Communication under these circumstances is an act of faith that we should cherish precisely for its fragility.

31. M. Mauss, *The Gift: The Form and Reason for Exchange in Archaic Societies* (Routledge & Kegan Paul, London, 1990; first pub. as *Essai sur le Don,* 1925).

32. F. Fukuyama, *The End of History and the Last Man* (Penguin, Harmondsworth, 1992). This book is the most notorious example of this.

33. M. Weber, *General Economic History* (Transaction Books, New Brunswick, NJ, 1981; first pub. 1922).

34. K. Marx, *Capital: A Critique of Political Economy* (3 vols., Lawrence & Wishart, London, 1970; first pub. 1867).

35. G.W.F. Hegel, *The Philosophy of Right* (Oxford University Press, Oxford, 1967; first pub. 1821).

36. C.L.R. James, *Notes on Dialectics: Hegel, Marx, Lenin* (Allison & Busby, London, 1980; first pub. 1948); S. Avineri, *Hegel's Theory of the Modern State* (Cambridge University Press, Cambridge, 1972).

37. No wonder that the Archbishop of Paris issued a *fatwah* against its author that unleashed the hit squads all over Europe, or that Rousseau was burned in effigy in Amsterdam, Geneva and Paris for writing *Emile* (note, not *The Social Contract* but a work on education that attacked the very premises of the Church's ascendancy). Receipt of *Emile* in the mail made Kant miss his famous midday walk—people set their clocks by him. He later wrote what may qualify as the most extravagant blurb ever (I paraphrase): "Two events stand out in the history of the struggle for human freedom: the French revolution and the publication of J.-J. Rousseau's *Emile*." J.-J. Rousseau, *A Discourse on Inequality (Discourse on the Origins and Foundations of Inequality among Men)* (Penguin, Harmondsworth, 1984; first pub. 1754); *Emile: or, On Education* (Basic Books, New York, 1979; first pub. 1762).

38. John Locke, *Two Treatises of Government* (Cambridge University Press, Cambridge, 1960; first pub. 1690); G. Caffentzis, *Clipped Coins, Abused Words and Civil Government: John Locke's Philosophy of Money* (Autonomedia, New York, 1989).

39. G. Simmel, *The Philosophy of Money* (Routledge & Kegan Paul, London, 1978; first pub. as *Die Philosophie des Geldes*, 1900); J.M. Keynes, *A Treatise on Money* (2 vols., Macmillan, London, 1930).

40. Sir J. Steuart, *Principles of Political Oeconomy* (2 vols, Miller & Cadell, London, 1767); Adam Smith, *An Inquiry into the Nature and Causes of the Wealth of Nations* (Methuen, London, 1961; first pub. 1776).

41. See note 16; M.K. Gandhi, *An Autobiography: or, My Experiments with Truth* (Penguin, Harmondsworth, 1982; first pub. 1927).

42. A. Grimshaw, ed., *The C.L.R. James Reader* (Blackwell, Oxford, 1992); C.L.R. James, *The Black Jacobins: Toussaint L'Ouverture and the San Domingo Revolution* (Secker & Warburg, London, 1938); see also notes 29, 36.

PART I:
MONEY AND MACHINES

Chapter 2
The Machine Revolution Today

The next three chapters attempt to articulate a vision of history. This is not history in the sense of that academic science where a suitable distance is maintained between the present and some part of the past conceived of as a dead object. For me history is the story of the movement of society and that means locating the present as a moment in transition between the past and the future. Since we are condemned always to write history from the perspective of a rolling present, we must make a virtue of starting concretely with the here and now, however far we subsequently travel within humanity's trajectory. By looking back to the past, we anchor any forward-looking vision of future possibility in self-conscious knowledge of what has already happened. It is of course easier to know what has gone than what is happening; and it is impossible to know what is to come. That is why those who prefer the certainty of being to the uncertainty of becoming live in the past.

If our time in history is unique, as it must be, that uniqueness lies principally in our reliance on machines for the means of everyday life. Regions vary greatly in this respect; indeed, that is one of the principal sources of inequality in our world. But by any reckoning the last two centuries of world history stand out from the rest by virtue of a machine revolution that throws the whole future of life on this planet into the balance. I approach this revolution from two angles. The first is to ask how its current phase, which I take to be characterized by the birth of the Internet in the 1990s, can be understood in relation to previous phases of mechanization. This inevitably means treating the history of modern technology as if it were separate from other social processes. Moreover, my aim in general is to uncover the potential of these changes for helping us to improve the human condition. This does not make me a gung-ho promoter of information technology as an unmitigated boon. I am as aware as anyone of the massive power discrepancies in this situation and of the processes of social exclusion involved. But I still want to ask what is special about the communications revolution and how it might be harnessed to the ends of economic democracy, if only by a few pioneers who are currently outnumbered by the forces of the dark side. And so I make this chapter my starting point for the book's substantive argument.

The second angle, however, is the main one of this section. It is that the machine revolution is itself an outcome of economic development, specifically of the age of money, or rather of that system of making money with money that we know as capitalism. In the course of the next three chapters I will outline how I think capitalism relates to the rest of world history and especially how it has evolved in the period of mechanization. It is one benefit of our situation that we can look back at two major distinctive phases of the conjuncture of money and machines that preceded this one. In general, however, I resist that modernist outlook that suggests that some sections of humanity at least have made a decisive break with the past as a result of capitalist mechanization. We are to a significant degree the creatures of five thousand years of agrarian civilization, and we must not forget that half of humanity still work with their hands in the fields. The burden of this section, which culminates in an analysis of the political economy of the Internet, is that we remain primitives who have recently stumbled into a machine revolution we don't know what to do with. This is why world society is stagnant and corrupt, allowing the obscenity of widespread poverty to co-exist with an elite lifestyle unimaginable two hundred years ago. This is why life on earth is threatened as never before. If the twenty-first century is governed by the same principles as the last century, there will not be a twenty-second.

I have said that I have extended the limits of this inquiry beyond my scholarly competence. This is particularly true of the present chapter. I have been engaged in economic anthropology for thirty years, but my exposure to the communications revolution dates back only to 1993–94, when the Internet went public and the world wide web was born. So, to the acknowledged difficulty of writing about an unfinished present, I add a lack of intellectual preparation for, or professional engagement with, the subject of machine technology. This may well be irritating to those who are more expert in such matters and confusing to those who are not. The paradox of this book is that I have chosen to privilege in my argument an aspect of modern history with which I am less familiar than others. But that too is a message I want to convey to my readers: We are in the early stages of the revolution linking machines and money to the formation of an increasingly unified world economy.

On an analogy with the invention of agriculture ten thousand years ago, we are like the first digging-stick operators in the process that culminated in Chinese civilization. We have little more chance than they did of anticipating what the results of current changes will eventually be. But we must try to work toward a better future somehow; and contemporary specialist knowledge may not be wholly adequate to the task.

A civilization built on machines

The half century since the Second World War has seen astonishing developments in technology. To begin with, we are the first generation to have seen the earth from outside. The impact of space travel on the human imagination is immeasurable. Then too for forty years the Cold War threatened to destroy us all with nuclear weapons. Television has unified the globe as never before, with audiences of up to half the population watching events like the Olympic Games men's 100 meters final. Transport has been revolutionized by the airplane and the automobile. Chemicals, plant genetics and synthetic substitutes have transformed the food chain. Human health and reproduction have been altered irrevocably by mechanization and molecular biology. And, of course, the convergence of television, telephones and computers in the 1990s, the communications revolution, strikes to the core of modern existence. All of this comes with an unknowable environmental, social and personal cost. It is unsurprising that what Edmund Leach called "a runaway world"[1] leaves many people wondering whether the consequences of this explosion of machine production are bearable.

The machine revolution has its origins in improvements made to the steam engine in the eighteenth century; but the period 1800 to 2000 may plausibly be described as "the age of mechanization." Although the penetration of machines into our lives has been a continuous process throughout this period, it is possible to identify three main phases, corresponding to steam power, electrical power and digitalization, respectively.[2] Each of these has been expressed in a distinctive organizational form: the factory, the office and the Internet. These phases in turn have been linked to growth in the power of the owners of money (capitalism) and to significant changes in the social forms of that power. At the same time the prime location of the economy has moved from the house via the city and the nation-state to the

33

world. It is therefore possible to identify schematically three sets of broad social changes associated with the development of machine production.

There is obviously considerable overlap between the stages; but it is evident that we are living in the transition from the dominant pattern of twentieth-century economy and technology to whatever will become its equivalent in the twenty-first. One principal aim of this chapter is thus to place the emergence of the Internet in the 1990s within a historical scheme that embraces not only the successive phases of the machine revolution but also the wider context of human development of which it is just the most recent part.

Marx and Engels correctly foresaw that machine production entailed the centralization of society, and they hoped that the newly formed industrial working class would seize the chance of being concentrated in the cities to organize effectively against the factory owners and their allies in government.[3] Instead, the bureaucratic revolution of state capitalism beat the workers to it, while harnessing the energies of the professional middle classes to the task of nation-building. The communications revolution is based on a more decentralized technology than before (at least at the level of use, rather than infrastructure), and it has accelerated the integration of world society, principally in the form of a network of markets. Does the emergence of a world market mediated by miniaturized machines contain new democratic possibilities for expressing general human interests; or are we merely witnessing the culmination of a global capitalism run by and for huge corporations?

Table 2.1   Three stages of the machine revolution

	C. 1800	C. 1900	C. 2000
Revolution	Industrial	Bureaucratic	Communications
Technology	Steam-power	Electrical power	Digitalization
Institution	Factory	Office	Internet
Capitalism	Market	State	Virtual
Economy	Urban	National	World

The key to understanding the part played by machines in the rapidly evolving human economy is to consider their consequences for the performance of work. In modern English usage, *work* is usually human effort made social by being paid for. It is the way most of us expect to make money. Mechanical aids to human labor are very ancient, but, for reasons that will become apparent, I reserve the term *machine* for the means of converting inanimate energy to human ends; whereas *tools* will be taken to be inert instruments handled by human beings in the course of their work. The growing number and sophistication of machines aiding human effort may be called *mechanization,* and it is this process that is the most distinctive feature of the modern economy (making money with money being as old as civilization itself, as we will see).

Because the first systematic application of machines to the objectives of production was the nineteenth-century factory system based on coal-fired steam engines, mechanization has been conventionally associated with smokestack industries and hence with what we generally call "the industrial revolution" or "industrialization." At the end of the twentieth century, when technological progress is focused on the mechanization of human brains rather than on muscle power, it is more appropriate to stress the relentless advance of machines without tying the idea to the imagery of industrial manufactures. Whatever else he may be responsible for, Karl Marx was the first major social theorist to notice the centrality of machines in modern economic development.[4] The cities we live in would be impossible without them, and in this sense the whole relationship between humanity and the natural world has been irreversibly changed by mechanization.

In two centuries, the differential rate of application of machines to production has been the single greatest indicator of uneven development in the global economy. Although there are few people in the world today who do not have access to the simpler machines in general use—fans, trucks, radios, corn mills—the majority still work with their hands in a production environment largely devoid of machines. Productivity, now a function of the machines supporting human labor, is a measure of the output generated by a worker in a period of time; it is the most direct guide to the growing gap between haves and have-nots in the world today. The staggering proliferation of machines on the whole reinforces this polarity. Machines use energy, mostly a dwindling supply of fossil fuels such as coal, oil and gas; and the world's population is divided increasingly by the degree to which everyday life is mediated by these mechanized sources of energy.

Thorstein Veblen, writing at the turn of the century in America,[5] believed that the "pecuniary" system of free enterprise and market competition was archaic, even barbaric. It stood opposed to an emergent civilization based on the qualities required for working with machines. These were: standardization, scientific precision, disciplined regularity, increased interdependence and a matter-of-fact rejection of conventional ways of thinking. He felt that such an ethos had already been embraced by industrial workers and, to a degree, by everyone in society, except for the bosses ("captains of industry") who were rather addicted to money profits and cultivated indifference to the real needs of society. In an impersonal world driven by an interlocking system of machines, personality was expressed in work only by a handful of destructive monopolists, of whom the literary prototype was Captain Ahab.[6]

In a sense, the bureaucratic capitalism that evolved in the first half of the twentieth century (sometimes called "Fordism" after Henry Ford's automobile plant near Detroit) could be said to have answered the need for a less chaotic approach, with corporate managers assuming authoritarian control of the production line and its "hands." C.L.R. James, echoing many radical critics of industrialism, caught the resulting alienation of workers when he wrote of the fearful mechanical power of an industrial civilization that makes incredible advances at the same time as destroying human personality.[7] In other words, faced with the regimentation and enormous scale of modern industry, most workers were reduced to being no more than "cogs in a machine," while an impersonal management hierarchy likewise took on the attributes of a machine technology to which human endeavour was relentlessly subordinated ("systems theory").

So, thanks to a line of polemicists, from the Luddite machine-breakers to Charlie Chaplin, the modern power of money is linked indelibly in our imaginations to its physical manifestation as belching, clanking behemoths, machines that reduce human labor to an almost pointless tending exercise. I grew up near Trafford Park, Manchester's pioneering industrial estate. Twice every day all the factory shifts in this huge engineering complex were ended together by an awesome sound, known as "The Buzzer," which told house-wives for miles around to get a meal ready for their husbands. The last trump of the Day of Wrath was a routine experience for us. The only comparable phenomenon was when Manchester United scored a goal on a Saturday after-noon and the unified roar of fifty thousand men was truly bestial, a reminder to women and children alike of what raw collective male power can be.

This kind of mechanization supported an imperialism in which the Western working class, itself oppressed by machines and the power of the owners' money, was invited to celebrate "our" collective dominance over colonial sub-jects who were unlucky enough to have no machines at all. Now the Fordist crisis of machine production is to some extent receding in the West, as an-other phase of mechanization ushers in new working conditions. The loss of smokestack industries to the communities built around them a century or more ago has spawned a poignant genre of films and literature in itself.[8] The millions of people who spend their days in front of computer screens are the coal-face or automobile workers of our times. Theirs is the central work ex-perience of an economy whose leading sectors are now driven by information technology. Following Veblen's analysis at the turn of the century or indeed those of Hegel and Marx earlier, we need to ask whether these new experi-ences of work contain the possibility of more or less personal satisfaction, more or less democracy. What kind of ethos do information technologies sup-port? Will the world be a more or less equal place as a result of their spread?

The answers to such questions are highly contested. Some argue that the historical alienation of machine workers is being reversed, with the empha-sis now being on the individual learning process and self-management of work; while others point just as plausibly to sweat-shop conditions and strict regimentation in the information industries.[9] The trend of machine technol-ogy over the last century has been on the whole toward miniaturization and domestication. In the process the scale of machines has become more human, more personal. Compare the first steam engines with what drives the average automobile today, the first IBM mainframe computers (only four decades ago!) with the laptop on which this book was written. It is a long way to your kitchen fridge from the ships that pioneered refrigeration to bring Argentinian meat to England in the last century; but this story has been repeated thousands of times. It is sometimes said disparagingly of the

1960s space race that its only useful by-product was the Teflon-coated frying pan. That seems quite a lot to me. But technology alone does not shape the conditions of work and we have not yet put the horrors of early industrialization definitively behind us.

The typical trajectory for machines, however, has been to start out as huge public monsters dominating the people working with them, then to become smaller and more efficient, allowing widespread diffusion into private domestic and public use. If the steam locomotive has served as a symbol of modern history from Tolstoy to Bertolucci, what kind of history is symbolized by the mobile phone? Of all the sectors of modern production, the increase in the efficiency of information processors has been staggering. An article in *Scientific American* once began with the observation that, if transportation had made the same improvements since 1945 (and it has hardly stood still in that period), we would now be able to fly around the world for $5 in thirty minutes on half a gallon of kerosene. Some comparable changes have taken place in the food chain, with more contradictory and potentially worrying results.

The implications of all this for the location and type of economic opportunities have been profound. There have always been hi-tech (well-paid) and low-tech (badly paid) variants of capitalism, sometimes in direct competition (as, for cxample, in the textiles industry), sometimes existing in parallel. Their relationship is a major theme here, to be discussed in the next chapter. In 1947 Lancashire's cotton textile exports, the culmination of the world's first industrial revolution, supplied one third of Britain's foreign exchange earnings. Its workers were contemptuous of cheap, shoddy competition from Japan. They felt they owned the world market. At about the same time, Hong Kong produced labor-intensive products for the colonies like enamelware and plastic flowers. No need to recapitulate what happened next in Japan. It is perhaps less well known that Hong Kong has since come to rival Europe's richest high-tech economies (Germany and Switzerland) in some of their most sophisticated production lines, like optical instruments. The relocation of the world's shipbuilding industry to Korea is another case in point. Meanwhile, the blackened textile mills of Lancashire lie derelict and abandoned, like the dockyards on Tyneside and the Clyde.

The shift to long-distance trade in information services obviously depends on an even higher, more integrated level of machine civilization than earlier phases of industrialization. The telecommunications corporations that control the infrastructure of this commerce and many of its specific products (AT&T, Microsoft, News International) obviously wield market power on a scale that J.D. Rockefeller would have envied. But the network of machines linked together by the Internet is more mobile and decentralized than before. If home-based production was traditionally associated with the exploitation of cheap family labor, the communications revolution now makes it possible for the most highly paid service workers to operate from home, if they choose. Many of the simpler tasks of data-processing have already been "put out" by satellite to Third World countries like India with a well-educated, low-wage workforce. San Diego doctors now have their medical notes made digital in Bangalore.

But this is just the beginning. Who knows where it will lead? Africa more or less missed out on the first and second industrial revolutions. Perhaps some Africans will make a more fruitful connection with this third phase; certainly the African market for telephony is attracting the attention of multinational suppliers. In any case, mechanization has been the source of large swings in global economic inequality over relatively short periods. Towns in Britain's northern and Celtic fringe now compete with well-educated, low-paid labor forces elsewhere for investments by Asian and American capital in assembly plants producing mass consumption goods for the European market. Meanwhile, in California, the best-paid, most sophisticated workforce in the world lives alongside illegal Chicano laborers whose conditions and pay are grotesquely inferior. And the nightmare of America's black inner cities builds to a climax that most Americans cannot bear to think about. It is not necessary to invoke the gap between rich and poor regions of the world; stark inequalities can be seen in every country.

So ours is a civilization built on machines; and it seems likely that the process of mechanization has brought with it much greater economic inequality, not less, especially in the last two decades leading up to the communications revolution. At every previous stage, critical social thinkers have been concerned to resolve the paradox of how technology designed to aid human work might be turned from a means of exclusion and oppression into a source of greater human freedom and equality. The same question preoccupies us today. Any answers are inseparable from the institutional forms taken by money, whether as capitalism or as the market. But first we must try to place the machine revolution in the context of human history as a whole.

In the long run: The age of mechanization

"In the long run we are all dead"
MAYNARD KEYNES

To recapitulate, the industrial revolution took place in the late eighteenth and early nineteenth centuries.[10] It was an integrated complex, centered on northern Britain, bringing together cotton, iron and coal. The commercial product was cotton textiles (clothing); production was based on the steam engine powered by coal; before long, railways provided the transport. The second stage saw America and Germany overtake Britain in the late nineteenth/early twentieth centuries with new large-scale industries: steel plants, chemicals, printing, shipyards and high-rise office blocks. This concentration of mass production in huge enterprises underlay the widespread assumption of the day that society was inexorably bent on a path of centralization. It was linked to the harnessing of electric power in what became national grids. The third stage is our own and the 1990s are certainly in the thick of it.

At the same time that the bureaucratic revolution was ushering in an era of mass production, discoveries were being made that led to the forms of machine technology that subsequently dominated the twentieth-century economy: petroleum, the electric motor, the telephone, cinema, radio and mass circulation newspapers, the automobile and the airplane, domestic appliances, steel-framed construction, office equipment such as copiers (without which new businesses like advertising would be unthinkable), and so on. The drive to occupy the center of mushrooming cities was reversed and suburbanization set in, increasing the distance between work and home, at least for male breadwinners.[11]

Similarly, the key discoveries underpinning the communications revolution were made in the 1940s during the Second World War (the transistor, computers, radar, etc.) and only now are they coming into general use. It could be said that the impact of information technology is still superficial, since the bulk of humanity is as yet left untouched by it. But how many people used telephones a century ago and how many use them now? And, in the 1840s, when Marx and Engels found a world revolution in a few Lancashire textile factories, what proportion of global production was organized in that way then? We can be sure that the principles of the technologies that will shape the way of life of most human beings in the twenty-first century have already been discovered. Our historical knowledge of earlier phases of mechanization should help us to make sense of our own transitional moment. Two centuries is a long time from the perspective of the human biological clock; but it is a blink of an eyelid in the scale of world history. We need to place the present within the widest context of time and space—human evolution and world population as a whole.

The project of imagining national communities, largely by means of statistical extrapolation, is a century and a half old. Even so, we now accept without question the idea that Italian and Spanish women have the lowest birth rates in Europe, or that Britain has sunk to being the eighteenth richest country in the world. Since the Second World War and the formation of the United Nations, it has become normal to collect statistics on the global population, but thinking about human society as a single entity has not yet taken hold. It is about time that it did. For now is the time when world society is being formed in a meaningful sense; and the fragmentation of perspective produced by national consciousness prevents us from imagining the human community as a whole. Numbers are one way of beginning that process.

The year 1800 may serve as an arbitrary marker of the beginning of the age of mechanization. In that year the world's human population has been estimated at 1 billion; only 1 in 40 people lived in cities (the largest, London

Table 2.2   Population, cities and energy 1800–2000

	C. 1800	C. 2000	ANNUAL INCREASE
Population	1 bil	6 bil	1.5%
Urban share of world population	1 in 40	1 in 2	2
Energy production	—	—	3

I have been using these figures in my lectures since the mid-1970s. At least some of them come from Carlo Cipolla's *Economic History of World Population,* 7th ed. (Penguin, Harmondsworth, 1968).

and Beijing, having populations of around 1 million); and animals and plants were responsible for almost all the energy produced and consumed by human beings. In 2000, world population is about 6 billion; half of us live in cities, many of them 10–20 million in size; and inanimate sources (mainly fossil fuels) account for the bulk of energy production. Seen as rates of increase over two centuries, the human population has been growing at an annual rate of 1.5%, while the rate of growth of cities has been 2%. This apparently small difference accounts for the huge rise in the proportion of city-dwellers. Energy production has been growing at around 3% a year since the mid-nineteenth century. The fact that this figure is double the rate of population increase indicates the considerable economic expansion of the last two centuries; but the distribution of this increment has been grossly unequal, with American citizens, for example, consuming on average four hundred times more energy than their Ugandan counterparts.[12]

Let us start with the population boom. It seems that births routinely exceeded deaths by 1% in agrarian societies. If left unchecked for the ten thousand years in which agriculture dominated the economy of the planet, this surplus would have led to the land mass being covered with a layer of human flesh thousands of miles deep and expanding into space at a speed fast approaching that of light. The reason why this did not happen was that periodic gluts of death (caused by war, famine and disease) wiped out the surplus, allowing instead for a modest net increase to around 1 billion by 1800.[13]

By modern standards, then, agrarian populations managed to tick over only by maintaining high birth rates to match equally high death rates. The modern demographic trend has been first toward lowering death rates and then eventually to reductions in birth rates, as people became more confident

Table 2.3 The demographic transition

	AGRICULTURE	EARLY MECHANIZATION	LATER MECHANIZATION
Death rate	High	Lower	Low
Birth rate	High	High	Low
Population	Static	Expanding	Static

in the survival prospects of their children. This trend has normally included a period of rapid population expansion when birth rates remained high while death rates were falling. Europe was the first to experience this "demographic transition," with births exceeding deaths significantly for a century from the 1830s to the 1930s, after which the current pattern of population stagnation and decline was established. In this same period Europeans grabbed most of the earth's land mass, controlling four-fifths of it by the time of the First World War, thereby allowing many of them to leave home for lands of new settlement overseas (50 million between the 1880s and the First World War, mostly to the United States).

A similar transition has been taking place in the rest of the world since 1945. Here too, sharp reductions in death rates as a result of better medicine and more secure food supplies have been accompanied by continuing high birth rates, especially in Africa. This is especially so when the conditions of habitat and production remain largely those of traditional agriculture. The result is that people of other than European descent have been reclaiming their share of world population; but this often appears to the Europeans as a threat to their recent ascendancy. The main difference between this wave and its predecessor is that, despite winning independence from colonial rule, non-Westerners have not been afforded the luxury of territorial expansion and have been subjected to highly restrictive controls over international migration. Even so, the movement of people from the poor to the rich countries has been a significant feature of the second half of this century, leading to quite marked changes in the latter's perceived racial composition, especially in the main urban centers.

One measure of the extraordinary shift in world population taking place during our epoch is the ratio of Europeans to Africans. In 1950 Greater Europe (including Soviet Central Asia) had twice the numbers of Africa. Today Africa has a population 120 million larger than Europe and Central Asia and is projected to be well on the way to double the size by 2010.[14] A glance at the map will reveal that the two regions are neighbors, a proximity that has sustained a history of slavery, imperialism and discrimination. And now immigration policies in Europe seem to be founded on a fortress mentality that not only seeks to keep Africans out, but even holds that the days of interdependence between Europe and Africa are over. Colonial

43

exploitation has been replaced with massive indifference to the inequalities between the regions. It is hard to imagine a peaceful denouement to such a blighted relationship.

A much more general feature of the modern period, however, has been the rise of the city as the normal human habitat, at the expense of the village. Whereas no region in the world could sustain more than a tenth of its population in urban centers during the agrarian era, today no country is less than 20% urbanized and many are less than 20% rural. Of the half of humanity that still does not live in cities, the vast bulk are Chinese, Indian and African peasants.

Marx and Engels claimed that human history was summed up in the changing relationship between town and countryside.[15] Until recently, agrarian inequality was sustained by states run by small urban elites. The life of the city—variously called urban commerce, the bourgeoisie, civil society or even politics—was the exceptional antithesis of rural drudgery. As the medieval Germans used to say, *Stadtluft machts frei* ("City air makes you free"). So far, the modern trend has been to live in cities, even in countries that so far have not incorporated machine production into their economies on any significant scale. While it is true that lack of spending power ("money") is the most tangible manifestation of Third World poverty, such a wholesale shift to urban living without a corresponding level of mechanization is fundamentally unstable. Cities have grown up there because modern states have been able to concentrate expenditure of revenues derived more from their monopoly of the international means of finance than from traditional exploitation of their own peasantries. As I have argued elsewhere for West Africa,[16] these states are built on thin air and must surely collapse if they cannot develop a sound basis for centralization in some mechanized sectors of the economy. But for now the expansion of Third World cities seems to be inexorable.

If we want to understand global demography (what Sir William Petty, the discipline's founder, called "political arithmetick"),[17] we must focus on production, on the application of animate and inanimate energy to the work purposes of human beings. The force propelling humanity to a new relationship with the natural world is the use of inanimate energy sources with machines as converters. From a modern perspective, human history seems to be divided into three periods—our own two centuries of mechanization,

44

the ten millennia when agriculture dominated world production, and the vast tracts of prehistory before we settled down on the land. Until very recently all economic activity rested on harnessing the energy stored in plants and animals, including the work of human beings themselves (energy fueled by consuming plants and animals). Other inanimate energy sources—water, wind, fossil fuels—and machines driven by them made a negligible contribution. The significance of agriculture lies in the change it brought about in the ratio of human to non-human energy deployed in production drawing on animate sources.

Before the invention of agriculture, human beings conserved their own efforts by letting plants and animals do most of the work involved in bringing products to the point of consumption. They moved to the locations where these sources grew naturally, leaving only the tasks of collection and processing to be performed by human labor. People who live this way today ("hunter-gatherers") allow large spaces to accommodate small mobile bands (generally no more than 1 person per square kilometer); and the food quest does not seem to absorb very much of their time. Marshall Sahlins has called them "the original affluent society," rich in leisure because they limit their material wants.[18]

Agriculture is perhaps best thought of as a system of food production in which the growth of plants and animals comes increasingly within the control of human beings. Human work is progressively substituted for natural processes of reproduction. By settling down in one place, human communities are obliged to protect animals and plants from threats to their well-being. The resulting pattern of irrigation, pest-scaring and weeding involves an intensification of labor input with diminishing returns. That is, people have to work harder and harder for proportionately less reward.

This logic of development through *intensification of labor* lent to agriculture a dynamic of inequality that eventually reduced the bulk of the population in most advanced centers to a life of coercion and servitude (slaves and peasants working under varying degrees of unfreedom). Thus the richest civilizations of the world in the late eighteenth century, Western Europe and China, rested on peasantries that could barely stay alive. Chinese peasants were once compared to people standing in a lake with the water fractionally below their noses: The merest ripple and they drown. This was also the time when Robert

Malthus developed a theory of population for Europe in which life and death were regulated by short-term fluctuations in the food supply.[19]

Because we are used to the neat hedgerows and paddy fields of "civilized" agriculture, it comes as something of a shock to learn that the untidy confusion of so-called "swidden" agriculture (shifting cultivation of plots often undertaken in semi-cleared forest by tribal peoples) conceals much higher levels of labor productivity, since so much of the work involved is left to natural regeneration and the amount of protection required is less.[20] When peasants work for absentee landlords, the emphasis is on maximizing yields from the land area owned, regardless of the drudgery involved in its cultivation.

It is a long way from the neolithic revolution (the expulsion from the Garden of Eden) to China's half-drowned peasants. Yet I would argue that the extremes of pre-industrial civilization, which erected splendid urban enclaves on the backs of impoverished country-dwellers, are entailed in the origins of domestication. The social forces necessary to bring animals and plants within a sphere of human regulation also were deployed to compel some parts of the population to work harder than their own immediate reward would justify. It took time; but eventually what we take to be civilizations were built on the systematic neglect of the interests of large sections of the workforce.

This argument has obvious affinities with Rousseau's.[21] Like him, I locate the turning point of human history in agriculture as a mode of production, even if the subsequent excesses of civilization cannot be explained solely by this means. I also join Marx in supposing that the mechanization of production holds out some hope for humanity. For the machine revolution introduced the possibility of releasing us all from the drudgery of village life, even if, as Marx showed, its immediate consequence was to make matters even worse for many workers. Indeed, in asserting that the world at the end of the twentieth century exhibits very similar conditions to those typical of the *ancien régime,* I support both Rousseau and Marx in opposing the triumphalist claim that humanity has already made the decisive leap to a progressive civilization.

Nevertheless, increased resort to machines converting inanimate energy sources did reverse the direction of the agricultural regime. Now human beings were able to produce much more for less work; more abundant means have been generated with less back-breaking toil. It is hardly surprising that peasants worldwide have voted with their feet to join the life of greater free-dom afforded by machine production in cities. At first, mechanization was almost exclusively an urban phenomenon and slow to penetrate agriculture. In fact, people were initially displaced from farming in Britain by horses. An-imals also dominated many sectors of transport throughout the nineteenth century, giving rise to the term "horsepower" as a measure of a machine's strength.[22] Only since 1945 has agriculture been truly mechanized, with consequences that we have still to discover.

The pursuit of human freedom, the idea that society is set on a course of material improvement, the rise of modern personality and of subjectivity it-self—all this is supported by the underlying trend I have noted, namely that inanimate energy sources are progressively being substituted for human labor. Many people live longer now; they work less and consume more—at least the majority of those who have escaped the rigors of traditional agri-culture. But a lot of peasants remain in our world, mostly in Asia and Africa. There are those (including Rousseau) who would turn the clock back to a pre-industrial way of life. They do not include this writer. Millions of Mexi-cans trying to emigrate to the United States can't all be wrong.

Apart from the quality-of-life issue, people throughout the modern period have feared that machines would displace human beings as well as animals from work. The machine-breakers of the early nineteenth century (Luddites) have their counterparts today, not least among intellectuals whose control over book knowledge is being undermined by television and computers. Mecha-nization is a hugely complex process, as well as being recent; at all stages there are undoubtedly winners and losers. The benefits and costs of machines cannot be understood independently of the social organization of production (the sub-ject of the next two chapters especially). The fact that the financial rewards of mechanization are distributed so unfairly should not be used to justify resist-ance to more effective ways of working. This ongoing contradiction, between increased efficiency and the unfair distribution of the benefits, underlies the economic divisions that make ours such an unequal world.

The origins of the communications revolution

A moment is a point in time when something moves. It may last several cen-turies (the end of the Roman Empire) or the nanosecond that it takes for a computer to flip from one binary digit (or *bit*) to the next. Moments are meaningful only as periods in stories that define what comes before and after them. Our moment in history, in my vision at least, is the birth of the Internet, a meaningful event in the communications revolution and the time when humanity as a whole became a single interactive network. The significance of this for human evolution is that, after two centuries when mechanization was an alienating burden for many people, it now becomes possible to imagine machines as instruments of human freedom, allowing us, separately and together, to make ourselves at home in the world to an extent that once seemed gone for ever.

If we are to grasp the significance of this moment, we must take further the reflections of the previous section on the place of humanity in life as a whole. Most of life divides into the two great classes of plants and animals. The principal difference between the two is that, while animals move to wherever their food supplies can be found, plants sit in one place waiting for the food to come to them. There are grounds for supposing that the primary function of the brain is to co-ordinate movement. There is a sea-anemone that is born with a vestigial brain. It needs this to search for the right spot on the sea-bed to put down its roots; but, once it is settled, the brain withers away and it becomes a plant. This allegory is useful since human beings are obviously animals with big brains and lots of capacity for movement; but we are also adapted to living with, off and like plants. The tension between staying in one place and moving about defines the main contradiction in society at this time and perhaps throughout human evolution. It has long been mediated by communication at distance.

A North African called Ibn Khaldun lived in Cordoba during the thirteenth century. A thousand years ago Cordoba, with Constantinople, was the center for civilization on the planet. Ibn Khaldun wrote a book, *The Muqaddimah,*[23] which entitles him to be thought of as the Max Weber of his day, since no one before and few since had such a comprehensive understanding of society and history. He lived at the far western edge of a civilization linked by dry spaces stretching from the Atlas Mountains to the gates of Beijing. Nomadic herders inhabited these spaces, moving with their animals in search of water and grass. They often developed ferocious military organization and, of course, Islam emerged as a thread unifying the region's many peoples. On the borders of the desert, usually in riverine and coastal areas, were to be found the world's first cities and their successors. The water allowed for continuous cultivation of plants, but was more important for the easy movement of trade goods. The lifestyle in these urban oases was luxurious compared with the rigors of herding animals. So, from time to time, the hard men would come sweeping in from the desert to take over the cities.[24] Ibn Khaldun calculated that the turnover rate in this sedentary/nomadic cycle was about four generations. A battle-hardened elite would establish a new dynasty, grow soft before long and be replaced by the next wave.

Another historical dynamic, to which we will return, is the tension between settled military occupation of the land and water-borne urban commerce. As the great French historian of the Mediterranean world, Fernand Braudel, made clear, that the sea provides another means of linkage between diverse territories.[25] And the struggle for political control between warrior aristocracies and maritime traders, between property in land and property in money, countryside and city, lasted a thousand years—from the Assyrians and Phoenicians, through the Persians and Greeks, the Peloponnesian war and Alexander's conquests, until the Romans, in defeating Carthage, made their world safe for landlords for almost another two thousand years.[26]

So here we have the theme of place and movement on a grand historical scale, with thin strips of urban civilization connected by deserts of sea and land, by water-borne commerce and territorial conquest. What lay behind this development of early cities and their hinterlands was the food-producing revolution, beginning about ten thousand years ago.[27] This is the epochal event that I liken to the machine revolution of the last two centuries and to the formation of a global communications network in particular. As long as we understand that more than just farming is involved, it is convenient to label it "the invention of agriculture." Before that human beings moved around to collect food from where it occurred naturally. Hunter-gatherers lived in small flexible bands spending relatively little energy on the food quest and much more on the elaboration of culture. They roamed the earth without limit or hindrance at very favorable ratios of food supplies to people. Their modern successors have been driven into the parts of the world that farmers and city-dwellers don't want to, or cannot, reach; but even so they work a lot less hard than the rest of us. Our greatest task is to grasp the significance of the relationship between these two revolutions, agriculture and mechanization. If we wish to be emancipated from the former, we must reflect on what life was like before it or is now without it. The comparison hinges on the relative emphasis we place on work and on the exchange of meanings as leading human preoccupations.

Domestication involves bringing some plants and animals within the protection of human groups who are thereby usually committed to maintaining a stronger attachment to one place. From the start it is probable that farming and herding were combined, since animals had to be fed and could be used for haulage. But once people grew plants for a living, they were stuck with protecting their fields and granaries from all sorts of predators. In a way they became like plants, fixed in the ground, unable to move. And the labor costs escalated: weeding, irrigation, storage. A question to which we will return is why such a development should be attractive and to whom. The standard answer is that food supplies became more reliable and that some presumed Malthusian threat was averted by agriculture. But settling down makes people easier to control and inequalities of wealth become more pronounced, since people can afford to accumulate property when they don't have to carry it everywhere. Whatever the reason, the way was now open for the reduction of the rural masses to a condition of unfree drudgery that is still the standard by which we measure work.

Hunter-gatherers seem not to draw sharp distinctions between themselves and others, or between themselves and the world around them. Their main mechanism of distribution is sharing rather than centralized allocation. Farmers especially see the world in strongly dualistic terms, as the domestic versus the wild. They struggle to maintain an internal order that is constantly threatened from the outside, and that threat is human (reinforcing an "us versus them" mentality) as well as natural and spiritual. Stability becomes the aim and *raison d'être* of their way of life; and memory is grounded in the timeless security of ancestral land. Nomads of all sorts—herders, travellers, merchants, sailors, outlaws—cherish their fixed points, but they have to develop habits adapted to movement. The interaction of the two is dramatized in countless Western movies, such as John Sturges's *The Magnificent Seven* (itself based on Kurosawa's *The Seven Samurai*), where peasants, made helpless by their sedentary way of life, secure the services of professional thugs to fight the bandits who terrorize them.

Communication is a word cognate with common and community. It appears to have at its root the ability of a group or network of people to share objects and ideas through interaction. This usually takes the form either of the circulation of material objects by means of money or the exchange of signs by means of language. The first of these is the main topic of this book, but the second is a submerged current of the argument that rises to the surface by the end. The two circuits are converging in the communications revolution of our day. In both cases the signs exchanged are now increasingly virtual, meaning that they are bits detached from persons and places that pass at the speed of light through the ether. The means of this convergence is digitalization, the process that lies at the core of our moment in history, but the precedents for it go back to the origin of writing and probably further than that.

Information is an intentional signal from the perspective of the sender, perhaps anything that reduces the uncertainty of a receiver. The transmission of information through machines has traditionally come in the form of waves, imperceptible gradations of light and sound. For communications engineers, *analog* and *digital* computation rest on measuring and counting, respectively: On the one hand, continuous changes in physical variables such as age, height, warmth or speed; on the other, discontinuous leaps between discrete entities, such as days of the week, dollars and cents, puppies in a litter, letters of the alphabet, named individuals. Analog processes, such as time and distance, can be represented digitally; but it was something of a breakthrough for early modern science to measure continuous physical change with precision. Before that the clarity of phenomena was generally enhanced and comparison facilitated by constructing bounded entities that could be counted, in other words by digitalization.

Digital numeration is at its clearest when the only possible signals are binary: on/off, yes/no, either/or, 0/1. And it is this reversion to an older system of simple enumeration that lies behind the latest revolution in communications. Digitalization greatly increases the speed and reliability of information processing and transmission; it also lies behind the rapid convergence of what were once distinct systems: television, telephones, computers. The last have been digital from the beginning, and telephones have almost completed the shift from sound waves to digital transmission. Television too is now beginning the process of digitalization. What it means is that any kind of information can be carried by any piece of equipment that becomes essentially substitutable. Communications technology in the future will consist in various combinations of screen, information processor and transmitter/receiver. The manufacturing monopolists will fight over whether the resulting hybrids most resemble a television, a PC or a telephone. But the process common to all is digitalization, and it is this precise moment of convergence that lends the decade of the 1990s its specificity.

It is wrong to stress information at the expense of people. For the relationships that people make with each other matter more than the content of the messages that pass between them or the means of their transmission. That is why I prefer to call what is going on a communications rather than an information revolution. It may, therefore, be worth stepping back and examining briefly the historical antecedents of this revolution, as a way of placing it within a broader context of social life.

Human communication starts out as speech, and the words exchanged are usually between people who can see as well as hear each other. A lot of non-verbal information accompanies the words—gestures, tone, emanations of feeling—and this helps us to interpret what is said and how to respond. This is surely what we mean when we say that social interaction is real. The words are abstract enough; but the exchange is face to face, grounding what passes between us in the exigency of place. Writing made it possible to detach meaning from the persons and places in which it was generated and to communicate at some distance in time and space, not only in the here and now. Even then, the signs were often highly particular, too many for all but a select few to understand and variable from one scribe to the next. The alphabet took the process of simplifying the signs a step further, one sound for one unambiguous letter, thereby making it possible for writing to be adopted more widely and reliably. It was, if you will, a cheapening of the cost of transmitting information.[28]

The Phoenician city-states, maritime traders of the Lebanese coast, were the main pioneers of alphabetic writing at the beginning of the first millennium BC; and it came into Europe through the Greeks. I like to speculate how books were received at first. For example, on Homer: "All today's youngsters want to do is read at home. You can't get them to go out or anything. They have no idea what it was like hearing the old boy in a torchlit barn on a Saturday night, with his voice echoing in the rafters. It brought tears to your eyes. Well, some of it was the smoke too." Many more people have had access to the bard over the last three thousand years than could ever have been in the same room as him during his lifetime, even if the experience of reading is less sensational than a live performance. Virtual communication takes place more in the mind than in actual fact. The only way people could escape from the restrictions of the present was through exercising their imagination, usually under the stimulus of story-telling. Alphabetic writing, ultimately the book, vastly increased the scope of the collective imagination. It also made possible more practical exchanges at a distance.

At more or less the same time as the alphabet (around 700 BC), coinage was invented in Lydia, now a part of Turkey. Alphabetic writing and this new form of money were profoundly subversive of old ways. Until then, wealth and power were concrete and visible, being attached to the people who had them. They took the form of cattle, vineyards, buildings, armed men and beautiful women. Now riches could be concealed as gold coins, allowing for a double detachment from persons—impersonal exchange at a distance and unaccountable (because hidden and private) economic power. From the beginning writing found a ready application in palace bureaucracy. The king could send messages while remaining himself invisible. It is one thing to be beaten up by thugs; but imagine the terror of receiving a written message saying "please commit suicide before tomorrow." We feel something of this dread whenever we receive a tax demand from the unseen hand of a remote authority.

Plato captures some of this in a story he tells in *The Republic*. Gyges was one of the Lydian king's servants. The king had a ring that made him invisible. He took Gyges with him one night to spy on his wife getting ready for bed. Gyges and the wife eventually ganged up to kill the king. Gyges got the ring, the wife and the kingdom, making him a precursor of legendary rich rulers like Midas. Marc Shell[29] argues persuasively that this myth expresses the contradictions widely felt at the time between visible/personal society and invisible/impersonal society. The Greeks were very concerned about the security of contracts between strangers. They insisted that each contract (for which they devised the word *symbolon*) should be marked by an object like a ring split in the presence of both parties and a witness. They didn't quite believe in pieces of paper.

As long as books were handwritten, their circulation was restricted to a small literate elite capable of copying and reading them. In my old university, Cambridge, until the sixteenth century teachers carried their own scrolls around in the deep pockets of their gowns and read them out for payment to students who thereby ended up with their own copies. Copying was not in itself a major obstacle to the diffusion of texts; it was the ability to interpret the texts that was scarce and costly. Printing made it possible for many more people to get hold of written material, and to an extent it eliminated some of the ambiguities of handwriting. It took a line of business away from the hacks with gowns and shifted the emphasis far more to the act of interpretation and hence to understanding. When my first-year students complained of "lack of structure" in my lectures, as they sometimes did, meaning that they wanted to be told the half dozen points that, when memorized by rote, would ensure a decent pass in the examinations, I used to ask them to consider the success of Cambridge University Press over the last four hundred and fifty years.[30] This was built on putting books directly into the hands of students, so they could make up their own minds what they meant, with the help of learned and hopefully inspiring teachers. Instead, some of them wanted me to recapitulate the role of a reader of scrolls before the print revolution, passing signs from one person to the next without touching the minds of either.

My grandmother was born before the car, radio, film, air travel and all the other transport and communications technologies that came to dominate twentieth-century society. I used to marvel at the way she adapted to all of them. Now I am beginning to grasp something of what she went through, for, having been alive every year since the Second World War, I realize how profoundly *my* world has changed in these respects. Having grown up without television in the home and with very limited opportunities for travel, I relied on books as my main way of transcending the limits of a particular place. It feels as if the intensive indoctrination I received then in the manipulation of words and numbers (Latin, Greek and maths) belongs to another age. Certainly, few of my students today share my mastery of spelling and grammar, nor do they care if they don't. I have managed to get a toehold on the communications revolution, largely through the tolerant assistance of very bright young people who have grown up with it. For them, the phase of national television that I largely missed is already a bygone era. We all enter this extraordinary time with a bundle of advantages and drawbacks. I take pride in a facility for writing coherent e-mail messages at a pace somewhere between essay-writing and a phone call. Yet I also know that communicating through keyboards will soon be replaced by audio-visual methods, thereby removing one point of convergence between the book and the screen. Many of my academic colleagues are still fighting the war against television, refusing to allow one into a living room designed to show off their books. It is quite a trip being a professional communicator right now.

One consequence of the rapid shift in the means of communication is a tendency for teachers and scholars to consider books and computers to be opposed, rather than complementary, technologies. Yet it is becoming increasingly clear that print media are expanding almost as fast as their new electronic counterparts. Face-to-face exchanges, instead of being displaced by telecommunications, take on an added value when one spends the working day in front of a computer screen. Simple pursuits like reading and conversation, which used to be taken for granted when they monopolized our means of communication, can be approached in a more analytical and creative frame of mind now that there are so many ways of acquiring and transmitting ideas. I wrote a large part of this book in a Paris flat, the traditional retreat into privacy of a long-distance writer; nothing new about that. But I maintained throughout e-mail dialogues with friends living all over the world. And no writer was able to do that before the 1990s. I also developed in recent years a virtual office to accommodate a life of movement; but then I was forced to recognize the value of my own memory when my laptop was stolen.

The present chapter is an attempt to make some sense of all this in terms of general ideas that might allow us to step back and consider the potential of what is happening in our world. Each of us experiences the communications revolution in our own way; yet there are palpable changes taking place that affect us all. The next section seeks to place the birth of the Internet within the context of the machine revolution as a whole; while the last one attempts to relate this process to previous turning points in the history of humanity, the invention of agriculture and of civilization, ten and five millennia ago.

The birth of the Internet

Computers have been with us for over fifty years, television for a bit longer and telephones for twice that long.[31] What is unique to the 1990s is the convergence of these technologies into an increasingly unified institutional pattern and the emergence of a worldwide network of communications, the Internet. Many people still do not understand what the term Internet refers to, nor how it relates to similar-sounding entities like "the world wide web." The Internet is the most inclusive term for all public electronic communication networks in the world. These are decentralized to a large extent, but they constitute a conceptual unity in much the same way as "the world market" does. Indeed, the transactions of the latter are increasingly carried out on the Internet. The "web" is a disembodied machine, a type of software, that emerged in 1994 for use on the Internet. It allows people to display messages in a non-interactive way through a multi-media format, employing words, pictures, sound, animation and video. At the time the big innovation was the move from words and numbers to visual images. All messages are transmitted between computers and television screens (hardware) by means of telephone and radio signals. The infrastructure for these transmissions in turn constitutes a rapidly evolving network of satellites, cable grids and other means.

The Internet was for several decades restricted in use to a strategic complex of military, academic and business interests, based in the United States and Europe. It was designed specifically to resist an all-out nuclear attack from the Soviet Union and so was decentralized. Being immune to a single strike, it was also impossible to control from a central point. For some time, the most intensive use of the Internet was between physicists located near the two main nuclear accelerators in Illinois and Geneva. These scientists lent to the medium its definitive style and content in the early decades: highly technical, closed and clubby. By the time that the Internet went public in 1993, there were only 3 million users in the world. In the next five years the number of users increased to 100 million. At the time of writing, Internet traffic is doubling every hundred days. Between 1993 and 1997 the number of domain names (the exclusive address of a computer terminal) rose from 26,000 to 1.3 million, a fiftyfold increase.

The Internet is an American invention. Certainly they behave as if they own it. Western Europe played a part from the beginning, and the Europeans are now trying hard to get a world regulatory authority for the Internet set up, preferably in Geneva. But the Americans still constitute over 60% of users, and most of the practical instruments for intervening in the network are located there. By 2002 several hundred satellites will make high-bandwidth communications available to users worldwide.[32] Only a handful of companies are capable of putting up those satellites. This side of the Internet revolution thus favors large corporations, even as it distributes the medium to an ever widening network of decentralized users. At present the fastest-growing use of the Internet, perhaps reflecting American priorities, is for electronic commerce, something almost unknown before the 1990s. At the same time companies and private individuals are forming *intranets,* exclusive circuits of information exchange offering higher security than the public medium. If ever there was a challenge to empiricism, the habit of extrapolating from previous experience, it is posed by trying to guess what the social impact of all this is likely to be.

Compare, for example, the adoption of iron in the lands bordering the eastern Mediterranean three thousand years ago.[33] Iron is the commonest metal ore on earth, and it is extremely robust and malleable. When the technique of smelting it was first discovered, small quantities of iron were used principally for prestigious ornaments worn by the ruling classes. Then it found a military use as weapons that allowed some groups to gain a temporary advantage over their neighbors. It took several hundred years in most cases for iron to find its most significant application, as tools used in the production of food and manufactures by the common people. If you had been living in Assyria, say, at the beginning of iron production, you would have guessed that its destiny was to be a symbolic and practical means of maintaining the dominance of a military caste. Much the same inference could have been drawn in relation to the Internet at any time during the Cold War.

So what is the communications revolution? It consists of rapid changes in the size, cost and especially speed of machines capable of processing information. This is now generally measured as millions of instructions per second, or

MIPS. The world's first computer, the Electronic Numerical Integrator and Computer (ENIAC), was built soon after the Second World War; it cost millions of dollars, was 50 meters wide and 3 meters tall, and processed 5,000 instructions per second. Twenty-five years later an Intel microprocessor chip, 12 mm square, cost $200 and processed 60,000 instructions per second (0.06 MIPS). Today Pentium PCs have a processing capacity of 4,000 MIPS, and this is expected to reach 100,000 MIPS by 2012. In 1980 copper phone wires transmitted information at the rate of a page of print a second; today hair-thin optical fibres can transmit the equivalent of almost a million encyclopedia volumes per second. The modems (linking computers and telephones) most commonly in use today take forty-six minutes to download a three and a half minute video; new technologies currently available can perform the same operation over copper wires in ten seconds.[34]

It may be helpful to contextualize this cascade of technical change by referring to Table 2.1, on the three stages of the machine revolution. These, it will be recalled, were inaugurated by steam power, electrical power and digitalization, respectively. The steam engine was invented in 1712, but it was another sixty years before James Watt's improvements made it feasible to power factories by this means; and the industrial revolution proper did not take off until after the Napoleonic wars (roughly a century after Newcomen's engine). Electricity was first identified and harnessed in 1831; just over fifty years later Thomas Edison began generating it for public use. Again, it was only in the first decades of the twentieth century that factories made the wholesale gains in efficiency that came with adoption of electric motors; and widespread domestic use of electrical appliances had to wait until the middle decades of this century. It took a hundred years from Faraday's discovery before 80% of Americans were supplied with electricity at home.

If ENIAC is analogous to the inventions of Newcomen and Faraday (its inventor being suitably anonymous for a bureaucratic age), our time bears comparison with those moments, half a century later, when the discovery first began to have widespread social application. It seems to us that the rate of change today is much faster and more general than those earlier revolutions; and this may be a justifiable impression. Certainly, a premise of this book is that the significance of this third phase is much more far-reaching than earlier phases, if only for its relationship to the formation of world society as a single interactive network. But we should remember that vast populations on this planet have not yet joined the steam or electrical power revolutions. In parts of Africa agriculture is currently being transformed by iron ox-ploughs replacing hand hoes, thereby bringing production in parts of the region to a technological level long considered normal in pre-industrial Eurasia. In the industrial West, as we have already seen, human labor was replaced for most of the nineteenth century not by machines but by horses; and full mechanization of food production had to wait until the second half of the twentieth century.

The main conclusion to be drawn from these comparisons is that it will be another fifty years at least before we can tell how society is affected in the regions most open to the adoption of information technology. Differences in the rate and manner of such adoption between the world's regions, classes and sectors of production will likewise only emerge in the course of the twenty-first century. Steam power allowed factories to be located away from their principal source of energy (once water and wood, now coal) and to deploy machines replacing manual labor. These factories were operated by a new class of industrial entrepreneurs, individuals like Richard Arkwright who were later parodied in Dickens's novels.[35] Electricity helped turn factory production into a streamlined system of managerial control, powered the office complexes of the bureaucratic revolution and eventually made domestic life more convenient. It required a physical network for its distribution, and this encouraged governments to own or license monopoly operators of grids that became among the most tangible symbols of the national economy.

The Internet harnesses light for almost instantaneous communication between machines using microscopic circuits to process and store information. It is not the aim of this book to give a comprehensive account of its likely social significance. But there are profound implications for the system of transactions involving money, for the market economy and its dark twin, capitalism. Now that the Internet is no longer primarily a research tool, its use is increasingly as a sphere of economic activity, as a link between and within businesses, and between businesses and their customers. It is becoming an electronic marketplace. The point about electricity is that it travels at the speed of light and the passage of information itself is essentially costless. This, then, is a market with unusual time and space dimensions, where the personal and impersonal aspects of economic life meet on new terms. It would not be surprising if it took us a while to adjust our expectations to this situation. In the meantime, however, the pioneers of cyberspace are getting on with making the most they can of these new opportunities. The world opening up to us is one in which borderless trade is transacted at the speed of light. Very little of social significance will be left untouched by it before long.

It is relevant to ask who is behind the expansion of the Internet and who its users are. But possible answers to that question require an analysis of the money system itself, beginning with the next chapter. Eventually, at the end of Chapter 6, I will summarize how this has already been transformed by the Internet. But some preliminary comments are in order here. The main player in the early stages of the Internet was the U.S. government, which funded its development in the interests of "national security" (the Cold War). Its expansion today is financed largely by private telecommunications corporations who plan to spend $27 billion between 1998 and 2002 on building a global broadband network in the sky capable of reaching that one-third of humanity that currently lacks access to phones and television. In the richer countries, companies operating with local licenses are laying thick cable wires with capacities ten times greater than high-speed phone connections. Radio and television companies are rapidly integrating their transmissions with the Internet (BBC on-line is the second most visited Web site in the world). This kind of infrastructure development is expensive, and there will not be many players in the global competition to provide it. But the power of these corporations (and of the governments with whom they have an increasingly ambivalent relationship) to extract payment from use of the Internet differs in important ways from the public service monopolies that supplied utilities in the twentieth century.

Almost two-thirds of Internet users today are Americans, but the country with the highest ratio of Internet users to the population is Finland (which also has the highest rate of mobile phone use in the world). America comes second (but first by a huge distance in the total number of machines connected to the Internet), followed by large countries of sparse settlement such as Canada, Australia and Sweden. The Dutch break with the trend as a small, densely occupied country, and the main European states, such as Britain, Germany and France come some way behind the leaders.

Table 2.4   The top ten Internet users (countries)

	HOSTS/POP.	HOSTS(THOUSANDS)
Finland	1:18	284
USA	1:26	10,113 (63% of world total)
Australia	1:35	515
Sweden	1:39	233
Canada	1:48	603
Netherlands	1:55	271
UK	1:98	592
Germany	1:114	722
Japan	1:170	734
France	1:236	233

Number of Internet hosts as a proportion of the national population in 1997.

The prominence of Scandinavia in the above league table is proof enough that, despite the size of America's lead in the communications revolution, others are adapting to the potential of the Internet at a rapid rate. These include smaller numbers of users in non-Western countries where already network communications are taking distinctive forms. Language is a hotly contested issue on the Internet, with English having emerged as the *lingua franca* by a long way. The words for describing participants are not yet established. Perhaps the most universal term is "wired," with its negation "the unwired" (echoes of "the great unwashed"). Aspirant poets of naming have the field relatively open at this time. Who will be the Homer, Dante or Shakespeare of the Internet? The prize is to enter the collective memory of humanity for all time.

Between agrarian civilization and the machine revolution

At the mid-point of the eighteenth century, Jean-Jacques Rousseau was walking down a lane in rural France, thinking about a possible entry for the Dijon Academy essay prize competition. The question to be addressed in 1750 concerned the contribution of the arts and sciences to the progress of civilization. A flash of intuition brought tears to his eyes and forced him to sit down. He suddenly realized that the answer was negative. Science was ruining the world; modern culture made us neither happier nor more virtuous; progress was an illusion. This was an extraordinary conclusion for an Enlightenment philosopher to reach; and, when he consulted his fellow *philosophe* Denis Diderot, the latter assured him that he had a good chance of winning, since no one else would be presenting that line of argument. Rousseau won. Four years later he entered another essay for the Dijon Academy prize, entitled *A Discourse on the Origins and Foundations of Inequality among Men.*[36] This time he lost. Yet *The Second Discourse* (as it is often called) deserves to be seen as the first great work of modern anthropology; it is the precursor of Rousseau's revolutionary contributions to our understanding of politics, education, personality and sexuality, written in the 1760s (*The Social Contract, Emile,* the *Confessions* and *La Nouvelle Héloïse*).

Rousseau was concerned, in his discourse, not with individual variations in natural endowments but with the artificial inequalities of wealth, honor and the capacity to command obedience that he derived from social convention. In order to construct a model of human equality, he imagined a pre-social state of nature, a sort of hominid phase of human evolution in which men were solitary, but healthy, happy and above all free. This freedom was metaphysical, anarchic and personal: Original human beings had free will, they were not subject to rules of any kind and they had no superiors. The essential human motives, according to him, are self-preservation, compassion and a desire for self-improvement. At some point humanity made the transition into what Rousseau calls "nascent society," a prolonged period whose economic base can best be summarized as hunter-gathering with huts. Why leave the state of nature at all? He speculates that disasters and economic shortage must have been involved. In any case, this second phase represents his ideal of life in society close to nature.

The rot set in with the invention of agriculture or, as Rousseau puts it, of wheat and iron. Cultivation of the land led to incipient property institutions whose culmination awaited the development of political society. "The first man who, having enclosed a piece of land, thought of saying "This is mine" and found people simple enough to believe him, was the true founder of civil society."[37]

The formation of a civil order (the state) was preceded by a Hobbesian condition, a war of all against all driven by inequality of all kinds and the absence of law. The key difference from Hobbes lay in Rousseau's insistence that such conflict was the result of social development, not an original state of nature. He believed that this new social contract to abide by the law was probably arrived at by consensus, but it was a fraudulent one in that the rich thereby gained legal sanction for transmitting unequal property rights in perpetuity. From this inauspicious beginning, political society then usually moved, via a series of revolutions, through three stages.

> *The establishment of law and the right of property was the first stage, the institution of magistrates the second, and the transformation of legitimate into arbitrary power the third and last stage. Thus the status of rich and poor was authorized by the first epoch, that of strong and weak by the second and by the third that of master and slave, which is the last degree of inequality and the stage to which all the others finally lead, until new revolutions dissolve the government altogether and bring it back to legitimacy.*[38]

One-man-rule closes the circle. "It is here that all individuals become equal again because they are nothing, here where subjects have no longer any law but the will of the master . . ."[39]

For Rousseau, the growth of inequality was just one aspect of human alienation in civil society. We need to return from division of labor and dependence on the opinion of others to subjective self-sufficiency. "The savage lives within himself; social man always lives outside himself."

> *The savage man breathes only peace and freedom; he desires only to live and stay idle and even the ataraxia of the Stoic does not approach his profound indifference toward every other object. Civil man, on the contrary, being always active, sweating and restless, torments himself endlessly in search of ever more laborious occupations; he works himself to death, he even runs toward the grave to put himself in shape to live, or renounces life in order to acquire immortality.*
>
> *Let the civilized man gather all his machines around him, and no doubt he will easily beat the savage; but if you would like to see an even more unequal match, pit the two together naked and unarmed, and you will soon see the advantages of having all one's forces constantly at one's command,*

of being always prepared for any eventuality, and of always being, so to speak, altogether complete in oneself.[40]

This subversive parable ends with a ringing indictment of economic inequality that could well serve as a warning to our world. "It is manifestly contrary to the law of nature, however defined . . . that a handful of people should gorge themselves with superfluities while the hungry multitude goes in want of necessities."[41]

Surely the stale odor of corruption that so revolted Rousseau is just as pervasive today. Dictatorship in one form or another has been normal for too long in many parts of the world, and we are all compromised by intolerable inequalities of wealth and power. Something has got to give; but our intellectual task today is to envisage a revolution that is universal, not just limited to individual states.

According to the United Nations *Human Development Report*,[42] the world's 225 richest men (and they are men) own more than one trillion dollars, the equivalent of the annual income of the world's 47% poorest people. Three of them have assets worth more than the Gross Domestic Product of the 48 least developed countries. The West spends $37 billion a year on pet food, perfumes and cosmetics ("let them eat Alpo"), almost the estimated additional cost of providing basic education, health, nutrition, water and sanitation for those deprived of them. The rate of car ownership in industrial countries is 400 per thousand, 16 in all developing countries. The rich pollute the world fifty times more than the poor, but it is the latter who are more likely to die from pollution. World consumption has increased six times in the last twenty years, but the richest fifth account for 86% of it.

As a thought experiment, we could conceive of humanity as a unit stratified by wealth, race, age and gender. Women everywhere are struggling with the legacy of patriarchy. The world's poor, however, are concentrated in what came to be called the Third World and latterly the South, the outcome of Western expansion over the last five hundred years and particularly of imperialism in the nineteenth century. The ideology sustaining this expansion was racism, the belief that the power of "white" people derived from a biologically founded superiority to the "darker races." Although racism is nowhere officially sanctioned today, it still plays a major part in organizing cultural responses to global inequality. Then also the world's young people are to be found predominantly in Africa, Asia and Latin America owing to a lag in the fall of birth rates there. For the age distributions of rich and poor countries are skewed heavily toward the old and young respectively.

There are tremendous inequalities within countries and regions (Bill Gates owns as much as the annual income of the 106 million least affluent Americans), but it is not difficult to summarize the above description in terms of a two-class model. A rich, mainly white, ageing minority (about 15%, if we take North America, Western Europe and Japan together) is surrounded by a majority (five-sixths of the total) that is on average a lot poorer, darker in color and especially much younger. Seen in terms of the reproduction of humanity as a whole, we can say that a stagnant Western elite is about to be replaced by a hugely proliferating generation of non-Westerners from whom it is separated by a tradition of cultural arrogance and by ingrained practices of social exclusion.

The situation is not unlike that found in agrarian civilizations, where small urban elites sought to maintain control over rural masses condemned to drudgery and political impotence. The main difference between the two cases lies in the fact that modern world society is supposed to be organized by an ideology of human freedom and equality. This is the legacy of a democratic revolution, begun in the seventeenth and eighteenth centuries, which aimed to install rule by the people in general as the only legitimate form of government. The industrial revolution, which closely followed its political counterpart, implied that humanity might now be released from material as well as social constraints on its development. But the evidence of global inequality today shows that this emancipatory rhetoric is an illusion.

World society today is at base as rotten as the aristocratic regimes that preceded the modern age. Power has been concentrated into forms held against the people, first in the hands of owners of big money (capitalists) and then in a revived and strengthened state apparatus. In the second half of the nineteenth century no major thinker envisaged the possibility of imposing state control on the restless energies of industrial/commercial society. Yet in the course of our own century, the rule of elites has been restored: State bureaucracy is absolute; and world society is divided into national fragments. There is no popular government anywhere, and most people have forgotten when they last took an active interest in such a possibility. The confusing part lies in the widespread use of a rhetoric derived from the democratic revolutions to cloak the purposes of those who reserve effective power to themselves. Western states are no more liberal than the Soviet Union was Marxist. At least the old regime of agrarian civilization called itself what it was. The vast majority of intellectuals are complicit in the lies needed to sustain this latterday revival of the state. Behind a smokescreen of democratic slogans, the bureaucracy relies on impersonal institutions to maintain grotesquely unfair levels of inequality.

One method for an anthropology of the contemporary human condition would thus be to conceive of world society as a single population divided into rich and poor, or, if you like, polarized between a remote elite and the undifferentiated masses. This society is unsustainable, in that most of its members are exposed to conditions of poverty and violence that are humanly unacceptable, while a few enjoy the benefits of wealth in forms that were unimaginable before the industrial revolution. Moreover, a society so cruel and indifferent to the general human interest is heading for ecological disaster. Ours is a corrupt *ancien régime*[43] that must soon find a new democratic revolution, if human intervention in the life of this planet is not to end in catastrophe.

The form of social organization underpinning this universal crisis for humanity in the twentieth century has been state capitalism, the attempt to manage markets and money through nation-states.[44] We know that agrarian civilizations ruled the earth for five thousand years before the machine revolution altered the conditions of human life irreversibly.

Today's societies everywhere claim to rest on science and democracy, the twin foundations of modernity and the lasting legacy of the eighteenth-century revolutions. This modern religion is similar in many ways to older claims made on behalf of God, and with the same plausibility: If society is omniscient and good, how can there be so much suffering in the world? The obvious answer to this question is that society is not run by and for the people as a whole, and, whatever its principles, they are not based on effective knowledge. Perhaps we are less emancipated from the past than we imagine and are further from a desirable future than we hope.

The institutions of agrarian civilization, developed over five millennia with a passive rural workforce in mind, are our institutions today: territorial states, landed property, warfare, embattled cities, objective money, long-distance trade, world religion, racism and the family. Consider what happened to all the wealth siphoned off by Western industrial states since the Second World War, the largest concentrations of money in the history of humanity. It went on subsidizing food supplies and armaments, the priorities of the bully through the ages, certainly not those of the modern urban consumers who paid the taxes. No, as Bruno Latour says,[45] we have never been modern. We are just primitives who stumbled recently into a machine revolution and cannot yet think of what do with it, beyond repeating the inhumanity of a society built unequally on agriculture.

The vision I have begun to sketch out in this chapter offers a number of angles from which we might perceive our moment in history. I have suggested that we are at the point when a third wave of mechanization, the communications revolution, first took on wider social use. This represents a new stage in the formation of world society as a single interactive network, and the evolutionary implications of that development are immense. It is also a time when the organization of capitalism by states may be moving to another, virtual stage driven by the possibilities inherent in digitalization. From the perspective of the human population as a whole, the course of the machine revolution has been very uneven, leaving large sections stranded in traditional agriculture. The problem of economic inequality, therefore, consists in the persistence of agriculture both as a mode of production and as the original matrix for institutions that still dominate our world. But it also consists in the forms of wealth and power specific to the modern age, to capitalism in its various guises.

The final chapter will address what might be done to accelerate the transition to a better world in which economic democracy is not just a figure of sham rhetoric. Certainly the issue of finding an appropriate time perspective for constructive change is a thorny one. I have been arguing here for a view of current developments as being rich in possibilities for far-reaching change in the relatively short run, yet also subject to institutional forces whose power to shape our lives has been greatly underestimated. Ours is a world of hectic movement and of remarkably stable institutions. The combination of a machine revolution and the legacy of agricultural society is potentially a lethal one.

Guide to further reading

The only anthropologist I know who tried to grasp the modern movement
of technology and society as a whole was Edmund Leach, whose Reith
Lectures, "A Runaway World?," were published in the mid-1960s (note 1).
This is still an inspirational work. Another of my teachers, C.L.R. James,
an itinerant revolutionary, made a brilliant stab at capturing the movement
of America at the beginning of the Cold War (note 7). I probably owe most
to the man who supervised all my early training, Jack Goody, whose
influence pervades this book. A recent example of his materialist approach
to culture in world history summarizes much of the rest, *The East in the
West;*[46] but no one has done more to investigate the consequences of that
earlier communications revolution, the invention of writing (note 28).

Since Karl Marx was the first major economist to notice the importance
of machines, it would obviously pay to read what he had to say on the
subject, particularly the long Chapter 15 of *Capital,* Volume 1, "Machinery
and Modern Industry" (note 4). A longer-term perspective on the
evolution of the relationship between city and countryside is provided by
his colleague, Engels (note 15). After them, the most significant writer on
capitalist industry was Thorstein Veblen. His *Theory of Business Enterprise*
(note 5) is just the best of several classic works on the contradiction
between machine production and markets.

Tom Kemp's overview of the literature on industrialization is
comprehensive; while David Landes's treatise is more personal and
engaging (note 10). Carlo Cipolla has the field to himself as the author of
The Economic History of World Population, even if the figures are now out of
date (note 13). I wish there were a history of twentieth-century
urbanization to match A.F. Weber's of the nineteenth (note 11); this book
has always been indispensable to me. Alvin Toffler is more than just a
popularizer; try his *The Third Wave* (note 2). I tried to assess the long-run
impact of the machine revolution on an underdeveloped region in my book
on West Africa (note 16). The annual reports of the World Bank and the
United Nations Development Program, especially that for 1998, provide a
global perspective on inequality.[47]

There are some classic works that bear on parts of the thesis advanced
here. The *Muqaddimah* of Ibn Khaldun (note 23) offers a fascinating view

of the social dynamics of the Mediterranean world six hundred years ago. This should be read with Fernand Braudel's amazing treatment of the same region a couple of centuries later (note 25). Gordon Childe (note 27) and Marshall Sahlins (note 18) offer very different but highly readable takes on the perennial questions of human social evolution. I believe that Rousseau's *Second Discourse* is the original source for such an evolutionary anthropology (note 21), and I find it to be still the most thought-provoking example of the genre. Sir William Petty (note 17) and Robert Malthus (note 19) inaugurated the modern taste for population economics, although Petty was probably more accurate in calling it *Political Arithmetick*. And, while we are on the subject of classics, don't forget to read Dickens's *Hard Times* for a jaundiced view of Manchester's pioneering industrial experiment (note 35).

If one of the main messages of this chapter is that contemporary world society is more like the old regime of pre-revolutionary France than anything else, I can only point to de Tocqueville's remarkable analysis of the antecedents and consequences of that decisive revolutionary moment (note 43). As for the idea that we are less modern than we think, Bruno Latour certainly got there first (note 45). But again, Rousseau seems to me to be the most modern thinker dealing with our dilemmas today.

I have disclaimed any authority as a guide to the information economy and the communications revolution of the 1990s. But the following would constitute a start for interested readers: Nicholas Negroponte *Being Digital;* Don Tapscott *The Digital Economy;* Carl Shapiro and Hal Varian *Information Rules.* The first two are set at a very popular level; the last advances the challenging thesis that mainstream economic principles apply to the Internet.[48] I like Negroponte's book best. To this I would now add John Naughton's *A Brief History of the Future* (note 31).

Notes

1. E. Leach, *A Runaway World? The 1967 Reith Lectures* (BBC, London, 1968).
2. A. Toffler, *The Third Wave* (Bantam Books, New York, 1981). The idea of periodizing the machine revolution is far from new. Economic historians have long distinguished the late-nineteenth-century industrial complex from what went before it. Alvin Toffler's *The Third Wave* is a recent, well-known example, combining recent and longer-term changes.

3. K. Marx and F. Engels, *The Manifesto of the Communist Party* in Marx–Engels, *Selected Works* (Lawrence & Wishart, London, 1968; first pub. 1848).

4. K. Marx, *Capital: A Critique of Political Economy. Volume 1* (Lawrence & Wishart, London, 1970; first pub. 1867).

5. T. Veblen, *The Theory of Business Enterprise* (Charles Scribner, New York, 1904).

6. C.L.R. James, *Mariners, Renegades and Castaways: The Story of Herman Melville and the World We Live In* (Allison & Busby, London, 1984; first pub. 1953).

7. C.L.R. James, *American Civilization* (Blackwell, Oxford, 1993).

8. The citizens of Paris, my adopted home, love working-class nostalgia films from northern Britain such as *Brassed Off* and *The Full Monty*. Perhaps it has something to do with French resistance to globalization.

9. Although there are many popular works emphasizing the positive side of the communications revolution, the balance of serious academic and left-wing opinion is, of course, the other way. For two recent exercises in the political economy of information, see O. Gandy, *The Panoptic Sort: A Political Economy of Personal Information* (Westview, Boulder, 1993); R. McChesney, E. Wood and J. Forster, eds., *Capitalism and the Information Age: The Political Economy of the Global Communication Revolution* (Monthly Review Press, New York, 1998).

10. T. Kemp, *Historical Patterns of Industrialization* (Longman, Harlow, 1993); D. Landes, *The Unbound Prometheus: Technical Change and Industrial Development in Western Europe from 1750 to the Present* (Cambridge University Press, Cambridge, 1969).

11. A.F. Weber, *The Growth of Cities in the Nineteenth Century* (Cornell Paperbacks, Ithaca, NY, 1967; first pub. 1899), p. 471. Adna Weber calculated in the first decade of this century that the maximum range for commuters was five miles, since no one would be willing to spend more than half an hour travelling each way and the average speed of trains was then ten miles per hour!

12. In 1995 Americans each consumed 8,000 kg of oil equivalent, compared with 22 kg in Uganda. World Bank, *Development Indicators 1998* (IBRD, Washington DC, 1998), p. 144.

13. C. Cipolla, *The Economic History of World Population* (7th ed., Penguin, Harmondsworth, 1968).

14. World Bank, *Development Indicators 1998* (IBRD, Washington DC, 1998), p. 44.

15. F. Engels, *The Origin of Private Property, the Family and the State* in Marx–Engels, *Selected Works* (Lawrence & Wishart, London, 1968; first pub. 1884).

16. K. Hart, *The Political Economy of West African Agriculture* (Cambridge University Press, Cambridge, 1982).

17. W. Petty, *Political Arithmetick: or, A Discourse Concerning the Extent of Lands, People, Power at Sea, etc.* (Clavel & Mortlock, London, 1691).

18. M. Sahlins, *Stone-age Economics* (Aldine, Chicago, 1972).

19. R. Malthus, *An Essay on the Principle of Population: or, A View of Its Past and Present Effects on Human Happiness* (Cambridge University Press, Cambridge, 1992; first pub. 1798).

20. H. Conklin, *Hanunoo Agriculture: A Report on an Integral System of Shifting Cultivation in the Philippines* (FAO, Rome, 1957).

21. J.-J. Rousseau, *A Discourse on Inequality* (Penguin, Harmondsworth, 1984; first pub. 1754).

22. It is worth recalling that there were 20 million working animals in the USA at the time of the First World War.

23. I. Khaldun, *The Muqaddimah: An Introduction to History* (Routledge & Kegan Paul, London, 1987).

24. For me the enduring image of this is taken from David Lean's film *Lawrence of Arabia,* when a Bedouin cavalry charge overruns the coastal town of Aqaba, whose guns are pointing uselessly towards the sea.

25. F. Braudel, *The Mediterranean and the Mediterranean World in the Age of Philip II* (Collins, London, 1973).

26. M. Weber, *The Agrarian Sociology of Ancient Civilizations* (New Left Books, London, 1976; first pub. 1904). Two millennia ago, as Max Weber pointed out, Marseilles was easier to reach from the eastern Mediterranean than from a hundred kilometers inland.

27. V.G. Childe, *Man Makes Himself* (Moonraker Press, London, 1981).

28. J. Goody, *The Domestication of the Savage Mind* (Cambridge University Press, Cambridge, 1977); *The Interface between the Written and the Oral* (Cambridge University Press, Cambridge, 1989).

29. Plato, *The Republic* (J.M. Dent, London, 1976); M. Shell, *The Economy of Literature* (Johns Hopkins University Press, Baltimore, 1978).

30. D. McKitterick, *A History of Cambridge University Press. Vol. 1: Printing and the Book Trade in Cambridge 1534–1698* (Cambridge University Press, Cambridge, 1992).

31. Since completing this book, I have come across John Naughton's excellent *A Brief History of the Future: The Origins of the Internet* (1999), which exposes the limitations of this summary, including my repetition of the myth of military origin. J. Naughton, *A Brief History of the Future: The Origins of the Internet* (Weidenfeld and Nicolson, London, 1999).

32. This matters now that the Internet is being used for a wide range of audio-visual transmissions, whereas not long ago it mainly carried handwritten messages. Pictures, especially moving pictures, take up a lot more bits than

alphabetic and numerical scripts. High-bandwidth transmissions are necessary if video, for example, is to be accessed quickly and cheaply.

33. I came across this issue when teaching an interdisciplinary seminar to graduate students at Yale during the late 1970s; it was called "The Transition from Bronze to Iron in the Eastern Mediterranean 1600–500 BC."

34. U.S. Department of Commerce, *The Emerging Digital Economy,* report published on the web in 1998 (www.commerce.gov).

35. C. Dickens, *Hard Times* (Bradbury & Evans, London, 1854); J. Crabtree, *Richard Arkwright* (Macmillan, New York, 1923).

36. See note 21.

37. J.-J. Rousseau, *A Discourse on Inequality,* p. 109 (see note 21).

38. Ibid., p. 131.

39. Ibid., p. 134.

40. Ibid., pp. 136, 82.

41. Ibid., p. 137.

42. United Nations Development Program, *Human Development Report 1998* (UNDP, New York, 1998).

43. A. de Tocqueville, *The Old Regime and the French Revolution* (Doubleday, New York, 1955; first pub. 1856).

44. C.L.R. James and associates, *State Capitalism and World Revolution* (Charles Kerr, Chicago, 1986; first pub. 1950).

45. B. Latour, *We Have Never Been Modern* (Harvester Wheatsheaf, Herts., 1993).

46. J. Goody, *The East in the West* (Cambridge University Press, Cambridge, 1996).

47. See note 12; *Human Development Report 1999* (UNDP, New York, 1999).

48. N. Negroponte, *Being Digital* (Hodder & Stoughton, London, 1995); D. Tapscott, *The Digital Economy: Promise and Peril in the Age of Networked Intelligence* (McGraw Hill, New York, 1996); C. Shapiro and H. Varian, *Information Rules: A Strategic Guide to the Network Economy* (Harvard Business School Press, Boston, Mass., 1999).

Chapter 3
Capitalism: Making Money with Money

Markets are networks of buyers and sellers using money to exchange goods and services. They are intrinsically democratic: All you need to participate is something to sell or the money to buy. Moreover, the market is based on movement: Its proliferating connections cannot easily be contained by political organization tied to a particular place. The extension of trade beyond the limits of locality has been a relatively benign means for the human economy to take on a global character in recent centuries (the less benign method being war and conquest, often in tandem with trade). It is not surprising, then, that the drive to form more democratic and inclusive societies has been linked with the expansion of markets. But there has always been a strong resistance to markets in ideology and practice. This has its roots in the interests that dominated agrarian civilization, but it also arose from what markets became in reality.

In the first place, an institution that depends on the freedom to spend money can hardly be said to be democratic, when some people have so much more of it than others. Owners of lots of money, capitalists who now take the form of public corporations rather than private individuals, have come to dominate the market economy, making it an experience of profound inequality and unfreedom for most participants. The second point is that markets have been closely associated in the modern period with the development of nation-states that, in the twentieth century, have concentrated impersonal power held against the people. To these social forces we should add the machine revolution that initially favored the centralization of economic and political power, leading to that alliance between money and bureaucracy that I call state capitalism. It is not surprising that, faced with the alienating forces of a capitalist world, many people took refuge in an anti-market ideology promising a society that would get rid of money altogether

73

from the core of economic life, substituting for purchase and sale the administration of resources by public officials. But in practice this collectivist alternative converged on the model it rejected, relying on political and economic bureaucracies, as well as on machines and money, in ways that were often more unequal and oppressive than the original.[1]

The failure of communism, coming after four decades of the Cold War for global supremacy, coincided with a shift in the ideology of Western capitalism. This was based on a recognition of the limits of welfare state bureaucracy and a revival of enthusiasm for the interplay of private interests in the market. The defeated peoples of Eastern Europe found themselves urged to embrace "privatization" as an economic panacea, a policy that quickly revealed itself to be a recipe for private misery, public decay and criminal enterprise. Nor is the initial euphoria over the West's "victory" in the Cold War much in evidence at the millennium. It is clear that markets are increasingly global, if only because of the extraordinary growth in the world market for money instruments. The communications revolution seems to have ushered in a virtual capitalism that is no longer securely grounded either in territorial states or in the exchange of real goods and services, being manifested rather as so many digits flashing between computer screens over the telephone wires. At the same time, over the last two decades, the gap between rich and poor has escalated at every level of world society, partly as a result of the decline of the state's powers of intervention both nationally and internationally.

Given the replacement of state capitalism by a commitment to the market, at least as dominant ideology, and growing confusion over the proper place of public and private interests in the organization of economic life, it would seem to be a good time to review the relationship between money, markets and political power in the modern era. The following two chapters take off from the idea that the age of mechanization has been dominated by money capital in several successive forms. In Chapter 3 the emphasis is on the origins of market capitalism and the early theories that have shaped our understanding of the modern economy. Both John Locke and Karl Marx conceived of their times as an age of money that left humanity suspended uneasily between a past dependency on nature and the possibility of building a just society in the future. Their contrasting views on the relationship between markets and money in such a future underpins the division that almost brought the world to catastrophe in the Cold War, even though neither envisaged the forms of capitalism and socialism that the antagonists actually took.

I then draw on Marx's work to define industrial capitalism's principles in its first Victorian phase and on Max Weber for the most suggestive alternative approach. If Marx emphasized the exchange of labor for capital as "free" forms of property, Weber took a broader cultural line focusing on "rational enterprise," the attempt to make the pursuit of uncertain economic futures more calculable. Both traced the origins of their idea of capitalism through the economic history of Britain; and their complementary theories are each indispensable to making sense of its continuing evolution. Before filling in subsequent developments, which is the task of Chapter 4, this chapter takes the analysis in a more ethnographic direction, reflecting my own knowledge of the emergent patterns of capitalist enterprise in the non-Western periphery. I argue that the evidence of Africa's small-scale societies throws light on the original conditions of capitalism's emergence in Europe, as living examples of processes that otherwise would be available to us only in dead theoretical texts. This in turn allows us to see the particular local variations that are always intrinsic to capitalism's general development. The chapter concludes with a detailed exposition of my own West African research into the personal face of capitalism, entrepreneurs, in preparation for later explorations of the re-emergence of personality in economic life.

In contrast to this miniaturizing approach, Chapter 4 returns to the broad outlines of twentieth-century history, to the formation of state capitalism and its decline as a result of conditions associated with the communications revolution. A major theme is the need to explain the growing gap between rich and poor regions of our world. This is taken up in a section dealing with the development of global inequality, especially in the period after the break-up of formal colonial empire. As a bridge between the first and subsequent phases of the machine revolution, I ask whether the classes identified by the political economists in the early nineteenth century help us to understand the struggle for the dividends of the Internet today. These classes, based respectively on control over the yields of the land, money capital and human creativity, derive their income from economic forms (rent, tax, profit, wages, equal exchange) that are evolving as capitalism has moved from an urban to a national and finally a global level.

Following the bureaucratic revolution of the late nineteenth century and the First World War, capitalism became, especially in the middle decades of the twentieth century, more or less synonymous with the nation-state and with Keynesian policies of demand management, "macro-economics." Toward the end of that period, the self-organized activities of people operating beyond the reach of state regulation were identified as "the informal economy." This was at first considered to be largely a phenomenon of Third World cities, but, in the face of waning state power, it has become a universal feature of the world economy. This dialectic of state and people is of interest as we move into the phase of virtual capitalism, a world where digitalized exchange of money and services at distance has ushered in a growing detachment of the money circuit from the real economy of production and trade. This is the source of, and possibly the solution to, growing economic inequality. For machines now offer ordinary people the chance to be in the forefront of technological change, while remaining for the first time independent of the owners of money and landed power. In general, these chapters cast doubt on the left's perennial belief that the demise of capitalism is imminent. But a more hopeful scenario pits the disorganized legions of "the wired" against the governments and corporations who threaten to dominate the future of the Internet.

The age of money

> "In the beginning all the world was America and more so than that is now; for no such thing as Money was any where known. Find out something that hath the use and value of money amongst his neighbors, you shall see the same man will begin presently to enlarge his possessions."[2]
> JOHN LOCKE

We have difficulty placing ourselves reliably in the schemes we construct to make sense of history. Most often, we conflate the pace of fundamental social change with our own biological clocks, imagining that we make the world anew in our own lifetimes while discounting the effects of long-established traditions. Commonly, modern writers have depicted a sequence in which the past was dominated by nature or the land, and the future will be a society made by ourselves fairly and reasonably in the interests of all. The present, conceived of as transitional between these two states, is simultaneously the dissolvent of the past and a bridge to a better future. Its main feature is money and the buying and selling that go with it. As I have noted, this can be called the market or capitalism, according to taste. But the idea is broadly the same in either case. What varies is whether money is taken to be indispensable to the just society or anathema to it.

John Locke and Karl Marx stand as the epitome of each strand: Locke has been credited with the theory underpinning the "bourgeois" revolution of property-owning or liberal democracy, while Marx has been claimed as the author of many twentieth-century experiments in "socialism." A case can be made that neither should be held responsible for the subsequent social developments they are supposed to have launched. For the philosophy and political programs of these thinkers have yet to be applied seriously in actual societies. But what concerns us here is their vision of the contradictory part played by money in human history. Certainly Marx's idea of an economic democracy run by and for all working people is hard to deny as a long-term goal; but at one level it is a question of whether we believe that Locke's middle-class revolution has yet run its course.

In the above quote, Locke was making his case that humanity originally lived in a state of nature, of which America was the closest contemporary example, where land was abundant and no one benefited from hoarding more goods than they needed for their own immediate use. Money changed all that by making it possible to store surpluses in a durable form; and accumulation of property, especially land, became the driving force of an increasingly unequal society. He was anxious to locate the origin of property in the state of nature and that of money in society before civil government (we might say before the centralized state). Accordingly, he made personal work the rightful source of property (the labor theory of value) and found the source of money in "fancy," an aesthetic preference for shiny metals in exchange as opposed to real use, and eventually in "mutual consent" rather than political authority.

In the recoinage crisis of the 1690s following King William's accession to the English throne, a time when Europe's religious war was at its height and

England's currency had been debased by civil war, criminality and corruption, money was the central plank of Locke's political project. He had a vision of an expanding world economy with England as its leading power and guarantor. He wanted sterling to be based on fixed quantities of precious metals, which meant pulling in the present debased coinage[3] and reissuing a smaller number with metal content up to face value. The state was necessary to regulate the currency, but was not its source. Locke's opponents, such as the London property speculator Nicholas Barbon, accused him of wishing to engineer a ruinous deflation of the national economy[4] for the sake of a few Portuguese wine merchants. They favored the reissue of the same number of coins at a lower metal content, in a word, devaluation. But this meant acknowledging that money was little more than the creature of government policy. In the words of Barbon's famous dictum, "money is a value made by law."[5] Locke wanted a state that guaranteed the property of the economically active and maintained a stable currency for international trade; he could not bring himself to sanction a policy that would effectively concede power to an implicit alliance of corrupt politicians and economic criminals.[6] He thus wanted government both to guarantee a standard of exchange and to separate that means of exchange from the aims and interests of government itself.

In retrospect it is easy enough to say that Locke's eyes were fixed on engineering society in the interest of a class whose detractors generally tend to call it "the bourgeoisie." I prefer the expression "middle-class revolution." He fought absolutist monarchy and a capricious political system dominated by the landed aristocracy (in other words, the old regime of agrarian civilization) in the name of everyone's natural right to accumulate property through their own efforts. In his day the poor or those lacking any property were a bit more than half of England's population, and their purchasing power amounted to around 20% of the market economy.[7] They would not see much of the silver coinage Locke was worried about. Compare that situation with England in the 1930s, when Keynes emerged to define another economic and political crisis, and wage employment accounted for two-thirds of national income. Even in the mid-nineteenth century when Marx was writing, the wages of workers were so low that the price of the wheat used for their bread was commonly understood to be a reliable proxy for their purchasing power.

When Locke came up with a three-stage theory of social development corresponding to the state of nature, an age of money and arbitrary political power, and constitutional government securing the property of market agents, he largely ignored the toiling masses even though he framed his analysis and proposals as human universals. Money had to be tamed in a number of senses, but it was indispensable to the emerging eighteenth-century world society whose contours he did more than any single person to shape. Money got humanity out of a state of nature, and it had to be rescued from those whose unaccountable power allowed them to steal from productive members of society. Establishing a reliable currency was thus at once an aid to the struggle of the middle classes against landed aristocracy and part of the effort to decriminalize an informal economy running out of control.

This project may be called "liberal democracy," a label that has been tarnished for many by the equally arbitrary accumulation of economic power it has sanctioned in its turn. This is less a condemnation of Locke than a recognition of the persisting inequality of a world society driven by money and lacking adequate political safeguards for the mass of humanity. Indeed, if America was the symbol of the state of nature in Locke's day, it has become the epitome of the age of money for us. Just as Locke confronted arbitrary state power, a money system running wild and a world lacking the guarantees of a stable and just civil society, so too do we; and America is that world's symbol. The task of constructing a society fit for human beings to live in seems as far ahead now as it did then. But for some time those who would do something about it have turned for inspiration not to John Locke but to Karl Marx.

If the main object of accumulation in Locke's time was still land, by the mid-nineteenth century money itself, in the form of capital used to organize industrial production, had become the driving force of society. Marx began his reconstruction of human history, in texts such as *Pre-capitalist Economic Formations,*[8] with settled agriculture, dismissing the hunter-gatherer phase of Locke's state of nature as a time when we were barely differentiated from the animals. All subsequent forms of society were in essence natural, emphasizing reliance on the land, food production, biological reproduction (the family) and kinship-based communities dominated by father-figures. The unity of the original herd was stretched but not broken by development toward greater complexity; and humanity, being passive in the face of nature, animated the world with spirits that became the object of religious devotion. Commerce, originating in cities, was the dissolvent of these primitive social forms and money succeeded God as the fetishized source of human agency.

Capitalism, as *The Manifesto of the Communist Party*[9] makes abundantly clear, was the ruin of traditional rural society. It achieved this result by drawing people into markets not only for goods, but also for their labor. Production was separated from the land and from social forms attached to it. Market contracts individualized property ownership and social relations. Centralization of production through widespread use of machinery concentrated the workers in urban areas. And this was the Achilles heel of capitalism, for an antidote to private property would grow out of the increased capacity of workers to organize themselves in the towns. The industrial proletariat was thus the vanguard of a society destined to arise out of the failure of capitalism's market anarchy to meet the needs of the majority. This society would revive the solidarity of pre-capitalist forms ("communism"), but this time with machine production as a means of mastering nature and self-conscious reason as a counterweight to religious alienation.

Since for Marx money was more or less synonymous with the contradictory transitional phase between pre-industrial and post-industrial society, how differently did he account for its origins and future, when compared with Locke? He begins *Capital* with a story taken from Adam Smith.[10] *The Wealth of Nations* is widely taken to be the foundation of modern economics, and, on this occasion, Marx saw no point in distancing himself from its origin myth. Smith considered the "propensity to truck and barter," that is, to exchange goods without money, to be part of human nature. He takes off from an example of two savages in North America exchanging deerskin for beaver pelts at a ratio of 2 to 1.[11] Money arises in stages as a way of making these exchanges more efficient. It does so by allowing the seller to buy in the future from someone other than the immediate buyer of his commodity, rather than be forced to find a buyer who is also selling what he wants. Money starts out as a commodity, such as cattle, salt or gold, which becomes specialized as a means of exchange and store of value. Marx repeats this account, even though he knew that barter in this form could not be original, since it assumes alienable private property in commodities exchanged between individuals; and that is a consequence of historical developments culminating in capitalism.

Unlike Locke, who believed that the appearance of money by itself encouraged accumulation, Marx distinguished between simple commodity exchange, where people used markets to meet their needs in use, and capitalist commodity exchange, where the aim was to increase the stock of money through profit. Finance and merchant capital, money-making through usury and trade, were as old as agrarian civilization; but industrial capital, the use of money to hire wage labor, was recent and revolutionary, since labor was the only commodity capable of producing more than the cost of its own purchase. The penetration of money and markets into the bulk of production was the distinctive feature of the capitalist age, since in earlier forms of society they had been restricted to minor enclaves that did not impinge directly on the system of landed property and power.[12]

Marx did not wish to grant to the apologists for bourgeois revolution the right to claim for it the decisive breakthrough in human history, important though it was in forcing the initial rupture with old society. For this reason, he set out in *Capital* to link the system of wage labor under capitalism to coercive extraction of the agricultural surplus from a servile labor force. Capitalist labor markets, including the reserve army of the unemployed that they generated, functioned as a source of economic coercion, allowing the owners of money to exploit their workers in ways analogous to feudalism. The concept of surplus value carried this connotation at the same time as it drew attention to the fact that workers only received a portion of the value of their output, just like serfs. It may well be that Marx's greatest contribution was to find a feudal metaphor for the idea of the *job* that has so dominated economic discourse in the last hundred years. In any case, he seized readily on Locke's labor theory of value to insist that a just society would grant control over the value of commodities to the workers who produced them, not to the owners of labor congealed in money.

Marx's writings on how a future communist society would work are nothing like as extensive as his critique of capitalism and of its apologists, the political economists. But it would not be excessive to say that he was as hostile to money and markets as he was to the institutions of agrarian civilization (states, religion, peasant agriculture, etc.). Indeed, by accepting Smith's origin myth of money in primitive barter, he was able to make capitalism an outgrowth of old society that loosened its bonds but remained fatally backward-looking in its social logic. This left the creation of a free and equal society to an imminent revolutionary future led by the workers. The age of money had unleashed mechanization and the means of social mobilization in cities, but it was not it-self capable of organizing a society adequate to the democratic needs of all humanity. Even if Marx left his own thoughts on communism largely implicit, his followers in the twentieth century remained hostile to money and markets, preferring to rely on the administration of economic resources by bureaucratic elites and to push commercial property to the illegal margins of society.

The collapse of Stalinism a decade ago led to the triumphalist celebration of capitalism in the West. The age of money was vindicated by the defeat of its socialist antagonist. Liberal democracy, with its bulwarks of private prop-erty, the market and representative democracy, was judged to be the only player left in the game, so much so that Francis Fukuyama earned short-lived fame as the author of a book whose main thesis was roughly that Locke's middle-class revolution had become universal and eternal.[13] Even before the 1990s concluded, this confidence could be seen to have been se-verely misplaced. So where are we today and how do we place ourselves in relation to money, the key element in both Locke's and Marx's historical schemes? One way of approaching that question is to examine the history of capitalism, the system of making money with money, which has changed its form in the course of the last two centuries. Its left-wing detractors have an-ticipated its early demise throughout that period; but, with the formation of world society in our time, it may just be coming into its own.

The theory of capitalism

If, in the last chapter, I may have given the impression that mechanization is the driving force of modern history, to do so would be to fetishize technol-ogy, to reproduce the notion that animated objects rule our world. Human beings make machines, and they make them under specific social conditions. What, then, is the form of society organizing our hectic march from the vil-lage to the city, toward the possibility of a global civilization? Since the last century the answer has been contained in a name that is at once a description and an explanation, the favorite label for our economic dynamism: capitalism.[14] Capitalism is above all that combination of money and machines whose special character underlies the polarizing tendencies of our world. Even naming this process is controversial, since its apologists prefer to mask its contradictions in polite talk of "business" and "the market."

In this section I will first examine the meaning of the term *capital,* showing how it is taken by some to be an objective and benign feature of human societies in general, by others a recent historical invention of dubious social value. Then I will turn to the two greatest commentators on capitalism as a general system, Marx and Weber, each of whom paid close attention to its specific origins in Europe, especially Britain. The origin of the modern economy is not, however, just a feature of Western history that passed long ago, something now preserved in the dry texts of dead writers. The conditions on which it has been built are still alive, taking root in the far corners of the world, as well as being renewed in its old heartlands. Later I offer a brief account of some African examples, before returning to the original case of modern capitalist development, Britain. The point of this comparison is that universal social processes are always modified by the concrete elements of their formation in particular places.

Capital is wealth used to make more wealth.[15] *Wealth* is all resources having economic value. *Value* is worth in general, but it tends to be measured in a universal equivalent, that is, *money.* So the essence of capital is that it is wealth (usually money in some form) capable of *increasing* its value. In both popular and scientific usage, the meaning of capital shifts uneasily between a material or technical emphasis on *stock* (produced means of production, physical equipment, nowadays notably machines) and identification with the kind of money prevailing in a modern economy. The analogy between capital increase and the natural reproduction of livestock is reinforced by the etymology of *cattle,* which suggests an ancient link between the two terms.[16] *Capitalis* (of the head) means important, chief, primary and, in the neuter form (*capitale*), refers to significant property, such as chattels and cattle. In this broad sense, then, capital, like the head, is most important to sustaining life (every body needs a head, every community a leader: hence heads and tails).[17]

The modern term *capital,* however, derives more specifically from a medieval banking expression (similar to the notion of "principal") implying an amount of money that grows through accumulating interest. There are thus two opposing camps, one of whom would assimilate capitalism into a wide, natural category with its technical basis in the domestication of plants and animals, while the other sees capitalism as a more ephemeral social arrangement devoted to making money with money. As a keyword of our civilization, capital reflects the contrasting ideologies that have arisen to represent it. As we will see below, Marx and his followers (which includes me in this context) consistently restrict the definition of capital to its form as money. Most modern economists, however, equate capital with, in one definition, "the stock of goods which are used in production and which are themselves produced."[18]

Marx viewed the piling up of riches by businessmen as a social relationship of exploitation that was mystified by equating capital with physical plant and profit with the reasonable income of its owners. For him, as for Locke, human labor was the source of wealth, and the addition of machines to that labor only made it more productive. Economists, however, tend to stress the notion of *sacrifice,* the withdrawal of goods from immediate consumption, and the enhanced productivity of factors other than labor in which the capitalist has invested. So that increase constitutes the reward for making the sacrifice. This argument makes sense in an industrial economy where money wealth comes most reliably from investment in mechanizing production. But there are forms of capital accumulation that do not necessarily involve physical plant (banking and trade, for example), and the broader usage tends to confuse money and machines by representing capital as a thing (that is, as *real*) and mystifying the social relations involved. The problem with the economists' definition is that it cannot deal with historical change in the relationship between production and the circuit of money, as Marx's dialectic can. Certainly it could not cope with the virtual capitalism of our day.

In this book, capitalism is taken to be that form of market economy in which the owners of large amounts of money get to direct the most significant sectors of production. They do so in the interest of adding to the amounts of money they already have. Competitive markets for industrial products meant that, for a time and perhaps also now, the most reliable way of making money with money lay in raising the productivity of labor through investment in machines. This is, roughly speaking, Marx's position.

So let us see how he developed it in the context of an historical analysis of Britain, the particular point of origin for the age of capitalist accumulation.

Writers from Aristotle to Polanyi have identified two distinct orientations to the market. The first is concerned with selling for money what is surplus to requirements in order to buy what one wants. Marx called this the "simple commodity circuit" (C-M-C).[19] The second, M-C-M', where M' > M, starts with money and has the aim of realizing more money through participation in the market as a "capitalist commodity circuit." According to Marx, there are three main versions of this capitalist circuit. The first two are as old as markets and money: Financial capital (M-M'), where profit takes the form of interest on money lent; and merchant capital (M-C-M'), where trade goods are bought cheaply to be sold dear and profit consists in the difference between buying and selling minus handling costs. In both cases the source of the money increase is mysterious, since the contribution of human work is hidden from view. The third form is distinctive to the modern age as a general economic system; and it consists in purchasing human labor for wages with the purpose of getting these workers to produce goods worth more than the cost of their hire. Marx called this industrial capital, not primarily with reference to the factories that were characteristic of the first industrial revolution, but in order to emphasize the penetration of money capital into production, whether that be agriculture, manufacturing or services.

In all agrarian societies, markets were peripheral to the organization of production. Once people routinely sold their labor for a livelihood, however, it undermined the traditional arrangements binding them to the land;

Figure 3.1   Two circuits of commodities and money

1. Simple circuit

Commodities　　⟶　　Money　　⟶　　Commodities

2. Capitalist circuit

Money　　⟶　　Commodities　　⟶　　More money

---

more importantly, it vastly expanded the market, since they depended on buying the means of their everyday subsistence. Moreover, only human creativity can produce goods valued at more than it costs to buy. This relationship of *surplus value* between owners of capital and workers held the key, in Marx's view, to the dramatic recent increases in the rate of accumulation. At the same time, unlike the case with finance and trading capital, it became clearer that workers generated the increase accruing to the capitalist. For Marx, then, modern capitalism was that form of making money with money in which free capital was exchanged with free wage labor. He sought to account, therefore, for the process whereby people's capacity to work was freed from the legal encumbrances of feudal agriculture and for the release of funds for investment in new forms of production. He discusses this process of "primitive accumulation" in the last section of Volume 1 of *Capital*.

Marx found that British capitalism had its origins in a long, drawn-out struggle to displace the peasants from their traditional occupation of the land. The enclosure movement began in Tudor times and was still going strong in the Scottish Highlands during the nineteenth century. It meant that large sections of the rural poor were forced to seek hire for wages, while the landlords were able to make over privatized land to lucrative activities such as sheep farming. Employment in capitalist textile factories was a natural outcome of this conjuncture. Marx deploys his full range as a writer to depict the brutal criminality of this history. So where did the money come from to finance industrial capitalism? Marx's answer is unequivocal: The expanded system of colonies, slavery and world trade that followed the explorations around 1500 and after. Here again he stresses villainy, the outrageous exploits of pirates and freebooters who stole the patrimony of people they often reduced to servitude. This is a key question of economic history. Did the industrial revolution rest on loot from the Third World or not? Max Weber thought that it did not; and neither do I. But this is only a secondary aspect of Marx's argument.[20]

Adam Smith had related profit levels to reduced costs achieved through raising the efficiency of workers; and he identified specialization and division of labor as the best way of doing this. Marx's great discovery was that this logic led to the introduction of more and better machines to the production process. Capitalists could stay ahead of their competitors by paying

86

proportionately lower wages than were justified by productivity increases. The changing ratio of wage costs to investment in machinery and plant ("the organic composition of capital") reflected this drive to cheapen unit labor costs: And its result was that centralization of production that Marx correctly saw as the underlying trend of nineteenth-century capitalism. But he also noticed that there were other trends; and he highlighted the alternative paths of accumulation in a long section of Volume 1 of *Capital* on absolute and relative surplus value.

It was one of Marx's aims to demonstrate that wage slavery under capitalism was fundamentally similar to feudal serfdom. In the latter case tied agricultural workers had to hand over a proportion of their product ("surplus labor") in some form, whether a share of their physical output, labor services or, occasionally, a money equivalent. Marx knew that feudal landlords had every interest in extracting the most they could from these workers by driving down to the limit what they retained for their own subsistence. Surplus labor becomes surplus value when workers are paid wages directly and the surplus retained by the capitalist takes the form of goods whose value is realized in the market as commodities. The most primitive type of industrial capitalism, therefore, is one in which the feudal approach is transferred to the industrial system of wage labor.

In Marx's terminology, one tendency of capital accumulation is thus concerned with extracting *absolute surplus value*. This means paying workers as little as possible and making them work as many hours as possible, for example by lengthening the working day without increasing wages. We call this phenomenon "sweat shop" capitalism, and it can be found anywhere that unprotected workers (often women, minorities or illegal aliens) are forced to endure low pay, long hours and oppressive conditions. The other tendency is the one we have already identified, marked by what Marx called *relative surplus value,* the improvement of workers' efficiency through increased scale of co-operation, division of labor and, above all, mechanization. This path leads to a high-wage, high-skill economy that Marx felt sure was the progressive side of capitalism and one that would inevitably win out in competition with the other tendency.

This distinction between absolute and relative surplus value contains one vital key to understanding the uneven development of the world economy.

In most sectors of production, but some more than others (textiles, say, more than nuclear submarines), there is direct competition between low-cost and high-cost producers. Thus Britain under the Tories offended its partners in the European Union by pursuing a strategy of attracting international investment with low wage costs. In France the emphasis is on reduced hours of working and improved social benefits, whereas Germany especially is committed to improving the skills and equipment of a high-cost labor force. Few doubt which of these countries has the more robust capitalism. The post-war rise of the South-East Asian "tigers" (Hong Kong, Singapore, Korea, Taiwan), and of Japan before that, began on the model of absolute surplus value and has subsequently switched to the relative path. In the meantime, the smokestack heartlands of the first industrial nations, which once led the way in machine production, now offer low-cost investment opportunities for Asian companies in a desperate attempt to regenerate employment. This restlessness of capitalism ensures that the original conditions of growth are always being renewed; there is nothing permanent about it.

It is increasingly commonplace for the two tendencies of modern capital accumulation to exist side by side in the same country. This is where formal and informal institutions dividing the labor force into high- and low-wage sectors are especially needed. Men have traditionally excluded women from better-paid work, with the consequence that the restricted areas available to women are overcrowded and poorly paid.[21] The same applies to the contrast between citizens and illegal aliens, providing the middle classes with the cheap domestic labor they need in order to pursue an affluent lifestyle. This leads to the embarrassment that President Clinton faced when trying to appoint an Attorney-General who wasn't employing illegal aliens as servants. And, of course, racial discrimination, even after emancipation from slavery, has acted as a color bar confining black people to menial, low-wage employment. So Marx's economic analysis, brilliant and far-reaching as it was, would not be complete without a broader framework capable of accounting for the specific ways in which inequality is institutionalized.

Max Weber did not disagree with Marx's account, although he did think that property relations were less important than most Marxists believed; and some might count such an emphasis consistent with his decision to line up on the side of the capitalist state. He just felt that it did not go far enough.

Agrarian societies and their urban enclaves had always relied on traditional certainties when organizing their economies; that is, they tended to repeat what they had done in the past. Hence the relative stagnation of society and technology during the agricultural phase of human history. He surmised that a massive cultural revolution must have been necessary to persuade people to place their economic lives in the hands of capitalists whose principal orientation was to the uncertainties of future profit. It followed that capitalism should be conceived of in terms of institutions whose meaning was not just narrowly economic but political, even religious, as well.

Weber's *General Economic History* was written under unusual circumstances. It was just after the First World War, when a defeated Germany was in the throes of revolution and Weber went to teach for a year at Munich. He died shortly afterwards, and this book was put together from students' notes taken on his last lecture course. Weber was a notoriously obscure writer, but this book reads easily. This transparent quality and the somewhat Marxist slant of the text may owe more to the students than to Weber's original intentions; or it could reflect a genuine change of heart, in the face of Germany's political calamity. However that may be, this is much the fullest account left of his explanation for the rise of capitalism.

For Weber, capitalism was an economic system based on *rational enterprise*. Both of these words were carefully chosen. Enterprise is something undertaken with a view to future profit. As such, it is intrinsically uncertain. Weber observed that, in most economies known to history, innovation was often explicitly discouraged and hedged around with magical deterrents. It was remarkable, therefore, that whole societies would commit their livelihood to the uncertainties of enterprise. As the American economist Paul Samuelson said in the introduction to his best-selling textbook,[22] ten million New Yorkers go to sleep every night confident that the economy will still be there the next morning; but how do they know?

Enterprise commonly takes two forms. The first is speculative and involves people gambling on a hunch that they will win. Keynes recognized that these "animal spirits" were central to the dynamism of capitalist markets, leading to a cycle of booms and busts as herds of investors chase the latest chance for windfall profit (from the tulip craze and the South Sea bubble of the seventeenth and eighteenth centuries onwards). Weber was interested in the second form of enterprise, a form driven by the compulsion to eliminate the risks entailed in reliance on uncertain futures. Rationality is the calculated pursuit of explicit ends by chosen means. Rational enterprise, according to Weber, rests above all on the entrepreneur's ability to calculate outcomes. For capitalism to take root, uncertainty has to be replaced, if not with certain knowledge, then with reliable calculation of the probabilities.

This explains the paradox that, while capitalists celebrate the risks of competition in their self-promoting ideologies, they will do everything in their power to avoid it in practice. Weber sets out, in the fourth and final part of the *General Economic History,* to show how the fledgling capitalist economy progressed by instituting the means of more reliable calculation. This meant improvements in book-keeping, working practices and technology. Above all it meant the development of a state alert to the needs of enterprises, securing their property and profits in law, stabilizing the conditions of market economy, ultimately at the expense of anyone else who got in the way. Weber did not think that mercantile colonialism was a sufficient explanation for the accumulation of a European capitalist fund, since several commercial empires (such as the Phoenicians) had developed similar systems of extraction without spawning modern industry. Rather, as everyone knows, he believed that capitalist culture owed its specificity to developments in the sphere of religion.

Weber explained the origins of capitalism in Western Europe by the Reformation and before it the rationalist ethos of the Judaeo-Christian tradition. He wrote his famous *Protestant Ethic and the Spirit of Capitalism* on a visit to the St Louis Great Exposition in 1904.[23] It deals specifically with the "elective affinity" (Goethe's phrase) of Protestant religion and rational enterprise, that is, with how each gets on partially with the other so as to produce a synergistic effect. But the last chapter of the *General Economic History* ("The Evolution of the Capitalist Spirit") covers more ground, reaching back into pre-Reformation Christianity and beyond to the Enlightenment and the secularism of the "Age of Iron," the nineteenth century.

The main source of uncertainty we face is death. Traditionally the Church placed responsibility for reaching the afterlife in the hands of a specialist class of experts. Protestantism, above all else, restored to individuals the right to make their own relationship with God. Weber held that rationality involved a similar form of means–end calculation, so that Protestants would be supported in their economic activities by a compatible religious outlook. Sects that stressed the election of members to the afterlife (Calvinists being the favorite example) provided a measure of certainty, but perhaps also of insecurity, which were transferred into the world of enterprise. Whatever the role of this factor in the origins of capitalism, Weber was gloomy about the prospects for a disenchanted world in which exploited workers could no longer fall back on hopes for a better life after death. If Marx successfully linked capital accumulation to mechanization and the wage-labor system, these considerations of rationality, magic and religion are indispensable to an analysis of the cultural revolution affecting money and exchange in our times, as we will see.

The ongoing origins of capitalism

It can be seen from the above account that both Marx and Weber explained the origins of capitalism as the emergence of the elements that each took to be central to its definition: The free exchange of capital and labor and rational enterprise, respectively. When we turn to consider more recent developments outside Europe, the inescapable conclusion is that capitalism as a general system is always modified by the specific conditions in which it grows. Thus Italian capitalism is not Japanese capitalism is not Brazilian capitalism, and so on. There is a sense in which the modern economy has become in retrospect an abstract general system enshrined in texts that have become disembodied from the living history in which they were originally created.[24] Contemporary investigations of social realities ("ethnography") can restore that sense of living particulars to what remains a search for the universal principles of economic organization in our world. For we need to explain not only the common form, but also its infinite differentiation. If we wish to understand and to help make economic civilization on a planetary scale, such an exercise is indispensable. Modern anthropologists have recorded a decisive moment in history, when non-Western peoples began to participate in the world economy on their own terms. In the decades after the Second World War, a few of them set out to investigate the experience of economic development in the predominantly rural societies of the Third World. The most distinguished of these was Polly Hill. But, before turning to consider her work, an East African case study may serve to introduce the genre.

The Giriama are a people who live on the east coast of Kenya. They were studied in the 1970s by David Parkin, whose subsequent book has the great merit of being both well written and only a hundred pages long.[25] The story is as general and as specific as all the others we will encounter. The Giriama once kept cattle and, during the colonial period, often worked as migrant laborers. Now, an export market for copra (coconuts) had arisen that was attracting a new class of entrepreneurs. Palm trees had been used principally to make palm wine, and this was drunk on many social occasions, especially marriages and funerals. People worked for each other on the basis of reciprocity and need, paying close attention to the kinship ties between them. Extraction of copra required the acquisition of property in coconut trees and control of an adequate labor supply. From the first, entrepreneurs had to win the support of elders who could act as witnesses to the land transactions involved. This ensured that traditional sources of authority had to be accommodated by this incipient capitalist process. Nor was labor unproblematic, since the expectation of handing over profits to an owner was not built into kinship-based labor relations. Moreover, the community at large had a diffuse interest in any such profits being spent on public ceremony—involving much consumption of palm wine, of course.

So far the story upholds Marx's focus on the exchange of money for land and labor. But there is a Weberian element too. For some of the entrepreneurs sought to extricate themselves from the entanglements of traditional institutions by embracing a new religion. This took the form of conversion to Islam, often after consulting a diviner about dreams that revealed a calling in that direction. The great advantage of Islam was that it prohibited joining in the drinking that was such a prominent part of marriages and funerals. This may not have the cognitive force of the Protestant ethic thesis; but it is clear that emancipation from the diffuse social ties of community life is compatible with greater calculation of capitalist profit.

Parkin's narrative implies that the march of this new capitalist class is inexorable and that Giriama society is well on the way to being irreversibly transformed. But a longer-term and wider perspective might lead us to revise such a prediction. Colonial political economy was organized as a racial division of labor. The British ran the government and owned the most profitable estates; the Africans were expected to work for them and were excluded, where possible, from profitable alternatives to wage employment. The Indians, having first been brought as indentured labor to build the ports and railways, were allowed to fill the commercial niches between the two, but were denied the right to buy land. After independence in 1962, this hierarchy of white, brown and black came under pressure, as might be expected.

The Giriama ethnography belongs, then, to a period when Kenya sought to establish itself as one of Africa's leading capitalist economies, allowing for some rearrangement of the racial division of labor.[26] For a time, redistribution of wealth and power toward some Africans induced an atmosphere of commercial prosperity. The world economy in the 1960s and early 1970s was also favorable. This climate did not last, however, and for some two decades now economic conditions have deteriorated in Kenya. This is not the first time that Africans have experienced a boom only to repent at leisure during a long recession. In the Giriama case, it is by no means obvious that the forces of nascent capitalism have triumphed in the face of conditions reinforcing traditional norms of rural self-sufficiency.

West Africa offers one of the most striking histories of indigenous capitalism in modern economic development—one, moreover, that had to wait a long time for its ethnographer. The period from the 1880s to the First World War saw an explosion in the mass production and consumption of commodities, much of it based on raw materials located in territories that were rapidly being acquired as colonies. In most cases, this meant European-owned mines (gold, copper, bauxite) and plantations (tea, rubber, oil palm) employing a mixture of local and indentured Asian labor. The cocoa industry was an exception. It arose during this period in the rainforests of the Gold Coast (now Ghana) without the benefit or knowledge of any European interest, beyond the Liverpool and Manchester traders who were happy to buy the raw material of chocolate from its indigenous producers. Although many other countries eventually joined in, Ghana still supplied almost half of the world market until its economic and political reverses of the mid-1960s.

Despite Ghana's standing as the world's leading cocoa producer, little was known about the indigenous producers. They were assumed to be African "peasants" earning a little extra by adding cocoa to their subsistence farms.

Polly Hill, Maynard Keynes's niece, traced the industry to its origins at the turn of the century.[27] She was able to show that the cocoa farmers were an authentic modern class, migrant entrepreneurs opening up virgin forest often in companies capable of hiring Swiss construction firms to develop the infrastructure that they needed and the colonial authorities could not provide.

Hill's study, combining historical records with fieldwork, documented the complexity of the social organization that ensued after a local man brought knowledge of cocoa from the Portuguese dependency of São Tomé. All of the new farmers were migrants; most of them came from families that had accumulated wealth from earlier export trades, such as slavery and rubber; their level of education was often high. Some of them drew on existing matrilineal kinship to organize the collective appropriation of the rainforest; others, especially those from patrilineal areas, formed companies that allocated land rights among members. They invented a new institution, *abusua,* a means of recruiting migrant laborers to work on a one-third, two-thirds division of the crop. Hill is sure that Ghana's cocoa industry was capitalist from the beginning, and she is probably right. But this capitalist class did not capture the state. The first post-independence government, led by Kwame Nkrumah, was based on a coalition of interests opposed to the Ashanti region where the majority of cocoa farmers lived. Their wealth was squandered by this new ruling class, with inevitable consequences for the industry's decline.[28]

It would be hard to exaggerate the contrast between Hill's discovery and the conventional thinking of development economists and administrators at the time (and since).[29] Her work has barely been absorbed into the modern anthropological tradition because it contradicts deep-seated convictions about Western economic leadership and African backwardness. But more is at stake than revising racist perspectives on Africa. The core history of capitalism may have to be modified in the light of such ethnographic examples. Pierre-Philippe Rey sought to bring the West African colonial experience of capitalism and the original British case within the scope of a single theory.[30] He argued that, wherever capitalism developed, the new class was forced into making compromises with the old property-owning classes in ways that made the resulting hybrid something specific to that society. Thus the British industrialists had to make an alliance with the landowning aristocracy in order for the factory system to flourish at the expense of feudal agriculture. (Compare Marx's account of the enclosure movement above.) Similarly, in West Africa the indigenous lineage elders made an alliance with the colonial authorities to supply the labor of young men to plantations and mines.

This kind of class alliance is depressingly familiar in the transition to capitalism. It is an example of the institutional complexity that more abstract economic theories tend to ignore. In Britain the industrial bourgeoisie was separated from the traditional landed aristocracy by regional location (North versus South), but their influence on national government was always limited by its location in London, the home of the mercantile and colonial ruling class. In the late nineteenth century, the industrial civilization of independent regional cities (led by Manchester's liberalism) was undermined by a combination of nationalism and financial imperialism based in London. The industrial economy never recovered from this process of political centralization.

In this brief summary of a complex history, I have come full circle. For there is no doubt that, in a lifetime of journeys to strange places, nothing compares with the shock I had at the age of eighteen, when I had to alternate living as a student in Cambridge and at home in Manchester. They did seem to me, then and now, entirely different civilizations, and I was much exercised by the problem of uniting them in a viable identity. Later I transposed the problem to Africa. Again I found it difficult to understand how a displaced poor boy like me could wield so much social power there. I have spent much of the time since trying to bridge that gap in my knowledge of the world. I realized that, whereas I knew life in Accra's slums concretely, my ideas about "the West" were very abstract, being taken largely from social theory. This was the beginning of an attempt to place myself within a unified vision of world history. The preceding paragraph and indeed the historical perspective informing this book as a whole indicate where that journey has taken me so far.

In principle, it probably pays to do the same for other instances of intellectual history. Thus Weber's sociology is inseparable from the history of the newly formed German state. Here a very different kind of story needs to be told, emphasizing the alliance between Prussian *Junkers* (a military landowning class) and the Rhineland bourgeoisie. Weber's insistence that the institutional forms of rationality are twofold reflects the particular compromise reached in his home country, where the state bureaucracy and market-based capitalism forged an alliance that underlies the contrast between German and Anglo-Saxon models of capitalist development throughout the modern era. As pioneers of state capitalism, the Germans drew on their specific institutional history, just as the British had in inaugurating the first, market-based, form of industrial capitalism. We can be sure that state capitalism's successor is currently incubating in conditions particular to many different places. But this is to jump the gun. Before addressing the forms and consequences of global capitalist development in this century, the subject matter of Chapter 4, it is necessary to consider first its personal side, in the spirit of local differentiation emphasized here.

The personal face of capitalism: Entrepreneurs

The system of making money with money, capitalism, also has a personal face. It is called entrepreneurship, a term that roughly stands for economic leadership. We have already seen that Weber thought the distinctive feature of the modern economy is enterprise, the ability to imagine and to realize a future that does not already exist. This ability is a characteristic of certain individuals, and much attention has been paid in the literature to their qualities. For most writers, entrepreneurs are the heroes of capitalism, boldly going where no man went before. For others, however, they are the villains who cruelly sacrifice the general interest to their personal greed or megalomania. Bill Gates or Henry Ford would be contested cases in point.

When I first became interested in this question in the 1960s, the Cold War was at its height. Supporters of American "free enterprise" held that modernization of the former colonial peoples would come if a cluster of institutions, what I call "the middle-class package," could be successfully transplanted from the West: cities, education, science and technology, the rule of law, democracy and, of course, capitalist enterprise personified as a type, the entrepreneur. By the 1970s, however, a climate of economic failure reinforced the opposite view, that development was the primary responsibility of the state, not least because only political power could redress the inequalities intrinsic to world capitalism. In the 1980s an unfettered Western capitalism undermined its Soviet antagonist and subjected Third World states to a regime of free markets, public retrenchment and debt repayments that made survival difficult and development impossible. Finally, in the 1990s, while most Third World countries stagnated in appalling poverty, the "enterprise culture" was once again alive and well in the Western heartlands, while the former Eastern bloc was rapidly being taken over by its illegal variant, criminal mafias.

At the same time, the rise of Asian capitalism was until recently thought to be inexorable, led by Japan and the South-East Asian "tigers," with China lumbering into high gear behind. Some of these countries (Korea, Singapore) have made a virtue of strong state intervention, which may be represented as a Confucian collectivism in contrast with Western individualism. But in the West itself there has been belated recognition that relative failure may be due to a sclerosis induced by large-scale bureaucracy. And for some years now there has been a fashion for "downsizing" and "outsourcing," which at one extreme encourages small, dynamic work teams and decentralized decision-making. For a time in the 1980s the fastest-growing region in Europe was north-central Italy, where a pattern of innovative family firms predominated. This example was used to make the claim that the big corporations were dinosaurs, too rigid to compete with enterprises organized for "flexible specialization," that is, able to switch production techniques at will to meet the special needs of customers.[31]

Lately this anxiety for the future of the old Fordist model of mass production has led to pundits asking whether impersonal bureaucratic capitalism is about to be overtaken by a more personal form, "familistic capitalism."[32] This last phenomenon is held to consist of strong state intervention, high levels of political corruption, criminal mafias, reliance on personal networks in business, and a dominant ethos of family enterprise. Countries like Japan and even India are brought forward as exemplars; but the idea of Asian exceptionalism is usually modified to admit the European archetype, Italy. The USA and Britain are held to be ideally "bureaucratic" (and in the latter case on the way down), although the merest acquaintance with the political and business elites of those countries might lead us to suspect that the impersonal/personal contrast is overdrawn.

What all this overgeneralized debate adds up to is a suspicion that personality and personal relations are indispensable to modern economic organization and especially to building something new. The omnibus term "entrepreneur," inserted into a shifting theoretical debate over capitalism's historical trajectory, thus takes on many meanings, as we will see. The link of enterprise to the notion of the family may be in recognition of the actual predominance of families in business history. But I prefer to think of "family" as a metaphor for people you know very well and are stuck with, as it were. What matters from this point of view is not whether people are genetically related, but whether their mutual knowledge and trust can be the foundation of a durable partnership. Love and friendship can serve the same purpose, often more reliably. This aspect of the modern economy's contradictions therefore hinges on something more diffuse than enterprise as such, namely, the personal basis for making durable economic relations.

In what follows I draw extensively on my own ethnographic researches in Ghana.[33] The idea of capitalism employed here is not located in an imaginary space known as "the West." It is global in scope, and people everywhere must respond to being drawn into its complications. My study, based on fieldwork carried out thirty years ago, concerns a translocal ethnic community, "Frafras," especially migrants from the dry savanna who lived in a slum quarter of Accra, Ghana's capital city. Out of this field research I developed the concept of "the informal economy." This idea refers to the mass of economic transactions that takes place beyond effective state regulation. But my first focus was on entrepreneurs. By any standards they were small fry; but I take their enterprises nevertheless to be part of the general economic movement of our times.

The value of closely observed ethnography on the margins of the world capitalist economy is that the distinction between personal and impersonal institutions is clearer there than it normally is for people who have become inured to bureaucracy. The properties of relating to a person rather than to a thing or an idea have become blurred for us who barely distinguish between trusting a salesman, a dollar bill or the free market. The Frafra migrants brought a vivid appreciation of personalized social relations to their economic enterprises, just as they often missed the point of bureaucracy, since the state was for them a remote, sometimes threatening, presence but not an intrinsic part of everyday life. It is now less certain than it was three decades ago that corporate investments and state guarantees offer most people a more prosperous and secure future than small-scale enterprises and intimate relationships. Thinking about this contrast in how people in different places construct the personal/impersonal pair thus has considerable salience for us today.

The Frafras were fighting hill tribesmen who grew sorghum and raised livestock, an egalitarian people huddled together in densely packed settlements.[34] Only a small minority had converted to Islam or Christianity, and even fewer adults had a modicum of education. Their traditional society was based on descent groups, earth cults, clan alliances and marriage exchange. A pervasive ideology of kinship and ancestor worship provided the social glue linking larger corporate units to the flux of domestic life. Elders controlled most collective assets, such as land and cattle, and raiding between neighbors had traditionally reinforced group solidarity; but individual accumulation and self-made men were commonplace.

By the 1960s the Frafras were dispersed throughout Ghana. They worked as domestic servants, soldiers, petty traders and general laborers; they were widely considered to be thieves. They circulated between town and countryside, usually retaining an extended family network based on their home village. Out of a total of a quarter million, some 10,000 Frafras then lived in Accra, many of them in a sprawling slum called Nima. This was a shanty town, the main red-light district for the city's lower classes, and a criminal "badlands" that the police entered only sporadically. I lived with a "fence" (receiver of stolen goods) and joined in the life of the underworld to the extent of sharing in my landlord's criminal enterprise. My research gravitated toward the self-organized economic activities that sustained the majority of Nima's inhabitants. In the course of a stay of over two years, I became a local big man, redistributing my ill-gotten gains to an army of field assistants, throwing large parties and making handouts to the indigent. The alternative, nonparticipation in the criminal economy, left me vulnerable to accusations of being a police spy.[35]

I was captivated by what seemed a paradox: On the one hand the banal individualism of a Dickensian mob of water carriers, bread sellers, shit shovelers, taxi drivers, pickpockets and bartenders; on the other the communal spirit of hill tribesmen whose fathers were earth priests and who expected to end their days as custodians of ancestral shrines. I was impressed by the energy and ingenuity of their efforts to enrich themselves and by the inevitable failure of all but a few. It seemed as if the economy were being made, unmade and remade from day to day. The central task for everyone was to find a durable basis for livelihood and perhaps for accumulation. That was why even a poorly paid job was valued, as a stable core in the chaos of everyday life, an island in a sea of ephemeral opportunities. I came to think of this as the search for *form,* for the invariant in the variable, for regularity in a world constituted by flux, emergence, informality.

Over the period of fieldwork I built up case records on 71 individuals, members of this translocal ethnic community.[36] They lived both in the cities of the south and in their homeland. One in five had assets of more than £10,000 at a time when people working for the minimum wage earned £100 ($250) a year; half had accumulated more than £2,000, or twenty years' unskilled work. These were substantial sums by Frafra standards, but only three were rich on a national scale. They usually maintained a diversified portfolio of investments on a part-time basis; few were committed to managing a single enterprise. In Nima a third were still employed for wages and a further half had been employed recently. The most common medium of investment was housing for rent, followed by trade, bars, construction, machinery for hire and moneylending. A third of the sample owned commercial transport, the riskiest and most lucrative form of investment. Many included an illegal element in their enterprises. There were many more Muslims and Christians than the national average for Frafras. These are some of the people I was most closely associated with in Nima.

Anaba was forty years old, the second son of a poor farmer, and now a soldier in charge of army meat supplies. He owned five houses and nine commercial vehicles that, together with numerous trading and investment activities, brought in an annual income of around £20,000. He had eleven wives and seventeen children, a household of eighty people, scores of clients and dependants. In addition to these outgoings, he financed a successful bid by his brother for the chiefship of their village. Soon afterwards he left the army and went home to farm. There he suffered a catastrophic economic decline and lost most of his wives and hangers-on.

Atibila was a little older and also an army sergeant in Accra. His father had been a soldier. In his youth he had known great hardship; but, during the 1950s and 1960s, he had accumulated two houses, a minibus, a corn mill and several other income-bearing assets. A monogamous Christian, he lived with his wife, a trader, while his five children attended missionary schools. He tended to stay aloof from the migrant community.

Ananga had left home at the age of twelve. After three decades working as a cook/steward, while plying a number of ancillary trades (most of them illegal), he now lived in his own house in Nima with two wives, four children and several younger male relatives. Although at one stage he had £2,000 in the bank and owned two commercial vehicles, in the mid-1960s Ananga's fortunes were recovering slowly after a short jail sentence had all but smashed his entrepreneurial career. He maintained strong links with migrants from his own village.

In all relatively open economic systems it is possible for a few individuals to enrich themselves through their own efforts. The relationship between individual enrichment and community well-being, however, is a matter of dispute. One set of ideas is associated with the new rich themselves and those who endorse them. Success is attributed to hard work, abstinence, ambition, initiative and perseverance, perhaps to luck and a quick eye for opportunities. No one really suffers in the process. Even if some people do get hurt, the public good is enhanced in the long run by economic growth and charitable redistribution. The opponents of the new rich tell a contrasting story: of greed, exploitation, theft, lack of scruple and numerous other antisocial vices. Wealth is seen as a transfer of value, grabbed by force or sneaked by deception. The price of such accumulation is the damage done to the community. When we turn to social theory, we find again two broad political camps corresponding roughly to the opposed ideologies set out above, often identified with Weber and Marx respectively. Who can forget that for some forty years we were all threatened with nuclear annihilation in the name of a contest between these same ideas for global supremacy?

The problem is a general one in history. "Emphasis on accumulating money as against meeting social obligations worried many people in the United States and Europe in the early years of industrialization. John D. Rockefeller was highly unpopular most of his life. English literature is filled with hostile references to the new men, such as Dickens's *Hard Times*."[37] I wondered whether some practices of accumulation lead to the disruption of the social fabric, while others are compatible with an enduring framework of co-operation. Accordingly I examined my ethnographic material to see if perceptions of individual entrepreneurs could be traced to their objective strategies of accumulation.

"When they see this man is better," Amoro said, "they want him to be worse; and they will always keep on coming, coming and you are giving, giving, giving. And then you will stand in the same shoes as them. You will have nothing to give and they cannot give you anything. So you are poor and that is the level they really want to bring you to." The theme of a contradiction between accumulation and social obligation was a common one, highlighted by Atibila, who simplified his life history along classic Weberian lines. He portrayed himself as a poor boy who, bereft of any help from kin and cast adrift by misfortune in Accra, had managed to pull himself up by his own bootstraps only through systematic self-denial, reliance on his wife and the rejection of all other social ties.

A soldier and a Christian, Atibila had not been home for twenty years, wanted to have nothing to do with other Frafras and sought only to provide for his conjugal nuclear family's security through his own endeavors. He rejected traditional religion ("You cannot vote for two parties at the same time"), as well as co-operation with kinsmen and all the institutions, like mutual aid societies and funeral parties, that promoted ethnic solidarity in the city. Rather, he was a model exponent of rational economic behavior, monogamous seclusion and personal asceticism. Atibila had not been reading Talcott Parsons at night classes.[38] There was enough observable fact to make his story credible. He was certainly perceived as being socially isolated. But I later discovered that he was heavily involved with kinsmen and other Frafras; visited home regularly; wanted his children to retain their ethnic identity; and, as a lineage elder back home, had a much more equivocal attitude toward traditional religion in practice.

The point is that one-sided self-portraits, just like the ideal types of Western social theory, should never be mistaken for the reality they purport to depict. Atibila identified a strong underlying tendency in his own behavior; but he was in fact engaged in a far more complex process of seeking to reconcile a contradiction in his life without ever being able to eliminate either pole. It would be hard to overstress the importance of this theme for a humanist anthropology: People are never reducible to simple ideas, even or especially to those they hold of themselves. Rather, they put together flexible combinations of opposed strategies in order to cope with the fluctuations of their lives. With this in mind, I now turn to the different strategies employed by Frafra entrepreneurs in resolving the contradiction between individual accumulation and community consumption.

The term "entrepreneur" is used in social science and history to denote a bewildering variety of types. In anthropology anyone who does something novel or manipulative, seeks profit or "maximizes" his own interest is likely to be called an entrepreneur.[39] Even in economics, "some writers have identified entrepreneurship with the function of uncertainty-bearing, others with the co-ordination of productive resources, others with the introduction of innovations and still others with the provision of capital."[40] The classical definition, however, was designed to identify that human agency that combined the factors of production (land, labor, capital, technology) in working enterprises. Later Joseph Schumpeter concentrated on entrepreneurial innovation as the main factor in economic development.[41] I use the term here to denote not even a status (never mind a class), but rather an economic role that may be only an aspect of an individual's behavior. Entrepreneurship refers in this context to accumulation of an expanding capital fund managed by the owner. It is thus virtually synonymous with personalized capitalism.

If an entrepreneur is to maintain effective links with his community, he has to maintain a balance in his career between private accumulation and collective consumption. Not all forms of accumulation have the same social effects. The first requirement is an investible surplus. This can be generated in one of two ways: either by saving from domestic income and working more effectively, or by securing a transfer of income from elsewhere. One involves producing a surplus without apparently making anyone worse off, while the other involves the circulation of value in what could be represented as a zero-sum game. In the Frafra case, savings could be generated by abstention; working harder; increasing family labor inputs; improved efficiency; a stroke of good fortune. Transfers might take the form of inheritance; gift; credit; rent and interest payments; tribute; theft; favorable market trends. Finally, control over labor producing surplus value in Marx's sense combines elements of both production and transfer. The transfer of income to the entrepreneur may not always be counted as a cost to the community. When surpluses are derived from outside or by internal methods considered legitimate, little opprobrium may be incurred.

The perceived social benefits of accumulated surpluses thus depend heavily on their source, as well as on their destination. They may be used for further investment or consumed, directly by the entrepreneur and his family or through redistribution to the community (e.g., charitable donation). Two further considerations are crucial: the time dimension and the openness of the community. Negative transfers now may be justified in terms of jam for everyone tomorrow. The more open the community the less powerful are its sanctions on members and the more difficult is assessment of the net consequences of entrepreneurial activities.

The balance between accumulation, consumption and redistribution is likely to be highly variable in an individual's career. Moreover, not all exchanges between entrepreneurs and others are economic. A moral atmosphere of public service and political correctness may sometimes be maintained without material cost. The contradiction between public and private interests may thus be resolved in any of a number of ways: by enriching oneself at no one else's expense; by generating economic growth in the community and keeping up a fair level of redistribution; by adopting the symbols and conventions of community membership and service; by escaping to a more permissive or supportive social milieu; and by single-minded profit-seeking through any means, however disreputable, which is not a resolution of the dilemma but rather conformity to the one-sided negative stereotype. Since people like to think of themselves as good, there are few takers for this option outside moralizing fiction.

The normal platform for Frafra migrant entrepreneurship was a secure job. This could be a source of extra income (through bribes and theft of supplies), but was often intrinsic to the organization of enterprises and to their markets. They believed with some reason that the poor only get rich by means of trickery. Certainly, criminal activities were commonplace and scarcely disapproved of in the community. Apart from wages and illegal enterprise, self-employment offered a bewildering variety of opportunities on Nima's streets. Larger enterprises ranged from risky investments in public transport to the relative safety of rented housing. In addition to keeping their jobs, most entrepreneurs diversified their investments. Sudden reversals of fortune were common. A corrupt bureaucracy always posed serious obstacles to migrants who were mostly illiterate, as did the existence of monopolistic trading rings dominated by other religious and ethnic minorities. Most Frafras found it extremely difficult to hire workers who would not consume whatever money they generated: So that close family members, especially wives, were indispensable as assistants or even partners.

In general, surpluses were generated more often by transfer of value than by its production. Thrift, hard work, use of family labor and innovation were obvious enough in many cases; but the vast bulk of income came from the sphere of circulation. Moreover, most of it came from outside the Frafras' community of origin: Traders, transporters, moneylenders and thieves did their business with the general public, only a fraction of whom were their own people. A distinction was often drawn between "clean" and "dirty" money, and this entered into moral exchanges within the community. Inheritance, gifts and loans played a negligible role in generating investible surpluses. There were a few instances of benevolent patronage. The poor do not have so much that they can afford to make large donations to each other; nor do the rich often transfer their wealth voluntarily to a young man in need of a lucky break. The only way the poor can acquire surpluses, short of working impossibly hard, is to fiddle a slice of the social cake to which they would not ordinarily be entitled.

There was not much conflict over the origin of surpluses; indeed, the more successful entrepreneurs were usually celebrated as heroes. What really mattered was the destination of these surpluses and how the successful managed their relations with close kin and other members of the ethnic community. The problem was particularly acute in hiring labor. Strangers would disappear with the proceeds of their work, and kinsmen often failed to observe the distinction between private and communal property. Marx was right to focus on the contradiction of trying to get a worker to hand over more value than he produces. This was a cleft stick from which only a few geniuses managed to escape. Beyond that, the demands for redistribution of surpluses to family and community consumption were insistent. The egalitarian ethos of sharing was hard to reconcile with personal accumulation; and this was the site of most social conflict, as Amoro's complaint above testifies.

The social ties of Frafra entrepreneurs to their ethnic community had varying significance at different stages of their life career. They needed lineage kin at first for the bridewealth to get married; the social security of an ethnic brotherhood and a home village to fall back on, in case the strategy of accumulation failed utterly; the co-operation of kinsmen as workers who might be more reliable than strangers. As members of a despised ethnic group, they had to look close to home for political advancement and prestige; and finally most of them were bound by the exigencies of the ancestor cult, which helps to explain why so many Frafra entrepreneurs were converts to world religions.

Unable to recruit reliable employees or partners, Frafra migrants had to secure the co-operation of kinsmen and others from their community of origin whom they felt they could trust.[42] But, in order to be successful, that trust must be based on recognition of an ethic of open-ended reciprocity, sharing and mutual obligation that diverts income from investment toward the maintenance of these solidary relationships. The central paradox is the struggle to reconcile the demands of personal accumulation and social equity. The entrepreneurs considered here do not constitute a stable psychological or sociological type, but should instead be seen as persons enmeshed in a variety of social exchanges throughout their lives. Their efforts to stabilize successful adaptations were often frustrated by fluctuations in their circumstances. But it is nevertheless worth asking what alternative forms of economic organization were available to Frafra migrants who sought a durable foundation for enterprise. Let me approach this question through two case studies from Nima.

Atia had been hawking a camera around with intermittent success: The problem was that his customers did not like to wait for the film to be completed and business was often slow. His breakthrough came when he persuaded the principal of a girls' secondary school to let him take the girls' photographs at weekends. Many others had tried without success, but his own "sweet" approach worked. He spent £10 on chickens, eggs and gifts of money before receiving permission. Trade was brisk: Every weekend he got through two or three rolls of film "cutting" the girls. Whenever they saw him, they all wanted to send photos to their boyfriends and families. Some asked to be taken in the nude: "I was trusted by all of them. They knew that I was there for the money, that's all. If one of them asked me to stay and do something with her, another would call for a photo before anything happened." He generally asked for an advance payment of half the cost. Those who paid an advance wrote their names in a book, although he was himself illiterate. This was to stop any false claims; but he usually worked on the basis of mutual trust. If the photos he had developed were refused, he could not force them to pay. He rejected force, he said, because they might gang up on him and stop buying his pictures altogether. So he relied on good will. If he heard that a girl had paid for a picture she did not like and later tore it up, he would do her a new set free.

Sometimes Atia "fell down" when he spoiled the whole negative and had to refund all the advances. He claimed that his average profit was 50%. Good photos fetched more or less whatever he asked for. If a customer was pleased, she might not ask for change from a large banknote. He reduced his production costs by buying from the same wholesale supplier and using one enlarger, both of whom sometimes extended credit. So the profit from two films in a single weekend, although variable, could be substantial, adding up to more than a full week's wages as a domestic servant. Later Atia had to give up photography after joining the army. He was put on a charge for spending too many weekends outside the barracks. Despite the increases in army pay after the 1966 coup, he was chronically in debt and looked back with nostalgia to those secondary school weekends as a time when he was free. Be that as it may, Atia's enterprise was short-lived and unstable. He depended on the patronage of a headmistress and on his ability to step through a minefield of adolescent girls. Having failed to place his enterprise on a more secure footing, he fell back on a reliable job. Even so, his willingness to invent the conditions of participation in the market economy, rather than to accept passively whatever its formal institutions had to offer, was typical of Frafra migrants in Nima.

At the other end of the spectrum of migrant enterprise is the transport industry. The abandoned hulks that litter Ghana's roadsides offer silent testimony to the risks involved in running a truck, an estate wagon (Peugeot) or a minibus (Benz). But the potential rewards are high. If you buy a commercial vehicle, there are three things you can do with it: drive it yourself, hire a driver, or sell to a driver on a hire-purchase basis ("work and pay"). No one who spends his days behind a wheel is in a position to accumulate. Most naive operators would opt for hiring a driver, since the prospective profit is greater and the wage costs are fixed. This is why they often fail: A wage employee has no incentive to maintain the vehicle or to be honest with the takings. One alternative is to make a driver pay the owner an agreed sum daily; but again he has no stake in the vehicle and there is nothing to stop him making common cause with a fitter to supply inflated repair bills or to say that the truck was off the road when it wasn't. The most secure method is to sell the vehicle to its driver on an instalment plan and make him responsible for maintenance. This method was pioneered in Ghana by Lebanese businessmen.[43] Some owners would run the risk of paying wages to a driver while a vehicle was new and later sell it second-hand on the work-and-pay basis.

Anaba, the entrepreneur whose rags-to-riches and riches-to-rags story was mentioned above, evolved his own method of running a transport business after several false starts. He would buy driving licenses for young men from his home area and let them serve an apprenticeship on someone else's taxi until he was convinced they were a good risk. When he had enough cash in hand to buy a vehicle for £2,000 to £3,000, he would pick out one from his pool of clients, many of whom lived in his large household. He would then write up a contract, adding £1,000 to the sale price, selling it to the driver at a rate of repayment of £10 a day, with a clause giving him the right to seize the bus if the driver missed three successive days' payments. The driver was responsible for maintenance, but, if he got into difficulties, Anaba would pay for the repairs and add the cost to the total bill. This arrangement minimized the length of time a vehicle might lie idle. Most drivers took up to one and a half years to buy their bus or taxi. Anaba was remarkable for remaining aloof from the lorry park system in Ghana, which was controlled by Muslims. Kinship ties, self-reinforcing agreements and legal contracts played a more important role in his enterprise than friendship or trust. He was not a trusting man, in contrast to Atia, the unsuccessful photographer; and this was why he preferred hire purchase over wage employment.

Three basic models presented themselves to Frafra entrepreneurs for how to go about establishing reliable economic relations in the slum. The most obvious and apparently profitable of these was the system of *contract* fostered by the civil society they may have thought they had joined, the middle-class package of city life whereby rational individuals enter market contracts freely and accept the binding obligations sanctioned by impersonal state laws. In practice, things turned out differently. The state was hardly an effective presence in Nima and illiterate Frafras were in a poor position to make the bureaucracy work for them. The conditions of rational calculation were subverted by a general shortage of money, which pushed people into credit relations of a highly personal nature. In any case, they had to learn the impersonal disciplines of contractual behavior from scratch, and they were not very good at it (timekeeping, for instance).

Looking for some alternative form of guarantee, Frafra migrants turned to the opposite of modern civilization, their own customary morality based on the identities of *kinship* and a shared language, reinforced as they were by the certainties of birth and religious community. They were in many ways preadapted to the statelessness of the slum, but it was not easy to transfer their customary rural institutions to the city. At home, lineage organization lent the full authority of ancestors to elders, fathers and husbands. The ancestor cult was never practiced away from home and genealogical differences of generation were collapsed into a single brotherhood, so that the sheer unequal power of parenthood was mainly absent in the slum. Ethnic solidarity found expression in beer talk, and kinship was a domestic relationship of uncertain moral provenance.

The migrant community was an egalitarian brotherhood of young men attached as clients to a few resident big men. It was not closed or powerful enough to make kinship ties reliable. Kinship is a poor foundation for the reckoning of two-sided economic relations, especially hierarchical relations such as employer–employee, since it is based on an assumption of sameness, collective identity in opposition to the generalized other. The idea of shared but separate interests cannot easily be expressed in a kinship idiom. So traditional forms were ill adapted to the needs of migrant economic life. Inevitably they fell back on free-floating *association,* that sphere of social relations that Mauss identified as the true locus of society,[44] where self and other meet in some reciprocal understanding, and interest is negotiated within relations formed by shared experience, even friendship. Society in this sense is always personal, active and concrete, straddling as it does the poles of the primitive and the modern. The currency of this sphere is *trust,* a willingness to endure risk and uncertainty in human relations based on some degree of prior knowledge. Frafras were often forced to rely on an idiom of trust, although usually with the reinforcement of some other social interest. Moneylending was a case in point.

Loans in Nima were never made to strangers. Landlords lent to tenants, patrons to clients. The borrower often invoked friendship as a way of soliciting a loan; the rhetoric of familiarity was commonplace there. Kinsmen make poor borrowers, as they identify the lender's interests with their own. Again, small traders sold to strangers for cash. Once their customers became more familiar, they granted them special privileges (extras and, more importantly, credit). In this way trust is engendered by means of the gift, making a kind of friendship between buyer and seller, even when this was not a precondition for their association. Regular clients with substantial debts were few and traders had to pick them carefully. In this respect they were as selective as most Westerners in their personal friendships. The migrants usually failed to transcend their origins as fighting hill tribesmen in the social chaos of the slum. But some of them did. It helped if they could make a break with traditional religion, for positive and negative reasons. They needed some distance from customs that hedged in personal freedom with kinship obligations on all sides.

The world religions conferred membership of new associations that lent organization and sanctions to negotiated social relations. In Accra, Islamic brotherhoods controlled much of the intermediate business between state-regulated corporations and the informal economy of the slum.[45] Christians, at least the few Frafra Christians, did not join organizations relevant to their enterprises, such as the Freemasons, Rotary, Lions, etc. But they were encouraged to elevate their wives to the position of friend, partner and equal (see Atibila's story above), as an antidote to the macho complex of public familism and private patriarchy. The idea of two working as one, the ancient but often abused notion of wife as friend, was a recurrent theme in the life histories of several Christian entrepreneurs.

Most impersonal written contracts were worthless. But personal relationships are created over time, so that exchange in Nima was largely a learning process. People found out by trial and error what worked for them, and the failure rate was extremely high. Accordingly, although the market economy was what most economists would think of as competitive, ease of entry was severely restricted by the need to develop effective social tactics and techniques of information management. The contrasting cases of Atia and Anaba make it clear that there is no straightforward relationship between successful enterprise and an ability to make friends or engender trust. Anaba, the rich transport entrepreneur, relied on a combination of kinship and contract, while Atia the hustler made trust the cornerstone of his activities. Frafras relied on trust as a last resort, for good reasons. Trust is essential to dealing, as the game theorists know, with their suckers, free-riders and lemons. But the routines of productive enterprise are not easily managed by an ethos of personal freedom. Kinship and contract each offer a durable model for hierarchy and control, parental and legal sanctions respectively. This is why traditional rural society has room only on the margins for achieved relations of friendship and why trust accumulates in the cracks of mass societies organized by states and markets.

Trust is central to social life when neither traditional certainties nor modern probabilities hold: in weak states or lawless zones and in the transition to capitalism or its breakdown, especially in the mercantile sphere of circulation where credit is so important. Trust is not particularly relevant to industrial production and division of labor. In other words, trust is the negotiation of risk occasioned by the freedom of others, whom we know personally, to act against our interest in the relative absence of constraints imposed by kinship identity and legal contract. Domination and interest offer a more pervasive and durable basis for enterprise than friendship and trust. It is of some interest that, at this time when state capitalism's certainties are on the wane, the economists have rediscovered the problem of trust.[46]

If kinship and friendship are in some senses opposed, in several parts of the world, especially the Mediterranean and its offshoots, key social relations are a fusion of the polar types, both obligatory and free, the pseudo-familism of the kinsman/friend: the godfather, the patron and in-laws in general. Something similar is at work in religious brotherhoods and in secret societies where free associates take on the attributes of shared blood and common substance in their rituals. Again, as Durkheim insisted,[47] contracts rest on a non-contractual element that is prior and irreducible to their logic.

Hence capitalist firms do not simply rely on state-made sanctions for exploitation, but often have recourse to ideologies of paternalism and trust in their labor relations.

Real economic organization depends on creative combinations of the types that I have highlighted here. Successful mixtures vary in their situational effectiveness. It is only the intellectuals who believe that the modern economy could ever be founded on rational choice alone or that the simple-minded identities of societies based on kinship have no room for the person or the individual. Ethnography forces us to confront the complexities of society as ordinary people live it. I hope to have shown that the ideas of kinship, contract and trust are powerful guides to our understanding of economic relations; but people like the Frafra migrants I studied some time ago are faced with the need to develop practical strategies that give them a tenuous foothold in the shifting terrain of a world that is always moving on. As the next chapter shows, the static abstractions that underpin most theories of capitalism fail to address the palpable movement manifested in the history of the last century. The main lesson of this section, to be revisited at length in Chapter 5 on the market, is that ideas move when we view them through the activities of living people.

Guide to further reading

Marx and Engels were a genuine double act. Engels deferred to his partner's colossal ego, but he was a polymath in his own right. They wrote *The Manifesto of the Communist Party* (note 9) to be widely read and understood. Start there. *The German Ideology,* taken with Engels' brilliant ethnography of Manchester in the 1840s,[48] provides the theoretical and empirical background. Marx's *Pre-Capitalist Economic Formations* (note 8) gives his overview of economic evolution; and the "Introduction" to *Grundrisse*[49] is perhaps the best short discussion of his method. But there is no substitute for tackling the first volume of *Capital* (note 10). The last section, Part 8, is a knockabout history of accumulation before the industrial revolution. The opening chapter is crucial, but in some important respects opaque. In my view, Parts 3–5 on absolute and relative surplus value, some 350 pages, are the most important. I would avoid commentaries that invariably have a slant particular to the author; but

Anthony Giddens's *Capitalism and Modern Social Theory,* on Marx, Weber and Durkheim, is reliable.[50] I also like Ernest Mandel's *Marxist Economic Theory,*[51] but it is pretty idiosyncratic.

At least Marx was a practicing journalist. Max Weber's prose is often impossibly dense and his commentators are, if anything, even more ideological. The *General Economic History* (note 12) is by far his most accessible work on capitalism; read Part 4 and especially the final chapter, "The Evolution of the Capitalist Spirit," which is more comprehensive than the famous *Protestant Ethic and the Spirit of Capitalism* (note 23). Dip into his great work, *Wirtschaft und Gesellchaft,* in the Roth and Wittich translation, *Economy and Society,* not the Parsons and Henderson version, *Theory of Social and Economic Organization,* which is seriously flawed. Reinhard Bendix's *Max Weber: An Intellectual Portrait* is the best of the American bowdlerizers of Weber.[52]

For John Locke, again it is better to go to the original, *Two Treatises of Government* (note 3); but John Dunn's *Locke* is a readable short introduction to the man and his philosophy.[53] Macpherson's *The Political Theory of Possessive Individualism* has been very influential,[54] but I prefer Caffentzis's wackier treatment of Locke's approach to money (note 7).

The literature of economic anthropology is very large. I suggest you start with the four texts that I have cited: Gudeman and Rivera's *Conversations in Colombia* (note 24), Parkin's Giriama ethnography (note 25), Polly Hill's masterpiece on Ghanaian cocoa farmers (note 27) and my own comparative treatment of the West African literature (note 28). The French Marxist anthropologists are accessible through David Seddon's translation of several important articles.[55] Claude Meillassoux's seminal Gouro ethnography is not translated, nor is Pierre-Philippe Rey's magisterial Congo study; but Meillassoux's *Maidens, Meal and Money* is available in English.[56]

If anyone wants to know more about the Frafras (Tallensi) of northern Ghana, I recommend the works cited in note 34, especially Meyer Fortes's classic *The Web of Kinship.* The anthropology of enterprise is on the whole not rewarding. The Barth collection (note 39) is dated but good, as is Clifford Geertz's *Peddlers and Princes.*[57] The literature on trust is growing rapidly, as the West rediscovers the virtue of durable human relationships. I recommend the Gambetta volume of essays (note 42); Fukuyama's massive tome asks the right questions and makes interesting comparisons, but his sociology is unreliable (note 32).

Notes

1. C.L.R. James and associates, *State Capitalism and World Revolution* (Charles Kerr, Chicago, 1986; first pub. 1950).

2. J. Locke, *Two Treatises of Government* (Cambridge University Press, Cambridge, 1960, p. 301 (Locke's emphasis).

3. The silver content of English coins had been reduced by clipping, counterfeit and smuggling to the point where they were no longer a standard likely to be used by international traders.

4. Locke's own quantity theory of money predicts that a lower supply or velocity of money would reduce market demand and prices. But his priority (as Caffentzis argues convincingly) was to stabilize the infrastructure of a national economy increasingly driven by international expansion.

5. J. Schumpeter, *History of Economic Analysis* (Oxford University Press, London, 1954), pp. 647–8.

6. He was instrumental in securing the appointment of Isaac Newton to be Master of the Mint, a post where, in addition to employing his scientific talents to improve the metallic standard of coins, he could pursue counterfeiters and hang them at Tyburn. It is interesting that England's two greatest intellectuals should have been obsessed with money in this practical way.

7. G. Caffentzis, *Clipped Coins, Abused Words and Civil Government: John Locke's Philosophy of Money* (Autonomedia, New York, 1989), p. 92.

8. K. Marx, *Pre-capitalist Economic Formations* (Lawrence & Wishart, London, 1978).

9. K. Marx and F. Engels, *The Manifesto of the Communist Party* in Marx–Engels, *Selected Works* (Lawrence & Wishart, London, 1968; first pub. 1848).

10. K. Marx, *Capital: A Critique of Political Economy. Volume 1* (Lawrence & Wishart, London, 1970; first pub. 1867); A. Smith, *An Enquiry into the Nature and Causes of the Wealth of Nations* (Methuen, London, 1961; first pub. 1776).

11. Clearly America was still a powerful stimulus to the philosophical imagination almost a century after Locke. It is ironic that this example, taken as indicative of primitive exchange, was drawn from the contemporary North American fur trade, where scarcity of cash meant

that barter was often an initial source for skins whose commodity value was ultimately determined by demand in a world market whose growth Locke had worked so hard to promote.

12. M. Weber, *General Economic History* (Transaction Books, New Brunswick, NJ, 1981; first pub. 1922); K. Polanyi, *The Great Transformation: The Political and Economic Origins of Our Time* (Beacon Books, Boston, Mass., 1944). Hence the strategy frequently adopted by the rulers of agrarian civilizations to grant control of the money complex to pariah minorities (like the Jews in medieval Europe) who lacked political and property rights. As Weber and Polanyi insisted, the market was for a long time kept *outside* mainstream society. Our period is historically specific for its centrality to the internal functioning of society.

13. F. Fukuyama, *The End of History and the Last Man* (Penguin, Harmondsworth, 1992).

14. The term was popularized by Werner Sombart. W. Sombart, *Der Moderne Kapitalismus* (Duncker & Humboldt, Munich, 1928).

15. The following section is taken largely from K. Hart and L. Sperling, "Cattle as Capital," *Ethnos,* vol. 52, 1987.

16. The Latin for money, *pecunia,* is derived from *pecus,* livestock. C. Menger, *Principles of Economics* (New York University Press, New York, 1976; first pub. 1871), pp. 312–14.

17. A major theme of Chapter 6. Compare Chapter 2, where it was suggested that the main difference between animals and plants was the possession of a brain.

18. G. Bannock, R. Baxter and E. Davies, *The Penguin Dictionary of Economics* (third edition, Penguin, Harmondsworth, 1984), p. 63.

19. C = commodity; M = money; M′ = m prime (more money).

20. West Indian writers, such as C.L.R. James and, most notably, Eric Williams, have argued the case for seeing the Atlantic slave trade as the source of Britain's industrial capital fund. C.L.R. James, *The Black Jacobins: Toussaint L'Ouverture and the San Domingo Revolution* (Secker & Warburg, London, 1938); E. Williams, *Capitalism and Slavery* (Deutsch, London, 1964; first pub. 1944).

21. A point made strikingly by Ester Boserup in her pioneering book, *Women's Role in Economic Development* (Allen & Unwin, London, 1970).

22. P. Samuelson, *Economics* (thirteenth edition, McGraw-Hill, New York, 1989).

23. M. Weber, *The Protestant Ethic and the Spirit of Capitalism* (Allen & Unwin, London, 1970; first pub. 1904).

24. This point has been made in a vigorous and original way by Gudeman and Rivera (1990), who argue that Andean peasantries maintain as living

institutions the conditions that shaped the historical context of the great texts of the modern economic tradition. S. Gudeman and A. Rivera, *Conversations in Colombia: The Domestic Economy in Life and Text* (Cambridge University Press, Cambridge, 1990).

25. D. Parkin, *Palms, Wine and Witnesses: Public Spirit and Private Gain in an African Farming Community* (Intertext, London, 1972).

26. C. Leys, *Underdevelopment in Kenya: The Political Economy of Neo-colonialism* (Heinemann, London, 1975).

27. P. Hill, *Migrant Cocoa Farmers of Southern Ghana* (Cambridge University Press, Cambridge, 1963).

28. K. Hart, *The Political Economy of West African Agriculture* (Cambridge University Press, Cambridge, 1982).

29. P. Hill, *Development Economics on Trial* (Cambridge University Press, Cambridge, 1986).

30. P.-P. Rey, *Les Alliances de Classes* (Maspero, Paris, 1973).

31. Curiously, this phenomenon attracted more attention outside Italy, particularly in America, than within that country. C. Sabel and M. Piore, *The Second Industrial Divide: Possibilities for Prosperity* (Basic Books, New York, 1984); R. Putnam, *Making Democracy Work: Civic Traditions in Modern Italy* (Princeton University Press, Princeton, NJ, 1994).

32. F. Fukuyama, *Trust: The Social Virtues and the Creation of Prosperity* (Hamish Hamilton, London, 1995).

33. K. Hart, "Migrants and Entrepreneurs: A Study of Modernization among the Frafras of Ghana" (University of Cambridge Ph.D. dissertation, 1969).

34. The Frafras, whom I studied both at home and as migrants to southern cities, included the Tallensi, subjects of a classic ethnographic study carried out by my Cambridge professor Meyer Fortes in the 1930s. K. Hart, "The Economic Basis of Tallensi Social History in the Early Twentieth Century," *Research in Economic Anthropology, Volume 1* (JAI Press, Greenwich, CT, 1978); M. Fortes, *The Dynamics of Clanship among the Tallensi* (Oxford University Press, London, 1945); *The Web of Kinship among the Tallensi* (Oxford University Press, London, 1949).

35. I was arrested four times during the course of fieldwork in Nima, twice by the police and twice by the army. The only costs I suffered from these arrests were money for bribes and, on one occasion, considerable physical damage. I did not consider the option of staying clean to be viable, at least on the evidence of the first weeks of fieldwork. After that, there was no way back. The problem then was to avoid accumulating material wealth; hence, without really trying, my assumption of the role of the redistributive entrepreneur. K. Hart, "L'entreprise africaine et

l'économie informelle: réflexions autobiographiques" in S. Ellis and Yves Fauré, eds, *Entreprises et Entrepreneurs Africains* (Karthala et ORSTOM, Paris, 1995).

36. The next few pages are a condensation of an article I published in the 1970s entitled "Swindler or Public Benefactor? The Entrepreneur in His Community." K. Hart, "Swindler or Public Benefactor? The Entrepreneur in His Community" in J. Goody, ed., *Changing Social Structure of Modern Ghana* (International African Institute, London, 1975).

37. A. Kamarck, *The Economics of African Development* (Pall Mall, London, 1967), p. 51.

38. T. Parsons, *The Structure of Social Action: A Study in Social Theory with Special Reference to a Group of Recent European Writers* (Free Press, Glencoe, Ill., 1937).

39. F. Barth, ed., *The Role of the Entrepreneur in Social Change in Northern Norway* (Acta Universitatis Bergensis, Series Humaniorum Litterarum, No. 3, 1963).

40. B. Hoselitz, *The Progress of Underdeveloped Areas* (University of Chicago Press, Chicago, 1952), p. 98.

41. J. Schumpeter, *The Theory of Economic Development: An Inquiry into Profits, Capital, Credit, Interest and the Business Cycle* (Harvard University Press, Cambridge, Mass., 1934; first pub. 1912).

42. K. Hart, "Kinship, Contract and Trust: The Economic Organization of Migrants in an African City Slum" in D. Gambetta, ed., *Trust: Making and Breaking Co-operative Relations* (Blackwell, Oxford, 1988).

43. K. Hancock, *Survey of British Commonwealth Affairs 1919–1939. Volume 2* (Oxford University Press, London, 1941), Part 2.

44. M. Mauss, *The Gift: The Form and Reason for Exchange in Archaic Societies* (Routledge & Kegan Paul, London, 1990; first pub. as *Essai sur le Don*, 1925).

45. They did so in ways that have been documented brilliantly for the Hausa trading diaspora by Abner Cohen, *Custom and Politics in Urban Africa: A Study of Hausa Migrants in Yoruba Towns* (University of California Press, Berkeley, 1969).

46. See note 26 and DasGupta's contribution to D. Gambetta, ed., *Trust: Making and Breaking Co-operative Relations* (Blackwell, Oxford, 1988).

47. E. Durkheim, *The Division of Labour in Society* (Free Press, Glencoe, Ill., 1960; first pub. 1933).

48. K. Marx and F. Engels, *The German Ideology* (Lawrence & Wishart, London, 1970; first pub. 1846–7); F. Engels, *The Condition of the Working Class in England in 1844* (Lovell, New York, 1887).

49. K. Marx, *Grundrisse* (Vintage Books, New York, 1973; first pub. 1857–8).

50. A. Giddens, *Capitalism and Modern Social Theory* (Cambridge University Press, Cambridge, 1971).

51. E. Mandel, *Marxist Economic Theory* (Merlin, London, 1968).

52. M. Weber, *Economy and Society* (2 vols, G. Roth and C. Wittich, eds., University of California Press, Berkeley, 1978); *The Theory of Social and Economic Organization* (T. Parsons, ed., Oxford University Press, New York, 1947); R. Bendix, *Max Weber: An Intellectual Portrait* (Heinemann, London, 1960).

53. J. Dunn, *Locke* (Oxford University Press, London, 1984).

54. C.B. Macpherson, *The Political Theory of Possessive Individualism: Hobbes to Locke* (Clarendon Press, Oxford, 1964).

55. D. Seddon, ed., *Relations of Production: Marxist Approaches to Economic Anthropology* (Frank Cass, London, 1978).

56. C. Meillassoux, *Anthropologie Economique des Gouro de Côte d'Ivoire* (Mouton, Paris, 1964); C. Meillassoux, *Maidens, Meal and Money: Capitalism and the Domestic Community* (Cambridge University Press, Cambridge, 1981; first pub. as *Femmes, greniers et capitaux,* Maspero, Paris, 1975); P.-P. Rey, *Colonialisme, néo-colonialisme et transition au capitalisme: exemple de la Camilog au Congo-Brazzaville* (Maspero, Paris, 1971).

57. C. Geertz, *Peddlers and Princes: Social Development and Economic Change in Two Indonesian Towns* (University of Chicago Press, Chicago, 1963).

Chapter 4
Capitalism: The Political Economy of Development

Modern knowledge, as organized by the universities, falls into three broad classes: the natural sciences, the social sciences and the humanities. This is to say that the academic division of labor in our day is concerned with nature, society and humanity, of which the first two are thought to be governed by objective laws, but knowledge of the last requires the exercise of subjectivity or critical judgement. Whereas nature and society may be known by means of impersonal disciplines, human experience is communicated between persons, between individual artists and their audiences.

Nature and humanity are represented conventionally through science and art, but the best way of approaching society is moot, since social science is a recent (and, in my view, failed) attempt to bring the methods of the natural sciences to bear on a task that previously had fallen to religion. If science is the commitment to know the world objectively and art the means of expressing oneself subjectively, religion was and is a bridge between subject and object, a way of making meaningful connection between something inside oneself and the world outside. Now that science has driven religion from the government of modern societies, we must find new forms of religion capable of reconciling scientific laws with personal experience.

The onset of the age of machines coincided with various attempts to develop a science of society, of which British political economy (Ricardo), French sociology (Comte) and German philosophy (Hegel) all achieved a high level of definition in the years immediately following the end of the Napoleonic wars (the Congress of Vienna in 1815).[1] What interests me here is classical political economy, since it was more closely attuned to the rise of capitalism, the subject of these two chapters. Political economy was an argument about how the distribution of the value generated by an expanding market economy might best be deployed in the interest of economic growth. Smith, Ricardo and their followers identified three types of resources, each thought to be endowed with the power of increase: nature (land), money (capital) and human creativity (labor). These in turn were represented by their respective owners: landlords, capitalists and workers (the latter rapidly taking the form of an industrial proletariat). Their interest was in specific sources of income, the distribution of which contained the key to the laws of political economy: rent, profit and wages. The main conflict was at that time seen to be between landlords and capitalists; and the policy recommendation was to ensure that the value of market sales was not diverted from the capital fund to high rents. Only later did the issue of the conflict between the interests of capitalists and workers arise.

I contend that the basic division between classes formed by an interest in land, money and human creativity persists today. Indeed, as we saw, writers as diverse as Locke and Marx have constructed visions of history in which a state of nature or society based on the land gives way to an age of money (our own) whose contradictions should lead to a just society based on fair reward for human creativity. So the question posed by our latest phase of the machine revolution, whose symbolic and practical expression is the Internet, is how these broad classes of interest are manifested in the struggle for the value generated by electronic commerce. If the class alliance was first presumed to be between the owners of money and labor against the landlords (industrial capitalism) and then took the form of landlords and capitalists against the people (state capitalism), how are the classes aligned in the present phase of virtual capitalism? I will return to this question in the final section of the present chapter.

The original claims made by the classical political economists arose from a perception that the rising forces of industrial capitalism were running up

Table 4.1 The three classes of political economy

World	Nature	Society	Humanity
Knowledge	Science	Religion	Art
Subject-Object Relations	Object	Subject–Object	Subject
Resources	Land (Nature)	Capital (Money)	Labor (Creativity)
Income	Rent	Profit	Wages
Classes	Landlords	Capitalists	Workers

against the entrenched institutions of agrarian civilization. They found that the land was in the hands of an hereditary aristocracy who could charge what they wanted for its use, and that the price of the food eaten by their workers was similarly tied up in traditional agriculture. They sought to change both. But they soon found themselves faced with two potential antagonists, not just the traditional ruling class but, increasingly, the industrial working class that the combination of money and machines had called into being. In Britain the capitalists ended up sharing power with the aristocracy in order to keep the workers tied to an unequal labor contract. This class compromise ensured that the country's lead in the industrial revolution would soon be lost.

The moneyed class was at first in the vanguard of the struggle against agrarian hierarchy, before they eventually formed a reactionary alliance with its representatives against the people they employed. Put simply, mechanization is the consequence of human effort being put into improving the efficiency of production rather than into controlling the distribution of whatever is produced. All agrarian civilizations were ruled by groups who owed their power to control over distribution. They cared little for the effectiveness of production and even less for the material welfare of producers, many of whom were serfs or slaves. That is why technology was broadly stagnant in such societies. Many parts of the world retain regimes that reward those with the power to grab what has been produced by others. It can be argued that even the industrializers have relapsed into an economic condition where distribution dominates production.

For a brief period, in Britain and a few other places, a class emerged that saw profit in cheapening the costs of production, mainly through the introduction of machines. If, as was normal before the machine revolution, producers received, let us say, a seventh of what consumers pay for commodities, there was little point in an enterprising young man busying himself with making goods. The largest slice of the action lay in distribution processes (banking, haulage, protection rackets, middle-men's profits, taxation, theft, etc). Better by far to become an agent of those who wield political power or, failing that, to become a highway robber. The middle-class revolution, with its emphasis on the autonomy of "civil society," sought a radical reduction in rents, interest rates, transport costs and political extraction that, at least temporarily, shifted the emphasis of money-making toward improvements in the efficiency of production.

The theory of political economy held that competitive markets lowered the margins available to distributive agents and forced capitalists to reduce their production costs through innovations aimed at improving efficiency. This was achieved through economies of scale, division of labor and ultimately the introduction of machines to factories. The productivity of labor was thereby raised, allowing the resulting profits to be ploughed back into an expanded level of operations. By lowering the cost of producing basic goods such as clothing, society's manpower was freed up for more elaborate forms of commercial production. The only threat to this upward spiral was if those who controlled the land raised their rents to take advantage of these newly profitable industries. This meant that value would be diverted into wasteful consumption of imported luxuries. Worse, whereas the capital fund was inherently limitless, land was very definitely in limited supply. Economic expansion meant population growth, thereby driving up food prices and squeezing the capital fund on the other side through wages. The solution was to expose Britain's landowners to competition with cheap overseas suppliers of food like America; and this made free trade, specifically the repeal of the Corn Laws, the great political issue of the mid-nineteenth century.

Later, when capitalist power was thoroughly consolidated, the economists came up with a theory that claimed that distribution in the old sense had been replaced by competitive market exchange.[2] The question of who gets what was now reduced to an allocative process that was both rational and fair: Everyone gets what they are worth in the market. Any residual anomalies of distribution were best resolved by ensuring greater market competition. There is an underlying truth (as well as a lot of mystification) in this. The economic historian Douglas North has argued convincingly that a large part of America's economic growth may be attributed to reductions in "transaction costs," in other words, to innovations lowering the share of consumer prices accountable to distributive processes.[3] At the same time, Jean-François Bayart has argued that all African ruling classes, precolonial and modern, have been exercised to preserve the sources of revenue they live off—what he calls "the politics of the belly."[4] This is undoubtedly true, but there is nothing specifically African about it.

What is abnormal is the political experiment, launched by people like Locke in seventeenth-century Britain, to build an economy favoring production. The success of mechanization in a few countries since then has reinforced the value of that experiment, but it is still insecure. The social forces that concentrated economic power in the state during the twentieth century had a strong distributive logic, derived in part from a mission to protect the weak; and latterly the ability of virtual capitalism's protagonists to make money with money in a circuit that is increasingly independent of production may also have shifted economic power back to those who place themselves between producers and consumers. Most of this chapter is concerned with these two phases of capitalist development and their significance for global political economy. The twentieth century itself may be conceived of as having been framed by these stages in the evolving relationship between capitalism and the machine revolution: at one end, by the bureaucratic revolution and the shift from market to state capitalism; at the other, by the communications revolution and the shift from state to virtual capitalism. This in turn can be understood in terms of changing relationships of alliance and conflict between the three classes of political economy. An alliance of capitalists and workers against the landlords was replaced by an alliance of capitalists and landlords against the workers. The last section of this chapter will ask how they shape up in the struggle for the resources of the Internet.

The twentieth century

Hegel's owl has been winging it through the gathering twilight for some years now. The debacle of the Balkans has brought back memories of genocide in Europe and of events like the Spanish civil war; and Yeltsin's resistible rise has forced us to reassess the events of 1917. But, if Hegel's famous remark about the wisdom of hindsight has never seemed more apt than today, it is hard to avoid concluding that the dominant feature of our world has been violence on an unprecedented scale. The twentieth century has been, in effect, one long war, a war to rule the world, waged by rival versions of the modern state. We would be justified in asking, as it draws to a close with yet another European war, how we might avoid repeating the experience in the future. So far, Eric Hobsbawm has weighed in with a 600-page retrospective account, *Age of Extremes: The Short Twentieth Century 1914–1991*.[5] He is right to see the First World War as the formative moment of the century's dominant form of political economy, state capitalism (although he wouldn't call it that); and the collapse of Stalinism and apartheid in the period 1989–91 was obviously a watershed of some kind, even if we don't yet know what. The heyday of the modern state was, according to Hobsbawm, 1947–73; and, as a former communist, he cannot resist feeling nostalgic for those "golden years."

In order to sketch out my own version of recent history, I need to talk of the *long* twentieth century. Its origin was the revolutionary decade of the 1860s and it is by no means over yet, although we can but hope that the 1990s were at least the beginning of the end. All the major powers of the twentieth century took a political form conducive to state capitalism in the decade that began in 1861 with the American civil war, the completion of Italy's *Risorgimento* and the abolition of serfdom in Russia. It ended with German unification, the Franco-Prussian war, the Paris Commune and its successor, the French Third Republic. In between, Britain passed the second Reform Act, the cornerstone of Victorian democracy, and Japan's Meiji restoration took place. In all these cases a deal was struck between military landowners, industrial capitalists and the professional middle classes; and a deadly struggle began between this new ruling coalition and the growing mass of urban workers. The latter in turn began to organize: The First International was formed and Marx published *Capital*.

The transport and communications revolution of the 1860s laid the basis for a rapid expansion of the world market in subsequent decades. This in turn stimulated imperialist rivalry between the newly formed industrial states. Marx and Engels were almost alone at first in recognizing that the overwhelming movement of society was toward centralization. This had its roots in machine production and the concentration of people in cities. They believed that capitalism was undermining itself by giving working people an unprecedented opportunity to organize themselves in the new centers of mass production and consumption. But there was a corresponding mobilization at the top of society, based on the resources of capital and machines, which gave the state, an archaic agrarian institution, a new lease of life.

The period from the 1870s to the First World War saw an economic revolution. It had several aspects. Most important was the development of mass production for an expanded mass market of consumers. Mass production entailed standardization and an increased scale of operations. New forms of corporate enterprise dominated the economic stage: joint stock companies whose directors had limited liability for their firms' losses (i.e., they were no longer ruined when a company they owned went bankrupt). This was the age of the first department stores, concentrating under one roof a wide range of commodities that would previously have been sold in separate shops. It was also the age of the modern office block, when bureaucracy came to dominate both commerce and government.

The shift toward more impersonal forms of economic organization had important consequences for marketing. Bureaucracies limit the personal discretion of employees, hedging their activities around with rules that can only be broken at risk of dismissal. In the new stores, customers dealt face to face with assistants who had no power to negotiate. That power rested with owners and managers who were now removed from the point of sale, unlike the small shopkeeper who had retained a personal relationship with his clientele. The main imperative of management was to control subordinates; and this ethos stretched back to the production lines as well as outwards to an anonymous market of consumers whose tastes were manipulated by public advertising.

This bureaucratic revolution passed unnoticed by the economists, who chose the same moment (the end of the nineteenth century) to reinvent their discipline as the study of individuals making rational decisions in competitive markets. When economics was born two centuries earlier, a new system of "natural rights" linking political citizenship to private property in production protected the interests of the small property owners who made up the new middle classes. Later, the science of political economy addressed the historical struggle between broad classes of economic agents for control of the wealth realized in production. Now the second machine revolution in Western Europe and America launched giant corporations onto the economic stage whose successors dominate the world market today. Through an extraordinary act of legal manipulation, these corporations were granted the privileges won by individual citizens in the seventeenth and eighteenth centuries, so that General Motors, for example, is in legal fiction an individual with the same rights as you and me.

At the same time the concentration of workers in rapidly expanding cities gave impetus to their drive for political recognition; and the heirs of Marx and Engels were not slow to offer that drive a revolutionary content. The period leading up to the outbreak of the First World War was touch-and-go. Fifty million Europeans left for lands of temperate-zone new settlement, and the same number of Indians and Chinese were shipped to the tropical colonies. The ruling classes did not know how to cope with all the people piling up in the cities. The brilliant moment of modernism lit up the intellectual and artistic firmament. Global humanity was on the move and the scent of revolution was everywhere. The newly organized parties of the working class were wooed by promises of greater security. The middle classes prepared themselves for service in an expanded welfare state, Hegel's recipe for containing the contradictions of capitalism;[6] and in the process they invented the social sciences. But it could have gone either way. In the event, revolution was headed off, and a massive counter-revolution reasserted the power of the few to control the behavior of the many.

The modern era had been ushered in by a series of revolutions of which the French version had by far the greatest impact. Here Napoleon led the movement to restore elite rule against the popular democracy unleashed by the revolution. In England too the monarchy was restored after a period of parliamentary rule in the seventeenth century. This reaction has been called a *counter-revolution,* a term I find extremely useful in trying to understand how our twentieth-century world has maintained the rhetoric of freedom and equality, while instituting societies controlled from the top by state-made elites. How else can one explain a situation in which despotisms more powerful than any known to history are able to persuade their victims that they are the beneficiaries of modern freedom?

There have been two moments of general social upheaval that defined the course of the twentieth century. Each spawned a major revolution and an even more decisive counter-revolution. We call them the First and Second World Wars. The carnage of 1914–18 revealed state powers that no one before had imagined could exist. Governments raised and killed off huge armies; they organized production; controlled markets and prices;

discovered propaganda. The Russian revolution threatened to undermine the transfer of these powers into peacetime control of economy and society; and, for a couple of years after the war, Europe hung on the edge of revolution. Then the 1920s saw such an effective reinstatement of centralized bureaucracy (not least by Stalin) that the political question was no longer whether the people would revolt, but which form of state—fascist, communist, welfare-state democracy—would prevail universally. The period 1914–45 was named by Winston Churchill "the second thirty years war" and he should know. It was an unmitigated disaster for humanity, with economic misery compounded by brutality of an unprecedented kind.

The outcome of the Second World War was determined by the duel between Hitler and Stalin, pioneers in the use of state terrorism against their own people and various out-groups. Once again whole societies were set in irreversible movement around the globe. Once again a major revolution was unleashed, this time the revolt against European colonial empire in Asia and ultimately in Africa. Once again the immediate aftermath of the war was a rocky period for the governing establishments in Europe. And once again a counter-revolution was launched to preserve the power of rule from above. Its name was the United States of America. The USA used its new-found leadership to put down every popular movement it encountered and to prop up every unsavory dictator whose support made the world safer for nation-states and capital. At the same time the threat of communism was wildly exaggerated in order to institute the Cold War, a regime of nuclear terror lasting four decades.

This was Hobsbawm's golden age. It is true that the co-ordination of public policy in the leading industrial states generated the biggest economic boom the world has ever seen. Moreover, I can attest to the fact that many of us found the end of empire exhilarating: Students challenged the authorities in the name of Third World leaders like Fidel Castro, Kwame Nkrumah and Mao Tse-tung. Historical judgement on the political significance of the sixties is still out. Edmund Leach argued that there was a lot of fear and conservatism beneath the brave talk of liberation then; and he may have been right.[7] Even so, we have to make up our minds as to what was right and wrong about that decade, which I would place as 1964–72, if we are thinking of a general uprising of the young in America and Western Europe.

My short answer is that patriarchy (the dominance of father-figures at all levels of society) was fatally undermined in the 1960s, with its one irrefutable legacy being the women's movement. There was an expansion of subjectivity and consciousness, mainly among college kids who could look forward to well-remunerated careers whenever they chose to resume normal middle-class existence. But domestic life will never be the same again. What was wrong was the political analysis of the scope for change in state capitalism. The bureaucracy was never stronger than at that time, the state's management of the economy never more legitimate. Inflation, interest rates, unemployment and taxation were all low, and incomes were rising fast. Personal liberation without an adequate historical perspective on society at large usually ends in tears.

There is a watershed in post-war history and its moment is the mid-1970s. Some would point to the two OPEC oil price hikes of 1973 and 1979 as marking the end of the economic boom; others to the end of empire, the American defeat in Vietnam and the Portuguese revolution; perhaps the most important change in the long run was the invention of money markets in Chicago in 1975. In any case, soon after Richard Nixon announced in 1972 that "We are all Keynesians now," the economic mechanism of the welfare state began to show the strain of lifting the Western economies out of the Great Depression for four decades. This was manifested chiefly as general rates of inflation well above normal. In 1975 the global rate was 15% per annum and almost double that in part of Europe; when shoppers find that supermarket prices are regularly increased by 2% a month, they get nervous. This nervousness was noticed first by the right, who, through a series of national leaders such as Reagan, Thatcher and Kohl, found a winning message by the end of the 1970s: a retreat from state intervention and a return to sound money through the revival of market disciplines. These politicians heard and amplified the rumble of the tax revolt gathering momentum in Western societies.

In any case, before the mid-seventies the state was universally strong and the world economy was booming; afterwards the state became weaker and the world economy stagnated. Before, there was an attempt to reduce the gap between rich and poor nations; after, the gap widened rapidly. The end of the Cold War and now the communications revolution have exacerbated these trends, so that we are entitled at the millennium to ask whether state capitalism is now on its last legs and what its successor is likely to be. In recent decades it has become obvious that the promise of universal state provision cannot be fulfilled; and the revival of a Victorian faith in free markets has produced too many crooks and too many losers for most people's liking. As Daniel Bell said, the nation-state now seems to be too big for the small things and too small for the big things.[8] It is probable that power will leak upwards and downwards, into more inclusive political associations and to more devolved local arrangements. But there is a dearth of radical thinking about such possibilities. The left has had so much at stake in the nation-state as a means of defence against the power and mobility of capital that it leaves discussion of this terrain largely to right-wing thinkers. We will return to this question in Chapter 7.

The salient fact of society today is the communications revolution brought about by the convergence of digital telephones, television and computers. This also sets up a terrain for political debate in which the right currently predominates. For the first time, the machine revolution may be swinging toward decentralization, thereby lending technological support for greater democracy. Although its contours are too close to us to be obvious, it seems likely that capitalism is also being reformed to take advantage of new global conditions. I discuss the possibility of a stage tentatively identified as "virtual capitalism" below. It is, in any case, abundantly clear that the major players in our world economy are a handful of transnational corporations and that Bill Gates deserves to be seen as the most successful monopolist since Rockefeller. We need to ask, in the aftermath of the Cold War, which forms of political association are best placed to check the powers of these corporations. I doubt if many would now say the existing nation-states.

There is, then, a universal history of the twentieth century, and its periodization is summarized below. But every place and individual has their own particular trajectory through it, so that our experience of that history is highly variable. To repeat the conclusions of the last chapter, the causes of the variations are as important as the overall pattern. But we need a sense of that pattern, especially as we approach a phase in which the need for common regulation of world society and ecology is likely to take on a degree of

Table 4.2　The long twentieth century

1860s	Formation of leading capitalist states
	Transport and communications revolution
1870s–1914	The bureaucratic revolution
	Corporations, mass production/consumption
	Formation of the modern world market
	Imperialism and mass migration
1914–1945	"The second thirty years war"
	The Russian revolution and the rise of fascism
	The counter-revolution of corporate states
	Collapse of the nineteenth-century economic system
1930s–1970s	The welfare-state consensus
1945–mid-1970s	The long post-war economic boom
	The Cold War at its hottest
	End of European empire; American hegemony
	The heyday of state capitalism ("golden age")
1960s	The youth rebellion
mid-1970s–now	Stagnation and polarization of the world economy
	Money markets and the rise of virtual capitalism
	Decline of state capitalism
1980s	Neo-liberal conservatism
	The market revival
1989–1991	Collapse of Stalinism and apartheid
	End of Cold War
1990s	The communications revolution, the Internet
	World society as a single interactive network

urgency. The greatest obstacle to any such co-ordinated program for humanity is global inequality; and it is to the twentieth-century sources of that inequality that we now turn.

The development of global inequality

West Africa is separated from the Mediterranean world and Europe by the Sahara desert and an inhospitable Atlantic coastline.[9] Despite sporadic

contacts with Carthaginians and Romans, the region remained largely isolated from the north until the spread of Islam in the late first millennium
provided a common ideological framework for trade and migration. One
reason for this isolation lies in the rich ecological diversity of West Africa itself, including rainforest and savanna, the sea and major rivers, substantial
mineral deposits and a long history of interlocal trade in textiles, ironware,
pottery, vegetable products, animals and slaves.

A thousand years ago, the gold-rich West African state of Awdaghust produced traders with bills of credit larger than any known to Islamic civilization. When the Malian king Mansa Musah went on a pilgrimage to Mecca in
the Middle Ages, his expenditures in Egypt caused runaway inflation there
for thirty years. For more than three centuries after they reached West
Africa around 1500, European trading settlements on the coast exchanged
manufactures for slaves on terms of rough political equality with African societies (such as Ashanti and Dahomey), which themselves grew strong as a
result of the trade. The Atlantic slave trade may have been bad for West
Africa's economic development; but, if so, it was because it reinforced the
wrong indigenous elements, predatory aristocracies who were full partners
in the trade. It was only in the late nineteenth century that the Europeans
were emboldened by their new industrial power (specifically, the machine-
gun) to establish colonies inland.

The last century (roughly sixty years of colonial rule and forty years of
independence) has seen a rapidly widening gap between West Africa and Europe. The former's governments have been reduced to economic and strategic impotence, leaving them prey to any policy the rich countries wish to
impose. This uneven pattern of development cannot be explained in terms
of a colonial exploitation model alone. West Africa did not have to suffer a
settler class or an extensive mining industry, and, as we saw in the last chapter, it generated an indigenous export sector of capitalist and peasant production. The highest rates of wealth extraction have been as a result of
international debts incurred long after the region became nominally independent. There was an indigenous pattern of urbanization, especially in
western Nigeria;[10] and in the course of the twentieth century this has now
grown to levels of 30–40%. The main reason West Africans have slipped so
far behind is that they have failed to mechanize production to any significant

extent. Their countries have acquired modern states, but these have not lifted the productivity of at least some sectors of their economies to a level capable of sustaining such a superstructure. Is it any wonder, then, that West Africans are leaving their home region in droves to find work where the prospects are better, if necessary as illegal migrants?

The post-war population boom in the Third World has, for the most part, spawned an urban revolution without that rate of mechanization that accompanied the rise of cities in Europe and America during the nineteenth century.[11] This means that the economies of these cities must sustain proliferating numbers of people living by their own efforts at a very low standard of living ("the informal economy"). The poverty of the inhabitants of large modern cities has always provoked more anxiety in their rulers than the plight of the peasantry, since the city mob is closer to home and less easily controlled. Moreover, these cities contain in microcosm all the pathologies of global economic inequality exaggerated to tragicomic effect. Gilded palaces protected by bars, dogs and guns look down on squalid slums familiar to middle-class readers since the publication of *Oliver Twist*. A poem I wrote while spending a couple of years in Jamaica in the 1980s expresses something of this contrast. You might say it is a considered reaction to the encounter with Alvin (see the prologue).

VIEW FROM A BALCONY

I   *The evening sky parades its wonders just for me:*
Here towering columns, residue of rainclouds,
Boiling black smoke, hellfire of blast furnaces;
There thin purple islands, feathered archipelago
Floating in an unmapped, turquoise lake.
Encircling hills, reduced to pristine dormant shapes,
Stretch out familiar fingers to the golden sea.
A forest city spreads its winking lights beneath my feet.
This surge of elevated power intoxicates,
Brings on wild fantasies of flight,
Makes all things possible from here.

2   *We clasp cold Red Stripe in the still warm air,*
Hands slipping on the bottles' icy dew,
Our senses captive to the evanescent spell
Of sunset's lurid melodrama,
Brief recapitulation, daytime's curtain call.
But Herman was uneasy. "It isn't right
To be up here when they are all down there."
The godlike seeming was dissolved
And cooling beer now mixed with clammy sweat.

3   *My home's a hillside fastness, garden paradise,*
Container walls like fortress ramparts,
Far more lovely, twice as safe as any bank.
Here yelping curs outnumber people,
Harass dark strangers night and day.
White mansions show the world a surly shuttered face.
Grim burglar bars, sham rococo,
Cannot disguise the prisons that they make.
Guns guard the inmates, rich inviolate,
From unseen dangers, bleak reminder of their wealth.

4   *The restful cool of breezy night*
Is shattered by rounds of canine choirs,
Redundant drone of air-conditioners
And TV movies broadcast for the world to hear.
Then daylight brings the peaceful sun
To light this magical profusion—
Royal palms, wild ferns and clinging vines,
Banana's crazy leaves, cascading banks of flowers—
And then at last to lull abandoned dogs to sleep.

5   *Each morning sleek new German cars,*
Evading potholes and debris of rainstorms,
Carry the masters down the winding, unkept road,

Past servants trudging slowly up that steep incline,
Eyes averted from their rulers and the sun,
Their unpaid journey almost done,
An hour or more from Kingston slum
To bright, fantastic cages on the hill.

6 *For all their fortifying bulk*
This colony's foundations are not firm.
The fluid earth escapes the shoring walls
And leaks away in swift corrosive streams.
The race threat grasps them by the throat.
The sound of distant jungle drums
Drifts up to fill the owners' restless dreams
Of dread invasions, crime and death.
Subversive nightmares are transformed
In frantic talk of hurricanes and land slides,
Elemental cataclysms, nature's revolutions,
Displaced symbols of a deeper terror,
Monstrous fear of fellow men.

7 *This fragile platform on the edge of empty space*
Suspends me over chasms of despair,
Until the evening sky parades its wonders once again
And idle torment shifts to fantasies of flight
Where contradiction's black and white,
Made gaudy by the dying sun's strange light,
Fade into nothing and the night.

The beleaguered elites are afraid of the poor majority whom they only see from afar or in threatening circumstances on the streets. Should they anticipate an explosion or can the cracks in the social façade be papered over? In the nineteenth century, the journalist Henry Mayhew ventured into the vast unknown desert of London's East End to report on *London Labour and the London Poor* for the benefit of his readers' curiosity.[12] His conclusion was that they were extraordinarily busy and enterprising. Even so, the incorporation of what Gareth Steadman Jones calls *Outcast London* into mainstream twentieth-century society has itself been an uneven process and was never completed.[13] The crisis of America's inner-city ghettos is as acute today as at any time before. The contradictions of massive inequality are intrinsic to the huge urban agglomerations growing everywhere from Lagos to Los Angeles.

In the Great Depression of the 1930s, Maynard Keynes offered a solution to national elites concerned that their ability to govern would be overwhelmed by the mass of poor and unemployed generated by the economic system they supervised.[14] The rich countries today are similarly cast adrift in a sea of human misery that includes most people alive, but especially the inhabitants of Africa and South Asia. Marx used to say that "the social relations of production act as so many fetters on the development of the productive forces," by which he meant that capitalist markets could not organize machine production for the benefit of society as a whole. At the most inclusive level the main fetter on human development today is a United Nations world order (dominated by the USA) that prevents the evolution of new forms of economic life more appropriate to the conditions of mechanization and global integration into which we have so recently stumbled. It also, of course, prevents the implementation of a Keynesian program aimed at alleviating world poverty by means of redistribution of purchasing power.

In the film *Annie Hall,* Woody Allen says that he doesn't feel like eating out tonight because of all those starving millions in the Third World.[15] The audience laughs, uneasily. The gesture rings false: Why tonight and not every night? No one could live consistently with that proposition—could they? We might well ask how people live with economic inequality. And the short answer is that they don't, not if they can help it. Most human beings like to think of themselves as good. This normally involves being compassionate in the face of others' suffering. The worst thing would be to imagine that we are responsible for that suffering in some way. Better to explain it away as having some other cause: Perhaps the people deserve to suffer or are just pretending to be poor. Better still not to have to think about it in the first place. In the last resort it is possible to ignore them by defining them as less than fully human (not like us). Distance (in every sense—physical, social, intellectual, emotional) is the answer to the unwelcome conflict between inequality and human compassion. And, while each of us engages in thousands of voluntary acts distancing ourselves from the suffering of others, the task is performed more reliably, at the communal level, by institutions.

An *institution* is an established practice in the life of a community or it is the organization that carries it out.[16] What they have in common is the idea of a place to stay, in opposition to the movement, flux and process of life itself. Institutions and agriculture go together. The conflict between fixing society in the ground and reinventing it on the move underlies our contemporary global crisis. The maintenance of inequality depends on controlling the movement of people. If the poor are to be kept at a proper distance, it would not do to have them invade the protected zones of privilege established by the rich. Better by far that they should know their place and stay there.

The two principal institutions for upholding inequality, therefore, are formal political organization (laws administered by states) and informal customary practices widely shared by members of a community (culture). The most important task of both is to separate and divide people in the interest of maintaining rule by the privileged few. Classifying people is as old as language and society themselves; and, as Durkheim and Mauss pointed out, it can be constructive in defining solidarity within and between groups.[17] But it is equally well-known that labelling people differently is a means of preventing them from combining. One of the main ways that modern ruling elites everywhere have come to terms with the anonymous masses they wish to govern is to pigeon-hole them through systems of classification. The intellectuals have devoted their efforts overwhelmingly to devising and maintaining such categories. Social science itself would be impossible if individuals were not subordinated to these impersonal systems of thought and enumeration.

To the extent that society has become a depersonalized interaction between strangers, an important class of categories rests on overt signs that can be recognized without prior knowledge of the persons involved. These are usually visual—physical and cultural characteristics like color or dress; speech styles may also sometimes be taken as revealing social identity. Modern states are addicted to documentation, identity cards, preferably with a photograph of the bearer.[18] By a standard symbolic logic, these sign systems are often taken to reveal underlying causes of behavior—trustworthiness, ability and much besides. On this arbitrary basis:

- personal destinies are decided,
- people are routinely included and excluded from society's benefits,
- inequality is both made legitimate and policed,
- the world is divided into an endless series of "us" and "them,"
- monstrous crimes against humanity (like genocide) are carried out.

After the Second World War, South Africa's ruling National Party set out to institute what they called *apartheid*. Despite the close integration of people of European and African origin in the country's economic system, they decided to separate the "races," by allocating to "blacks" a series of homelands (themselves fragmented according to "tribal" origin) and denying them the right to reside in the cities, where the "whites" mainly lived, except with a pass (work permit). Within the cities, black and white areas were kept apart and were very unequally endowed with resources. Establishing and maintaining such a system required the systematic use of force, although collaborators were, as usual, not hard to find. Internal resistance built up gradually, and the rest of the world expressed variable degrees of outrage, eventually translated into an intermittent boycott. The release of Nelson Mandela in 1990 signalled a retreat from this policy, and African majority rule soon resulted. An end to apartheid perhaps? Or perhaps not.

The South African experiment was ugly, but not the most extreme form of inhumanity known to the twentieth century. Stalin and Hitler between them were responsible for much worse; and even as the ANC was being peacefully elected, a million people lost their lives in Rwanda, while Bosnia revealed that genocide was alive and kicking in Europe. Yet the Afrikaners managed to provoke the most co-ordinated international opposition since the Second World War. Why? What they did was obnoxious, but was it so exceptional?

Perhaps their main crime was to be explicit, even boastful, about their method of maintaining inequality. For the same method could be said to operate everywhere, without being acknowledged so openly or practiced so violently. I believe that South Africa became a symbol of a universal institution that people were feeling generally uneasy about. It offered a limited target, outside the societies of its international critics, that could be vilified and rejected as an alternative to more painful introspection. For do not people like to think of themselves as good? Opposing evil elsewhere is a way of displacing our ambivalence over how we handle inequality closer to home. Whether this analysis holds true or not, it is indisputable that, after the official demise of apartheid in South Africa, something similar to it is the ruling principle of organization by which the inequalities of world society are managed today.

This principle can be stated briefly as follows. Inequality is intrinsic to the functioning of the modern economy at all levels from the global to the local. The rich and poor are separated physically, kept apart in areas that differ greatly in their standards of living. It is impossible to prevent movement between the two areas in any absolute sense, if only for the fact that the rich need the poor to perform certain tasks for them on the spot (especially personal services and dirty work of all kinds). But movement of this sort is severely restricted, by the use of formal administrative procedures (state law) or by a variety of informal institutions based on cultural prejudice. These rest on systems of classification of which racism is the prototype and still the single most important means of inclusion and exclusion in our world.

There is a great lie at the heart of modern politics. We live in self-proclaimed democracies where all are equally free; and we are committed to these principles on a universal basis. Yet we must justify granting some people inferior rights; otherwise functional economic inequalities would be threatened. This double-think is enshrined at the heart of the modern nation-state. Nationalism is racism without the pretension to being as systematic or global. So-called nations, themselves often the outcome of centuries of unequal struggle, link cultural difference to birth and define citizens' rights in opposition to all comers. The resulting national consciousness, built on territorial segmentation and regulation of movement across borders, justifies the unfair treatment of non-citizens and makes people blind to the common interests of humanity.

There are other ways of classifying the poor besides visible signs of "natural" difference encoded as race. Nationality, ethnicity, religion, region and class can be signalled in many other ways. But the pervasive dualism of modern economies derives from the need to keep apart people whose life-chances are profoundly unequal. Engels noticed it when he came to Manchester in the 1840s.[19] In medieval cities the rich and poor lived together. Here the rich lived in the suburbs and worked in the city center; and they rode to and from their businesses along avenues whose facades of shops concealed the terrible housing conditions of the slums that lay behind. Post-apartheid Johannesburg takes this to a latter-day extreme, with its rich white northern suburbs policed by private security firms and poor blacks still crowded in monochrome townships like Soweto.

The apartheid principle is to be found everywhere in local systems of discrimination, more or less blatantly. But there are also grounds for asserting that twentieth-century world society has been constructed along the same lines. Arthur Lewis makes a plausible case for this as follows.[20] In the period from the 1880s to the First World War, as we have seen, 50 million Europeans left home to go to the lands of temperate-zone new settlement (37 million to the USA, the rest to Australia, Argentina, etc.). A similar number of Indians and Chinese (coolies) were shipped to the tropical colonies as plantation and transport workers, indentured laborers who signed away their freedom for a sea passage. These two streams of migrants had to be kept separate, since, although their work was often similar, the first was paid on average nine shillings a day, the second a single shilling a day. And in the areas where Asian workers were allowed to settle, the price of local wage labor was driven down to the same level. Seen in this light, the paranoid fear of Asian immigration that was then common among Australian workers of European origin makes a lot of sense.

Lewis goes on to argue that this division of the world by Western imperialism into countries of dear and cheap labor had profound consequences for their subsequent economic development. For high-wage economies sustain higher levels of demand than their low-wage counterparts. Moreover, world trade has been organized ever since in the interests of the better-paid, with tax-rich states subsidizing their farmers to dump cheap food overseas at the expense of agricultural development there and preventing the imported manufactures of poor countries from undermining the wages of home industrial workers. South Africa and the United States were two countries that allowed heavy immigration of working-class Europeans, while seeking to retain a reserve of poorly paid, mainly black, labor. The resulting dualism is inscribed on their shared twentieth-century history of racist urbanization. That is not hard to see. Lewis's feat was to show how we might think of contemporary world society as a whole in similar terms.

The unequal world made by Victorian imperialism was sustained by a cultural theory based on presumed biological difference. Our late twentieth-century world is more unequal. Underlying this process is the uneven development of mechanization and money-making (capitalism). The boundaries between rich and poor in this world are not static: Some Asian countries have begun to challenge Western hegemony, for example. The cultural theory is now more overtly nationalist than racist, but the coercion and prejudice exercised in its name are much the same. They maintain economic inequality at the local level and block any appropriate response to human misery on a world scale. People may be less triumphalist about their sense of superiority these days, but it is their culture, with its curious mix of self-congratulation and indifference, of rationalism and mystification, that enables them to sleep at night.

How can a world that has seen the end of formal colonial empire maintain racial inequality at the heart of its economy? The answers lie in the failure of post-colonial development. Kwame Nkrumah, leader of Africa's first state to win independence from colonial rule (Ghana in 1957), told his followers, "seek ye first the political kingdom."[21] If the anti-colonial revolution posed the main threat to the prevailing world order in the second half of the twentieth century, it was also widely assumed that political emancipation would be a source of economic liberation for the impoverished masses of the Third World. Quite the opposite has been the case, however; and now, four or five decades after independence, the gap between rich and poor countries has grown wider. Many parts of Africa are in real terms worse off now than in 1960.[22] At the same time the world economy, which boomed in the decades immediately after the Second World War, has been stagnating for over two decades now, since the turning point of the mid-seventies identified above.

The financial crisis of 1929 triggered a general slump (the Great Depression) that was felt acutely in the West but affected the whole world. The discovery of demand management by governments (welfare-state capitalism) and the boost to production provided by the Second World War ended the slump. After the war America pumped aid into a shattered

Europe (the Marshall plan), but economic growth was slow and took off only in the early 1950s under the stimulus of the Korean war. Now, with the world in thrall to a potentially terminal conflict between the Western and Eastern blocs, the global economy enjoyed two continuous decades of expansion. This was the context both for the anti-colonial revolution and for the youth rebellion in the West, with its links to the civil rights and women's movements, especially in America. It should be remembered that, until well into the 1970s, many intellectuals believed that the communist experiment would prove to be economically superior to the "free enterprise" system.

Under these circumstances the essence of political economy everywhere came to be known as "development." At one level, this meant the relationship between rich and poor countries, a new contract sponsored by the United Nations world order whereby the richer countries agreed to help the newly independent Third World to close the gap between them. This involved the transfer of money, technology and skills ("aid") that people imagined could be afforded out of an economic growth many thought of as permanent. At first, the recipe for development offered by the Americans was called "modernization."[23] Societies considered to be traditionally backward needed an infusion of what I have called "the middle-class package": cities, capital, technology, democracy, education and the rule of law. There was some optimism in the 1960s that prosperity could be diffused in this fashion.

But by around 1970 it was clear that something was wrong. Most poor countries were not getting any richer, and for some the situation was deteriorating. This provided the context for a critical analysis, rooted in Marxism, the other side's ideology in the Cold War, which was known variously as underdevelopment or dependency theory, eventually as "world systems" theory.[24] The common core of these approaches was the idea that the poor were poor because their economies had been structured by Western capitalism in the interests of accumulation, which effectively transferred wealth to the rich countries from the Third World. It followed that involvement with the West in the hope of becoming modern was the problem, not the solution. The latter required some form of isolationism or withdrawal from the capitalist system. This theory was associated at first with certain Middle Eastern and Latin American writers.[25]

Cracks were already beginning to show in the West's post-war boom by 1970. The Vietnam war introduced financial instability to world markets, as well as indicating that American pretensions to global hegemony had clay feet. The oil price hike of 1973 then threw the world economy into a depression from which it has never recovered. The OPEC countries were a cartel dominated by a group of small countries in the Persian Gulf with a lot of sand and next to no people, led by the Saudis. Oil production was organized by American and one or two European companies ("the seven sisters"). It is not for this book to investigate how an economic disaster of this magnitude could be pulled off by a few Arab sheiks sheltering under the military umbrella of the United States. Let us infer that the collusion of the oil companies and of the U.S. government implies that their interests were also served by what transpired.[26]

The consequence of the oil price rise was an immediate reduction in aggregate demand within the industrial economies, as consumers were forced to pay substantially more for energy. The oil producers received a windfall surplus that most of them could not spend, since their populations were too small and there is a limit to how many fancy weapons they could buy. They made huge transfers to the U.S. government, their patron, in the form of purchasing Treasury bonds;[27] which meant that U.S. citizens were indirectly financing additional government expenditures by paying more for gasoline, a tax hike by the back door. There was still a lot of money left over that was deposited by the producers in the banking system, much of it the new offshore eurodollar circuit that offered higher interest rates. In order to pay the interest, the banks had to lend on the money. There were few takers in the West, since the sharp reduction in demand discouraged investment there. The communist bloc at this time was not considered to be reliable and had little to sell that the rest of the world wanted. So the bankers turned to the Third World.[28]

If the oil price rise was bad for the industrial countries, it was a full-scale disaster for the non-oil producing Third World countries. These had been encouraged by the World Bank and other international agencies to concentrate on exporting a few primary products. The resulting oversupply kept prices down, while rapid urbanization in their countries raised demand for the manufacturing exports of the industrial countries. As a result the terms of trade between the two blocs were worsening from the perspective of the poor agricultural economies. The oil shock depressed demand in the rich countries for Third World exports; yet when the latter were faced with increased energy bills, all they could do was to try to sell more of their traditional exports, thereby driving world prices even further downwards.

Into this desperate situation came the Western banks looking for ways of lending on the oil surplus. They found takers, usually corrupt leaders of bankrupt governments who were prepared to sign any piece of paper to get their hands on some money. The premise of the loans was that they would be invested in productive projects out of whose yields the interest and capital repayments would be made. But, more often than not, the money went into private Swiss bank accounts or the projects failed, as most "development" projects did at the time.[29] By the end of the 1970s there was a huge banking crisis, since Third World debtors were in no position to pay off the loans. This was exacerbated by the second oil price hike, in 1979. The gains of 1973 had been eroded in the meantime; so the producers tried to claw some of them back. This time, the dollar was undermined and the Federal Reserve responded by raising interest rates to around 20%. The subsequent regime of high interest rates coincided with the shift from post-war Keynesian demand management to the "monetarist" (sound money = deflationary) policies identified with Reagan and Thatcher.

The 1980s and afterwards saw a massive transfer of money from the Third World to the West in the form of interest repayments that often amounted to as much as a third of government revenues in any given year.[30] This drain of income from the poor countries was greater than any extracted under previous colonial and neo-colonial arrangements. The International Monetary Fund and the World Bank imposed draconian measures known as "structural adjustment," designed to reduce each government's financial obligations. The threat to the Western banking system was averted by a combination of rescheduling agreements (which only increased Third World liabilities) and covert support to the most vulnerable banks. The governments of poor countries were caught without any alternative to playing along. In any case they had long ago abandoned any sense of responsibility toward their own people in exchange for dependency on their foreign creditors.

In the process of this catastrophe, which is the specific context for escalating impoverishment in much of Africa, Asia and Latin America, the idea of
"development" was quietly dropped. The international agencies now have
just one goal, the survival of governments whose task is to supervise passively the international flow of money into the coffers of Western banks and
corporations. Aid levels have been much reduced since the 1960s; indeed,
non-governmental organizations of a bewildering number and variety have
stepped in to perform functions that neither Third World states nor their international sponsors are prepared to undertake any more. But the obscene
transfer of wealth from the poor to the rich, honoring debts contracted
under highly dubious circumstances, reveals how far world society has de-
generated from the high ideals produced by the defeat of fascism and colonial empire in mid-century.

A brief note should be added on the communist bloc.[31] That great states-
man, Richard Nixon, made a sort of peace with Brezhnev's Soviet Union, as
well as with China, at the beginning of the 1970s. This opened up the possibility of trade between East and West. Nixon's solution was the so-called
"vodka–cola" strategy; the point being that there was no way that Americans
could drink enough vodka to pay for all the Coke that Russians would want
to buy. What was it that the communists had plenty of? Docile, reasonably
skilled, cheap labor. They could buy Western goods with the proceeds from
selling that labor to Western corporations. Consequently, the World Bank
and other institutions lent money to the Poles, Hungarians, and so on, to go
in for joint sponsoring deals with these companies, setting up factories
there, for example making up clothes for sale in the West. The hard currency
earned by repressing their own labor force was spent by the political elites
in special shops for whisky and Marlboro cigarettes, which served to mark
off their status from that of the masses, who ate bread and potatoes if they
were lucky.

There was a snag. World trade was rigged to prevent countries with cheap
labor, like Taiwan or Poland, undermining their high-cost Western competitors. North America and Western Europe erected tariff barriers against such
competition that were potentially prohibitive for the trade initiated under the
auspices of the vodka–cola strategy. A solution was found. When West Germany signed the Treaty of Rome, to join the European Common Market, it

signed in the name of Germany as a whole, so that East Germany was in theory a member of the Western trading circle. Manufactures from the communist bloc were shipped into the West through East Germany acting as a sort of port-of-trade. When the Berlin Wall fell, several Eastern European countries had accumulated billions of dollars in debts to finance this scheme. The resulting popular governments then embarked on a privatization program that ruined their economies; and the attention of the Western powers shifted to doing what they could to protect their trade and investment there. It may eventually dawn on them that, having participated actively in the economic ruin of the second and third blocs of post-war humanity (which is to say, the great majority), they are merely preparing the way for their own downfall. Certainly, there are fewer triumphalists around today ready to claim that the West "won" the Cold War. The shadow of the 1930s presses closer in on us all.

In the meantime, whether they actively sought it or not, many countries have effectively been ejected from the movement of world trade. At the time of the First World War, when Lenin claimed that accumulation through the colonies was the main concern of Western capitalism,[32] these accounted for something like a third of world trade. It was still the heyday of a world market based on exchange of raw materials for simple manufactures. By the end of the 1970s the Third World's share of international trade had fallen to 10%, and in the last two decades this has fallen sharply even further. Increasingly, world trade is dominated by exchange between a few countries capable of entering the sophisticated system of money, information services and hi-tech manufactures that constitutes "virtual capitalism." If the underdevelopment theorists once advocated withdrawal from the world system as a positive strategy, most non-Western governments are now desperate to keep a toe-hold in a market that threatens to exclude them for good. The priorities of ordinary people in these countries may be somewhat different, however. They at least, unlike their governments, have the option of leaving home and trying their luck in the centers of world economy.

State capitalism and the informal economy

In the twentieth century, capitalism took the specific form of being organized through the state. Three world wars were fought to determine which form of state would predominate, but in the end it was the state itself that lost. Now there is not a popular government in the world, and people every-where are looking for ways of getting the state off their backs, especially by reducing their obligations to pay taxes. The antithesis of state capitalism is the so-called "informal economy," a term that originated in the early seventies. Beginning as a way of conceptualizing the unregulated activities of the marginal poor in Third World cities, "the informal sector" has become recognized as a universal feature of the modern economy.[33] Evasion of the state's rules unites practices as diverse as home brewing, street trade, the drugs traffic, political corruption and offshore banking. The issue of informal economic activities is thus intimately tied up with the crisis of state capitalism in our times.[34]

In nineteenth-century Britain, the "nightwatchman state" was content to provide the conditions in which market capitalism could flourish. This included putting down workers' riots, when necessary. The Germans and later the Japanese pioneered a national system of closer co-operation between government, the banks and industry. But no one then dreamed of the state being able to regulate the workings of the economy in fine detail, down to fixing prices and taking on responsibility for boosting the number of jobs. A capitalism whose principal organ of reproduction was the state itself arose out of the conditions of the First World War. During the Great War of 1914–18 millions of working people were killed in the trenches, which in one way solved the problem of popular pressure for change. But the greatest discovery of their rulers lay in the powers of intervention unleashed by the bureaucratic revolution of recent decades.

For a century or more, intellectuals had been grappling with the problem of how to rule the anonymous masses of the new industrial cities. Statistics, classification and professional specialization were part of the answer. Hegel proposed, around the end of the Napoleonic wars, a state-made "universal class" of bureaucrats trained in universities to administer the common good. Not long afterwards, Marx and Engels argued that, if there was to be a universal class taking responsibility for the guidance of society, it would be the mass of ordinary working people themselves.[35] This set the stage for a gigantic struggle to determine the locus of power in modern society. The industrial working classes flirted with revolutionary politics, but eventually settled for a welfare state administered by professionals—an army of doctors, teachers, lawyers, social workers and, eventually, economists. In other words, it was Hegel's vision that won out in our century, not Marx's.

This was obscured by the revolutionary consequences of the First World War, which exploded in Russia and for a time (1917–19) threatened everywhere to overturn the system of rule in the interests of big money. Less noticeably, however, the rulers of the industrial countries acquired massive powers of direction and mobilization in the course of the war. Faced with the possibility of universal insurrection afterwards, they deployed these new powers to launch a counter-revolution, a reassertion of the state's right to rule, if necessary by taking on its own people. This was true even of Russia, which, after Lenin's death in 1923, was ruled by Stalin as a totalitarian bureaucracy only nominally committed to world revolution. From the 1920s to the end of the 1980s, there was one system of political economy in the world and several variants bent on winning overall control.

After 1945, the rhetoric of the Cold War did not disguise the convergence of the American and Russian systems toward a common model of accumulation. C.L.R. James pointed out that both sides organized workers in factories to produce surpluses that were ultimately managed by the state.[36] The difference between public and private ownership of the means of production was more important in ideology than in practice. A similar conclusion was reached by Clark Kerr and his associates writing from the perspective of life in post-war California (the "logic of industrialism" thesis of the 1950s).[37] Many people thought that the Russian economy was more robust than the American and would soon overtake the West. It turned out otherwise, and Stalinism faded away after 1989 with much less turmoil than anyone would have expected.

The economic theory that underpinned the welfare-state democracies was called "macro-economics" and its inventor in the Great Depression was Maynard Keynes. This theory (along with the economic stimulus of rearmament) rescued the Western societies from a severe decline manifested as high levels of unemployment. It rested on the assumption that only the state could regenerate a damaged market economy, mainly by spending money it did not have in order to reflate consumer demand. After the Second World War, the strongest economic boom in history depended in no little part on the co-ordinated efforts of the leading industrial states to expand their own public sectors. When Richard Nixon said, "We are all Keynesians now," he meant that Western voters were unanimous in expecting their governments to intervene in the economy for the general good. It all began to unravel soon afterwards. The neo-liberal conservative politicians who dominated the 1980s claimed to be opposed to state control of the market economy, but their policies often combined "privatization" with a strengthening of state power. Even so, it was the end of the twentieth-century consensus that I have called "state capitalism."

The idea of an "informal economy" has run as a submerged commentary on these developments during the last quarter-century. If state capitalism is now in crisis, it is because it failed to deliver economic democracy in adequate measure; and because its negation, the activities of ordinary people making their own daily life, contains the seeds of a more humane alternative. Moreover, although the informal economy is acknowledged to be a universal phenomenon, the idea came out of the lives of Third World people, whose lack of money makes them about as conventionally poor as it is possible to be in our mechanized world. The way they each set about redressing their personal situation, hedged around with insuperable difficulties as they often were, is the concrete experience of economic life on which this book is founded.[38]

By the 1970s it was becoming clear that development in the accepted sense was a pipedream for Third World countries. Populations had exploded; cities were growing rapidly; mechanization was weak; and productivity in predominantly agricultural economies remained low; the gap between rich and poor was widening. Even so, there was a consensus that the only institution capable of mobilizing economic resources on an appropriate scale was the state. Marxists and Keynesians agreed on this; free-market liberals had no effective voice at this time. The malaise was conceived of as "urban unemployment." Third World economies were supposed to deliver jobs, but, in the absence of machine-based industry, employment creation was left largely to the only economic agent of any significance in most of these countries, state bureaucracy. The number of corporate firms offering jobs was embarrassingly small. What, then, could all the other new inhabitants of the major cities be up to? They must be unemployed. Figures of 50% unemployment and more were conjured up by economists. The spectre of the 1930s—broken men huddling on street corners ("Buddy, can you spare a dime?"), the rise of fascism and ultimately war—dominated the discourse of interested Western intellectuals.

Anyone who visited, not to mention lived in, these sprawling cities would get a rather different picture. Their streets were teeming with life, a constantly shifting crowd of hawkers, porters, taxi-drivers, beggars, pimps, pickpockets, hustlers—all of them doing their best to get by without the benefit of a real job of the sort found in national economic statistics. There was no shortage of names and descriptions for this kind of early-modern street economy. Terms such as "underground," "unregulated," "hidden," "black" and "second" economies abounded. But the antithesis of the state-made modern economy had not yet found its academic name. This came about through a paper, based on my Accra fieldwork, that I presented at a Sussex conference on "Urban employment in Africa" in 1971.[39]

The main message of the paper was that Accra's poor were not "unemployed." They worked, often casually, for erratic and generally low returns; but they were definitely working. What distinguished these self-employed earnings from wage employment was the degree of *rationalization* of working conditions. Following Weber (and Geertz[40]), I argued that the ability to stabilize economic activity within a bureaucratic form made returns more calculable and regular. That stability was in turn guaranteed by the state's laws and rules, which only extended so far into the depths of Ghana's economy. The "formal" sector consisted of regulated economic activities and the "informal" sector of all those lying beyond the scope of regulation, both legal and illegal. I did not identify the informal sector with a place or a class or even whole persons. Everyone in Accra, but especially the inhabitants of slums like Nima, tried to combine the two sources of income. Informal opportunities ranged from market gardening and brewing through every kind of trade to gambling, theft and political corruption. What makes this concept of interest here is its roots in what people generate out of the circumstances of their everyday life. They do this despite being apparently confined to choosing between the scarce opportunities offered by an impersonal system and the meagre pickings left in the cracks of that system. The laws and offices of state bureaucracy served only to make their efforts at self-preservation and even improvement more difficult.

The idea of an informal economy was taken up quickly by some economists, so quickly indeed that a report by the International Labor Office applying the concept to Kenya came out in 1972 before my own article had been published.[41] The ILO report suggested that self-employed, or "informal," incomes might be able to reduce the gap between those with and without jobs and might even be a means to achieving a more equitable income distribution. Following the "growth or bust" policies of the 1960s, which had often had very unequal results, they advocated "growth with redistribution," that is, helping the poor out of the proceeds of economic expansion. This reflected a shift in World Bank policy announced by its president, Robert MacNamara, a year later. By now the international economic authorities were worried about potential explosions, and they felt that more attention should be paid to the peasants and to the urban poor. A vogue for promoting the "informal sector" as a device for employment creation fitted in with this shift.

Of course no one could agree on what the term meant. Most economists saw it in quantitative terms as a sector of small-scale, low productivity, low-income activities without benefit of advanced machines; whereas my notion stressed the reliability of income generated by work, the presence or absence of bureaucratic *form*. The problem with trying to use the bureaucracy to promote the informal sector—by providing credit, government buildings or new technologies, for example—was that these initiatives killed off the informality of the enterprises concerned and, moreover, exposed participants to the very thing they wanted to avoid, taxation. The association with the sprawling slums of Third World cities was very strong; but the "commanding heights" of the informal economy lie at the centers of political power itself, in the corrupt fortunes of state officials who often own the taxis or the rented accommodation that are operated by the small fry. The Marxists rejected the concept (which they preferred to call "petty commodity production"),[42] since they believed that it put a positive gloss on exploitation, the poor subsidizing capital accumulation with their cheap goods and services.

That was the 1970s. The following decade saw another major shift in world economic policy following the lead of Reagan and Thatcher. Now the state was no longer seen as the great provider; "the market," freed of as many encumbrances as possible, was the only engine of growth. The informal economy took on a new lease of life with institutions like the World Bank as a zone of free commerce, competitive because unregulated. This coincided with the imposition of structural adjustment policies that reduced public expenditures and threw the responsibility onto the invisible self-help schemes of the citizens themselves. By now, even the rhetoric of development had been abandoned as the Third World suffered the largest income drain to the rich countries in its history, in the form of repayment of debts incurred during the wild banking boom of the 1970s.

So is it possible to assess the part played by the informal economy in Third World development? Many parts of the Third World have undergone an urban revolution since 1945 linked to the concentration of state economic power (and expenditure) in a few cities, often just one, the national capital.[43] Rural–urban migration has vastly exceeded the growth of a bureaucratic or modern sector of employment. Even those who have jobs must often supplement them with extra earnings. The growth of cities has not stimulated local agriculture as much as it should, since cheap food imports have been available from the subsidized farmers of the rich countries. This has only encouraged more of a stagnating peasantry to leave home for the city. The informal economy has in some cases been a source of economic dynamism, even capital accumulation. At the very least, as the following story shows, it has allowed people to maintain themselves in the urban areas.

Atinga's bar

Atinga lived in the same house as me in Nima; in return for occasional loans, he allowed me to keep records of his economic transactions. He was given a medical discharge from the army at Christmas 1965. He was twenty-eight years old, had been in southern Ghana for nine years and now lived with his wife and a brother's teenage son. He was without work and had not yet been paid any gratuity or pension; but he had £10 from his last pay packet. At first he thought of going home to farm in the remote north-east of the country, but the prospect of getting another job in Accra was more attractive. This meant he had to finance the period of his unemployment, and he decided to set up as a retailer of crude gin (*akpeteshi*).

First he converted his room (for which he paid £3 a month in rent) into a bar-cum-living quarters by the simple expedient of hanging a cloth down the center and piling his possessions on both sides. Chairs and a table, bought for 15s. (twenty shillings to the pound), occupied the public section. For next to nothing he got hold of some small plastic glasses, an assortment of used bottles and an old, rusting funnel. These were placed on the table. Atinga then went to a distiller nearby and bought a four-gallon drum of *akpeteshi* for £5.10s. He handed over what was left (just under £4) to his wife for food, borrowed £4 from me to help pay the rent and opened up his business on New Year's Eve.

The retail price of gin was fixed throughout Nima at 6s. a bottle and smaller quantities were priced in proportion. Allowing for wastage, receipts from a drum ought to have come to £8 or a bit less. Profit margins could be increased by buying the gin for as cheaply as £4 a drum, depending on quality and method of payment (cash or credit). Atinga bought the best gin at first, in order to attract a clientele and because he knew that high turnover compensated for reduced profit.

His main problem was with extending credit. Because his customers were poor and improvident, he could keep up sales only by offering generous credit facilities. But he also needed cash to replenish his stock and feed his family. His average daily expenditure was 7–8s. or £14–15 a month, including rent. So he had to sell a lot of gin. He also tried to diversify; but his wife's attempt to sell sugar lumps foundered under a saturation of local competition, and his own Coca-Cola business failed for lack of a refrigerator.

After a few weeks Atinga faced a major crisis. He had overextended credit to the tune of £14 (a third of total sales) in order to keep up a turnover of one gallon a day. Some of his customers were clearly out to take him for a ride before they moved on to the next inexperienced operator. Others simply did not have the money to pay. His gin supply ran out just before January pay-day, and he lacked the means of replenishing it. He weathered this crisis by borrowing again; otherwise his clients would have taken their custom and their debts away. He secured enough repayment of credit to go on with and started insisting more often on cash from his customers. This naturally slowed down business, but he was able to keep a small, regular clientele (mostly young men from his home village) who came to him whatever the quality of his gin. This enabled him to economize by buying gin at £4 a drum.

By now Atinga saw that his bar could only ever be a sideline, a supplement to a more substantial source of income—in other words, a job. Moreover, his wife was pregnant. He tried to get back into the army, leaving his wife to look after the bar. Attempts to diversify in trade failed for lack of capital and expertise. When things were bad, his landlord's wives helped out with food. Meanwhile he lent and borrowed money to roughly equal effect, in the hope that he could pass on his creditors to his debtors. A backlog of rent was his greatest debt. After his narrow escape, turnover steadied out at four or five drums a month, giving him a monthly income of between £10 and £12, rather more than the minimum wage. Moreover, this income was being eventually realized as cash, since he was only owed £12 in April (of which some £5 had been written off as bad debts).

The remainder of 1966 saw a gradual decline in the fortunes of Atinga's bar, if not in his total income. In September he took a job as a watchman at 8s. a day, leaving his wife to look after their customers. Turnover, however, slowed to a trickle, and his wife consumed most of the gin. Occasionally trade was boosted by a one-off enterprise, like the purchase of a stray dog for sale as meat and soup. At times like this the bar did roaring business for a brief spell. More often, it was empty at night because he had no gin to sell or his customers no money or, more likely, both.

In December Atinga's wife gave birth to a son. In February 1967 the military bureaucracy got round to paying him £40 as an advance on his gratuity. The bar took on a new lease of life, £20 being spent on wood for a counter, partition, door and shelves. Atinga even bought a gin-seller's license. He did not, however, pay off any of his accumulated debts. For a few weeks he used the remainder of his capital to keep up an artificial rate of business, but he was soon back in the vicious circle of credit and turnover.

In May he lost his job as a watchman, but was lucky to be accepted almost immediately for training as an escort policeman (a colonial hangover distinguished by wearing a red fez and khaki puttees). This took him off to Winneba in June, and he could only visit his wife and child at weekends. On one of these visits, in August 1967, his landlord threw him out of the house on suspicion that he had been the informer behind a police raid on the premises. The room and all its wooden fittings were seized in partial compensation for over £32 owed in rent.

Atinga left Nima with his family, and the gin bar enterprise was at an end. His landlord's wife took it over, but, as she offered no credit whatsoever, she was unsuccessful. Some twenty months of unemployment and intermittent wage employment had been negotiated by means of an informal operation that was always rickety, but that had been the main basis of Atinga's family's survival in the city. His story shows that being "out of work" in a society entirely devoid of social security benefits need not lead to destitution or dependence on others. As it happens, Atinga was extremely unimaginative, well suited to the lower orders of an army or police force. Even so, he showed some economic initiative in the face of adversity. As we saw in the last chapter, there were more spectacular examples of Frafra enterprise, but this one was more typical of the general run.

The idea of the informal economy was wedded from the beginning to the heyday of state capitalism. It could almost be described as the conceptual negation of Keynesian macro-economics, the decentralized activities of ordinary people as opposed to the economic policies of governments. There is widespread agreement that the powers of nation-states have been in decline since at least the mid-1970s. Many commentators attribute this to globalization,[44] the rapid integration of world markets for goods and services, money, information and even people themselves. The market for money is the most important of these in view of the traditional association of currency with states. So powerful have "the markets" become that it is no longer an option for governments to implement policies disapproved of by those who buy and sell the national currency.[45] We will take up this topic in the next section.

Another way of pointing to this relative decline of state economic power is to focus on the informalization of the world economy in recent decades. By far the most valuable commodity traded internationally is drugs, a predominantly illegal traffic. Finance has been slipping its political shackles, for example by relocating offshore where money transactions can hardly be monitored or taxed. The armaments industry is a sea of corruption reaching, as we know thanks to Irangate, Iraqgate and all the other scandals, to the core of Western governments. Then there are the so-called "grey markets" for goods imitating well-known brands and the outright criminal duplication of videos, CDs and tapes. The irrational borders of nation-states are often principally sites for smuggling. These are just the commanding heights of an informalized world economy, much of it illegal, all of it defying state regulation. The term has become widely used in the industrialized countries. Raymond Pahl has explored just how much economic activity in Britain might be said to be informal, from allotments and do-it-yourself to the more criminalized economy of disaffected youth.[46] Even before the collapse of Stalinist bureaucracy in the Soviet Union and its satellites, it was clear that collectivization had spawned a flourishing "black market," antecedent of the criminal mafias that now dominate much of the Russian economy. In Europe, the dissident left has long had a slogan: "Think red, work black, vote green."

Meanwhile, the collapse of any orderly version of the state in many Third World countries has led to the informal economy becoming the whole economy, a contradiction of terms. One only has to think of Congo (Zaire),[47] which, before Kabila's revolution, President Mobutu reduced to a shambles where soldiers looted at will and many hangers-on had a large foreign bank account. The amount of paved road fell from 62,000 km at independence from Belgium (not one of the world's most enlightened colonial powers) to less than 8,000 km three decades later; Mobutu boasted of being one of the richest men in the world and once hired a train for a lavish party in New York. Or take Jamaica, which in the 1970s was a model "middle-income" developing economy. Not long ago the value of illegal marijuana sales (*ganja*) was higher than the country's three leading legitimate industries (tourism, bauxite, garments) taken together. No wonder that politics often seemed to be carried out by armed gangsters and that youths left school in droves to learn hustling on the street.

When so much of the economy is "informal," we are entitled to ask whether the term has outgrown its usefulness. Certainly there is some point in looking for positive ways of identifying social forces that may be concealed beneath the formal/informal label. The poetry underlying the term's longevity may perhaps be attributed to the stand-off of the Cold War. The opposition between state socialism and the free market was frozen by the unthinkable prospect of a nuclear resolution to the conflict. At the same time the universality of state capitalism had taken on a timeless quality by the early 1970s. The activities of little people in the interstices of a state-dominated economy were at best a defensive reaction to exclusion and a possible bulwark against destitution—surely not the basis for any serious alternative. So, it did not seem likely that the dialectic of informality contained much movement. The last decades have exposed the limitations of such a perspective.

The popularity of the label "informal" may derive from its being negative. It says what people are *not* doing—not wearing conventional dress, not being regulated by the state—but it does not point to any active principles they may have for doing it. In this sense it is a passive and conservative concept that acknowledges a world outside the bureaucracy, but endows it with no positive identity. The informal sector allowed academics and bureaucrats to incorporate the teeming street life of exotic cities into their models without having to confront the specificity of what the people were really up to. In sacrificing my own ethnographic encounter with real persons to the generalizing jargon of development economics, I played my own part in this process of rationalization and cover-up.

We can see all this now thanks to the "velvet revolution" of Eastern Europe and the Soviet Union, which demonstrated that ordinary people could get rid of the most awesome bureaucratic states with remarkably little violence. Who can now think of the state as eternal when Stalin's successors were dispensed with so completely and quickly? Nor are the conclusions to be drawn from this cataclysmic event all that straightforward. We may want to romanticize the informal economy as a little people's alternative, but would we want to live in a Moscow run by gangsters?

West Africa's former colonies were among the last admitted to state capitalism and among the first to leave. Ghana was already in an advanced condition of political and economic decay in the mid-1960s when I did my fieldwork. Seen in that light, Nima may be thought of as a harbinger of state capitalism's decline. After much of the Third World dropped out of the movement of the world economy, the communist bloc followed suit, leaving America, Western Europe and a resurgent East Asia to contemplate the consequences for their own societies of a comparable decline. The informal economy was nothing less than the self-organized energies of people, biding their time to escape from the strictures of state rule. The question remains whether those energies might take on a more constructive dynamic under the conditions unleashed by the communications revolution.

Virtual capitalism

Virtual reality: *The experience of a computer simulation in real time.*[48]

When I was twelve years old, I took stock of my situation. I did not want a job like my father's when I grew up. He worked for wages in a public bureaucracy, and every night we were silent witnesses as he told his wife about his frustrations: How he knew his job better than his superiors, but had to suffer their interventions and obstruction anyway. One alternative seemed to be entailed in my career at Manchester Grammar School: I would pass enough examinations to join the free professions, jobs that allowed people a lot of say in making the conditions of their own work. I imagined academic life to be like that. But this option filled me with dread. What if I failed to pass the exams? Looking around for something else to fall back on, I could only think of making money with money and, at the time, that meant betting. I set out to make money by betting on horses; but I did not have any money. So, for the first three years, I used my grandmother's *Daily Express* (tipsters The Scout and Peter O'Sullevan) to keep a record of bets made only in a notebook, restricting myself, we might now say, to virtual betting.

At the end of that period I was making a regular profit on paper, and I also had a part-time job delivering newspapers. I managed to save out of the money I was given for lunch and bus fares. Later I took better-paid jobs in factories and warehouses during the holidays. So I had the means of making real bets. By the time I arrived in Cambridge at the age of eighteen, I had six years' knowledge of the horses under my belt and a small income from winnings. But I never had enough money to bet with. When I received my first advance from the education authority for a whole term's subsistence, I realized that I was now the owner of capital. This opened the way to scientific gambling, and I devised a statistical method (of which more below) that eventually produced highly predictable earnings, when combined with the expertise I had accumulated in the world of horse-racing. In my years as an undergraduate student, I lived quite well without ever working for wages or taking any money from my parents. I calculate that I more or less doubled my grant by betting. (I also won consistently at card games, especially bridge for high stakes). I eventually gave it up, after two years in Africa interrupted my knowledge of the horse-racing scene. I decided that I was better off trying to finish my Ph.D thesis than spending all my afternoons in the betting shops. And so the examination passer took over from the gambler.

Later, during an eight-year stay in America, I adapted my betting strategy to gambling on cocoa futures and money markets. In this time I developed a more abstract understanding of the process that I suppose has informed the writing of this book. Let me begin by outlining my horse-racing methods. I started from the binomial theorem. If two outcomes have equal probability (0.5 each), then the chance of repeating a sequence of such outcomes is the probability raised to the power of the number of tries. If you toss a coin ten times, the chance that it will come out ten successive heads is 0.5 to the power of 10 or 1 in 1,024. Assuming a bet has an evens chance, I calculated that the probability of my losing ten successive evens bets was just over 1,000 to 1. This meant that I had to have a fund 1,000 times larger than the size of the initial bet, £1,000 for every evens bet of £1, and that would allow me to double up bets to cover my losses. So that, if the first bet lost, the second bet would be £2 to recover the first stake and still win £1 net; if the second bet lost, the third would be £4, the fourth £8 and so on until the tenth bet was £1,024 to recover what I had lost and still make £1.

I restricted my bets to favorites starting at odds of between evens and 2 to 1. The fact that their odds were on average better than evens provided a margin with which to pay a 10% betting tax. Odds-on (less than evens) carried too great a risk of escalating the sum I had to lay out if they lost. The crucial variable in this system was to maintain the highest possible turnover of bets. Favorites tended to win 1 in 3 races, so that my average run before I won was three. I made bets automatically until I had lost four times, so that I did not have to waste effort selecting a horse after reviewing the form of all runners. In the bulk of cases, therefore, I was limited only by the frequency of races, every half hour over three hours in an afternoon or evening, usually at two or more meetings with starts, if I was lucky, staggered on the quarter hour. If the fourth bet lost, I slowed down subsequent bets, taking time to exercise critical judgement, picking horses I really thought would win. This is where memory, experience and skill came in, improving the purely statistical odds in my favor. The longest losing betting sequence I ever suffered was seven, meaning that I had to spend over £100 to win £1; even so, this was a lot less than 1,000 to 1, and I began to make bets assuming a much lower margin of risk that I might lose everything.

On average I laid out £5–10 to win £1, with 20 wins out of 50–70 bets a week (many more chances to bet on Saturdays, especially in the summer). A profit rate of £20 a week from a stake of £1,000 doubles the fund in a year for the time it takes to make those bets. My earnings increased as I took higher risks of exhausting my betting fund. Working by telephone with a credit account involves much less effort than sitting in a betting shop all afternoon. In any case, my income from betting stabilized at a very predictable level. I had established three principles. What matters is:

1. The size of your initial fund;

2. The risk you will take of losing the lot; and

3. The speed with which you can place the bets.

Since my fund was small and my life depended on keeping it, the third factor was paramount. There was a fourth factor. Access to making bets is regulated by gatekeepers (bookmakers or, in other gambling pursuits, casinos) who have the legal right to refuse a bet for whatever reason. If they realize that the punter is using a statistical method that puts the odds on his side rather than on theirs, they simply close him down (an example would be card counters at blackjack). So that it is not enough to overcome generations of superstition and learn to gamble scientifically; you also have to get past the gatekeepers. I found that, by switching bets at random between three betting shops, I came across as a high-volume punter who seemed to break even. If they had seen the regularity of my positive returns, that would have been the end of my enterprise.

Later, in America, I applied this method to cocoa futures in New York.[49] But it was only when I took the method to money markets in their home town, Chicago, that I realized its potential under the conditions of the communications revolution. The principles I had first worked out clumsily in an unfavorable medium and with inadequate resources are central to the workings of virtual capitalism. On both occasions, my capital fund was very much greater than it had been at first ($25,000); and I ran a risk of losing my fund nearer to 100 than to 1,000 to 1. In order to maintain a high turnover of bets, I had to identify a range of fluctuations in prices that occurred frequently in a day's trading. I was not betting on the long-run trend in cocoa prices or the exchange rate between dollars and deutschmarks; rather, a win or loss was when the price deviated up or down by a predetermined amount from my purchasing price. Making bets by telephone via a computer screen, in the case of money markets up to twenty-four hours a day (thanks to the London, New York and Tokyo exchanges), is certainly more efficient than waiting for a few horses to run a race. There were also barriers to overcome: fees, minimum purchases, club rules of various sorts designed to keep the small punter out. But the main deterrent in the end was boredom.

Gambling for most people is an opportunity to win a lot with a little occasionally. This means that they must normally lose. And in a way, they want to lose, treating the "flutter" as a form of consumption, a chance for a rare buzz of excitement. I loved to go to Newmarket racecourse for an afternoon of this kind of gambling, always making sure that I set a limit to how much I was prepared to lose. Betting under these circumstances is like taking a holiday. It is nice while it lasts, but real life consists of the daily grind. Scientific gambling depends on making the opportunity to *win a little with a lot often.* This means in most cases sacrificing the pleasure even of exercising judgement, following strict statistical rules. Nowadays, computers are programed to invest money in equities and derivatives on a basis similar to that which I laboriously evolved.[50] It is mind-bogglingly tedious to sit in front of a computer screen for hours on end making mechanical decisions. That is why I always took up the offer of an academic job rather than devote myself to money-making full time. Believe it or not, it was more fun. I was glad to have mastered, in a small way, something of how to make money in our world; but I would rather study money than make it.

I have mentioned that not long ago I wrote a textbook on economic anthropology that I didn't publish because it seemed to contain so little of what I actually knew about the economy. The account I have just given is not based on academic research. Many people would say it is impossible or a fiction. But I believe that I learned more about capitalism in this way than by any other method. For the formula for making money with money, "win a little with a lot often," making as little contact as possible with events in the real world, is driving the latest phase of capitalist development. If you were the treasurer of a multinational corporation or the governor of a central bank or a very rich speculator, what would you put your money in, remembering that your potential fund for rectifying mistakes is huge? Surely making things and persuading people to part with their cash for them is much too onerous. Better to play the money markets at calculable odds. That is why capitalism in our day is a vast river of money flooding around the world at high speed. Markets for the goods that most people need are stagnant because they do not have the money to buy, and capitalists have more reliable ways of increasing their money than by making them.

In 1975 Milton Friedman, favorite economist of Ronald Reagan and Margaret Thatcher, set out, with a partner from the Chicago Mercantile Exchange, to prove that the age of Keynesian macro-economics was over.[51] He was outraged by the pretension of governments that they could determine the rates at which their currencies were exchanged and could intervene in markets in the national interest. As a free trader and sound money fundamentalist in the tradition of John Locke, he took heart from the financial crises that affected international exchange in the early seventies and from the persistent inflation caused by governments trying to spend themselves out of trouble. The instrument he devised was intended to alleviate the uncertainties inflicted on Midwestern farmers by wide fluctuations in exchange rates. If you sell your pork bellies to Germany six months ahead of delivery time, the dollar/deutschmark exchange rate may deteriorate in the meantime and your actual earnings will be less than anticipated. A futures market in money allows you to determine that exchange rate six months in advance and to stabilize your expectations as a result. Others can speculate for the sake of making money (as I did); but the farmer gets paid reliably for his pork bellies.

From this unremarkable beginning, a new phase of capitalism emerged. In the mid-seventies almost all currency exchanges were to finance the international purchase of goods and services (like pork bellies or tourist holidays). Today less than 0.1% of international money transactions are for that purpose; the rest is just money, in a bewildering variety of instruments and forms, being exchanged for money. It is now possible to buy futures in anything, such as the likely level to be reached by the index of a major stock exchange.[52] This was how a Singapore trader broke the British bank, Barings, by betting on the Tokyo Nikkei Index at a time when an earthquake depressed prices unpredictably. Of course, not all investment in these money markets is scientific. There is plenty of scope for the "animal spirits" (Keynes) involved in speculating on a hunch, especially when the backing funds are large. There is a magical and a rational side to this development, and it is by no means obvious which will win out.

"Virtual" means "as good as." I have already claimed that the communications revolution is driven by the desire to replicate, at distance or by means of computers, experiences that we normally associate with face-to-face encounters. All communication, whether the exchange of words or money, has a virtual aspect in that symbols and their media of circulation stand for what people really do for each other. It usually involves the exercise of imagination, an ability to construct meanings across the gap between symbol and reality. The power of the book for so long depended on sustaining that leap of faith in the possibility of human communication. In that sense, capitalism was always virtual. Indeed, Marx's intellectual effort was devoted to revealing how the power of money was mystified through its appearance as things (coins, products, machinery) rather than as relations between living men.[53] Both Marx and Weber were at pains to show how capitalists sought to detach their money-making activities, as far as possible, from real conditions obstructing their purposes. Moneylending, the practice of charging interest on loans without any intervening act of production or exchange, is one of the oldest forms of capitalism. So the idea of the money circuit becoming separated from reality is hardly new. Yet there are changes taking place that deserve a distinctive label, and, for the time being, "virtual capitalism" will have to do.

The point of virtualism[54] is abstraction, and this in turn is a function of the shift to ever more inclusive levels of exchange, to the world market as principal point of reference for economic activity, rather than the nation-state. But, as I insist throughout this book, reliance on more abstract forms of communication carries with it the potential for real persons to be involved with each other at a distance in very concrete ways. The idea of "virtual reality" expresses this double movement: On the one hand machines whose complexity their users cannot possibly understand, on the other live experiences "as good as" real. It is the same with money. Capitalism has become virtual in two main senses: the shift from material production (agriculture and manufacturing) to information services; and the corresponding detachment of the circulation of money from production and trade. This in turn is an aspect of the latest stage of mechanization, the communications revolution of the late twentieth century. The question is whether the same developments that have been responsible for the recent integration of world society are also the cause of its increasing polarization. The answer is certainly yes.

Long-distance trade in information services requires a substantial technical infrastructure. The Internet, as we have seen, has its origins in scientific collaboration between America and Europe during the Cold War. Its main language is English. Each stage of mechanization has been first concentrated in a narrow enclave of world society; and this one is no different. Equally, diffusion of new techniques has often been quite rapid. Satellite and cellular telephony, as well as videotape, have brought telecommunications to many parts of the world where the old infrastructure of electric power was underdeveloped. There is even talk of the Western market for the means of communication (telephones, computers, television) being saturated or nearly, leading to a new version of the scramble for Africa, this time for shares in a largely untapped telecommunications market. But, for all this talk, the short conclusion is that many poorer regions appear to be stuck in phases of production that have been marginalized by this latest round of uneven development.

The most problematic issue concerns the spiralling markets for money in countless notional forms that have injected a new instability into global capitalism. The East Asian bubble of endlessly rising stock markets has recently burst, precipitating unprecedented upheavals on Wall Street and pushing the Japanese banking system into a tailspin. Billions of paper assets have been wiped out overnight. Mismanagement by the banks has reached colossal proportions. (Crédit Lyonnais made "errors of judgement" that amounted to losses equal to the deficit on the French national social security fund!) This apotheosis of capital, its effective detachment from what real people do, has made many huge fortunes, often for individuals controlling billions of dollars, more than the annual budgets of some Third World countries. Here is certainly one of the motors of global inequality, money being made with money.

The situation is comparable to that between the First and Second World Wars in America, especially, and also in Europe. A stock market boom ended with the Wall Street crash of 1929. The resulting depression lasted a decade. This was the opportunity for states to assert their own dominance over a capitalism that was then still more national than international. The subsequent period of about four decades was the heyday of state capitalism. What political forces are adequate to regulate the present money madness in the interest of people in general? The world organization of money has now reached a social scale and technical form that makes it impossible for states to control it. This may be good news for democrats and anarchists in the long run; but in the meantime Hegel's recipe for state moderation of capitalism has been subverted, with inevitable results: rampant inequality at all levels and appalling human distress without any apparent remedy.

We are obviously at a turning-point in human affairs. The present situation cannot continue indefinitely. It is no longer self-evident that being inside the virtual economy is a privilege. If the balloon goes up, people sitting on little plots of land in the countryside will count themselves lucky to have missed the bonanza. In another sense, development is no longer conceivable of as a linear process describing unequivocal winners and losers in the global economy, advanced and backward producers. The rules of the game are being rewritten so fast and with such uncertain consequences that it is unclear who is best placed to benefit from them. The populations of America and Europe, which have grown passively dependent on the impersonal institutions of state capitalism, may be less well placed than many West Africans, who have never known the relatively painless security of a welfare state.

The political economy of the Internet

Now that the Internet is no longer primarily a research tool, it is becoming increasingly an electronic marketplace. The point about electricity is that it travels at the speed of light and the passage of information itself is virtually costless. This, then, is a market with unusual time and space co-ordinates, where the personal and impersonal dimensions of economic life meet on new terms. Most of us will take some time to get used to the implications of such developments; in the meantime, the pioneers of cyberspace are making the most of these new opportunities.[55] Is the analysis of classical political economy appropriate to these circumstances? There are broad and narrow answers to that question. In the former case, we need to talk about the distribution of value in the global economy as a whole; in the latter, only of the Internet conceived of as a contested site of virtual capitalism or the world market. It is easy to conflate the two, as Marx and Engels did when they chose to interpret a few Lancashire factories as the vanguard of capitalist development. I have suggested that the three classes of political economy may even have represented the divisions of our worldly knowledge (ecology, economy, anthropology) or the overlapping stages of history in which land, money and human creativity are respectively dominant.[56]

So where are the three classes today? The landlord class has by no means rolled over and died, at least in Britain where politics retain a distinctly feudal tone.[57] But if one thing can be said with confidence about the Internet, it is that it offers a means of escape from land shortage, indeed from spatial constraints in all their forms. The part originally played by the landed aristocracy in maintaining the right to control people by virtue of occupation of territory has largely now passed to national governments. Territorial states are able to extract taxes and rents from all those economic activities involving money that take place inside or across the boundaries of their jurisdiction. Their ability to do so has been greatly facilitated by the advances made in bureaucracy during this century. But this becomes more difficult when the source of value shifts from car factories and downtown shopping centers to transactions of money and commodities conducted at the speed of light without regard to borders. The system of involuntary transfers could once be justified as a source of economic security for all. But that principle has been under attack from the right for at least two decades now; and the governments of rich countries are now more likely to legitimate their activities in terms of keeping the poor majority out.

The capitalists have come a long way too. Having formed an alliance with the traditional rulers from the 1860s onwards, they absorbed and ultimately defeated the challenge posed by the working class. It is not hard to see in the recent revival of free-market liberalism triumphal evidence of that victory. But the relationship of capital to the state has become increasingly moot.

Money has always had an international dimension, and the corporations that dominate world capitalism today are less obviously tied to their nations of origin than they once were. There are today some 34 firms with an annual turnover of $30–50 billion, larger than the Gross Domestic Product of all but eight countries in the world (the same countries being the home base of these corporations).[58] Moreover, despite an apparent trend in the 1980s for Asian countries to challenge Western hegemony, by the end of the nineties half of the world's 500 largest firms were American (244, up 22 on the previous year), more than a third were European, and the rest of the world's representatives shrank in numbers and influence as a result of the financial upheavals of 1998.[59] In other words, the evidence is that an ever larger proportion of the world economy is controlled by a few firms of Western origin but dubious national loyalties.

The relationship between capital and the nation-state has always been one of conflict and co-operation. The wave of anti-trust legislation that accompanied the rise of monopolists like John D. Rockefeller at the beginning of the century is matched today by the feebler efforts of governments at various levels (mostly in America) to contain the economic power of Microsoft and a few companies like it. A lot rides on whether bureaucracies and legislatures can impede Bill Gates's dream of extracting payment for use of his Internet software worldwide. The idea of profit as a form of rent (income from property) is confirmed, even if the burden has shifted from workers to consumers. The state competes for a share of the value of commodities in the form of taxes. But both rent and tax depend on a system of legal coercion, on a realistic threat of punishment, to make people pay up. This remains a shared concern of governments and corporations alike.

So where does that leave the rest of us, allowing for the fact that many ordinary people would side with the big players for quite mundane reasons? If Marx could identify the general interest with a growing body of factory workers tied to machines owned by capitalists, it has been true for some time now that the majority of us enter the economic process mainly in the role of consumers. Economic agency is for most of us a matter of spending money. Despite the collapse of traditional industries in recent decades, there are still those who argue that workers' associations, unions, remain the best hope for organized resistance to big business. It was an achievement of state capitalism to make people believe in society as a place with one fixed point. But this is giving way to a more plural and shifting terrain in which the Internet may well be breaking new ground. The mass of ordinary users have a common interest, as individuals and pressure groups of various kinds, in avoiding unreasonable regulation of their activities and in retaining the economic benefits of their exchanges (conducted on an equal basis). In this formulation, we may provisionally accord to the wired, netties, internauts or what have you a class identity in opposition to governments and corporations. But this has to be demonstrated rather than assumed.

To summarize, then, the main players in the political economy of the Internet are governments, corporations and the rest of us, the people (in this case the small minority who are wired). The landed interest, following a class alliance between landlords and capitalists in the nineteenth century, now takes the principal form of territorial power, the coercive capacity of states to extract taxes and rents on threat of punishment or by right of eminent domain. Capitalist profit is now concentrated in a handful of huge transnational corporations whose interest is not only in keeping up the price of commodities, but often in deriving rent (income from property) in the face of resistance to payment. It is problematic to identify the class that represents the general human interest in retaining the benefits of our own creativity; but, on an analogy with the workers who tended the factory machines (themselves initially a very small minority), we could start by looking at the wired, the ordinary people who exchange services as equals on the Internet.

Governments and corporations need each other, for sure, but their interests are far from coincident. Both may be vulnerable to self-conscious use of Internet resources by a democratic movement, which is the premise of this book. How does this triadic classification relate to historical periodization of

Table 4.3   The three classes today

Resources	Land	Money	Human creativity
Classes 1	Landlords	Capitalists	Workers
Income	Rent	Profit	Wages
Classes 2	Government	Corporations	Ordinary people ("the wired")
Income	Tax/rent	Profit/rent	Equal exchange

the age of money? I have argued that two revolutions in transport and communications, belonging to the 1860s and the 1990s respectively, mark the
beginning and end of state capitalism. Each was a decisive stage in the formation of the world market. If this present phase of opening up to the world
goes the same way as the previous one, toward ruinous conflict, the twenty-
first century could well be our last.

The institutional enemy of humanity is the jealous concentration of state
and corporate power, the retention of agrarian hierarchy to block humanity's potential to build a just society capable of exercising our collective responsibility for life on this planet. We could do worse, then, than return to
Ricardo and focus attention on the means through which wealth is distributed in human society, in particular on the contradiction between the unequal and coercive imposition of tax and rent demands and the formation of
a market in which people, reflecting the plurality of their associations as
equals, freely exchange services using money instruments of their own devising. This means separating capitalism conceptually and practically from
the market.

Guide to further reading

If you read only one book on twentieth-century economic development, it
should be the West Indian Nobel laureate, Arthur Lewis's *Evolution of the
International Economic Order* (note 20), for its theoretical insight, grasp of
history, subdued passion and lucid brevity. A good short guide to the
principles and categories of classical political economy and to the contrast
with modern economics is the opening section of Robinson and Eatwell's
Introduction to Economics (note 2). There are few competitors as yet of
Hobsbawm's one-volume history of the twentieth century and it is well
regarded (note 5). The anguish of Angola, where a million people have died
in thirty years, sums up the horrors of the contemporary "world economic
order" and is captured vividly in *Why Angola Matters* (note 15).

The 1998 edition of the United Nations *Human Development Report*
contains the most wide-ranging critique yet of escalating global inequality
from an official body, as well as a lot of interesting tables compiled from a
broader perspective on the human condition than the economic statistics
provided by the World Bank in its annual *Development Report*.[60] The

ideological extremes of development theory at the peak of the Cold War are well illustrated by Gunder Frank's devastating critique (note 25) of Rostow's megalomaniac *The Stages of Growth* (note 23). Wallerstein's *The Modern World System* (note 24) has been influential, but I find its historical vision rather mechanical.

"State capitalism" is a Trotskyist notion from the time when it was necessary to point out that there was nothing very socialist about the Soviet Union. The 1950 book (note 36) put out by the Johnson Forest Tendency was prescient but limited in its scope. I prefer to cite my own occasional writings on the informal economy (notes 34, 38, 39, 43) to the many volumes published on the topic. Bromley and Gery (note 42) offer a critical and varied selection of papers on Third World urban poverty. Janet MacGaffey's exemplary ethnography of enterprise and the "real economy" in Zaire (note 47) has recently been complemented by a major study of the illegal trade linking West Africa to Paris.[61]

The literature on globalization, virtual capitalism and *fin de siècle* money madness is breaking so fast that I have not been able to work out what is classical yet. Roland Robertson has managed to get his name associated with the term "globalization" (note 44). George Soros, as predator-turned-critic, personifies the capitalism of the era (note 45). Two recent books on Wall Street, by Frank Partnoy (note 50) and by Doug Henwood (note 52), caught my fancy. In anthropology, James Carrier and Daniel Miller are pioneering the post-capitalist term *virtualism* (note 54). It is debatable whether capitalism has yet reached its apogee. The best bet for keeping up with the latest developments is to read the *Financial Times* and surf the Internet. The only way to find out about the political economy of the Internet is to be there.

Notes

1. D. Ricardo, *Principles of Political Economy and Taxation* (Penguin, Harmondsworth, 1971; first pub. 1817); A. Comte, *Cours de philosophie positive* (Hermann, Paris, 1975; first pub. 1830–42); G. W. F. Hegel, *The Philosophy of Right* (Oxford University Press, London, 1952; first pub. 1821).
2. J. Robinson and J. Eatwell, *An Introduction to Economics* (McGraw Hill, New York, 1973, Book 1).

3. D. North, *Structure and Change in Economic History* (Norton, New York, 1981).

4. J.-F. Bayart, *The State in Africa: Politics of the Belly* (Longman, London, 1993).

5. E. Hobsbawm, *Age of Extremes: The Short Twentieth Century 1914–1991* (Michael Joseph, London, 1994).

6. See Hegel in note 1.

7. E. Leach, *A Runaway World? The 1967 Reith Lectures* (BBC, London, 1968).

8. D. Bell, *The Cultural Contradictions of Capitalism* (Basic Books, New York, 1975).

9. K. Hart, *The Political Economy of West African Agriculture* (Cambridge University Press, Cambridge, 1982), Chapter 2.

10. P. Wheatley, *The Pivot of the Four Quarters: A Preliminary Inquiry into the Origins and Character of the Ancient Chinese City* (Edinburgh University Press, Edinburgh, 1971).

11. A.F. Weber, *The Growth of Cities in the Nineteenth Century* (Cornell University Press, Ithaca, NY, 1965; first pub. 1899).

12. H. Mayhew, *London Labour and the London Poor* (4 vols, Dover, London, 1968; first pub. 1861–2).

13. G.S. Jones, *Outcast London: A Study in the Relationship between Classes in Victorian Society* (Penguin, Harmondsworth, 1984; first pub. 1973).

14. J.M. Keynes, *The General Theory of Employment, Interest and Money* (Macmillan, London, 1936).

15. K. Hart, "Angola and the World Order: The Political Economy of Integration and Division" in K. Hart and J. Lewis, eds, *Why Angola Matters* (James Currey, London, 1995).

16. Notice the root *sta-* (stand, set up), which "institution" shares with "establish" and, of course, with the "state," the institution that secures all others in society.

17. E. Durkheim and M. Mauss, *Primitive Classification* (Cohen & West, London, 1970; first pub. 1905).

18. It is hard to credit, given their universality today, that passports were only introduced on a general basis after the First World War.

19. F. Engels, *The Condition of the Working Class in England in 1844* (Lovell, New York, 1887).

20. W.A. Lewis, *The Evolution of the International Economic Order* (Princeton University Press, Princeton, NJ, 1978).

21. K. Nkrumah, *Africa Must Unite* (Heinemann, London, 1963).

22. D. Sparks, "Economic Trends in Africa South of the Sahara, 1998" in *Africa South of the Sahara 1999* (twenty-eighth edition, Europa, London, 1999).

23. W. Rostow, *The Stages of Growth: A Non-Communist Manifesto* (Cambridge University Press, Cambridge, 1960).

24. I. Wallerstein, *The Modern World System: Capitalist Agriculture and the Origins of the European World Economy in the Sixteenth Century* (Academic Press, New York, 1974).

25. S. Amin, *Unequal Development: An Essay on the Social Formations of Peripheral Capitalism* (Harvester Press, Hassocks, 1976; first pub. in *Le Développement inégal,* Minuit, Paris, 1973); A.G. Frank, *Latin America Underdevelopment or Revolution: Essays on the Development of Underdevelopment and the Immediate Enemy* (Monthly Review Press, New York, 1969), Chapter 2, "The Sociology of Development and the Underdevelopment of Sociology."

26. A. Samson, *The Seven Sisters: The Great Oil Companies and the World They Made* (Coronet Books, London, 1976).

27. The Saudis bought some $20 billion of these in 1974, according to my memory. Soon afterwards came the Carter government and the appointment of a Trilateral Commission that, in revealing the close connections between that government and the Rockefellers, lent support to those who saw a growing identity of interest between the U.S. Federal Government and the energy corporations.

28. A. Samson, *The Moneylenders* (Hodder & Stoughton, London, 1981).

29. K. Hart, *The Political Economy of West African Agriculture* (Cambridge University Press, Cambridge, 1982), Chapter 4, "The State in Agricultural Development."

30. S. George, *A Fate Worse than Debt* (Penguin, London, 1990).

31. The evidence for statements in this section is even more flimsy than usual. I include the story because its point of view is not often expressed in public and there might be some truth to it.

32. V.I. Lenin, *Imperialism, the Highest Stage of Capitalism: A Popular Outline* (Lawrence & Wishart, London, 1948; first pub. 1916).

33. A. Portes, M. Castells and L. Benton, eds., *The Informal Economy: Studies in Advanced and Less Developed Countries* (Johns Hopkins University Press, Baltimore, 1989).

34. K. Hart, "The Informal Economy" in J. Eatwell, M. Milgate and P. Newman, eds, *New Palgrave Dictionary of Economic Theory and Doctrine. Volume 2* (Macmillan, London, 1987); "The Informal Economy," *Cambridge Anthropology,* 1986.

35. K. Marx and F. Engels, *The German Ideology* (Lawrence & Wishart, London, 1974; first pub. 1846–7).

36. C.L.R. James and associates, *State Capitalism and World Revolution* (Charles Kerr, Chicago, 1986; first pub. 1950).

37. C. Kerr et al., *Industrialism and Industrial Man: The Problems of Labor and Management in Economic Growth* (Harvard University Press, Cambridge, Mass., 1960).

38. K. Hart, "Market and State after the Cold War: The Informal Economy Reconsidered" in R. Dilley, ed., *Contesting Markets* (Edinburgh University Press, Edinburgh, 1993).

39. My paper was called "Informal Income Opportunities and Urban Employment in Ghana," later published under the same title in the *Journal of Modern African Studies* (1973). This is now commonly cited as a classic source.

40. Clifford Geertz divided the economy of an Indonesian town into "firm" and "bazaar" sectors, according to the presence and absence of that bureaucratic form that is indispensable to calculation of money profits. C. Geertz, *Peddlers and Princes* (University of Chicago Press, Chicago, 1963).

41. International Labor Office, *Incomes, Employment and Equality in Kenya* (ILO, Geneva, 1972).

42. R. Bromley and C. Gery, eds, *Casual Work and Poverty in Third World Cities* (John Wiley, Chichester, 1979).

43. K. Hart, "Rural–urban Migration in West Africa" in J. Eades, ed., *Migrants, Workers and Social Order* (Tavistock, London, 1988).

44. R. Robertson, *Globalization: Social Theory and Global Culture* (Sage, London, 1992).

45. G. Soros, *The Crisis of Global Capitalism: Open Society Endangered* (Little, Brown, London, 1998).

46. R. Pahl, *Divisions of Labour* (Blackwell, Oxford, 1984).

47. J. MacGaffey, *Entrepreneurs and Parasites: The Struggle for Indigenous Capitalism in Zaire* (Cambridge University Press, Cambridge, 1987); *The Real Economy of Zaire: The Contribution of Smuggling and Other Unofficial Activities to National Wealth* (James Currey, London, 1991).

48. *American Heritage Dictionary* (third edition, 1993).

49. I had spent three years as a journalist for the Economist Intelligence Unit, reporting on West African export commodities, 1972–5.

50. If we are to believe Frank Partnoy, such staid methods, which ought to favor holders of large investment funds, have been abandoned in favor of wild gambling on derivatives. Such gambling often leads to major losses, but always generates large fees for the bankers. F. Partnoy, *F.I.A.S.C.O.: Blood in the Water on Wall Street* (Profile Books, London, 1997).

51. A. Hirsch and N. de Marchi, *Milton Friedman: Economics in Theory and Practice* (Harvester Wheatsheaf, London, 1990).

52. See note 50 and D. Henwood, *Wall Street: How It Works and for Whom* (Verso, London, 1997).

53. K. Marx, *Capital: A Critique of Political Economy. Volume 1* (Lawrence & Wishart, London, 1970), "The Fetishism of Commodities and the Secret Thereof," pp. 71–83.

54. J. Carrier and D. Miller, eds, *Virtualism: A New Political Economy* (Berg, Oxford, 1998). Carrier and Miller have hit on the expression "virtualism" to describe the current stage of economic and social development. I would not go as far as they do in claiming that capitalism itself has been superseded by a new virtual economy.

55. P. Uimonen, "Transnational Networks of Internet Pioneers. A Study of Technology, Modernity and Globalization" in *Antropologiska Studier,* special issue on culture and technology, January 1999.

56. The capacity of our categories to move between universal and particular applications may irritate positivist readers, but it is a style that I borrow from Marx. This admission is unlikely to make the irritation less.

57. Land reform, sometimes represented as "putting an end to feudalism," was high on the agenda of all parties contesting seats in the new Scottish parliament of 1999. Scotland has one of the highest concentrations of land ownership in the industrial world and a set of laws to match.

58. My source is Alexandra Ouroussoff, speaking at the annual conference of the Association of Social Anthropologists on "Elite Cultures: Anthropological Perspectives" in March 1999. I could have looked it up, but I like to sustain the oral tradition.

59. According to the *FT 500* survey of the world's largest firms in 1998, 49%, or 244, were American (up 22 on the previous year) and 35% were from Western Europe (with Britain represented by more firms than France and Germany combined). Only 46 Japanese firms made the list, compared with 71 in 1997. Hong Kong, Singapore, Taiwan and Malaysia went from 25 to 10 of the top firms in one year. Countries like Russia, Brazil and South Africa experienced a similar drop. All of this reflected financial instability in these places and a radical revaluation of the dollar against their currencies. *Financial Times,* 28 January 1999.

60. United Nations Development Program, *Human Development Report 1998* (UNDP, New York, 1998); *The World Bank World Development Report 1996: From Plan to Market* (Oxford University Press, New York, 1996). Both annual publications; see also the latest.

61. Janet MacGaffey and Rémy Bazenguissa-Ganga, *Congo-Paris: Transnational Traders on the Margins of the Law* (James Currey, Oxford, 2000).

PART II:
MONEY AND THE MARKET

Chapter 5
The Market from a Humanist
Point of View

As soon as I was old enough, I received threepence a week as spending money. The coin itself was a chunky polygon, but there was also in circulation an earlier round version called the "silver joey" and, because of its scarcity, I felt it was more precious. In any case, I rarely kept the money long. I spent it on sweets, which seem to have dominated this aspect of my economy then. In retrospect, these coins symbolize the idea of money as an external object of unknown social origin, passing much too quickly through my hands, a tantalizing reminder of my childish powerlessness. I was a regular customer at Mrs Hewitt's sweetshop. There were many such shops in the neighborhood, but I always went there with my weekly spending money. This meant that she reserved my favorites for me and sometimes gave me extra measure. When she sold the shop, she spent two weeks with the new owner introducing regular customers and their tastes: "This is Keith and he likes wine gums, pear drops and liqorice allsorts."

We will consider below whether this sort of behavior was already archaic when I was young or is a more durable feature of modern markets. But there was more to it. This was a time of rationing, the "age of austerity" following the Second World War; and everyone was entitled to the same meagre share. So, in addition to my threepence, which bought two ounces of sweets, I handed over a coupon entitling the bearer to that precise quantity. One day, when I was six or so, my mother announced that sugar rationing was over. From now on, people could buy as many sweets as they liked. I rushed to Mrs Hewitt's and ordered sweets up to the limit of my imagination, three bags of two ounces each. "That will be ninepence, please." "But I only have threepence. They said you could now have as much as you like." "Well, you need the money too." And that is how I learned the bitter lesson that money, at least money as the traditional stuff I grew up with, is also a rationing device. Markets are democratically open to anybody. All you need is the money. Some people have lots of it and most people hardly any. But that is a deep mystery we should not seek to penetrate. As my Grandma used to say, "If you can't pay, don't go."

My next formative experience in this regard occurred when I was nine years old. I was admitted to a children's hospital to have my tonsils removed. Consistent with well-established family practice, my bribe for compliance was now two four-ounce packets of my favorite sweets. (I was going up in the world.) Almost as soon as I arrived, I was sedated, operated on and woke up sans tonsils the following morning. My mood was not great, but it was made worse by the discovery that my sweets, carefully stowed away in my bedside cabinet, were gone! I hunted high and low for them. I started shouting for the nurses and eventually one of them came. She seemed perplexed by my distress, pointing out that it was hospital policy for sweets to be pooled for the benefit of all the children, many of whom were too poor to buy their own. She knew I would be glad to learn that my sweets were enjoyed by the poor children. I was not. I was outraged. These people had knocked me out in order to rob me of my property while I was unconscious. I missed the sweets much more than my tonsils. I demanded restitution. She returned with a handful of sweets, but they were not my favorites. Ah, the National Health Service in its heyday, how decent it all was then.

Readers may be relieved (or disappointed) to learn that the next three chapters do not rest on personal anecdotes of this kind. I introduce Part II in this way because the aim and style of its contents differ quite substantially from what has come before. In Part I, I put together a vision of modern history as the development of capitalism, in which the process of making money with money became tied to successive stages of a machine revolution. This vision was, if anything, more pessimistic than the opposite. The big battalions of government and corporate bureaucracy have ensured that the world is still largely ruled by a remote elite in a way that condemns the bulk of humanity to lives of poverty and violence. The rest of us (and I include myself as someone who probably qualifies for membership in such an elite) are not powerless, however; and I argued that contemporary developments offer some limited prospect for greater economic democracy. This next section takes off from such a possibility. Money conceived of as buying and selling, as the market in other words, expresses our hope that humanity might be connected by means of equal exchange. I argue that, for this to be so, we need to approach markets and money as the result of human agency, as actual persons doing things with each other. This means developing an analytical method that incorporates a humanist perspective into its abstractions.

This chapter, therefore, lays the foundation for a normative approach that might be capable of leading us beyond the inequality endemic to capitalism. Starting from an anthropological critique of economic individualism, I try to show what happens when we consider markets from the point of view of their human participants. This perspective shows that market economy is more fluid and mobile in practice than its representation as ideas would suggest. And this opens up the prospect of a piecemeal approach to economic reform, building on the substantive changes that have already taken place in the way living people encounter the structures they live by. The chapter following this one argues that money might increasingly come to be seen as a source of personal credit, with each of us playing a more creative role in managing its supply than was thought possible until recently. This chapter could be said to be an attempt to rescue the liberal tradition of Locke, Simmel and Keynes from the romantic and socialist critiques offered by Rousseau and Marx (which underpin much of Part I).

The general arguments made in both of these chapters are firmly anchored in the present and recent past, whereas Part I took its impetus from a much longer-term account of the historical past. The final chapter has its eyes fixed firmly on the future. What scenarios might inform the construction of a better world in the twenty-first century? Again the perspective is humanist and therefore individualistic in spirit. Social movements may arise from any quarter of global society, but this book is aimed at a middle-class, largely Western readership with a view to making history (that is, society in movement) more personally accessible. These concluding remarks are aimed at promoting the possibility of self and the world being brought into a more meaningful relationship, one that encourages us to behave as economic agents, alone and in co-ordination with others. The trajectory from my childhood reminiscences above to the forward-looking collective agenda articulated in the final chapter may or may not be adequately supported by the chapters in between. The point, however, is to try to place oneself in history, setting a personal example that others of like mind may care to follow in their own way.

The market, private property and liberal democracy

We experience the economy in modern society as a network of exchange relations. Most often these exchanges take place through the medium of money: The buyer hands over money to the seller in return for commodities. The sum total of these transactions is sometimes referred to as "the market," an abstract entity whose extent is unknowable. It is only in recent decades that people everywhere have become linked up in a single nexus of exchange, "the world market." There are no isolated pockets of humanity any more; and, in that sense, we are witnesses to the birth of world society in the form of a market. We cannot tell how such a society will evolve, although we can be sure that the properties of exchange will be central to that process. One major problem with thinking about markets is the part that money plays in them. We are aware of massive discrepancies in purchasing power. This inequality is so overwhelming that, for many people, the idea of a just society would require us to do away with money altogether and, with it, the system of buying and selling itself. But we may not have exhausted the potential of markets to support equal exchange.

What can the professionals tell us about markets? Economists generally approach markets as quantified abstractions, even as idealized curves on a graph. According to Marcel Mauss, the essence of such an approach is to assume that in market transactions the reciprocal acts of giving and making a return gift are collapsed into a single moment of instant equivalence.[1] Yet, despite the formal equality of the two sides, we distinguish in our language and thought between those who give in trade (sellers exchanging commodities for money) and those who take in trade (buyers exchanging money for commodities). In the hands of economists this transaction, when multiplied indefinitely, becomes the point of intersection between two curves representing the supply of and demand for specific commodities.[2] The equivalence of the exchange is symbolized by the agreed price at which the commodity is transferred from one party to the other. This price is considered to be fair when many sellers compete to find buyers. The condition of monopoly, where the absence of competition allows the seller to set the price, is taken to be abnormal. Prices are expected to move in response to short-term fluctuations in supply and demand; yet, as we will see below, fixed prices are normal in modern markets. Any particular market is held to be efficient when available supplies are cleared and buyers get what they want at a price they can afford.

It is part of the ideology of modern markets that they can take place any time, anywhere, and that the individuals involved are independent and unknown to each other. This assumption (economic individualism) enables economists to construct mathematical models of great generality, since they are conceived of initially as referring to behavior outside time, place and society. Moreover, there is indeed now a tendency for markets to take on these properties, with money itself being exchanged as a commodity twenty-four hours a day through telephones linking computers from all corners of the world. The institutional conditions that make the assumption of economic individualism even remotely plausible are quite abnormal and were won at first in a few countries only after centuries of political struggle. The idea of buyers and sellers being free to make decisions concerning the price and volume of commodities to be transferred between them is pretty remarkable, even when all that is at stake is an artifact like a pair of shoes; but imagine the complications when the commodity being traded is someone's ability to work or a place for a family to live in. This led Karl Polanyi to insist that market transactions are usually "embedded" in social life, whatever efforts the accountants may make to treat them as "fictitious commodities."[3]

It is hard for workers to understand why they must lose jobs they are still perfectly capable of performing with skill, just because "the bottom line" says a firm is losing money. The Anglo-Saxon countries have gone further than the rest toward the acceptance of market forces as somehow inescapable. I was talking not long ago to a school janitor in a Paris suburb about the closure of a Renault car factory. He thought it was scandalous. I asked him whether the factory was losing money or not. He replied yes, but added, "If it was making a loss, that was the bosses' fault and they should be sacked. But the workers did what they were told to and they did it well. There is no way they should lose their jobs." His response was based on a cultural belief that the French people had won certain rights irreversibly grounded in natural justice, such as the right to work. But the question of employment in a world of capitalist markets is a mystery that cannot be abolished merely by clinging to beliefs of this sort. The answer lies partly in the system of private property and the power of public institutions to override the interplay of private interests entailed in that system.

Private property is the ability of an individual owner to command exclusive rights over something against the rest of the world.[4] We assume that, once we have bought an item, we can do what we like with it; the seller in turn has even greater freedom to dispose of the money we paid for it. Take a look at your personal possessions. They are yours. How did you get them and what gives you the right to think of them as your own? Your watch, for example, is clearly your own private property. It feels as if it is yours simply by virtue of being worn next to your skin. You probably bought it or it was a gift from someone who bought it somewhere. Market exchange is therefore the source of your right to claim the watch. But what secures the market exchange? Most people barely think about this, until something goes wrong. You get mugged on a dark night and the stranger demands your watch. In your fear and anger you now realize that it is the state that underwrites your claim to own the watch and promises to restrict violent assaults on persons and property. Perhaps you resent the inadequate level of policing for a time; but eventually you settle back into thinking of your possessions as your own and forget about the social conditions that make it possible.

This idea of private property being secured by an anonymous state apparatus has been very rare in human history. More typically it was understood that ownership is relative to membership of concrete social groups capable of stopping others from infringing the right to control what belongs to us. In the extreme case of what Mauss called "total prestations,"[5] exchange is carried out by clans or similar groups acting as undifferentiated units. More usually individual claims to ownership are modified by such groups asserting a collective overright, in contrast with the presumptively absolute individual ownership characteristic of private property. Take the following fictitious example as a case in point.

A Masai warrior works as a nightwatchman in Kenya's capital, Nairobi. The Masai are famous for having maintained a traditional way of life based on cattle-herding, and young men are formed into groups of warriors whose task it is to defend the herds against all comers. Nowadays many of them work temporarily for wages, often in jobs that require a watered-down version of their warrior training. This migrant saves money and, before returning home, buys some commodities, including a watch that he wears on his wrist. On arriving back at his village, he meets an age-mate who says, "I like your watch: Give it to me" and he must give it up. Why? Because all property in the village is held by virtue of the ability of warriors to ward off predators, both animal and human; and their solidarity, essential in battle, is undermined by any tendency of individuals to differentiate their own interests from those of the rest. They assert that a man's wife belongs to all his age-mates, even though it would be rare for sexual access to be demanded by one of them as a right. Our ex-nightwatchman must be taught to recognize that life in the village still rests on different principles from those obtaining in Nairobi, and he hands over the watch.

In Western legal history the Romans are credited with having invented private property. Before they achieved a strong state linked to extensive markets, property rights were based on the same ability of local kin-groups to assert their interests against similar groups. This was called *ius in personam,* and it stated that rights over things are always mediated by concrete personal ties.[6] In societies such as this, ownership was derived from either production or consumption: Something belonged to you because you had made it or because you needed to use it; and both kinds of right were exercised through membership of local groups. Traders, on the other hand, wanted to hold property in a wholly different sense: They needed to secure the right to own something they had neither produced themselves nor would use personally, but rather intended to sell for money. Moreover, they were exposed to the brigandage of any small group wishing to enforce its own local monopoly of violence. In the interest of furthering long-distance trade, the Roman state offered military protection to these private merchants. It supported their claim to *ius in rem,* rights over things unmediated by personal relationships, in other words, the same system of private property that we now take so much for granted.[7]

To summarize, in order to allow the free circulation of commodities in exchange for money, both the connection between persons and objects and that between persons in groups were weakened in law. Yet physical association between persons and objects is still quite strong for modern English-speakers ("possession is nine-tenths of the law"), even if the social ties that make ownership possible have receded to the point of invisibility in the face of an atomizing economic ideology. What if there is more to market exchange than meets the eye? Unfortunately, as a result of what amounts to a wholesale conspiracy of Western intellectuals, especially the anthropologists, to leave core modern institutions largely uninspected, empirically informed theoretical analysis of market relations remains at a stage that has not advanced far beyond Emile Durkheim writing a hundred years ago.[8] But, before embarking on this task in however limited a fashion, we should at least touch on the historical and theoretical relationship claimed to exist between markets and the political project of liberal democracy. And this in turn requires us to consider the thought and times of John Locke.[9]

I have only come to John Locke while writing this book. It is hard to recall just how important he was. In 1683, at the age of fifty-one, Locke was an unpublished Oxford academic and the client of a discredited politician. During the exclusion crisis of the Catholic James II's accession to the throne, he fled for his life to Holland and was sacked by his college. He returned to England six years later after William's establishment of a Protestant monarchy in the Glorious Revolution of 1688. In that same year he published *Two Treatises of Government* and *An Essay Concerning Human Understanding,* both of them considered classics of philosophy today.[10] In 1693 he published *Some Thoughts Concerning Education,* which shaped eighteenth-century thinking on this topic in Britain.[11] He was appointed to the Board of Trade and wrote influential pamphlets on money that helped to resolve the recoinage crisis of the 1690s.[12] Long before his death in 1704 he had become so famous that one of his correspondents could describe him without irony as "the greatest man in the world."[13] He was certainly the leading public intellectual in the period when the United Kingdom was formed. As an architect of the middle-class revolution, he sought to build the stable infrastructure of a new world economy with England at its center. The eighteenth-century Enlightenment was largely a response outside England to the achievements of Locke (and Newton). The Americans wrote their constitution (fruit of the first anti-colonial revolution) on the basis of his ideas. Now he is merely credited with theorizing the narrow economic individualism on which neo-classical economics is founded. My interest, however, is in recovering something of what he discovered to such amazing social and intellectual effect; and I know that it can't be just that he found a way of mystifying capitalist exploitation.

When I finally got round to Locke's *Two Treatises of Government,* I did not find in them the story of possessive individualism I had been led to expect.[14] I found that the purpose of his Commonwealth was to preserve everyone's property in themselves and their possessions. "The end of law is . . . to preserve and enlarge freedom." Freedom is "a liberty to dispose and order, as he lists, his person, actions, possessions and his whole property within the allowance of those laws under which he is, and therein not to be subject to the arbitrary will of another, but freely follow his own."[15] The main emphasis is on the political conditions of personal autonomy. Both treatises turn out, in my view, to be extended essays on the theme of parent–child relations. In the first Locke denies the right of absolute monarchs to claim to be the father of their subjects. In the second, he allows only one exception to the rule of autonomy of citizens and that is childhood. He poses the question, how can we protect children so that they grow up to be independent? This is a contradiction that no society has yet solved, and it explains why he was known for his educational theories rather than for his politics or epistemology in eighteenth-century England.

Locke also anticipated Kant's concerns when he asked how a single Commonwealth can protect the property of foreigners passing through it (Who or what secures the property of the Dutchman in London?), thereby opening up the issue of cosmopolitan society beyond the boundaries of states. Yet Locke deserves to be seen as the founder of state capitalism, long before Bismarck and the rest. He anticipated and worked for a world economy with England as its guarantor. In the recoinage crisis of the 1690s, he insisted on the state securing the currency according to an internationally reliable metallic content against proto-Keynesians who just wanted to keep domestic prices and employment up.[16] Locke's project was nothing less than the establishment of the infrastructure of global trade for the following century, emphasizing the need to stabilize the means of communication and exchange, words and money. For him, there were economic criminals and semantic criminals. The state can hang counterfeiters, but what do you do with people who never say what they mean? Each undermines confidence in civil society. Remember that seventeenth-century England had been a very turbulent place, and by the end of it a sort of criminal informal economy was threatening to get out of control, while resources were stretched to fight the most expensive war in English history against Louis XIV.

It is only with hindsight that this urgent and far-sighted political project could come to be regarded as an essential plank in the establishment of an ideology of economic individualism, cloaking the inequalities of an emergent capitalism in a rhetoric of market democracy and natural rights.[17] I will return in the final chapter to the question of whether liberal democracy can be salvaged from its association with economic individualism, as manifested today in the modern discipline of economics. But first we should consider the critique of that ideology launched from the perspective of the founders of economic anthropology.

The anthropological critique of economic individualism

The First World War posed a shattering challenge to notions of civilization that had been prevalent in the nineteenth century. The founders of modern economic anthropology, Bronislaw Malinowski and Marcel Mauss, responded to that challenge in the 1920s by suggesting that Western conventions of economic rationality were neither universal nor inevitable. Moreover, each found in the idea of the gift an appeal to a fuller conception of humanity than that enshrined in modern markets. Each was influenced by the critical work of sociological theory carried out by Emile Durkheim in the decades leading up to the war (which, in the case of Mauss, was hardly surprising, since he was his nephew). And each was a major influence in turn on Karl Polanyi, whose *The Great Transformation* (1944; see later in this section) was written in the belief that the attempt to build civilization on the basis of the market had been a disastrous failure.

Rarely have writers been confounded so completely or quickly as Polanyi was by the revival of the world market under American leadership in the immediate post-war period. Perhaps the financial turbulence of the late 1990s has brought back echoes of the Wall Street crash of 1929 to undermine our confidence in the market regime. But it is hard for us, who have seen the triumphant march of commerce in recent decades, to imagine the faith placed by these writers of the early twentieth century in non-market mechanisms of economic life. Any forward-looking anthropology of exchange must be rooted in their work, and it is as well to bear in mind the historical circumstances of their writing. For texts are not just dead ideas embalmed for ever on a library shelf; they once took life from the purposes of a human being engaged with a specific social context. And they can live again when read with similar purposes in mind.

Durkheim

The way for Malinowski and Mauss was prepared by Emile Durkheim, who sought, in work published in the decades around the turn of the century, to establish a science of society with which to counteract the market liberalism of his day. He identified the ideology of economic individualism with the English thinker Herbert Spencer, whose ideas enjoyed enormous popularity at the turn of the century in a form that has come to be known as "social Darwinism."[18] This doctrine combined evolutionary biology and the economic theory of competitive markets to explain riches and poverty as the outcome of innate individual differences. Durkheim had no time for the self-serving racism and class triumphalism of the bourgeoisie; his target was a broader and more elusive one.

He believed that, although society is not easily visible to us, we must strive to understand its influence on our individual behavior. We live normally in an everyday world made up of small events and pragmatic decisions, never pausing to ask how our ability to do these things rests on a largely invisible framework of shared social life. Durkheim despised economic individualism not because it was wrong, but because it left out the parts of human existence that we most need to understand, if we are to escape from the narrow treadmill of an unreflecting daily routine. In *The Division of Labour in Society*[19] he focused on the core of everyday business practice, contracts. The exchange of contracts between individuals depends on a collective tradition of customary law, forms of government, social institutions and shared culture that might not always be visible but are essential none the less. It may seem that, when you pay a few pence to a street vendor for a newspaper, only the immediate interests of the two parties are involved and then only for a transient moment. But try the thought experiment of locating the transaction in a largely uninhabited jungle and you can imagine what might be missing from that fleeting urban encounter. Durkheim called this social background to in-dividual acts of exchange "the non-contractual element in the contract," and it was central to his vision of the world.

His main inquiry was into the sources of common moral sentiments or social solidarity. France's experience of modern history had been highly dis-ruptive, to say the least, with wars, invasions and revolutions punctuating at-tempts to stabilize political order. Durkheim's interest was in securing the foundations of the Third Republic; and to this end he constructed two types corresponding roughly to primitive and modern societies. In the first, which he called "mechanical solidarity," people thought alike and hung together be-cause they were in essence the same, lived the same kind of life; whereas in the second, "organic solidarity," division of labor made people interdepend-ent precisely because they were different, did different things. The organic solidarity of industrial societies was potentially more durable than the me-chanical form because specialized producers need each other and people who are self-sufficient do not. Implicit in this analysis was a critique of na-tionalism, the attempt to build solidarity on a primitive appeal to sameness.

Durkheim, like many of his contemporaries, noticed that the world was rapidly becoming centralized, as large-scale industry concentrated people in mushrooming cities and governments acquired unprecedented powers of control over these anonymous masses. Economic individualism seemed anachronistic in such a world and, with the intellectuals at least, Herbert Spencer fell out of favor, so that in the 1930s Talcott Parsons, the founder of modern American sociology, was able to write: "Spencer is dead. But who killed him and how? This is the problem,"[20] listing Durkheim himself as the principal suspect.

When the Romans were still Latins living as part of a disorganized rabble in west-central Italy, they invented the word "society" (*societas*). Only much later, as the medieval French word *société,* did this come to mean a bounded entity with a fixed center. Originally it meant a loose network of allies, a confederation of equals pledged to follow any group whose need in an emergency gave them temporary leadership.[21] This was the context for an-other invention, the word "distribution." At some stage it was felt that the as-sociation needed greater coherence. Accordingly, the confederation was divided into three parts (*tribes* or thirds), and in this form its members met from time to time to perform a ritual in which a cow was split into three and eaten by them separately and together. This process of division and allocation was called *distributio,* a sharing out between the tribes.

I mention this origin myth because it illustrates something important. Division is not just a way of separating parts from wholes; it can also be preliminary to their recombination as a whole made stronger by having well-defined complementary parts. The model of division of labor promoted by Adam Smith and his successors argues that economic efficiency is advanced by specialization. The good of us all is increased by leaving each to do what they can do best. Countries and regions should trade only in what they are naturally suited to produce ("comparative advantage"). Within work organizations, tasks should be broken down into their minimal components in order to benefit from smooth repetition. Competitive markets will weed out the inefficient operations. This is all very well, but most people and social groups fear the consequences of going out of business; they resent performing mindless tasks; and they wish to ensure that provision of basic needs remains within their own control. This version of division of labor seems to rest on a distribution mechanism that is inadequately social.

Emile Durkheim argued that the point of division is to increase the cohesion of the whole, as in the case of the Latin tribes mentioned above. To divide is not just to separate, but potentially to unify on the basis of complementary difference. So that one reason for the traditional division of tasks between men and women might be to add strength to their union over long periods (in marriage, for example), when otherwise they would drift apart. In this scenario, markets induced by specialization create the conditions for interdependence that could mitigate war. Europeans made a common market not least because they did not want to repeat the experience of two world wars fought largely on their territory. Division of labor can thus also be seen as a matter of life and death. Our future as a species depends on how the evolutionary questions raised here are resolved.

Malinowski

The high point of Victorian rationalism was long gone by the time Durkheim set to work. The ranks of those capable of exercising reason had begun to seem rather narrow, since women, children, servants, uneducated workers,

madmen, criminals, savages and the darker races were all excluded. Then
Freud pointed out that even the enlightened few were probably the unconscious victims of irrational forces laid down in childhood. And Frazer's *The
Golden Bough* made it obvious to his many readers that magic and religion
had not been banished from their own scientific cosmology.[22] Belief in the
superiority of Western civilization had thus been seriously undermined by
the time that the First World War brought about its collapse.

For how could societies claim to be based on reason when they sent millions of their citizens to an appalling death in the trenches? When the war
was over, several countries seemed on the brink of emulating Russia's revolution. And, even when that moment passed, there was a popular thirst for
new visions of civilization less restrictive than the last. This was Bronislaw
Malinowski's opportunity, and the year (1922) in which he published his
book *Argonauts of the Western Pacific*[23] saw a remarkable outpouring of literary
and artistic innovation. The death of a civilization was commemorated in
T.S. Eliot's *The Waste Land,* while Joyce's *Ulysses* and Wittgenstein's *Tractatus
Logico-Philosophicus* are now seen as twentieth-century landmarks; and
crowds flocked to admire the resilience of the Eskimo protagonist in Robert
Flaherty's movie, *Nanook of the North.*

Malinowski's title evoked the mythical journeys of discovery undertaken
by Jason and the Argonauts. He had spent much of the war in the Trobriand
Islands, off the coast of Papua New Guinea. These islands were linked by
trade to a number of others, creating a regional interdependence that
evoked in microcosm the global maritime economy of the day. Malinowski
retained and made famous the indigenous term for the social mechanism
that made this exchange possible, the *kula.* His intention was explicit. He
wanted to show that a complex system of interlocal trade flourished without
benefit of merchants, markets or money and without centralized authority
(states). Moreover, this system made sense, even though the natives despised
commercial motives and based their conduct on an ethos of generosity in
giving. Malinowski's aim was thus to show that the stereotype of economic
man (*homo oeconomicus*) was not universal; that Western notions of civilization were restrictive, even narrow-minded; and that a fuller conception of
rational humanity would include the customs of people who had hitherto
been dismissed as "savages."

The peoples of the Western Pacific have a common culture with elaborated material needs that cannot usually be met out of local resources alone. The islands are not self-sufficient: One will be rich in sago palms, another in stone or clay, while yet another may be noted for a particular kind of fish. The question is: How to ensure the circulation of these specialist items between islands that lack any overarching guarantee of the peace? The islanders do trade with each other by means of individual haggling, a form of two-way exchange (e.g., so many fish for an equivalent number of yams) in which the ratio of the commodities is negotiated without benefit of money prices. But it is not always the case that each side has what the other wants at the time; and longer-distance trips are too fraught with danger to allow for the unrestrained competition of commercial barter. So an alternative method has evolved based on the exchange of valuables between leaders of expeditions and their respective followers. *Kula* is both the practice of exchanging these valuables and the name for the tokens themselves. A good deal also goes on under the umbrella of *kula* whose importance is frequently denied by the leaders.

It works like this. Very few communities in the region have official chiefs. Instead there is an unstable pattern of political leadership in which "big men" (leaders without office) compete for followers. If people from island A want to acquire a commodity *x* from island B, they organize a canoe expedition under the leadership of a big man who has a long-standing partnership with a big man in island B. They take with them *kula* valuables, of which there are two types: red necklaces and white armshells. These valuables are named and the history of transactions involving the more famous ones is well known. Big men vie with each other to attract the best pieces to themselves. On this occasion the big man from A will set out carrying, say, red necklaces only and no other commodities. The canoes arrive empty-handed except for the necklaces. The big men from A and B will discuss which white armshell the latter may bring the next time he visits A. In the meantime their followers strike up partnerships, make promises of valuable exchange and load up the canoes with commodity *x*. They may also haggle over other individual items, safe in the peace secured by their leaders. The canoes return home and, when an expedition from B arrives some time later, carrying white armshells, the process is enacted again in reverse, with commodity *y* being loaded into B's canoes.

It can be seen from this brief description that the *kula* is at one level a method of ranking political actors in a climate of unstable competition for power. At another level, acts of utilitarian exchange are carried out through an institution that stresses the generosity of givers rather than narrow calculation of profit. What the Melanesians are afraid of is appearing to be cheap, lest their attractiveness as potential exchange partners be diminished. They therefore affect to despise barter for its selfishness, standing on its head the economic ethos that underlies modern Western civilization. More than once in his narrative, Malinowski draws attention to the parallels with aristocracy in the Western tradition; hence his allusion to the mythical heroes of ancient Greece.

Mauss

Marcel Mauss, Durkheim's nephew, started in the mid-1920s with the recent ethnography of gift-exchange produced by Malinowski for the Pacific and by Franz Boas and his students for America's north-west coast. In the latter case, an institution known as *potlatch* pitted indigenous leaders against each other in an orgy of competitive giving and material destruction.[24] Mauss saw that there were parallels in Western history, and he proposed to outline a general theory of exchange based on these examples. Many people have subsequently read his *Essai sur le Don (The Gift)*[25] as offering a model of the gift economy to set in opposition to modern commerce, much as Malinowski's *Argonauts* did. In fact, Mauss's intentions were the opposite. He wanted to show that the contrast between primitive and modern economy was a false one, being based on a split between society and the individual that has to be integrated if human beings of any time or place are to enjoy full lives.

The simple contrastive approach to markets and gift-exchange rests on the notion that whereas "we" moderns are selfish individuals, "they," the primitives, serve only the interests of their communities. Hence they prefer the generosity—even altruism and self-sacrifice—of the gift, while we base our contracts on the pursuit of narrow personal advantage. By labelling one practice "primitive" and the other "modern," we imply that the direction of social evolution is, however regrettably, toward economic individualism. Mauss profoundly rejected this argument. First of all, his uncle had already shown that market economy rests on social institutions as well as on individual interests. Then again, the gift still flourishes in pockets such as Christmas and weddings, and can be shown to underlie some of the contracts most central to capitalism, such as wages. Equally, the *kula* and the *potlatch* reveal a rampant egotism on the part of competing leaders that hardly squares with the stereotype of primitive communism. No, this attempt to separate individual and society as a developmental sequence just will not do. Mauss held that there are two prerequisites for being human: We each have to learn to be self-reliant to a high degree and we have to belong to others in order to survive, merging our identities in a bewildering variety of social relationships. Managing to be both at once is extraordinarily difficult, and this accounts for how few truly successful human beings there are. Even so, we must try, and this means that we all carry around in our heads knowledge of the principles of exchange, whether or not we succeed in practising them.

Mauss asked how we create society where it did not exist before; and by this he meant every new instance of social connection from falling in love and bringing up baby to registering a business and establishing international relations. His answer was reciprocity, the idea that exchange must be two-sided. He broke reciprocity down into three rules that he believed were common to all humanity: the obligation to give; the obligation to receive the gift; and the obligation to make a return gift in time. All forms of exchange are variants of this logic, which is as universal as parent–child relations. Mauss wrote of a spiritual bond between persons and material objects that extended to relationships formed through the circulation of these objects. In every way modern markets deny this premise, separating individuals from the object world and from each other, banishing the spirituality and social substance from exchange. Yet our humanity inserts the spirit of the gift into market economy in profound ways.

Mauss believed that reciprocity probably had its origin in sacrifice: *do ut des,* I give so that you will give to me. Faced with the overwhelming forces of the natural world, primitive man gave up something material in the hope of making a spiritual connection that would be translated into a reciprocal social relationship with unseen powers, the gods.[26] The next stage in this speculative evolutionary sequence he called "total prestations," meetings between whole communities in which everything was exchanged, much in the manner of medieval fairs. Mauss imagined that gift-exchange might be a step toward individuation of these collective encounters, leading as it does to the threshold of authoritarian rule. Giving in the form of alms or charity exchanges material support for moral deference in evolved systems of social stratification. Finally, individuals confront each other as equals in markets, without benefit of social or spiritual ties. And this enables, on the face of it, a clean separation of persons and things to occur, so that buyers can walk away from sellers, knowing that any obligation between them has been wiped out by the equivalence of whatever has been paid.

In this account, the human story begins with religious alienation and culminates in a secular version of the same condition with which we are all too familiar. Mauss sought to provide us with the means of rediscovering the common basis of reciprocity that underlies market economy, since the logic of the gift persists at all sorts of levels unknown to the prevailing ideology. The big difference between gifts and market contracts, according to Mauss, lies in the timing of the return. A gift must be returned at some time in the future, whereas a contract is defined by the instant equivalence of the exchange. Mauss noted that givers are superior to receivers as long as their gift stays unreciprocated; if recipients cannot make a material return, they owe spiritual deference. This points to the conclusion that giving is intrinsically unequal, leading to the contests between participants in gift-exchange, each striving to outdo the other in order to cancel outstanding debts and to establish a temporary advantage as the last one to give. If anyone should doubt the inequality of the gift (as in the Innuit proverb: "Gifts make slaves as whips make dogs"),[27] remember that the archetypal gift relationship is that between parents and children, and they don't come more unequal than that.

It follows that Mauss thought markets were a force for greater social equality. The idea that "my money is as good as yours" and that people walk away from contracts, having established their mutual equality, was quite widespread in the Manchester of my childhood. My grandmother, whose family was not long emancipated from a feudal estate, refused to join the "free" library or to accept National Health spectacles, since they smacked of the gift and charity. She had no intention of going back to the world of handouts from the lord and master. Today we are more sensitive perhaps to the fact that people enter the market with huge discrepancies in the amount of money at their disposal; and we vote for governments pledged to redressing such inequalities through the power of the state. Mauss was prescient (as was my grandmother) in recognizing the potential of the welfare state to reproduce a new class system based on the superiority of tax donors to the recipients of benefits.

His more general point was that we all understand the principles of exchange, whether we objectify them or not. A young woman who goes out with a man to the cinema has a stock repertoire of responses to his offer to buy both tickets. Going dutch means that she refuses social obligation at this stage; accepting the offer leaves open the question of how the gift will be returned . . . On other occasions we make compromises, perhaps offering to pay the tip while one's companion picks up the bill for a shared meal. This retains the social and spiritual companionship of the gift, while asserting an underlying willingness and ability to reciprocate as an equal in future.

Seen in this light, the pure types of selfish and generous economic action obscure the complex interplay of human reciprocity as we seek to define our individuality while belonging in subtle ways to others. Immature individuals have problems with subtlety, and commonly have resort instead to one extreme or the other. Consider, for example, the baby in its stroller. One moment it clings to its toy as a matter of life or death, refusing to part with it, person and thing wedded together in a parody of possessive individualism. The next moment it throws the toy overboard, supremely indifferent to its fate or perhaps altruistically sharing it with the world. It says little for our ideologies that they rest on a similar childishness. Consider again how lovers behave, especially at the beginning of an affair. One moment he will insist on controlling her every movement, the next he will be offering himself, heart and soul for ever, with no thought for his own independence. It is a sad reflection on our society that many people never get beyond this stage. If learning to be two-sided, to be reciprocal, is the means of becoming human, then the lesson is clearly hard to learn.

The ideology Mauss fought has made a strong recovery in the second half of the twentieth century. So much so that most readers of his essay still think that it is about an alternative to capitalism called the gift economy.[28] His mission was to show people who live by markets that they too belong to each other in society. This is not the opposite of individualism, since no one is of any use to society if they can't look after themselves. The same imperatives hold in so-called "primitive" societies, as Malinowski's ethnography showed, even if his rhetoric favored a more extreme contrast with the West. Mauss concluded that the gift was still present in such market contracts as wages, for does not the worker give his labor on the promise of future payment? Even more profoundly, the linguistic distinction between sellers and buyers, between those who give and take in trade,[29] suggests an older inequality beneath the surface of equal exchange. And, as a personal example of the kind of society he wanted to live in, he labored to publish the research of colleagues killed needlessly in the First World War.

I often wondered why Mauss wrote so little, a handful of essays only; and the idea of selfless labor on behalf of dead colleagues filled that gap. But recently a huge volume of his occasional political writings was published, 800 pages, two-thirds of them written in the period 1920–25.[30] Here Mauss is revealed as a passionate advocate of the co-operative labor movement and prescient critic of Bolshevism. The societies he was concerned with (in rough order of index citations) were France, Russia, England, Germany, the United States, Switzerland, Italy, Belgium, Holland, Scotland, Morocco and Denmark. Not much on the *kula* or the *potlatch* here. It is something of a tragedy that Mauss's academic admirers in the late twentieth century should have been oblivious of what was clearly his greater commitment, to the political causes of his day. This separation of engagement and exoticism, of the personal and the impersonal, which Mauss reproduced even as he transcended it, is one legacy of modern anthropology that we must put behind us.

Polanyi

Karl Polanyi wrote *The Great Transformation*[31] toward the end of the Second World War. The transformation he referred to was the attempt to build a civilization on the basis of self-regulating markets. This attempt appeared to be successful for the hundred years that separated the Congress of Vienna in 1815 (the formal end of the Napoleonic wars) and the outbreak of the First World War. The last thirty years, however, had been an unmitigated disaster, with two world wars separated by the collapse of the gold standard, the Wall Street crash and the Great Depression, the rise of totalitarian states, the Spanish civil war and many other catastrophes. In Polanyi's overview this depressing sequence was the outcome of the nineteenth century's experiment in market economy. The repair of civilization now required nothing less than a return to economic principles that had underpinned society since time immemorial.

The civilization of the nineteenth century, with its center in Britain, had rested on unsustainable institutional premises. These were four: the balance of power; the gold standard; the liberal state; and the self-regulating market. The hundred years of peace (1815–1914) depended on a balance of power between the major European nations that on the whole made them hold back from waging war on each other. Underlying this truce was a growing economic interdependence manifested in trade and finance (a sort of organic solidarity, if you like), which in turn required the operation of a stable international monetary system, the gold standard. The idea that money was a commodity, convertible to gold and thereby freed from government interference, was matched by the liberal norm of a minimal, or "nightwatchman," state whose principal function was to leave the economy to its own devices. This last was, of course, based on the market, whose operations were guided, not by conscious human intervention, but rather by a "hidden hand," a natural tendency toward equilibrium that ensured prosperity for all in the long run. (But, as the great man said, in the long run we are all dead . . .)

In Polanyi's view, this scheme was at best utopian and at worst a cynical cover for anti-social accumulation of wealth. States were ultimately obliged to give vent to the social interests of their people. This meant that they could not disguise their internal social conflicts indefinitely, and they could not sit idly by while commodity-based money (immune to manipulation in the public interest) destroyed their economies. The collapse of the gold standard in the face of national protectionism after the First World War was inevitable. The liberal state had no moral authority, since its *laissez-faire* ideology disguised strong intervention in the interests of capital at everyone else's expense. Worst of all, there was nothing in the market mechanism to stop it ruining economies when left unchecked. The Great Depression was proof of this, and fascism and communism were the political result.

Like Max Weber before him, Polanyi was aware that the market had always been kept on the periphery of pre-industrial societies. People exchanged commodities in the form of manufactured objects (shoes, hats, etc.) or small agricultural surpluses, but the main means of production and reproduction (food, housing, working the land) were kept largely outside the circuit of commerce and money. This meant that the economy was "embedded" in social relations that owed little or nothing to the market. In the age of mechanization, markets had arisen for what Polanyi called the "fictitious commodities." Nature, society and humanity are not themselves produced by people, as normal commodities are. The political economy of the nineteenth century, by calling them land, capital (society as money) and labor, commodities to be bought and sold just like artefacts, subjected the very substance of human survival to the forces of unregulated commerce. In the process, environment, social life and human creativity were casually destroyed in the name of the market's unfettered progress.

Individual freedom, for Polanyi, was meaningless unless it was based on recognizing the necessity of society as the precondition for decision-making at any level. Aristotle had been right to make our social nature the central premise of his philosophy ("man is a political animal"). Material survival itself depends on observing the rules of social interdependence. What, then, are these rules? Polanyi turned to the evidence of anthropology and economic history. Where transactions take place between equals, the norm is one of reciprocity (see Mauss's *The Gift* throughout). Where a hierarchy exists, fairness is secured by a norm of redistribution: An agent reallocates the pooled resources of the group according to need. To these timeless economic rules, Polanyi also proposed that the principle of "householding," budgeting for self-sufficiency, should normally take precedence over markets, which would consequently be made marginal to basic livelihood or at least regulated in the public interest. This was the basis for a discipline to which he devoted much personal effort: social planning.

Polanyi had all the makings of a great prophet except one—his timing was terrible. For the end of the Second World War signalled America's emergence as the dominant power of a world economy that once more was driven by market expansion. As we have seen, the 25-year period 1948–73 saw the biggest economic boom in world history. And, even when the boom ended, neo-liberal conservatives (Reagan, Thatcher and their ilk) acquired a hegemony that has only recently given way to a period of center-left governments practicing similar policies but with an interventionist rhetoric. In the process, Stalinism has withered away and with it the Cold War rivalry between state socialism and "the free market." The triumphalism of 1989, which proclaimed a victory for the market and private property, has not lasted long, and at the millennium there are far fewer takers for the idea that self-regulating markets hold the key to global prosperity.

Of the four thinkers considered above, Durkheim and Polanyi concentrated on the market end of the primitive/modern pair at a high level of theoretical abstraction, while Malinowski and Mauss approached the gift as a concrete ethnographic phenomenon, allowing their commentaries on market economy to remain largely implicit. This leaves an obvious hole that the following section begins to fill, namely the need for a concrete analysis of market relations in modern societies.

Market relations in time and space

We have already seen that markets are constituted by acts of sale and purchase that economists collapse into a single timeless moment when the two sides achieve equivalence. But if we look more closely, the moment is always embedded in social processes that both precede and succeed it. Thus the commodity being sold had to be produced and brought to the point of sale; and, once it is bought, it is taken away to be consumed by the buyer. The chain of production and consumption may be called into question for any number of reasons, such as when the buyer has a complaint against the seller or original producer owing to the goods being faulty when used.

There is a further major consideration. Market relations involve money. In Marx's classical formulation (see Figure 3.1), this may be represented as a sequence, C-M-C (where C = commodity and M = money); a seller exchanges commodities for money and later uses that money to buy commodities. But the money involved is also subject to complex social procedures. The seller may offer credit, allowing the buyer to delay payment. Or, if cash is handed over, there is a time when the seller is holding money that can be put to several alternative uses, ranging from personal consumption to investment in other forms of enterprise. It is therefore a particularly strong assumption to isolate the frozen moment when something is bought and sold; and it separates economists from all the rest of us. Put simply, market relations in the real world involve considerations of time and social complexity.

As Mauss pointed out, many of the contracts central to modern economy have a time element built into them that expresses the variable social relations linking buyers and sellers. Have you ever considered why, if you work for wages, you only get paid after you have done the work; or why, if you rent accommodation, you normally have to pay before you use it? This inequality reflects the social superiority of employers and landlords, their ability to regulate who bears the risk of non-payment. But the area in which time and social inequality enters most strongly into modern economies is finance, the market for money itself. The essence of credit is that a buyer gets something for nothing initially and pays later, usually with interest. This may take the form of a loan of money or an advance of commodities. In either case, time is intrinsic to the transaction and the social relations entailed in credit/debt are fraught with difficulty. We have all experienced the social embarrassment of an unrepaid loan. Credit inevitably invokes the personal side of market transactions, in a way that impersonal purchases with cash need not.

One variant of the stereotypical contrast between primitive exchange and modern markets is the notion that traditional markets, of the kind found in peasant societies or the oriental bazaar, rely on personalized transactions (typified by bargaining) that have been largely displaced from the modern economy. Thus, in many non-industrial societies it is normal for individuals to form long-standing partnerships based on the loyalty of customers to particular traders. Yet recourse to even casual introspection reveals that such a personalized approach to market relations is not foreign to industrial societies. I have already mentioned my childhood addiction to sweets and choice of a single seller, Mrs Hewitt, as purveyor of my weekly fix. Maybe that kind of commerce is now archaic in Western economies. But I cannot help noticing how many people, especially those who feel vulnerable when faced with the need to maintain an essential good, such as their car or computer, try to build a sense of interdependence with particular companies and even persons.

It is nevertheless the case that the personal dimension of economic life is more obvious in many non-Western societies. When I went to Ghana as an anthropological fieldworker in the 1960s, I was initially slow to recognize how the pervasiveness of credit altered the working of market relations. For example, a small number of women brewers catered at weekends for the drinking needs of young male migrants to the city. Their profit levels at first seemed to be staggering. I worked it out that sales of millet beer were valued at eight times the costs of production. Like everyone else, I assumed that these women must be rich; but they were not. The vast bulk of sales were on credit, and the rate of payment was so poor that the women often found it difficult to raise the cash to buy the ingredients for another brew. Instead they had a large retinue of regular customers in their debt, young men whom they could call upon for various services. Some of these women were politically influential; they had substantial investments in social ties, but they had little more money to spend than the majority of their customers.

For the truth is that most people in our world do not have enough money in hand to make markets a paying proposition without widespread extension of credit facilities. As it is, levels of market activity are depressed in many poorer regions, and buying now in order to pay later is indispensable to maintaining even those levels. In Ghana a fruit or vegetables trader would typically sit in a part of the market surrounded by women selling the same commodity. She would take her supply for the day and put one third in a basket under the table. The rest would be divided into small bundles for a few pence each, adding in total to a sum that left her some margin of profit over her costs. Every customer paid the same amount, but she would use the stuff in the basket to give extras to regulars or as a way of attracting new customers. Contrary to Western stereotypes, haggling was rare under these circumstances and a high proportion of sales would be on credit, with each customer's record locked away safely in her capacious memory.

In my experience, everyday comestibles like food were bought and sold in this way. The obvious interest of the client was in gaining access to regular supplies even when he had no money (which was normal) or when supplies were scarce (which was often). The trader's interest lay in attracting a stable clientele from competitors and in having a regular outlet even when the market was oversupplied and prices would otherwise tumble. One reason for traders sticking together in the same place is that they can pool information about credit risks and are less likely to be played off against each other by unscrupulous customers. You do not usually haggle when relations are circumscribed in this way. Bargaining occurred more naturally when people made occasional purchases of consumer durables, such as a chair. Here long-term association between buyer and seller is unnecessary, and the business of getting the best possible deal can take up a lot of time.

To sum up this part of the argument, models of supply and demand require prices to adjust up and down for markets to clear. There is no need for this process to involve direct haggling between individual buyers and sellers, yet such bargaining would be a natural expression of the conflicting interests of the two sides. In economic orthodoxy, however, emphasis is placed on competition between sellers, and the idea of conflict between buyer and seller is associated with less developed markets. This assertion is clearly ideological, since it abstracts from the real social relations that inevitably arise in modern markets when a time dimension is involved. Credit, wherever it occurs (and it is indispensable to the functioning of markets everywhere), introduces a bias toward greater co-operation between buyer and seller, and reduced competition between sellers. These patterns of association, taken to be anomalous in economic theory, are intrinsic to the way markets work.

This discussion of market relations in time should have done enough to indicate why it is dangerous to make a glib contrast between Western impersonal markets and their personalized "peasant" equivalents. It is also often claimed that, whereas traditional commerce occurs mainly in real market places, in modern societies "the market" has become an abstract or virtual network whose functioning is largely independent of place. Karl Polanyi, writing some years after *The Great Transformation,* held that in industrial societies "the market" had become an idea abstracted from real social relations and therefore, as an autonomous sphere, was amenable to the form of analysis devised by modern economists. But in all other societies, past and present, markets were located in real places where they were kept marginal and subject to regulation by the agents of dominant social institutions.[32] This was the main theme of an edited volume, *Markets in Africa,*[33] which, following Polanyi, emphasized the spatial dimension of markets and linked this to a simple theory of development. In Africa, markets were traditionally restricted to specific times and places, thereby leaving the bulk of production and consumption to be organized by kinship ties. The development of more broadly based colonial markets for export crops and wage labor meant that the market principle became more pervasive, undermining traditional authorities.

Why are markets supposed to be subversive of traditional social arrangements? In essence it is because commerce knows no bounds, and most local societies are predicated on maintaining a measure of control over their members that is threatened by that lack of limitation. All markets are in a sense world markets in that they link specific places to a proliferating network of infinite scope. In the face of this unknowable extension of human sociability, the ruling elements of local societies seek to keep markets and those who specialize in them at arm's length. Often the concrete symbol of the threat posed by markets lies in merchants' greater command of money, which in turn is just a measure of their access to a wider world. Markets likewise offer a potential means of escape to the dominated classes: women, young people, serfs and slaves, ethnic minorities. In this sense, the money to be gained from buying and selling offers relative freedom from local social obligations, at the same time as making much wider social connections possible.

In historical reality, the power of long-distance merchants has frequently modified the autonomy of local rulers; and markets have not always been peripheral, as the latter may have wished. Rather, the dialectic of local and global economy has defined the struggle between these co-existing interests long before they emerged as prominent features of the way we perceive the modern world. Traditional societies have varied in the methods they adopted to tackle the problem of markets. But one common ploy has been the restriction of mercantile activities to excluded ethnic groups, thereby ensuring that local citizens had no access to money and that those who did lacked political power. The most famous example was the pariah status of Jews in medieval Europe (also, at varying times and places, other mercantile groups such as Greeks and Syrians). The British, as we have seen, gave Indians in colonial East Africa a trading monopoly, but debarred them from owning any land, which was restricted to whites and blacks. The pre-industrial civilizations of Asia and the Near East habitually prevented merchants from investing in production, with the same ultimate intention of protecting local monopolies of power from the disruptive influence of markets and money.

Nor is this tension an insignificant feature of the modern world. For nation-states have habitually struggled to defend local economic priorities against the forces of the world market (sometimes called just "the markets").

This battle between territorial nationalism and cosmopolitan commerce has its roots in the traditional opposition between local societies and market places. Max Weber was intrigued to know how Western societies came to allow markets to be central to their functioning. Yet this process is far from complete. One conclusion concerning the spatial dimensions of exchange is that, just as traditional rural societies were always linked by markets to world civilization, modern markets have not yet transcended the attempts of political society to place physical restrictions on their operations. The emergence of the Internet as a site for commerce brings this contradictory relationship to a new level.

As I have said, the contrast between fixed and sliding prices, between the absence and presence of bargaining, has often been taken to be the distinguishing feature of modern and traditional markets respectively. The Alexanders, anthropologists who studied Indonesian markets, asked why many American tourists in Bali choose Western-style shops, with their posted (and higher) prices, over the local bazaar, with its haggling and generally lower prices.[34] Obviously, because they find them more familiar and feel more comfortable there. But this is merely to say that people are programed to stay within their own culture, even when travelling abroad. Where does the institution of fixed, posted prices come from? Or, to put the boot on the other foot for a change, instead of looking on bargaining as abnormal, what happens if we treat fixed prices as an anomaly of recent history?

In a novel of life in the English Potteries at the end of the last century,[35] Arnold Bennett describes the appearance of the phenomenon of posted prices. People were used to engaging with shopkeepers personally; and each purchase took place under particular circumstances, involving variable price, quality and credit terms, all of them based on the specific relationship between trader and customer. Bennett recalls the shock of encountering for the first time goods identified by little white cards with nonnegotiable prices on them. That was little more than a hundred years ago, yet the descendants of these pioneers now find sliding prices to be almost as threatening as beggars in the street.

The period from the 1880s to the First World War, which I have identified with the origins of twentieth-century state capitalism and the bureaucratic revolution, was the age of the first department stores, concentrating under one roof a wide range of commodities that would previously have been sold in separate shops. This is where fixed prices came from. The shift toward more impersonal forms of economic organization had important consequences for marketing. Bureaucracies limit the personal discretion of employees, hedging their activities around with rules that can only be broken at risk of dismissal. In the new stores, customers dealt face-to-face with assistants who had no power to negotiate. That power rested with owners and managers who were now removed from the point of sale, unlike the small shopkeeper. The main imperative of management was to control subordinates; and this ethos stretched back to the production lines as well as outwards to an anonymous market of consumers whose tastes were there to be manipulated.

The remarkable thing is that this bureaucratic revolution was ignored by the economists, who chose the same moment (the end of the nineteenth century) to reinvent their discipline as the study of individuals making rational decisions in competitive markets. Political economy's embarrassing emphasis on class divisions was disposed of, and the overwhelming social trend toward centralization (which so impressed Durkheim and his contemporaries, from Engels to Weber) was ignored. It is a short step from here to an economic ideology that represents the modern world as a competitive market driven by the independent decisions of a mass of individuals. Now we can perhaps see dimly through the fog of a modern rhetoric that systematically misrepresents the corporations of our day as individual agents with an economic profile that would not be out of place in an Eastern bazaar. At the heart of the confusion is the systematic refusal of Western intellectuals to analyse the institutions of modern economy. Above all, what is needed is an effort to distinguish between the properties of markets, of buying and selling as a form of human activity, and those of a capitalism increasingly organized by states and bureaucracy.

If the trend a century ago was toward centralization, the reorganization of society from the top in an era of mass production and consumption, there is some evidence to support the idea that today the technological trend supports decentralization of economic and political power, even as the world market becomes more integrated. It is impossible to address such a proposition by means of orthodox economics, since the discipline is based on a systematic attempt to misrepresent the truth of that earlier transition. Even sadder, resistance to the power of big money and its political representatives has led many ordinary people, especially on the left, to regard markets and money as intrinsically anti-social institutions, along with the capitalism that has flourished on their foundation. Yet it is inconceivable that modern citizens could do all the things they would like to in a day without having recourse to buying and selling in some form. Moreover, I would argue that it is conceivable they could do so with a greater sense of personal involvement and without accepting the predations of capitalists as inevitable. Disentangling the potential of market relations from their embodiment in capitalism will take more than intellectual effort, but we must begin to do so.

The moral economy of paid and unpaid labor

Most of us "make" money by working. Work is a very modern concept. For one thing, it is usually performed in a special time and place, away from home. For another, it is not really work unless it is paid, thereby generating another contrast between wage employment and unpaid work. Finally, work is effort, the expenditure of energy; and in the modern period that energy is usually supplemented by machines. In this section I will consider the social question of working for money, the division between an impersonal, public sphere of work and the personal world of home and private life. This separation lies at the roots of modern culture and consciousness, so much so that it seems almost natural for most of us. Yet we will see that it is historically recent and, in an important sense, anomalous. There are already signs that it is giving way to new patterns of economic life.

Money, time and energy constitute the essential infrastructure of the market economy. All three lend themselves to quantification; they have become embedded in our collective consciousness as so many numbers. We are used to calculating the costs of alternative courses of action in terms of these variable elements. Should I take the car or catch the train? How long will it take? Can I get someone to share the fuel? We are even slowly becoming aware of the collective energy costs involved in choosing between public and private transport. Money, time, energy—the calculus of modern life. But it is highly unusual for human beings to divide up the components of their world in such a precise manner. A lot of it has to do with the distinctive way in which we now work.

We have seen above that Emile Durkheim made a rough contrast between primitive and modern societies in terms of the development of the division of labor. It was based on the observation that, while simple organisms do everything they need for themselves, more complex forms of life (notably ourselves) split up necessary tasks between specialists, who thereby become interdependent. Adam Smith took the idea further in *The Wealth of Nations* when he suggested that this process of specialization in production held the key to increased efficiency and economic progress. The Victorian social philosopher Herbert Spencer turned this into a general theory of evolution in which forms of life advanced toward greater complexity and internal difference.[36]

All of these writers were trying to come to grips with a fundamental change in the way people now experienced the world. Before the industrial revolution, with the exception of some systems of slave-based agriculture, work was quite closely integrated with domestic life. Although some sectors of production were organized in a socially complex manner, most work was carried out in loosely co-operative teams containing a high proportion of members of the same family. Roles were diffusely defined and easily switched according to the fluctuating rhythms of personal, domestic and community life. Very little of this work earned direct money payment, and hence there was less concern with time spent on particular tasks. In any case, there was little social pressure to improve the efficiency of production; people were generally content to carry on doing what they had done before. In a traditional context like this, it was hard to distinguish one aspect of life from any other.

As the factory system of industrial production grew in significance from the late eighteenth century and throughout the nineteenth, it became clear that traditional work patterns had to be broken up in order to get people to endure the new disciplines associated with wage employment. This process was analysed by Max Weber,[37] but the fullest account is to be found in E.P. Thompson's *The Making of the English Working Class*.[38] At first the new wage laborers brought peasant attitudes into the factories. If a sheep was sick, they stayed at home to tend it. The owners could not put up with such slackness; the steam-driven machines used up fuel continuously and human work patterns had to be adapted to this. As Thompson and others have shown, the imposition of time discipline was often brutal. Gradually it became established that workers were paid for precisely how long they worked and how much they produced. They did this under strict supervision in a special place sharply demarcated from their homes. The modern world of work was ideally impersonal. Men were "hands," and, if they were given the sack, it was inappropriate to take this as a personal affront from their boss. For one of the most important disciplines of industrial employment was acceptance of an ideology that attributed such calamities to the inscrutable forces of "the market."

Impersonal social institutions were the hallmark of the early modern city. Max Weber, in *The City*,[39] pointed out that relations in pre-modern societies were personal. All authority figures from God and the king to priests and landlords cloaked themselves in the symbolism of male heads of families, the father or patriarch. This lent a moral dimension to social order, but it also encouraged arbitrary treatment according to the superior party's disposition. The medieval cities of northern Italy and the Netherlands committed themselves to founding public life on written rules that applied to everyone equally. This is the origin of bureaucracy, rule by office rather than by persons, and it is well to remember that its initial impulse was democratic and egalitarian, an attempt to escape from the corruption and violence of a feudal regime. The problem was and is that, in carving out a sphere of impersonal law, the subjective basis for a moral connection between self and society was ruptured, generating a permanent crisis of legitimacy for modern governments.

We have seen that the market nexus also rests on a degree of impersonality, breaking the intimate connection between persons and things and, by emphasizing the equivalence of the exchange, reducing the need for ongoing social ties between buyers and sellers. But, as Polanyi insisted, we also saw that this anonymous ideal was stretched to its limit when what was bought and sold was inseparable from persons, namely human creativity itself ("labor"). If someone buys a hat, it is not hard to imagine that the hat ceases to have any connection with the seller. But how do you persuade a paid worker that his work no longer belongs to him once it has been bought, that the impersonal rules of the labor market take over at the expense of his own personality? Buying and selling human beings is an old practice. We call it slavery. Typically a slave was a war captive or a victim of debt who was eventually sold on to a master who had command over his or her labor for life. In the Roman tradition, the slave was an object, not a subject with personality, an *instrumentum vocale* ("speaking tool"), part of the family property along with the animals. Even so, slaves had some rights as family members, and it was in the interest of the owner to maintain the value of a life-time asset. This is the Achilles heel of slavery: Why buy labor for a lump sum in advance when you can hire it piecemeal as needed?[40]

A wage is a pledge, a promise to pay when the work is done. As long as there are people ready to sell their labor, hiring for wages is more flexible than slavery and it ties up much less capital, just whatever it costs for a day's or week's work. Wage employment[41] was not invented by the industrial revolution. Indeed, recent work by economic historians shows that the institution was widespread in rural England as early as the thirteenth century, a relative exception in medieval Europe.[42] Nevertheless there was something of a crisis in the late eighteenth century when the numbers of so-called vagrants, migrants in search of work, began to overwhelm the poor-relief system.[43] And the subsequent flood of rural–urban migrants into industrial employment established wage labor as the norm. It is worth remembering, however, that there were still many peasants, servants and self-employed workers in nineteenth-century Europe; and the wage system never took over completely.

The growth of wage labor in the modern economy led to an attempt to separate the spheres in which paid and unpaid work predominated. The first was ideally objective and impersonal, specialized and calculated; the second was subjective and personal, diffuse, based on long-term interdependence. Inevitably, the one was associated with the payment of money in a public place, the other with "home," so that "work" without a marker usually meant outside activities and the business of maintaining families became known as "housework." It is a short step from this conceptual separation to the idea that the real work of production is supported by domestic reproduction; that the energies used up in work are restored by leisure at home, giving rise to a marked oscillation between work and rest (evenings, weekends and holidays).

This is how the citizens of modern societies now live. We earn money when we work and we spend it in our spare time, which is focused on the home. Production and consumption are linked in an endless cycle of complementary activities. But it is not easy. Work still has a strong element of compulsion in it. It is necessary, whereas consumption is notionally a sphere of freedom—we can choose what to spend our money on. Perhaps it is extreme to label our normal condition *wage slavery*; perhaps not. In any case we have to knuckle under to regimes of varying rigidity. And we do so under the threat of losing our job, often for unexplained and anonymous reasons. Job loss, of course, means a massive reduction in our ability to spend. Especially at times of crisis, it is difficult to keep the personal and the impersonal apart; yet our economic culture demands nothing less of us, day in, day out, for most of our adult lives.

The system of paid and unpaid labor has been until recently gendered. The separation of the two was made clearer if men worked for money outside and women were responsible for the home. Returning from a hard day at the factory or office, the patriarch beat the kids, ate a meal, put his feet up and enjoyed free sex before sleep completed the process of restoring him for the next day's work. This was the moral universe of early industrial society. It rested on a strong opposition between the money sphere of buying and selling and the domestic sphere of give-and-take. This is why money has a sharp cultural resonance for us that it lacks in societies that have not instituted such a strong polarity between (outside) work and home.[44] For example, I was once talking to a Ghanaian student about exchanges between lovers, and he said that it was quite common for a boy who had slept with a girl after a party to leave some money as a gift and token of esteem. Once he had done this with a visiting American student and the resulting explosion was gigantic: "Do you imagine that I am a prostitute?", etc. Prostitution is at the contradictory core of the modern economic system and its moral defenses. What could be more personal than sex and more impersonal than a money payment? The combination of the two strikes at the heart of the attempt to separate male and female spheres of work. No wonder women sex workers often provoke a moral panic. When the institutional division of work and home is itself breaking down, occasions for moral outrage multiply daily.

Let me spell out why the division between paid and unpaid labor lies at the core of capitalism's moral economy. At the end of the twentieth century, people have never been more conscious of themselves as unique personalities seeking full expression of their subjectivity in the world. Scientific knowledge has lent to that consciousness the promise of increased collective control over material conditions that before placed severe limits on human aspirations. Why, then, do most people feel so powerless in the face of the forces governing their co-existence? The answer is obvious. Society is unknowably large and complex, being driven by impersonal institutions whose effects can be devastating (war, mass unemployment), while the actions of individuals are trivial and meaningless. Between self and society there is an apparently unbridgeable gap that leaves most of us alienated from the sources of our collective being, confining our energies and ambitions to the petty projects of everyday life. It was once the task of religion to fill that gap; and, for many of the world's dispossessed, it still is. Today money is both a principal reason for our vulnerability in experiencing society as a remote external object and a means of connection between the two, a practical symbol allowing each of us to make an impersonal world meaningful. If Durkheim said we worship society and call it God,[45] money is the God of capitalist society.

The modern economy consists of two complementary spheres that have to be kept separate, despite their interdependence. One of them is a zone of infinite scope where things and, increasingly, human creativity are bought and sold for money, *the market*. The second is a protected zone of domestic life where intimate personal relations hold sway, *home*. The market is unbounded and, in a sense, unknowable, whereas the bounds of domestic life are known only too well. The normal link between the two is that some adults—traditionally men more often than women—go out to *work*, to "make" the money on which the household subsists. The economy of the home rests on spending this money and performing services without payment. The result is a heightened sense of division between an outside world in which our humanity feels swamped and a precarious zone of protected personality at home. This duality is the moral and practical foundation of capitalist society. It is reflected in the institutional segregation of selling and buying, production and consumption, income and expenditure, *work* and *home*.

We have seen that the attempt to construct a market in which commodities are exchanged instantly and impersonally as alienable private property is utopian. The idea of civil society in this sense was to grant a measure of independence for market agents from the arbitrary interventions of personalized rule. Relations in such a system between owners of property and workers without property ("servants" for John Locke) were left obscure, leaving it to Marx to make their opposed interests brutally clear. All the efforts of economists to insist on the autonomy of an abstract market logic cannot disguise the fact that market relations inevitably have a personal and social component. This is particularly the case when the commodity being bought and sold is human creativity.

Markets and money were until recently minor appendages of agricultural society, largely external to relations organizing the performance of work on the land and to the distribution of its product. The owners of money capital were in turn excluded from political power. Even though the rulers needed money to fight wars and to buy imported luxuries, markets remained on the margins of mainstream society. The middle-class revolution of the seventeenth and eighteenth centuries changed all that, by preparing the way for markets to be accepted at the center of society, a process given intellectual weight by Adam Smith in particular. But it was the industrial revolution and subsequent mechanization that made selling one's labor for wages the main source of livelihood. Only now did the market, more especially that for human services, become the principal means of connecting families to society at large.

Where does the social pressure come from to make markets impersonal, at least in theory? Max Weber's answer is as good as any: Rational calculation of profit in enterprises depends on the capitalist's ability to control the markets for his products and for the "factors of production," especially labor.[46] It is all right for the squire to have diffuse personal relations with his peasants, who are in any case going nowhere, but it will not do to let such considerations interfere with the running of a factory. The principle is that, once a commodity has been sold, the buyer is free to do with it what he likes. But, in the case of a wage contract, the human source of work is not an object separable from the work that has been bought. Nevertheless, people must be taught to submit to the impersonal disciplines of the workplace. The struggle to impose formal criteria of accountancy on people's economic lives has never been completely won. So, just as money is intrinsic to the home economy, personality remains intrinsic to the labor market. In consequence of this overlap in practice, the cultural effort required to keep the two spheres separate, if only at the conceptual level, is huge.

The members of societies that have been run on capitalist principles for some time maintain that the mere act of paying money transforms a relationship. Money stands for alienation, detachment, impersonal society, the outside; its origins lie beyond our control. Relations marked by the absence of money are the model of personal integration and free association, of what we take to be familiar, the inside. The issue is essentially a moral one. Commodities are "goods" because we consume them in person, but we find it difficult to embrace money, the means of their exchange, as "good" because it belongs to a sphere that is indifferent to morality and, in some sense, stays there. The good life, instead of uniting work and home, is restricted to what takes place in the latter. We live for the weekends and for holidays; the value of our jobs is to make home life enjoyable. There are those who commit themselves wholly to work or public life; but this reproduces the division between paid and unpaid labor, rather than subverting it.

Either markets are universal and everything is bought and sold, as some economists insist, or personality is universally acknowledged to be intrinsic to social relations, as most humanists would argue. But institutional dualism of the sort outlined here, *forcing individuals to divide themselves,* asks too much of us. Consequently, not only has the structure never been fully realized in practice, but it has been breaking down for some time in the face of people's need to integrate the personal and impersonal dimensions of their lives. They want to integrate division, to make some meaningful connection between themselves as subjects and society as an object. This process has been aided by the fact that money, as well as being the means of separating public and domestic life, was always the main bridge between the two. That is why the project of bringing together the different spheres of exchange into some meaningful unity is more likely to succeed through developing new approaches to money than by turning our backs on it.

Changing economic relations between men and women

In capitalist societies, then, production and reproduction have been separated into two spheres, one associated with the market, the other with home. But such a separation is only recent, partial and transient. To represent such an arrangement as eternal, as a culture of public and domestic life anchored in a sexual division of labor as old as the human species itself, masks the historical reality, which consists of continuous movement and cross-cultural variation. It is important to understand how people have already transformed static ideas into the practical dynamics of everyday life; for this makes contemplation of alternative economic forms less daunting than when change is conceived of as a leap from one abstract idea to its opposite. Accordingly, I now approach changing relations between work and home through an examination of gender divisions in three places I have lived and worked in: Britain, the Caribbean and West Africa.[47] The main theme of this history is the growing marginality of domestic life to social reproduction, as well as to production. I will finally address how the latest phase of the machine revolution potentially subverts the conventional division between work and home.

Britain

In the south-east heartlands of England's medieval civilization, the state and market were strong enough as early as the thirteenth century to sustain commercial agriculture and a rural wage-labor force on a significant scale. This allowed an unusual degree of individuation to develop within a general framework of peasant patriarchy.[48] Hence the long-standing British conception of the family as an individual household united under its male head. This early development of the labor market and of a family structure adapted to it no doubt facilitated Britain's pioneering breakthrough to industrial capitalism. The first phase of the machine revolution saw the wholesale transfer of peasant families into Lancashire's textile factories.[49] Men and women carried out their traditional tasks under the supervision of the former and children performed menial duties. But the factory owners turned increasingly to cheaper female and child labor in the drive to reduce costs. Patriarchy was, if anything, reinforced by the Victorians, and women were herded into domestic service, prostitution and badly paid wage labor. Their position in society deteriorated with the coming of industrial capitalism.

Social pressure built up against these early abuses of the industrial system. This was due in part to improvements in machinery that made it more profitable for some capitalists to raise the productivity of labor (Marx's relative surplus value) than to cheapen its absolute cost. The decades leading up to the First World War witnessed a shift toward heavy industries like shipbuilding and steel mills. This, coming on top of campaigns to release children for schooling and women for housework, consolidated the power of monopoly trade unions in key industries where male productivity was high enough to justify wages sufficient to support whole families. This is the specific origin of the "breadwinner/housewife" model of conjugal relations from which British women have been seeking to emancipate themselves in recent decades.[50] Before the 1880s only middle-class wives, supported by servants, restricted their attentions to the home. By the end of the century, a major plank of Labor Party and trade union policy was to seek similar privileges for working-class women. Europe's main Marxist party, the German Social Democrats, took a similar line; and the International Labor Office, from its foundation, promoted the aim of sparing women the burdens of wage labor. This coincided with a fall in the birth rate and the rise of family planning. It was also the period of maximum agitation for women's political rights (the suffragette movement).

It seems, therefore, that the emergence of a clear-cut sexual division of labor, identifying men with wage employment and women with housework, belongs to that second phase of mechanization that I have linked to the bureaucratic revolution and the rise of state capitalism. Moreover, working people themselves played a strong part in bringing it about, recognizing no doubt that as long as husbands and wives competed in the same labor market they drove down the wages of each. There are plenty of analogous examples of peasant societies where men have converted a new affluence into seclusion of their wives from working in public view (the institution of the veil, for instance).[51] This, then, was the general model of family life for a broad spectrum of middle- and working-class Britons until the 1960s. The extremes of rich and poor were largely untouched by these developments. The youth rebellion was the beginning of a decisive phase in women's emancipation. Now, with immigration being discouraged and the post-war economic boom at its height, women at home constituted the last great reserve of labor to which capitalists could turn.[52] Their subsequent mass re-entry into the wage-labor force led to struggles against discrimination that were soon seen to be as much cultural as economic. Eventually, British feminists, and after them gay men, took on marriage and the sexual division of labor itself, the idea that men and women perform complementary productive tasks that are rooted in their respective reproductive roles.

Throughout all this, the state has played a crucial part in promoting the concept of individual citizenship at the expense of traditional family responsibilities. An army of professionals—doctors, teachers, lawyers, social workers—now supervises the process whereby the young enter society; and they frequently exercise their legal powers to override parental control. There is resistance from conservatives; and the battle-ground that constitutes the future of the family is nowhere contested more keenly than in the controversy over the abortion laws. The link between reproduction in the home and production outside it has been substantially eroded in Britain as we approach the millennium; but it is not yet broken. That moral certainty, which for a remarkably short period of time underwrote the normative separation of work and home as a natural fact of marriage, is now on the wane, opening up new possibilities for the construction of economic life.

The Caribbean

Most societies in the modern world are long-established peasant civilizations in the early throes of the machine revolution. The Caribbean sugar islands were created as part of a precocious experiment in social engineering. The indigenous populations and their traditions were eliminated to make way for colonial plantation economies employing workers ripped out of their familiar environments (slaves and indentured laborers). Africans and Asians spoke variants of the languages of their European masters as they toiled in what were once the most advanced industrial enterprises in the

Western world. As the region's greatest writer, C.L.R. James, always insisted,[53] this peculiar history has thrown up a distinctive people, one of the
most modern in the world. This is no sleepy backwater, a tourist suntrap occupied by a few rum-drinking fishermen: It is a major crucible of the social
forms that are taking over contemporary society everywhere.

In the heyday of the Atlantic slave trade, owners did not need the Negro
family as a means of reproducing their labor supply. Some of them were hostile to the formation of kinship ties among the slaves, seeing in them the
seeds of autonomy and resistance. But, by the end of the eighteenth century,
most owners were indifferent to whether the slaves reproduced themselves.
The latter built up informal kinship systems, whatever their masters' attitudes, and these were strongest on large estates with stable workforces that
encouraged subsistence cultivation as a fallback when market demand for
sugar was weak. The notion of a patriarchal family was reserved for the estate as a whole. This meant that male slaves had no direct jural authority over
women and children, and their families had little or no official standing.
There was no social sanction for marriage or sexual division of labor between slaves; but work roles did follow a gender-specific pattern. Women
performed most of the unskilled field labor, while men held down the
skilled jobs offering a measure of privilege. Some women entered informal
unions with whites, thereby endowing their offspring with limited prospects
for upward mobility. Unions between slaves were consensual, usually involving visits to separate residences, and women undertook the bulk of family responsibilities.

The abolition of slavery made possible the emergence of an independent
black peasantry in the nineteenth century.[54] The former slaves tried to develop a subsistence base for patriarchal families, but not enough land was released by the owners to make that option viable and they remained
dependent on the plantations, this time as a wage-labor force. Some women
may have retreated from field labor to purely domestic tasks; certainly, in
some cases, African women were replaced by indentured Indian workers on
the plantations. The demise of slavery coincided with an upsurge of syn-
cretistic Christianity and this revival helped to consolidate socially sanctioned family life among the former slaves. The decades before the First

World War saw a sharp shift of population into urban areas, with women outnumbering men in the principal towns.[55] They performed domestic labor for the growing white and brown middle class and they dominated petty trade. It is probable that these women, like their counterparts elsewhere, had more to gain from escaping rural patriarchy.[56] At the same time, successive waves of men emigrated to Central America and the United States, establishing the twentieth-century pattern of male absenteeism and dependence of families on their female members.

In the past century a strongly dualistic family pattern has been established.[57] On the one hand, the Christian Churches endorse the middle-class ideal of marriage for all strata of the population, but without the norm of female seclusion that often goes with it. On the other hand, there is a working-class model of conjugal visiting, unstable unions and matrifocality, in which women put up with a culture of machismo and assume most of the responsibility for reproduction. The two types are often combined within individual family careers, with women pressing to make their unions and offspring official, when their men get older and perhaps tire of a predatory existence. Women stay in the education system longer than men and have the larger share of jobs in the bureaucracy.

Sex divisions are no more rigid in the Caribbean today than they were under slavery; and that synthesis of peasant patriarchy and middle-class family norms that briefly dominated Western industrial societies has not taken root there. In the absence of a viable local capitalism, wage employment is not an adequate staple for most families, so that the breadwinner/housewife model has scarcely been given a chance. High male unemployment rates undermine any improvements in men's jural status brought about by emancipation; and the women sustain a boom in evangelical Protestantism as a distraction from their menfolk's failings. As the Western nuclear family crumbles, giving rise to households resembling the fluid forms that have long been typical of the Caribbean, it becomes plausible to argue that the family pattern pioneered by the former slaves is better suited to modern conditions than the exaggerated sexual division of labor I grew up with in Britain. Caribbean families have never been organized by a strong separation of work and home, and to that extent their history may be prophetic of what happens to industrialized peasantries when that division breaks down.

West Africa

My concern here is with the region's traditional rural societies, excluding the Islamic savanna interior and the coastal trading towns. These societies were governed by peasant patriarchy, with and without the reinforcement of indigenous states. In some cases, group membership was traced though the female line, but this did not devolve authority from men to women.[58] Throughout West Africa, the division of labor rested on a combination of gender and age. Married men controlled the distribution of agricultural goods produced mainly by dependent women and young men. These "elders" disposed of movable wealth in the form of animals, cloth, precious metals and slaves.[59] They monopolized long-distance trade and restricted the movements of women. Each of the sexes was responsible for a long list of manufactures and services. Polygamy was normal, with the elders delaying marriage for their sons and junior brothers through control of bridewealth; girls married at puberty.

Urbanization and rural development in the twentieth century have introduced several modifications to this pattern.[60] Men have taken up most cash-cropping and wage employment opportunities; women are concentrated in small- and middle-level trade, giving them a reputation for controlling money. The upper echelons of both colonial and post-colonial society, however, have been dominated by men, who vastly outnumber women in government, the army, higher education, banking and international trade.[61] Women do have their secret societies, market chiefs and queen mothers; and they show scant deference to their menfolk. But they have further to go than their Caribbean sisters toward achieving social equality. They do often feel that they are better off than their European and American counterparts, and in this they may not be wrong.

An example from classical ethnography illustrates how West African gender divisions have fared in the face of twentieth-century developments.[62] Among the Nupe of northern Nigeria before colonial rule, married men controlled the essentials of life (food grains) and bridewealth tokens (cattle). Unmarried young men, who could be as old as their late thirties, worked on the farms of their elders in the hope of eventually being allowed to marry. Women, in addition to their domestic duties, kept small gardens in which they grew the relishes to relieve a monotonous diet, and they sometimes exchanged these peas, beans and tomatoes in local markets. British colonialism brought new markets, for wage laborers to build roads and towns, and for farmers cultivating export crops like groundnuts. These opportunities were taken up with alacrity by the young men, who left their villages in droves as migrants. Meanwhile, local markets expanded rapidly and many women found increased economic independence as traders.

To make matters worse for the elders, the colonial authorities levied taxes on heads of households, who were forced to turn to the women and young men for the cash. They raised the number of animals to be paid for a wife in a vain attempt to assert their control over their juniors. Witchcraft accusations escalated against women. Eventually they sought an accommodation with their colonial rulers, offering their services as labor recruiters and local crowd control. This alliance between traditional and modern authorities sparked off a vicious class conflict, and inequalities along lines of gender and age became more rigid as a consequence of colonial rule. West Africa is even more marginal to global capitalism than the Caribbean. Some feminist researchers have seen West African women as a model of independence, an inspiration to their downtrodden Western sisters. Others see only that they are victims of capitalist oppression, like most Third World women. In any case, there is even less evidence from this region of that sexual division of labor that briefly underpinned the moral economy of societies reorganized to meet the needs of state capitalism.

The family under state capitalism

The more I have pursued these comparative researches, the more anomalous the pattern of family life I witnessed as a boy now seems. Eternal and universal though it was made out to be, it can now be seen to have lasted from the 1890s to the 1950s in only a few countries. We should not be surprised that the attempt to separate work and home failed. It was an outlandish experiment, the domestic counterpart to state capitalism's reliance on bureaucracy and, at the same time, a vivid example of modern regression to the institutions of agrarian civilization. As we have seen, a way of life based on extracting energy from plants and animals is being rapidly replaced by one where goods and services are exchanged within built environments and even over telephone wires. The social patterns that have emerged under these circumstances represent an uneasy amalgam of agrarian and commercial institutions whose spread has been extremely uneven in geographical terms. The power of the money and machines at our disposal has been used to intensify old (and some new) patterns of exploitation, while reduction in exposure to back-breaking toil and premature death has been a source of liberation.

In the centers of capitalism, economic organization has been taken away from peasant families and concentrated in the hands of corporations large enough to control the labor force, capital and machinery needed for survival in a rapidly evolving world market. The relocation of much work and reproduction outside the home has introduced a new discontinuity between production and consumption. The sexual division of labor, which appeared as suitable sticking plaster for this alienating structure, was at first intensified and then undermined by the contradictions of state capitalism. Both states and markets are impersonal institutions, treating human beings as abstract individuals: citizens, voters, employees, households. The conception of society implied by both is composed of units endowed with the same atomized structure. Neither of them has much room for the mess of particularistic groupings on which agricultural and early urban society were founded.[63] This makes them profoundly egalitarian, while they reproduce agrarian hierarchy. Mobility is built into modern markets; the division of labor is complex and highly volatile, so that people must move in order to live. The state's job is to equip them with the education that makes this possible.[64] Less and less is left in the hands of families, whose responsibilities are taken over by an army of university-trained professionals. At the same time the right of men to control their women's property and beat them up has been abolished, making patriarchy less tenable as the foundation of family life.

The conjugal nuclear family (man, wife and 2.4 kids), whatever its agrarian antecedents, is an early and transient compromise between patriarchy and individualism. One solution to the problems entailed in habitual nomadism is to withdraw women and children from the labor market and make them tag along with the male breadwinner. In the 1950s, just before the deluge, this was being seriously touted by American sociologists as the functional answer to advanced capitalism's reproductive dilemmas.[65] No doubt the idea appeals to a certain type of atavistic male mentality, but it will not stand up long in the face of market penetration of domestic life and the relocation of much reproduction into the public sphere. The maintenance of a reserve army of cheap female labor also has its appeal in societies that are not committed to improving productivity through mechanization. But in general the family is becoming an almost contingent feature of capitalist societies. For these societies replenish their resources in ways that no longer depend on any particular division of labor between men and women.

People may still seek personal fulfillment in conjugal arrangements, but society does not really care any more how they do it. Parent–child relations have nothing like the significance they once had for how people expect to live. The majority of households contain only one or two people. The fastest-growing type of family in the world is the matrifocal one (mother alone with her kids) previously associated with poor black people and underdevelopment. There are major variations between the leading capitalist nations: Thus British women are still punished for trying to combine wage employment and motherhood, while their French counterparts have won cheap and effective sources of alternative childcare. We all inhabit a space between patriarchy and the possibility of more equal relations between men and women; and the permutations are infinite. The marginality of domestic life to the organization of social production and reproduction by states and markets leaves considerable scope for personal initiative. As family patterns are made increasingly consensual and voluntary, it seems likely that the sexual division of labor will be weakened to the point of being little more than a cultural memory. In this respect, the economic emancipation of women is the strongest sign that we may be entering a period when capitalism's moral economy can be remade.

Beyond wage slavery?

I have suggested that living in two strongly contrasted spheres of the economy, in the impersonal world of work and the personal world of home, poses intrinsic difficulties for our humanity. At the root of the problem is the way we work for each other through the market, when the buying and selling of services (as opposed to objects) is becoming by far the largest part of the human economy. A market economy may be said to be "capitalist" when people are paid to work, mainly outside the home in establishments controlled by the owners of money. There was always a tension between the needs of domestic or local organization and participation in market networks, but this was manageable, as long as the bulk of livelihood was generated outside the market. Wholesale conversion to the wage-labor system simultaneously made the market more central to economic life and reinforced the division between work and home. Morality itself was banished from public life, leaving individuals with no responsible or meaningful connection between private and public life. Yet the security of families depended on maintaining access to wage employment that was granted or withheld by remote agents in the public sphere. This is, of course, intolerable; and people responded in a number of ways.

One was to seek personal integration through the job itself. It is unreasonable to expect people to detach their long-term life expectations from their work, and one trend of the past two centuries has been to attach reproductive considerations to jobs. The Japanese are famous for the way that companies and their employees make a life-time commitment to each other; but the security of "jobs for life" has made its mark in most modern societies. The distinction between wages and salaries has often been one of class.[66] The salaried middle classes were quick to establish rights in pensions, health and education schemes, subsidies to housing, insurance and other supplements linking their direct income to security in the long run for themselves and their families. Later workers in protected and high-productivity industries like mining, steel and shipbuilding were able to win concessions that were similar but not as extensive. In the twentieth century a scaled-down version of these guarantees was provided by the welfare state. The result was a bureaucratic form of paternalism that modified wage employment in a direction reminiscent of the more benevolent versions of slavery.

The idea of the *job* is one of the chief examples of how the institutions of agrarian civilization have been adapted to conditions spawned by the machine revolution. A slave or serf depended for his livelihood on a landowner. A wage employee is likewise dependent on his boss, except that his contract is short-term and reversible; and it leaves the worker with more responsibility for his own security than before. Moreover, volatile labor markets pose a persistent challenge to the wages system. The whole point of paying workers on a short-term basis is to be able to lay them off when demand slackens.

This gave rise in some industries and trades (such as the docks and construction) to a pattern of casual hiring and firing that undermined attempts to build family life around a stable source of employment. Worse, it made redundancy and unemployment a fact of life for generations of workers. Sometimes groups of workers would forget that their livelihood depended on evanescent markets. The mill towns around Manchester dominated the world's trade in cotton textiles for a century and a half. Today the blackened centers of these towns are derelict; the market has moved on and they failed to adapt. The lesson is a deeply distressing one: Wage employment is at worst insecure and what seems secure can soon be wiped out, leaving ruined communities as mute testimony to the error of relying on jobs generated by capitalist markets. These fluctuations have always put pressure on the cultural program of stabilizing work and home as the twin bulwarks of a harmonious cycle of production and reproduction.

Only in retrospect will the work patterns of the twentieth century be revealed as the bizarre deviations from normal human life that they were: Men working outside the home for almost all the hours available to them in order to prove their devotion to their jobs; returning to wives who barely managed to get out of the house at any time; travelling to city offices from far suburbs daily in order to put as much distance as possible between work and home.[67] While well-paid workaholics cling to the few remaining jobs of a traditional kind, for most young people entering the labor market today the prospects are rather different. For there has been a revolution in the organization of production during the last two decades, mainly but not exclusively in America.[68] This has in turn been shaped by the developments in information technology and money markets discussed in the previous chapters. The literature dealing with these topics is vast and takes us beyond the scope of the present book. But a few points should be noted here.

The bureaucratic revolution was mainly about centralizing control of all the factors relevant to manufacturing a product. Thus Henry Ford not only made the paint for his cars, he even raised sheep in a neighboring county to feed and clothe his workers. Recently firms have been drastically reducing their workforces, for the first time at managerial as well as at lower levels. This is known as "downsizing" and, when it applies to senior- and middle-level management, as "delayering." Simultaneously, and in a related process, information technology has been introduced on a wide scale, especially to facilitate the development of networks and electronic data interchange systems within reorganized corporations. These are increasingly focused around their so-called "core competences" and have shed a range of support tasks to small specialist firms. This process of "outsourcing" has allowed the lead firms to become hubs of what are often giant networks of firms relying on deregulated markets to keep down internal costs while making it increasingly difficult for outsiders to compete effectively. This has led to a round of super-mergers across national boundaries that is rapidly reducing the number of corporate players in global markets.

Employees in "outsourced" firms are often temporary, get lower pay, have "flexible" working hours and do not enjoy the health and other benefits that are available to regular employees in the core firm. They are often located in Third World countries. If the scale and rapidity with which the twentieth-century system of manufacture is being reformed is remarkable, the process of "outsourcing" is not new. It used to be called "the putting-out system," and it is as ancient as the factory itself. This involved leaving parts of production to be performed at home by domestic workers, usually more cheaply than their hire as wage employees would be. The Japanese corporations who encouraged their core employees to embrace an ethos of lifetime commitment also relied heavily on casualized domestic workers; and this duality has been reproduced in countless ways throughout the short history of capitalism. What is new is the harnessing of information technology and networking to this process. At the very least we should be aware that the rigid separation of work and home in capitalism's moral economy has been more complicated in practice; and that contemporary developments have their analogies in the past.

It is hard to see the patterns emerging at this time. That is one reason for stepping back to look at the history of the modern period as a whole. It seems that whatever security workers were able to win under state capitalism is being eroded. Labor markets are less regulated, and the power of unions has been much diminished. The growth of employment in recent years has been largely in what are sometimes called "McJobs," after the hamburger retailing chain that specializes in hiring young, low-paid, part-time, temporary workers to perform unskilled tasks with no prospects of improvement. What is for sure is that any hope people once had that they could rely on "a good job" and state protection for their long-term security is less justified today than it ever was. The state capitalist experiment of linking human reproduction to anonymous bureaucratic structures seems to have failed.

At the same time, the communications revolution has opened up many new possibilities for reconfiguring the relationship between work and home. "Teleworking," the idea of working for one's employer from home on a flexible basis, has often been touted as an inevitable corollary of the new information technologies. The ramifications are infinite and lie beyond the scope of a book whose prime focus is on the means of exchange, not production and reproduction. The purpose of this chapter has been to establish that the money system, when considered as a market economy, has always been in movement, whatever attempts to stabilize the conditions of capital accumulation may have been made. This is for the good reason that it is people who animate economic life. In the next chapter we will see how they animate money itself.

Guide to further reading

The subject matter of this chapter is closest to my academic teaching of economic anthropology. There is only one place to start, with Marcel Mauss's *The Gift* (note 1). Readers of French should also look at his political journalism (note 30). Emile Durkheim's *The Division of Labour in Society* (note 8) provides the essential background to his nephew's efforts. Modern British social anthropology has its conventional origin in the publication of Malinowski's brilliant ethnography, *Argonauts of the Western Pacific* (note 23). Polanyi's *The Great Transformation* (note 3) is a wonderful, flawed critique of market capitalism. More recent contributions of note include Bohannan and Dalton's collection on African markets (note 33), Gregory's *Gifts and Commodities* and Strathern's *Gender of the Gift* (note 28); the Alexanders' article offers an engaging point of entry into the anthropology of markets (note 34). Marshall Sahlins's *Stone-age Economics* is an original *tour de force* and very accessible.[69] I have written a short polemical review of economic anthropology for a journal symposium.[70]

One anthropologist, Louis Dumont, has attempted the intellectual history of early-modern economic ideas (note 17). Otherwise, we depend heavily on Macpherson's efforts in the field of property (note 4, 14). Chris Hann has edited an impressive collection of articles by anthropologists on the subject.[71] Sir John Hicks' *Theory of Economic History* is a bit wild, but very stimulating and readable (note 7). And, for those who refuse to read John Locke in the original, I can only repeat my endorsement of Caffentzis's extraordinary study (note 16).

There is a vast literature on the social institutions of early capitalism. I would cite only four here: Weber's *General Economic History* (note 37), Engels's *The Condition of the Working Class in England in 1844,*[72] E.P. Thompson's *The Making of the English Working Class* (note 38) and Neil Smelser's *Social Change in the Industrial Revolution* (note 49). On money and moral principle, the Parry and Bloch collection points to major differences between the West and the rest (note 44). The collection I edited deals quite fully with the sexual division of labor in the Caribbean (note 47); but see also Smith's seminal Guiana study (note 57). Nadel's West African ethnography, *A Black Byzantium,* is the best I know, for changing sex divisions and much else (note 62). William Goode's survey of world family patterns in the early 1960s is still worth reading, if only as a reminder of social science's complacency before the deluge (note 65). Sandy Robertson's review of contemporary institutions of social reproduction is as forward-looking as any (note 66).

Notes

1. M. Mauss, *The Gift: The Form and Reason for Exchange in Archaic Societies* (Routledge & Kegan Paul, London, 1990; first pub. as *Essai sur le Don,* 1925).

2. I had in mind to include the sort of graph that illustrates the intersecting curves of supply and demand in elementary economic textbooks. But then I realized that most of my readers will already have seen one; and those who haven't could find one easily, if they wished.

3. K. Polanyi, *The Great Transformation: The Political and Economic Origins of Our Times* (Beacon Books, Boston, 1944), Chapter 6.

4. C.B. Macpherson, ed., *Property: Mainstream and Critical Positions* (University of Toronto Press, Toronto, 1978).

5. See note 1.

6. A.R. Radcliffe-Brown, *Structure and Function in Primitive Societies* (Oxford University Press, London, 1952).

7. The Nobel Prize-winning economist, Sir John Hicks, has written a speculative account of economic evolution that addresses the issues raised here in a manner that is at once analytically insightful and cheerfully indifferent to historical detail. J. Hicks, *A Theory of Economic History* (Oxford University Press, London, 1969).

8. E. Durkheim, *The Division of Labour in Society* (Free Press, Glencoe, Ill., 1960; first pub. 1933).

9. J. Dunn, *Locke* (Oxford University Press, Oxford, 1984).

10. J. Locke, *Two Treatises of Government* (Cambridge University Press, Cambridge, 1960; first pub. 1690); *An Essay Concerning Human Understanding* (Clarendon Press, Oxford, 1975; first pub. 1700, fourth edition).

11. Locke was the first writer to stress the importance of toilet training! J. Locke, *Some Thoughts Concerning Education* (Clarendon Press, Oxford, 1989; first pub. 1695, third edition).

12. J. Locke, *Several Papers Relating to Money, Interest and Trade, etc.,Writ upon Several Occasions and Published at Different Times* (A. & J. Churchill, London, 1696), especially "Some Considerations of Lowering the Interest and of Raising the Value of Money" and "Further Considerations Concerning Raising the Value of Money"; see also note 14.

13. See note 9, op. cit., p. 1.

14. C.B. Macpherson, *The Political Theory of Possessive Individualism* (University of Toronto Press, Toronto, 1963).

15. J. Locke, *Two Treatises of Government* (see note 9), p. 306.

16. I am grateful to Simon Schaffer for having pointed me to G. Caffentzis, *Clipped Coins, Abused Words and Civil Government: John Locke's Philosophy of Money,* a work that has done more to shape the present book than any other. G. Caffentzis, *Clipped Coins, Abused Words and Civil Government: John Locke's Philosophy of Money* (Autonomedia, New York, 1989).

17. This was rather a project of the eighteenth and nineteenth centuries, culminating in classical political economy. L. Dumont, *From Mandeville to Marx: The Genesis and Triumph of Economic Ideology* (University of Chicago Press, Chicago, 1977).

18. J.D.Y. Peel, ed., *Herbert Spencer on Social Evolution* (University of Chicago Press, Chicago, 1972); R. Hofstadter, *Social Darwinism in American Thought* (Beacon, Boston, Mass., 1992).

19. See note 8.

20. Durkheim was one of four assassins identified by Parsons, the others being Alfred Marshall, Vilfredo Pareto and Max Weber. His purpose was to establish the rise of a subjectivist and morally accountable social science in the early twentieth century, with himself as the founder of the

American branch. T. Parsons, *The Structure of Social Action: A Study in Social Theory with Special Reference to a Group of Recent European Writers* (Free Press, Glencoe, Ill., 1937), p. 3.

21. From *sokw-yo,* o-grade form of the Indo-European root, *sekw-,* "to follow" (*American Heritage Dictionary,* third edition).

22. J.G. Frazer, *The Golden Bough: A Study in Magic and Religion* (Macmillan, London, 1923).

23. B. Malinowski, *Argonauts of the Western Pacific: An Account of Native Enterprise and Adventure in the Archipelagos of Melanesian New Guinea* (Dutton, New York, 1961; first pub. 1922).

24. H. Codere, *Fighting with Property: A Study of Kwakiutl Potlatching and Warfare 1792–1930* (J.J. Augustin, Seattle, 1950).

25. See note 1.

26. This idea is close to the notion of "fetishism" associated with Marx.

27. M. Sahlins, *Stone-age Economics* (Aldine, Chicago, 1972), p. 133.

28. A mini-industry in economic anthropology was sparked off by Chris Gregory's *Gifts and Commodities* (Academic Press, London, 1982). He set out there to show how both types of exchange were combined in the practices of contemporary Papua New Guinea. But his readers generally preferred to identify the gift economy with "primitive societies" such as those he referred to. Marilyn Strathern, in her classic *The Gender of the Gift* (University of California Press, California, 1988), postulates a radical contrast between gift and commodity that she associates with that between "The West" and "Melanesia." Gregory has tried, in *Savage Money* (Harwood, Amsterdam, 1997, Chapter 2), to restate his position that the logical conceptualization of gift and commodity was not intended as a basis for ethnographic classification. But this argument too will probably fall on deaf ears, since modern anthropologists, following Malinowski, have too much at stake in claiming to derive special knowledge from their exotic encounters.

29. In the Indo-European tradition it is as common to identify the participants in trade as to differentiate them into buyers and sellers. C.S. Buck, *Dictionary of Selected Synonyms in the Principal Indo-European Languages* (University of Chicago Press, Chicago, 1949), p. 817.

30. M. Mauss, *Ecrits Politiques* (M. Fournier, ed., Fayard, Paris, 1997).

31. K. Polanyi, *The Great Transformation: The Political and Economic Origins of Our Time* (Beacon Books, Boston, Mass., 1944).

32. The collection *Trade and Market in the Early Empires* launched post-war economic anthropology as a fratricidal conflict between those who aped the methods of neo-classical economics ("formalists") and those who followed Polanyi in studying the institutions of pre-modern economies

("substantivists"). More profoundly, for Polanyi himself it represented a retreat from the splendid iconoclasm of 1944 into an academic division of labor respecting the economics profession's monopoly in "market" economies. K. Polanyi, "The Economy as Instituted Process" in K. Polanyi, C. Arensberg and H. Pearson, eds, *Trade and Market in the Early Empires* (Free Press, Glencoe, Ill., 1957); E. Leclair and H. Schneider, eds, *Economic Anthropology* (Holt, Rhinehart & Winstone, New York, 1968); K. Hart, "Comment on Pearson's 'Home economics goes native.'" *History of Political Economy,* Winter 2000, 1017–1025.

33. P. Bohannan and G. Dalton, eds, *Markets in Africa* (Northwestern University Press, Evanston, Ill., 1962).

34. J. and P. Alexander, "What's a Fair Price: Price-setting and Trading Partnerships in Javanese Markets," *Man,* September 1991.

35. A. Bennett, *The Old Wives' Tale* (Penguin, London, 1986; first pub. 1908).

36. See note 18.

37. M. Weber, *General Economic History* (Transaction Books, New Brunswick, NJ, 1981), Part 4.

38. E.P. Thompson, *The Making of the English Working Class* (Penguin, Harmondsworth, 1968).

39. M. Weber, *Economy and Society. Volume 2* (2 vols., G. Roth and C. Wittich, eds, University of California Press, Berkeley, 1978), Chapter 16, "The City (Non-legitimate Domination)," pp. 1212–372.

40. M. Weber, *The Agrarian Sociology of Ancient Civilizations* (New Left Books, London, 1976; first pub. 1904).

41. In case you wondered, "work" is Germanic, "labor" is Latin and "employment" is French—they are broadly substitutable. The oldest English term appears to be "job." The different resonance of these terms is associated with the historical periods and social strata that introduced them to the language.

42. E. Miller and J. Hatcher, *Medieval England: Towns, Commerce and Crafts 1086–1348* (Longman, London, 1995).

43. J. Townsend, *A Dissertation on the Poor Laws (by a Well-wisher to Mankind)* (University of California Press, Berkeley, 1971; first pub. 1786).

44. J. Parry and M. Bloch, eds, *Money and the Morality of Exchange* (Cambridge University Press, Cambridge, 1989).

45. E. Durkheim, *The Elementary Forms of the Religious Life* (Free Press, Glencoe, Ill., 1965; first pub. 1912).

46. See note 37.

47. This section is a condensed version of my lead article, "The Sexual Division of Labor," in the volume I edited, *Women and the Sexual Division of Labour in the Caribbean* (Canoe Press, Mona, Kingston, Jamaica, 1996; first

pub. 1989). In what follows, references are kept to the minimum, but a much wider range of references may be found in that earlier work.

48. Alan Macfarlane stresses this point in *The Origins of English Individualism* (1978). He tends to abstract the individualism of medieval England from its feudal context; but London's size as a market did stimulate precocious commercial development in the surrounding counties. A. Macfarlane, *The Origins of English Individualism: The Family, Property and Social Transition* (Blackwell, Oxford, 1978).

49. N. Smelser, *Social Change in the Industrial Revolution: An Application of Theory to the Lancashire Cotton Industry 1770–1840* (Routledge & Kegan Paul, London, 1967).

50. L. Tilly and J. Scott, *Women, Work and Family* (Routledge & Kegan Paul, London, 1989).

51. U. Wikan, *Behind the Veil in Arabia: Women in Oman* (Johns Hopkins University Press, Baltimore, 1982).

52. K. Hart, "Commoditization and the Standard of Living" in A. Sen, ed., *The Standard of Living* (Cambridge University Press, Cambridge, 1987).

53. Most notably in his masterpiece, *The Black Jacobins* (1938), a history of the world's only successful slave revolution in what became Haiti. C.L.R. James, *The Black Jacobins: Toussaint L'Ouverture and the San Domingo Revolution* (Secker & Warburg, London, 1938); K. Hart, "Introduction" in *Women and the Sexual Division of Labour* (see note 43).

54. M. Cross and G. Heuman, *Labour in the Caribbean from Emancipation to Independence* (Macmillan, London, 1988).

55. B. Higman, *Writing West Indian Histories* (Macmillan, London, 1999).

56. A.F. Weber writes of a *Frauenüberschuss* (an excess of women, literally an overshoot) in central Europe. A similar phenomenon could be found in twentieth-century Latin America. The common factor is the absence of wage opportunities for working-class men in major cities, along with high demand for domestics. Most African cities during this century supported an excess of men, many of them in domestic service. A.F. Weber, *The Growth of Cities in the Nineteenth Century* (Cornell University Press, Ithaca, NY, 1965; first pub. 1899), pp. 276–80.

57. Raymond T. Smith, *The Negro Family in British Guiana: Family Structure and Social Status in the Villages* (Cambridge University Press, Cambridge, 1958).

58. Matrilineal kinship was an egalitarian political device blocking the accumulation of male power through the father–son relationship. In states like Ashanti, the army and central bureaucracy rested on such father–son ties, while the villages were organized through matrilineages. The West African mammy, stereotype of the fearless female trader, was mainly a feature of the coastal enclaves before the twentieth century.

59. C. Meillassoux, *Maidens, Meal and Money: Capitalism and the Domestic Community* (Cambridge University Press, Cambridge, 1981).

60. J. Gugler and W. Flanagan, *Urbanization and Social Change in West Africa* (Cambridge University Press, Cambridge, 1978).

61. K. Hart, *The Political Economy of West African Agriculture* (Cambridge University Press, Cambridge, 1982), pp. 142–5.

62. S.F. Nadel, *A Black Byzantium: The Kingdom of Nupe in Nigeria* (Oxford University Press, London, 1942).

63. The great discovery of modern social anthropology was the importance of these complex sources of identity and organization in traditional societies, many of them extensions of the patriarchal family. The same finding was stressed by nineteenth-century historians of economy and jurisprudence, such as Vinogradoff and Maitland.

64. E. Gellner, *Nations and Nationalism* (Blackwell, Oxford, 1983).

65. Mainly by Talcott Parsons and his following of functionalist sociologists. W. Goode, *World Revolution and Family Patterns* (Collier-Macmillan, London, 1968).

66. I have benefited over the years from conversations with Sandy Robertson, and his *Beyond the Family* (1991) contains a much fuller treatment of this topic. A.F. Robertson, *Beyond the Family: The Social Organization of Human Reproduction* (Polity Press, Cambridge, 1991).

67. See note 56, op. cit., p. 471.

68. I am grateful to Don Robotham for showing me an unpublished paper, "Globalization: A Pivotal Process for Health and Environment in the Developing and Developed World," on which I have drawn freely at this point.

69. M. Sahlins, *Stone-age Economics* (Aldine, Chicago, 1972).

70. See note 32.

71. C. Hann, ed., *Property Relations: Renewing the Anthropological Tradition* (Cambridge University Press, Cambridge, 1998).

72. F. Engels, *The Condition of the Working Class in England in 1844* (Lovell, New York, 1887).

Chapter 6
The Changing Character
of Money

Money is often portrayed as a lifeless object separated from persons, whereas it is in fact a creation of human beings, imbued with the collective spirit of the living and the dead. We often recognize this aspect of money by speaking of it as if it had a life of its own, animating our lives for better or worse, more often the latter. For some people, money is the root of all evil; for others it is the source of modern freedom. In both cases it makes the world go round. And this leads to the second point: Money is associated with movement in space, with change, with the exchange of objects travelling great distances, in other words, with the market; and it is itself in movement through time, and hence the history of money is an essential part of the history of society. We will be asking in this chapter "What is money?", but the answer will not be one static thing or idea, much as we would all like money to stand still and be counted.

The standard definitions do not capture the most important feature of money, its evolution as a means of human interaction in society. Money is *made* by us, but for most people it has long been something scarce that we *take* passively whenever possible, without any sense of its being our collective creation. From having been an object produced by remote authorities, it is becoming more obviously a subjective expression of our own will; and this development is mirrored in the shift from "real" to "virtual" money. In the last three hundred years or so, the money form has evolved from metallic coins through paper notes to electronic digits. In the process, money has become dematerialized, losing any shred of a claim that it is founded on the natural scarcity of precious metals. Even the authority of states, which stamped coinage and issued the notes with which we are still most familiar as money, cannot long survive the electronic blizzard that is money in the age of the Internet.

Money has *character,* in the sense of having durable qualities, especially moral and ethical, which distinguish a person, a group or a thing from another. This word comes to us from the ancient Mediterranean: It meant originally a pointed stick for inscribing marks in the ground, hence a sign in a writing system, also a branding iron for cattle, a stamp for coins, an imprint on the soul and, in computing today, one of a set of symbols conveying information.[1] The idea of money as a vehicle for the transmission of information may seem new, but it is as old as the institution itself. Nor is the idea new to anthropology. Thus Malinowski says, of Trobriand *kula* valuables, "*Currency* as a rule means a medium of exchange and standard of value, and none of the Massim valuables fulfil these functions."[2] But Mauss replies, "On this reasoning . . . there has only been money when precious things . . . have been really made into currency—namely have been inscribed and impersonalized, and detached from any relationship with any legal entity, whether collective or individual, other than the state that mints them . . . One only defines in this way a second type of money—our own." He prefers to stress the purchasing power of primitive valuables like those used in the *kula* and argues that they are like money in that they "have purchasing power, and this power has a figure set on it."[3]

If the value of money does not lie in precious metals or in the power of governments, where does it lie? We will conclude, after the following investigation, that money is mainly, but not exclusively, an act of remembering, a way of keeping track of some of the exchanges we each enter into with the rest of humanity. And that is what makes money an instrument of collective memory. British conservatives who feel that the replacement of the pound sterling by the euro involves the loss of an important part of their cultural heritage have a point, even if it is a narrow one in a world that increasingly uses English as its common language. Once freed of a spurious claim to objectivity, money is revealed as a creature of our shared collective life, as necessary to it as language. Moreover, interpreted in a certain way, its history points to the possibility of economic democracy.

Contrary to the widespread belief that there is only one Western doctrine of money, economists have generated many theories on the subject.[4] For, while markets using money prices are perhaps the single most striking feature of contemporary life, this is the historical outcome of different institutional pressures and supports as many varieties of interpretation. Broadly speaking, these may be grouped into two classes, of which the first is by far the most common. In this *commodity* theory, money is a useful thing like a lump of coal and its price is the outcome of market evaluation. The second class may be subdivided into three types of theory that locate the value of money as a *token* of society—in the *state,* the *nation* and the *community,* respectively—placing variable emphasis on inequality and equality in social life (on vertical and horizontal relations between members). In this second group of theories, money is seen as a symbol of something intangible (society), rather than as a thing with an objective value. The community theory, the most informal and egalitarian of the three, with its emphasis on trust between people, leads directly to the idea that money is a kind of *personal credit,* generated by each of us in our social interactions. This in turn opens up an alternative to all standard theories of money as an impersonal object.

Ideas normally lag behind the movement of society; and this chapter begins with a brief history of concrete changes in the money form. Money today is more plural and dynamic than at any time previously. Banknotes and coins have become equally worthless in terms of the costs of their production; and private instruments of credit are multiplying. A short period when nation-states sought to manage their currencies in the public interest is rapidly giving way, under pressure from the international economy, to a phase where money markets, offshore banking and electronic payment systems have sharply reduced the autonomy of national governments. It may be premature to see the communications revolution as a stimulus to the middle-class tax revolt. But it is clear that the certainties of mid-twentieth century are being undermined at its close. Unprecedented developments are unfolding under our noses, so that an empirical approach to contemporary economic history is a salutary antidote to the welter of speculation that is the main subject-matter of this chapter.

The history of the money form

J.S.G. Boggs is an American artist who, since the mid-1980s, has been drawing pictures of money, of paper notes in the world's standard currencies.[5] He tries to exchange these pictures for goods and services; and in this he has been successful, having sold around a million dollars' worth so far. He once paid for an expensive meal in a London Chinese restaurant by drawing for the owners a non-existent £500 note; they gave him his change in normal cash. A collectors' market has arisen for his money pictures, and their prices have inflated considerably over time. His work is exhibited in museums. He also sells his signature for $100; and there is a trade in these too. As with Picasso, people don't cash his checks and sometimes sell them on at a substantial mark-up. The engraver of the heads on dollar bills has done a head of Boggs in the same style. The artist has reproduced this on a limited edition of $100,000 bills that he hopes to sell at face value to pay for most of his legal costs.

For he has, of course, been hounded by the authorities as a counterfeiter, even though his drawings could never be confused with the "real thing." At London's Old Bailey court in 1987 he was accused of "reproducing" sterling banknotes. His successful defense was that the banknotes were reproductions; his drawings were unique. In Australia he was acquitted on charges brought by the currency police and awarded A$20,000 in damages. Juries like Boggs and, in his home country, the United States, the Secret Service has waged a long campaign of legal harassment without going so far as to initiate a jury trial. His alleged crime is "uttering images in the similitude" of actual American currency. The Secret Service did manage to stop his plan to flood Pittsburgh with a million dollars in the form of photocopies of Boggs bills, by threatening all concerned with the direst consequences. In 1992 they seized the contents of his studio; and this led Boggs to engage in a series of appeals and civil suits that have so far cost him $800,000, without benefit of either a favorable ruling or a criminal prosecution that would require a jury trial. He cannot get his property back because the government has argued successfully that his drawings are contraband, like hard-core drugs, whose owner cannot demand them back, even if he is not prosecuted.

Boggs is funny, so what is the joke? And why are the authorities so worried about Boggs that the U.S. Secret Service will spend millions of taxpayers' dollars trying to disrupt his enterprise? Today's money, the measure of the value of everything, is intrinsically worthless. Not just that, value itself is so capricious that it can be whatever people will pay for something that catches their fancy. Money and art, especially when exchanged for each other, rest on values that are insubstantial or only as substantial as the shifting desires of the people who exchange them. Money, like art, is subjective.

Paper money is the successor of an earlier attempt to persuade people that money was worth what it claimed to be because of its precious metal content. This drive to establish the objective value of money foundered on a crime wave triggered by the English revolution or perhaps just by modernity. Counterfeiters, coin clippers, bullion smugglers and foreign imitators[6] contrived to make the actual metal content of coinage so unreliable that, eventually, Pitt's government, in the middle of an expensive war against Napoleon, decided to issue stylish, but almost costless, paper money (the famous black and white £5 note, or "fiver") backed only by its own power to enforce payment. This step away from the "real" to the "virtual" required the support of heavy-handed propaganda asserting that the paper money's value was immutable, even though, as we all know now, its objective purchasing power is not. The U.S. federal government is pursuing Boggs because, for them, his drawings are no laughing matter. Why, people might end up thinking that the mighty dollar was just a picture on a piece of paper and that a maverick artist was the government's equal. Worse, they might come to realize that money is a figment of their own collective imagination and not an object after all.

So what is money? All the textbooks give the same definitions: It is a means of payment; a unit of account; a standard of value; a store of wealth.[7] Above all, it oils the wheels of exchange by giving buyers something that any seller will accept in return for their goods or services. Dictionaries are even more limited, concentrating on the money form itself, which they usually refer to as "currency," whatever is in circulation: coins, banknotes and other instruments issued by governments. But then what about personal checks and savings accounts, private notes of bank credit and, more recently, plastic cards of all kinds linking us into electronic networks that greatly increase our spending options? The money form is not standing still, and that makes it even more imperative to probe beneath surface appearances and ask what the source of money's value is and what we can make it do for us.

To understand the significance of paper money, which has lasted roughly as long as the age of mechanization, we need to look at what came before it and is coming afterwards. For paper money looks back to coinage (state-money) and forward to electronic networks of personal credit (people-money). Its invention came from a combination of state-money and bank-money.[8] Alongside the circulation of the stuff minted by states, there has always been a market for written contracts specifying debts incurred between private persons. And it may be that the temporary convergence of these two circuits in the era of the nation-state is breaking down now. The issue of the money-form is a convenient way of expressing deeper anxieties about the risks involved in relying on markets. People want their market contracts to be secure and this crucially involves the stability of money's value over time. For we have seen in Chapter 5 that the exchange of goods for money in a single instant conceals the projection of contracts through time. The argument about what form money should take has often been about how to maintain the value of the standard, usually against its deterioration.

It follows from this that the citizens of societies based on markets would be seriously disturbed by rapid and unpredictable changes in the value of money. And such appears to be the case. The conservative governments of the 1980s and their center-left successors today have been universally committed to "sound" money, by which they mean low rates of inflation. This follows a period in mid-century, from the 1930s to the seventies, when ruling orthodoxy, inspired by the theories of Maynard Keynes, acknowledged the responsibility of states to stimulate their economies.[9] The method used was to issue more money than was warranted by existing levels of production. Nixon's statement, just before his downfall, that "We are all Keynesians now" expressed the idea that national government was inevitably the chief instrument of economic management.

Unfortunately, shortly afterwards, inflation rates of over 20% became normal in the leading Western economies. This may not seem very much by the standards of the German inflation of the 1920s or of Brazil not long ago, but the experience of finding prices in the supermarkets adjusted upwards by 2% every month was definitely unsettling. Businessmen do not like inflation because it makes it more difficult to calculate profits or perhaps because it symbolizes the ascendancy of the politicians. Ordinary people just get frightened when the value of money itself is unstable. Accordingly, around 1980, neo-liberal conservatives (Reagan, Thatcher, Kohl) were established in office throughout the Western world: Their creed was "monetarism," a rejection of state-made money and a return to the commodity theory that underpinned Victorian civilization (you are only allowed to spend the cash you have in hand).

In a remarkable article, Keynes once asked: Who gains and who loses from inflation or its opposite?[10] People who hold money in the form of savings or loan credit lose out from inflation, since it means literally the depreciation of their money. And this constituency includes not only bankers as a class, but also pensioners living off fixed annuities. The big winners from inflation, of course, are debtors and those holding real assets whose price appreciates faster than the cost of living. British middle-class home owners with mortgages once fell into this category. It is not obvious which side most capitalists would come down on, especially when demand for their products is stimulated by inflation. The deflationary lobby can count on an irrational fear of unstable money, but the general interest in this century has more often been met by governments pursuing mildly inflationary policies. Even so, Keynes concludes that any change in the standard rewards some and punishes others unfairly; and this is the best argument for sound money. But how to arrive at this utopia?

Keynes waged an unremitting campaign against the policy of the day to fix the value of money to an objective standard, gold. This had the consequence, especially after the slump of 1929–32, of engineering a ruinous deflation. Keynes could be said to have killed off the gold standard, Victorian civilization's legacy to the troubled decades that inaugurated our own century. This was itself a revival, after the experiment in free-floating paper of the first half of the nineteenth century, of British commitment to a metallic standard linking the pound sterling to an international economy of which it was both guarantor and principal beneficiary. And, to understand where that came from, we need to know more about "the father of the gold standard," John Locke, and his activities in the 1690s, when Britain was engaged in another French war, this one for religious ascendancy in Europe.[11]

The commodity theory of money has been labelled "metallism," for the simple reason that, if a currency was to be a reliable medium of exchange, it was thought that its value should be based on the metals it cost to produce the coinage, precious metals like gold and silver. Locke wrote a number of pamphlets on money in the period 1690–96, the same years in which his

major philosophical works were published.[12] The combination of war inflation (William III inaugurated the national debt in 1693) and the deterioration of the currency triggered a monetary crisis that threatened to
undermine the new regime. Everyone agreed that the old currency had to
be brought in and a new one issued ("recoinage"). But there were two opposed camps on how that should be done. One, associated with Lowndes
and Barbon, held in the latter's words to a proto-Keynesian position, "The
more every man earns, the more he consumes and the King's revenue is the
more increased,"[13] whereas Locke held that "civil government has its origin
and end in the regulation of money."[14] The crippled condition of the coinage
meant that money was outside state control and a way for the criminal
classes to undermine the state.

The two sides were also opposed in terms of the weight they gave to the
national and the international economy respectively. Here was what each
proposed:

Lowndes: *Remint the same number of coins with a reduced silver content*
(devaluation).

Locke: *Return fewer coins with the same weight and silver content as the*
currency was supposed to have but no longer did (revaluation).

His opponents accused Locke of favoring Portuguese wine merchants
(who would use a reliable international currency) over the national interest,
since, they claimed, his own quantity theory of money predicts that a reduced
money supply would cause prices and therefore employment to fall. To which
he replied that the business of business is making money, not giving pleasure;
people who put up with fraud are fools, but governments who endorse it undermine themselves; the world economy was the prime source of accumulation; and something had to be done to check the rise of the criminal economy.
For all these, and perhaps other reasons, Locke won the day.

Locke was trying to build an infrastructure for the eighteenth century,
and his monetary policies were just part, but a very significant part, of his
overall concern that the state should exercise the power and will to establish
standards. He wanted the state to secure the currency, but not to take it over

as an instrument of its own policy. He thought that adhering to an immutable metallic standard would ensure both these ends; and he helped recruit Isaac Newton to be Master of the Mint, where his scientific credentials could be brought to bear on maintaining the highest possible standards of coin production. Between them the two greatest English intellectuals of all time devoted their efforts to making the pound sterling the byword for reliability that it subsequently became.

As it happened, Locke succeeded in the aim of promoting sterling as an international currency, but he failed in his attempt to convince ordinary coin users that they were getting value for money. For, as long as value was based on the measurement of metal content, there were still many ways of illegally altering that measure (clipping, counterfeit, and so on). Moreover, the price of gold and silver was itself subject to fluctuations of market supply and demand. In consequence, a century later, the British government, following several Scottish precedents, decided to take the step of *counting* money rather than *measuring* it, going for a purely nominal approach, the £5 note. They hoped to persuade the public that the power of government was a better guarantee of stability than variable metal content. And with this, one of the great steps in the history of digitalization, they succeeded—for a time. Within half a century the pendulum had swung back and the Victorians rediscovered the virtues of the gold standard, a measure that, as Keynes pointed out acerbically, only lasted as long as it did because supplies from the South African mines were able to match the expansion of the world economy. Whether we have reached a stage when we can break out from this ruinous alternation between metal and paper, markets and states, remains to be seen in the sections that follow.

Ours is a time of unprecedented change in the form and organization of money. Most of us have access to six kinds: coins, banknotes, checks, savings accounts and a variety of plastic credit and debit cards. The relative significance of all of these is constantly shifting. Money is an index of our relations with society; it measures, to an important degree, the viability of our social connections. Becoming unemployed, for example, is a personal disaster from many perspectives, such as disposable income, public recognition, the opportunity to practise a skill, and much else; but the loss of a regular source of money is its most tangible manifestation. When the very techniques of paying and receiving money are in flux and each of us is continuously forced to learn a new monetary repertoire, more is at stake than just earning a living. We have to redefine our whole relationship to society almost on a daily basis.

An outline history of the money form may be summarized briefly for our present purposes. The traditional money form, known as "specie" (coins containing precious metals equivalent to their nominal value), now survives only in a specialist hoarders' market for gold coins. For two and a half thousand years the only alternative to specie was the note of credit, which took the precise form of bills of exchange in Europe about six hundred years ago. Coins were first mass-produced in Britain around 1800. At much the same time, national paper money emerged as a widespread substitute for both specie and promissory notes issued by private banks. Base metal coinage was introduced after the Second World War, so that both paper and metal versions of the national currency now became equally worthless, being distinguished largely by function rather than by cost of production. In the meantime, private individuals have continued to issue checks against their bank accounts; and this source of liquidity has been augmented recently by the issue of plastic credit and debit cards. These are the forerunners of electronic payment systems whose use has been boosted enormously by the convergence of telephones, television and computers in the 1990s (smart cards, e-money, banking by phone, etc.).

From the mid-nineteenth century, credit was based on the convertibility of money to gold. As we have seen, the gold standard broke down between the two world wars. It was replaced just over fifty years ago by the agreement known as Bretton Woods. This was a system of state-guaranteed money with fixed exchange rates tied to the main reserve currencies, especially the American dollar. In other words, international trade rested on confidence in the world's strongest economy, the United States. Bretton Woods broke down in the early 1970s as a result of the convulsions in world commodity markets and associated shocks to national finances brought about by the first OPEC oil price increase. This led to a hesitant acceptance of a free market in money, a process that was accelerated by the development of markets dealing in money futures. These were invented in Chicago in 1975, partly on the initiative of the liberal economist, Milton Friedman, who wanted to teach governments the lesson that "they could not buck the markets." Before long speculative buying and selling of currencies became the leading activity of international traders, a category that now embraces central-bank governors, the treasurers of multinational companies and pension-fund managers.

In this way, national governments have become subject to international financial pressures that make it less plausible than ever for them to pursue economic policies that do not meet the approval of the money markets. The eviction of several currencies, including the pound sterling, from the European monetary system on "Black Wednesday" in September 1993 provides the most dramatic evidence so far that individual speculators commanding the resources of a George Soros can bet against the declared policy of a nation-state and win.[15] Most governments (with some notable exceptions such as China and France) have got the message by now. The markets deal in such vast quantities of money every day (most of it exchanging money in one form for another) that the finances of individual states are too puny to make much of a difference.

Nor is money standing still on the home front. The virtue of traditional money forms—coinage and later banknotes—was that they could be spent anonymously in a wide variety of commodity transactions. Since their value was apparently objective, there was no need to introduce questions concerning an individual's creditworthiness. Moreover, governments levied the bulk of their internal revenues on transactions involving this kind of money. But all of this is being undermined by developments in electronic communications. It is now easier to evade state control at all levels of the economy, and money has become less anonymous, more attached to persons. The communications revolution offers the best chance to escape from state-made money since medieval merchants substituted private bills of exchange for coin of the realm as the preferred instrument of long-distance trade.

To sum up, the state monopoly of money has, in the late twentieth century, been subjected to pressure from above and below. Globalization of markets, including markets for financial instruments of growing complexity ("derivatives" and the like), has eroded the power exercised by governments over their national economies. In addition, internal devolution of state control over finance has been made inevitable by what are essentially decentralized instruments of credit. So, in a world that has seen national currencies become the plaything of increasingly erratic market speculation, we must look elsewhere for the source of money's value. What about the banks? What supports their claim to keep our money safe?

The real reserves of wealth supporting a bank's promise to pay are normally very small and, in the case of national banks, mostly illusory. A modicum of order was imposed on a country's residents until recently by regulation of the institutions, such as banks, using the national currency, for example, by insistence on the maintenance of minimum deposits. The last quarter-century, however, has seen the flowering of what was at first called eurodollar banking.[16] After the Second World War, the Russians and Chinese, fearing seizure of their New York dollar assets, transferred the money to London and Paris. The financial crisis of the early 1970s led to a more widespread use of this procedure, with London emerging as the main banking center for non-residents wanting to hold dollars outside the USA.

Offshore banking can afford to offer interest rates on average 1% higher than those banks that are subject to national regulation, because of the reduced costs entailed in avoiding the necessity for deposits. What, then, is the basis of the eurodollar banks' credit? Not gold or state power, to be sure. Their credit is based on the probability that they will recover outstanding loans. Default on any major loan would call into question the creditworthiness of all the offshore banks, which are often subsidiaries of the main domestic banks. The banks hedge against such a contingency by spreading each loan between a large number of them, so that the risk of any of them being declared bankrupt in isolation is reduced. They also make it known that they would seize the trade goods of any country involved in a major default. But this nightmare scenario could trigger a run on the bank that would make the financial failures of the Great Depression years look trivial in comparison. No wonder, then, that the high Third World debts incurred in the 1980s were endlessly rescheduled and, after two decades of outrageous interest payments, may now be graciously reduced. Neither side can afford a confrontation, although large countries like Brazil have contemplated it from time to time.

This brief attempt to introduce a measure of historical realism to the discussion of money should be enough to show that the pursuit of its objective foundation is illusory. Money is a measure of social interaction, no more, no less. We make it up, although most people prefer to think of it as already made. Above all, the consequences of examining what money really is are so shocking (because more metaphysical than physical) that the world prefers, for the most part, not to think about it. And the struggle for supremacy between states and markets is still very much with us.

Heads or tails? Two sides of the coin[17]

In a century that has seen three world wars fought over the form of state best suited to human economic progress, which is more important in determining the value of money—the state or the market? There are at least four contending answers to this question: States and markets may be seen as inherently opposed and in conflict (the Cold War); states and markets may be seen as being complementary, with one or the other definitely in the driving seat (mainstream socialism and liberalism respectively); or the state and the market may be seen as equally indispensable and forming a dialectical unity (German and Japanese nationalism, for example). The symbolism of the two sides of the coin (heads or tails?) provides a point of entry for an inquiry into the relationship between politics and exchange as the principal source of money's value. What therefore is the relationship between coins in particular and money in general?

Maynard Keynes did not think so much of coins, since they epitomized an outmoded adherence to objective money. In the brief history with which he launches his *A Treatise on Money,*[18] he dismisses the achievement of the kings of Lydia in allegedly first striking coins around 700 BC as follows:

> *. . . it may have been as a convenient certificate of fineness and weight, or a mere act of ostentation appropriate to the offspring of Croesus and the neighbors of Midas. The stamping of pieces of metal with a trade-mark was just a piece of local vanity, patriotism or advertisement with no far-reaching importance. It is a practice that never caught on in some important commercial areas . . . (for example, the Egyptians, the Carthaginians and the Chinese) . . . The Semitic races, whose instincts are keenest for the essential qualities of Money, have never paid much attention to the deceptive signatures of Mints, which content the financial amateurs of the North, and have cared only for the touch and weight of the metal. It*

was not necessary, therefore, that talents or shekels should be minted; it was sufficient that these units should be State-created in the sense that it was the State which defined . . . what weight and fineness of silver would, in the eyes of the law, satisfy a debt or a customary payment expressed in talents or in shekels of silver.[19]

Keynes held that modern money was as old as the invention of cities and, with them, the State (which he always capitalized), that is to say, as old as agrarian civilization:

The State, therefore, comes in first of all as the authority of law which enforces the payment of the thing which corresponds to the name or description in the contract . . . in addition, it claims the right to determine and declare what thing *corresponds to the name, and to vary its declaration from time to time—when, that is to say, it claims the right to re-edit the dictionary. This right is claimed by all modern States and has been so claimed for some four thousand years at least. It is when this stage in the evolution of money has been reached that Knapp's Chartalism—the doctrine that money is peculiarly a creation of the State—is fully realized. Thus the Age of Money has succeeded the Age of Barter . . .*[20]

The right to re-edit the dictionary! Keynes, a master of the art of writing who knew more about money than anyone in his day, was intimately aware of their connection as means of communication. He also knew of the state's jealous monopoly of the currency used by its citizens, the same monopoly that is called into question by the developments of our day. Language and money are both intrinsic to a society's collective memory or culture. But Keynes's aim in downgrading the significance of coinage was to establish that, as a social creation, money did not have to wait until coins were struck; and it is this aspect of *making money,* rather than *finding* it in the form of natural objects, that he wanted to stress. Money is a thing, but it also has to be named, and it is the act of naming that is more truly creative and social than manufacturing *per se.*

Figure 6.1 lays out Keynes's definitions of money.[21] These constitute at once a contemporary classification of what is in current circulation and an

Figure 6.1   Keynes's classification of money

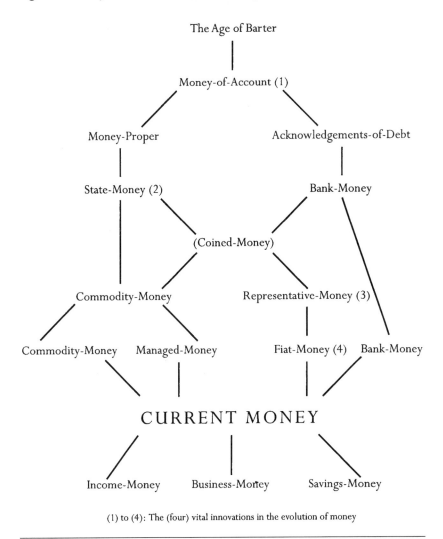

(1) to (4): The (four) vital innovations in the evolution of money

evolutionary scheme emphasizing the gradual replacement of an objective standard of value (commodity-money) with symbols of no intrinsic value (token or representative money). This evolution from substance to function, as Simmel puts it,[22] depends on distinguishing the way in which debts, prices or purchasing power are *expressed* ("money-of-account") from what is actually *discharged* or *held* ("money-proper")—the first being the title or description and the second the thing that answers to the description. The interest of the distinction lies in the possibility that the second may change while the first stays the same. The evolution of money as a convenient means of exchange on the spot, stressed by precursors such as Smith and Marx, seemed to Keynes less important than the emergence of a money standard named by law (the state) or custom (the community).

Money in the above sense, he believed, "like other essential elements of civilization, is a far more ancient institution than we were taught to believe some few years ago. Its origins are lost in the mists when the ice was melting, and may well stretch back into the paradisaic intervals in human history of the interglacial periods . . ." [23] But the first major step toward modern money was the state's exercise of its "chartalist" prerogative to establish a standard and to declare what answers to the money-of-account. [24] For almost as long as money-proper has existed, says Keynes, it has been recognized that private debts can just as well be used in the settlement of transactions expressed through the money-of-account; and he calls these acknowledgements of debt "bank-money."

The next stage consists in the convergence of state-money and bank-money as representative- (or, in my term, "token") money, such as occurs when a debt of the state is accepted in exchange for legal tender. This partial rupture with the principle of commodity-money, namely that its value is no longer wholly tied to an objective standard, leads to the last stage in Keynes's scheme, the invention of "fiat-money," such as paper currency, [25] whose value in terms of scarcity or cost of production is intrinsically worthless. In practice most of the currencies of his day took a hybrid form between commodity- and fiat-money; and they still do. He named this hybrid "managed-money," when a government seeks to maintain a relationship of its currency to an objective standard, while having a value that is intrinsically artificial. This can be confusing: "The public knows Commodity-Money and it knows Fiat-Money; but, readier to recognize the Standard than the Form, it is apt to consider a Managed-Money which has a familiar commodity as its standard as the same thing as a Commodity-Money, and a Managed-Money with an unfamiliar commodity as its standard as a Fiat-Money in disguise." [26] A familiar commodity might be gold, with the state holding far less than

100% equivalent in reserves, whereas an unfamiliar one might be the exchange rate of a powerful currency like the American dollar.

So token money begins when a currency is no longer composed wholly of its objective standard; it becomes fiat-money when the state abandons the objective standard altogether. Keynes admits that coinage may be a step on the road to token money, in that the state that has the minting monopoly may give coins a value higher than their objective precious metal content; but that is not essential to state-made money, which, as we have seen, predates coinage considerably. The Romans, he claims, pioneered debasement of the currency as a way of paying for wars; and subsequent debasements became common without constituting a break with commodity-money as such. Token money was rather an invention of modern banking, even though its origins in the settlement of private debts at distance was much older. The Scots took the lead in issuing banknotes in the eighteenth century, preferring to avoid the risks of transporting money-proper.[27] The invention of paper money followed closely. Although the Chinese are said to have used paper money long ago and John Law bankrupted Louis xv's France with his precocious experiments in paper instruments,[28] Keynes prefers to credit the French revolution and subsequent wars with responsibility for the move to paper money on the part of the two leading powers of the day, England and France.

Both countries subsequently reverted to managed currencies, for a while embracing at least the appearance of commodity-money in the form of the gold standard. Along the way, that supreme instrument of modern public finance, the bank rate, was invented, allowing states to regulate a vastly expanded sphere of private banking while retaining nominal control over the money-of-account.[29] Managed-money alone has a relationship to the other three principal forms current today, uniting within itself commodity and token, substance and function, the real and the virtual. This suggests an interdependence between the opposed principles and types of money that we can perhaps approach more easily through the symbolism of the money-form Keynes affected to disparage, coins.

Take a look at a coin from your pocket or purse. It has two sides. One side contains a symbol of political authority, most commonly the head of someone who is or was the head of government, hence *heads*.[30] The other side crucially contains the information about what it is worth, its quantitative value in exchange for other commodities. Rather less obviously, this is called *tails*. This example of money therefore has at least two aspects that are related to each other as top to bottom. One emphasizes that it is issued by society in the form of the state, here symbolized by a person; it is a *token* of relations between people. The other stresses that money is itself a *commodity*, lending precision to trade in an infinite range of commodities; it is a real thing with an objective existence that is independent of the persons who use it.

There is an obvious tension between the two sides of the coin that goes far deeper than appearances may suggest. For Victorian civilization made a concerted effort to base its market economy on money as a commodity, gold, whose value was allegedly immune to interference by states or any other social agencies. In our century, very much under Keynes's influence, political management of money became for a time normal and then again anathema. Now there is talk once more of the markets reigning supreme and of states losing control over national currencies in a process of globalization. At stake here is the project, repeatedly espoused by bankers and businessmen, of trying to liberate market economy from the political institutions that give expression to people's general social interest. Yet the evidence of our coinage is that states and markets are or *were* each indispensable to money; and some nations have long recognized the value of treating the two sides as symbiotic.

Most anthropologists, contrasting their own society with others they claim to know professionally, speak of "the West" or "Euroamerica" as if its economic culture were monolithic, being based on market logic alone. In this timeless version of the modern world, nothing has changed since the Victorians tried to impose the gold standard on the rest of humanity. Which is a pity—for it is precisely in the diversity of monetary theories and the historical conflicts they represent that the possibility of finding new ways forward lies. What states and markets share, despite the personal symbolism of heads, is a commitment to founding the economy on impersonal money. If you drop the coin and someone else picks it up, they can do exactly the same as you with it, whatever they like. This absence of personal information from the money itself is what recommends cash to people who prefer their transactions to be illegal: It conserves their anonymity. Yet, as I will argue, a more effective route to economic democracy lies through people participating in exchange as themselves, not just as the anonymous bearers of cash; and for such a move we need to examine the antecedents in monetary theory and history.

The commodity theory of money has been labelled *metallism,* as we have seen, for the reason (illusory as it turned out) that a reliable medium of exchange should be based on the precious metals it cost to produce the coinage. This ancient practice was elevated to the level of economic theory when the British argued in the 1850s for an international standard linking national currencies to the price of gold. But adherence to the gold standard made it impossible for governments to protect their citizens from wide fluctuations in markets. It did not escape notice that unemployment could be reduced and public misery alleviated, if governments spent money they did not strictly possess (i.e., by printing more of it). Indeed, the Wall Street crash of 1929 and the subsequent economic slump forced the British to abandon the gold standard in the early 1930s.

The voices of the anti-metallists (or *chartalists,* advocates of money as something issued by states) grew in strength as the twentieth-century crisis deepened. Their position was summed up long ago by Nicholas Barbon, Locke's antagonist, who said, "Money is a value made by law."[31] The most systematic challenge to the orthodox theory of money as an expression of market logic came from Germany. Adam Müller was the author of a fully fledged romantic approach, *A New Theory of Money,* in 1816. Müller negated everything British political economy stood for—free trade, specialization, international division of labor, etc.—in favor of national economic self-sufficiency, the virtues of working the land and maintaining the cultural integrity of a people. Money for him derived its value from the trust generated within a community and was more specifically an expression of national will.[32]

German monetary theory culminated in the publication of Knapp's *State Theory of Money.*[33] He set out to put flesh on Barbon's dictum, believing that money was a standard of credit issued by the state and that the latter's freedom in monetary policy should not be restricted by an international system anchored in the eternal exchangeability of gold. In this Knapp was building on a long-running "battle over methods" (*Methodenstreit*) that had pitted a historical approach against the timeless generalizations of marginalist economics.[34]

But it was not just a matter of English economism versus German romanticism. Writers from several countries, including England, felt that there was a moral dimension to money that went beyond the formalism of both market and state theories. For Victorian liberals like Bagehot,[35] the need for trust, credit, banking, "the Englishman's word," all of this defined money as an aspect of relations between persons, not as a thing, mere cash.

There were thus three types of theory opposed to the classical orthodoxy that regarded money solely as a *commodity* subject to the laws of competitive markets. These were all *token* theories that insist that money is a symbol of something intangible, an aspect of human agency, not just a thing. Money as the outcome of *state* policy emphasizes the role of law and government intervention; society in this version is composed of vertical relations between unequals, rulers and ruled, like the top and bottom of the two sides of the coin, heads and tails. A populist theory of money like Müller's stresses the framework for money constituted by the accumulated customs of a *nation* or people (*Volk*); while to conceive of money as an expression of trust locates value in the morality of civil society, evoking the notion of a *community* of equals to complement the selfishness of markets; its essence is the management of credit and debt in human relations.[36] Nationalism lies between the vertical and horizontal models of society contained in the other two, since it combines the formality of the state with the informal substance of community.

At the core of these opposed theories lies a contrast between the imaginary and the real. If only money could be tied to an object, a grain of gold for every dollar, we could all rest assured that our money is "real," a thing like the other objects we can touch. But what determines the price of gold? The answer lies in intangibles like how much some people desire it in relation to how much of it others choose to put in circulation rather than hoard it. An old conundrum asks why diamonds are more valuable than air, since we can live without them and not without the latter. We know now that diamonds maintain their price as a result of a complex international conspiracy organized by the South African firm, De Beers, in an uneasy alliance with the Russian government and rebel forces in Angola. And that is not to forget the subliminal effects of all that advertising reminding us that a diamond is a permanent guarantee of love.

The idea of money as merely a commodity depends above all for its credibility on a spurious realism. All the other theories of money acknowledge that the value of anything is inevitably symbolic. Society is something unknowably vast. Even the social networks that each of us enters reach a level of complexity that we could never document objectively. So we rely on symbols—words, ideas and things that stand for what we would like to convey. A red rose symbolizes the unfathomable depths of my love for you . . . Banks would not have to occupy impressive buildings if they contained the real resources adequate to meet their financial obligations. As we are constantly being told by the representatives of capitalism, it is confidence that rules the markets and that can be lost for the most imaginary (or perhaps, imaginative) reasons. We have only recently discovered the idea of "virtual reality," but in the world of money we have been living with nothing else for a long time.

In the nineteenth century, the world market consisted largely of things ripped out of the ground as raw materials for industrial manufacturing and mass consumption in the West. Hence "commodities" were (and still are in the financial sections of newspapers) things like tin, copper, wheat, cotton and coffee. The flow in the opposite direction consisted mainly of clothing and household utensils. Services were largely personal and restricted to local social interaction (haircutting, for example). Today, in a country like Britain, more than 4 out of 5 jobs are in services (increasingly information services), only 1 in 50 is in agriculture, and the rest work in industry.[37] Moreover, improvements in telecommunications allow a rapidly rising proportion of these services to be performed at long distance. This is to say that the human economy is now more concerned with what people do for each other than with the production and circulation of physical objects. And one measure of the poverty of Africa and South Asia is that so many people there still produce things for a living in a world market that for them remains obstinately tied to the conditions of the nineteenth century. For those regions that participate fully in the communications revolution, exchange is becoming both more personal and more abstract at the same time. The idea of money's value being objectively real is ever more untenable under these circumstances.

Theory is always likely to lag behind common experience, especially when its function is to uphold the powers-that-be. Maynard Keynes struggled against the cultural legacy of his Victorian parents to persuade policy-makers that the popular interest would better be served if they put more money into society (through demand inflation) and took less of it out (as savings). He tried to explain that there were not just two types of money, one based on a market for precious objects and the other paper notes made out of thin air, but rather that modern money must be the *managed* outcome of the interplay between states and markets. Because he gave some agency to the former, he was later represented by market fundamentalists as an advo-cate of fiat-money, of "*Monopoly* money."[38] We have seen that he was not, even though he believed that he was operating well within the Age of Money as defined by states. And so he was: The inter-war period was the heyday of the corporate state, if any time in recent history was. But he wrote, there-fore, as a spokesman for a controlling elite. In the age of electronic money, other possibilities than the hierarchy of heads and tails present themselves. For each of us money management must become a personal responsibility, with money assuming forms as diverse as the associations in which we each participate. In this respect, money could increasingly resemble language, as spoken by a diverse, cosmopolitan people.

In truth, the pursuit of objective certainty in the monetary sphere has wrecked many a modern economy, just as the stabilization programs of the World Bank and International Monetary Fund ("structural adjustment") have brought many Third World economies to their knees today. The interest of increasing international flows of commodities and money is impaired if indi-vidual states give priority in their financial affairs to internal political consid-erations. When impoverishment and chronic indebtedness drive these governments to the international agencies ("undertakers" might be a more ap-propriate expression than "bankers"), the price they pay to be bailed out of bankruptcy is to "stabilize" the currency by bringing spending in line with what they can afford. The medicine is more or less the same as that adminis-tered to any individual debtor or loss-making firm, despite the fact that the livelihood of millions hangs on the outcome, which is invariably very painful.

This practice was inaugurated at the expense of Austria after its defeat and loss of empire in the First World War.[39] Brutally stringent fiscal policies were introduced on the advice of an international team, unemployment mounted and eventually Hitler walked in. As someone said at the time, "The operation was successful, but unfortunately the patient died." It is no different now. Even though the imposition of market logic on public finances is manifestly unfair and irrational (how can a country come to be declared bankrupt or, for that matter, a multinational corporation be treated in law like an individual person?), the advocates of sound money can always represent their policies as realistic and alternative proposals as dangerous fictions.

We are afraid of taking responsibility for a world of exchanges that is based on nothing but our own ability to initiate relationships. For money is principally a way of keeping track of what people do with each other. It is above all a source of information, a measure of the value of transactions. The president of Citicorp Bank, Walter Wriston, once said (shortly before his own fall from grace), "The information standard has replaced the gold standard as the basis of world finance."[40] Well, not quite yet. But the time is surely ripe for us to grasp that money is not necessarily an objective cause or limitation of our economic action. The idea of determinate cause underlying Newtonian science (in popular terms, "the billiard ball theory") was long ago replaced by one of probability (nothing is certain, only more or less likely to happen), an idea permitting the infinite regress of matter in relativity theory and quantum mechanics.[41] In this sense, natural scientists reflect more closely the conditions of modern society than the metaphysical assumptions that still underpin contemporary ideology and social science, especially modern economics.

In Chapter 7, I will explore a scenario in which the communications revolution reintroduces greater personal flexibility to economic activities. The link between production and consumption through exchange would then be provided by money made by each of us. Money would no longer be left to impersonal agencies, to the death struggle of the disembodied twins, states and markets, heads or tails; rather, it would become a question of subjective judgement, a skill to be learned by persons capable of making and remaking society through the exercise of their own judgement of probabilities. In short, money might become more meaningful than it has been of late.

The meaning of money

The word *money*, as I mentioned at the beginning, comes from Moneta, a name by which the Roman queen of the gods, Juno, was known. It was in the temple of Juno Moneta that coins were struck, making it an early example of a *mint* (from Old English *mynet,* coin). Most European languages retain the word "money" for coinage (French *monnaie,* Spanish *moneda,* Dutch *munt,* etc.), using another word for money in general variously derived from silver, cattle, some specific coin or a broader category meaning payment, wealth or property. English has conflated the two, taking the word *coin* from the French word for a corner or wedge used as a stamp. *Cash* is the English term for ready money in the form of notes or coins; and this seems to be derived from Norman French for a money box, although the word also refers to an Asian coin (from Tamil and Portuguese).[42] But what does *moneta* come from?

Moneta was a translation of the Greek Mnemosyne, the goddess of memory and mother of the Muses, each of whom presided over one of the nine arts and sciences. Moneta in turn was clearly derived from the Latin verb *moneo,* whose first meaning is "to remind, put in mind of, bring to one's recollection" (other meanings include "to advise, warn, instruct or teach"; and later "to tell, inform, point out, announce, predict").[43] There seems little doubt that, for the Romans at least, money in the form of coinage was an instrument of collective memory that needed divine protection, like the arts. As such, it was both a memento of the past and a sign of the future.

I wish to explore here the possibility that a lot more circulates by means of money than the goods and services it buys. Money conveys meanings, and the meaning of money itself tells us a lot about the way human beings make the communities we live in. In a wonderful new book, *Frozen Desire,*[44] James Buchan has gone further than most toward rescuing the subject of money from the pseudo-scientists. Buchan's thesis is that money is principally a vehicle for the expression of human wishes. In order to realize our limitless desires, they are trapped for a moment, frozen in money transactions that allow us to meet others in society who are capable of satisfying them. "*Money is one of those human creations which make concrete a sensation, in this case a sensation of wanting . . . Quite early in its history, money . . . passed from being a mere conveyance of desire to the object of all desire." "For money is incarnate desire. Money takes wishes . . . and broadcasts them to the world . . . [It] offers a reward that is not in any sense fixed or finite . . . but that every person is free to imagine in the realm of his own desires. That process of wish and imagination, launched or completed a million times every second, is the engine of our civilization.*"[45]

This formulation is not wrong, but it does not go far enough. Like his main opponents, the economists of our day, Buchan emphasizes the subjective wants of individuals and the way these are made temporarily objective in acts of buying and selling. Money may well be evolving toward just such a condition. But it also expresses something social, about the way we belong to each other in communities. We need to understand better how we build the infrastructures of collective existence, or culture, if you like. How do meanings come to be shared, and how does memory come to transcend the minutiae of personal experience?

Giambattista Vico was an eighteenth-century Neapolitan who gave some thought to these matters. His career was something of a failure: He could not, for example, realize his ambition to win the chair in jurisprudence at his local university. In 1744 he published a book with the title of *Scienzia Nuova,* "The New Knowledge."[46] He believed (as it turned out, rightly) that he was breaking new ground in philosophy. Unfortunately, very few people read it during his lifetime, but, after his death, the book was popularized by the founder of German romanticism, Johann Gottfried Herder.[47] Vico was recognized posthumously as a pioneer of the Enlightenment after the Enlightenment itself had been succeeded by the Romantic movement. His aim in *Scienzia Nuova* had been to explain the rise and fall of nations with an analogy to the human life cycle. Beginnings, for him, mattered more than the ends (*telos*) of Aristotelian philosophy. The origin of nations, their birth (for nations are by definition born), was made (*poesis*) by great heroes and poets. The cultural capital, we might say, of this formative period underpinned a nation's maturity as it grew from the poetry of childhood to the rationality and routine of adulthood, became sclerotic and eventually died.

What concerns us here are Vico's ideas concerning memory. He points out that in the heyday of the Roman republic, the Latin word *memoria* meant not only remembering but also imagination.[48] Then, with the coming of the empire, a new word, *fantasia,* was invented by intellectuals and entertainers who believed that they could make things up without benefit of the collective memory, thereby breaking the link between the two meanings of *memoria.* He asks us to recall how vivid were the memories of childhood, when compared with their adult successors (David Hume called ideas "pale sensations"). This is because the child relies on the imagination to bring lived experiences to mind and reshape them. This process owes nothing to reasoning. Only later do we learn to rely on rationalizations. We remember the rules we have been taught to abide by and these supersede the act of remembering for ourselves. We pay entertainers to imagine for us. Money may give expression to the child in each of us, by giving vent to our desires. But it is also one of the principal ways through which we learn as adults to participate in normal society.

This was why memory played such an important part in John Locke's philosophy of money.[49] We have already seen that, when considerations of time are introduced to market transactions, the abstract models of economics take on greater human and social complexity. Locke's theory of property rested on the idea of a *person* who, by performing labor on the things given by nature to us in common, made them his own. "Man, by being master of himself and proprietor of his own person, and the actions and labor of it, has still in himself the great foundation of property."[50] But, in order to sustain a claim on his property through time, that person has to remain the same; and personal identity depends on consciousness:

> *For, since consciousness always accompanies thinking, and it is that which makes everyone to be what he calls self, and thereby distinguishes himself from all other thinking things, in this alone consists personal identity, i.e., the sameness of a rational being: and as far as this consciousness can be extended backwards to any past action or thought, so far reaches the identity of that person; it is the same self now as it was then; and it is by the same self with this present one that now reflects on it, that that action was done.*[51]

Property must endure in order to be property, and that depends on memory. In Caffentzis's words, "The great enemy of property is oblivion, since the loss of conscious mastery over time and succession leads inevitably to the breakdown of property. Thus the forces of oblivion are antagonistic to the self and property, while all the techniques of mnemonics are their essential allies."[52] In the state of nature, private appropriation of the commonwealth through individual labor was limited by the needs of the person and by the transitory character of the goods. What drove society to the social contract and civil government was the invention of money (and with it the invention of crime). "Scarcity, for Locke, is not natural. It was only with the invention of money that wealth stopped being defined and bounded by use. With money a man could own more land and produce more than he needed for his own necessities. While still abiding by the natural law, he could accumulate wealth in a quasi-eternal form which he need not share with others." The impetus to accumulation and to theft was the same. "Money, its possessor, whether legal or illegal, in abstractness as well as in the potential infinity of satisfaction. The accumulation of money is thus the exercise of our power to suspend our determination, which is for Locke the highest expression of our liberty, before an infinity of choices, while for the thief it is the door to Paradise Now."[53]

It follows from this that money considerably expands the capacity of individuals to stabilize their own personal identity by holding something durable that embodies the desires and wealth of all the other members of society. An aid to memory, indeed. I would go further. Communities exist by virtue of their members' ability to exchange meanings that are substantially shared between them. There seems little doubt that money is an important vehicle for this. Commonwealths (or communities) communicate common meanings. It is worth exploring briefly the etymological roots these words share.

The first four of the above are known to share a root: *kom-*, "with," and *moin-*, "held in common." See also municipality, communism, etc. The *American Heritage Dictionary* gives as the Indo-European root *mei-*, "to change or move, with derivatives referring to the exchange of goods and services within a society as regulated by custom or law."[54] It also includes under this heading the word *mean* in the sense of low or poor, the common people as seen by an elite looking down (cf. German *gemein*). There are two other senses of *mean,* which are usually treated as being independent: *mean* as in medium or average, to which is linked *means,* method of achieving something or property/wealth. Then there is the one we are interested in, to which *meaning* is linked: To *mean* as to denote, signify, intend, bring about. What if they all three share the same root? It would then be that the common people share meanings (symbols) as means of achieving their purposes together. They form communities to the extent that people understand each other for practical purposes. And that is why communities operate through culture (meanings held in common).[55]

Communities operate through implicit rules (customs) rather than state-made laws. They may be large (the European Economic Community) or small (the village community). To the extent that they regulate their members, they usually do it informally, relying on the sanction of exclusion and not on punishment *per se*. Social anthropology in its prime focused on the study of small-scale societies ruled by custom, people who exchanged meanings specific to themselves.[56] In the second half of the nineteenth century, when no one believed that states, an archaic institution of agrarian civilization, could govern the restless energies of urban commercial society, the study of "primitive" communities was thought to throw light on the construction of modern societies according to the principles of liberalism, socialism, anarchism and communism, etc. The First World War put an end to that. Since then the comparative side of social anthropology has been more or less meaningless, as the modern state seemed inevitable and small-scale alternatives were hardly relevant.[57]

But now, centralized states are in disarray to a variable extent, even though their bureaucracies remain powerful. The word is out for devolution to less rigidly organized "communities" or regions. The networks of market economy, amplified by the Internet and cheap transport/telecoms, offer more direct access to the world at large. Cheap information allows relations at distance to be made more personal. Now we have to think again about how societies can be organized for their self-improvement or development. And it may pay us to consider money as part of this process of building communities. If money comes from the mother of the Muses, it follows that it is an instrument of collective memory, not far in fact from *meaning*. It is certainly an important *means* in several senses noted above. I wouldn't be surprised if communities, in their linguistic origin, once held money in common too, as a special kind of meaning. Even if they did not, there is nothing to stop us running with the idea now. But that requires us to overcome the legacy of alienation, which still bears heavily down on how people think of money.

The modern economy, as we have seen, is from one perspective a market, a proliferating network of buyers and sellers. And money is intrinsic to how markets work. We all need it and there is never enough of it. This gives money an almost godlike power—with money all things are possible; without it, most things are beyond our reach. You might think that something so important would be well understood by now, but the opposite is the case. Economists are traditionally committed to obfuscation, while anthropologists prefer to look the other way. The maverick economist J.K. Galbraith, in his unusually readable book about money, gives us a clue as to why we are ignorant about something so vital.[58]

He tells a story from the 1960s about a member of Kennedy's administration being paid off with a directorship of a bank. After his first meeting as a director, he was seen walking down Wall Street in a daze, muttering, "I never knew. I never knew." What hadn't he known? Galbraith surmises that he may have learned the first principle of modern banking: Take money from one party and lend it to another, then persuade both that they still have it. Perhaps money truly is a phantom conjured up by unscrupulous wizards. In which case, most of us would rather not know. We prefer to think that we are standing on solid ground, that the money we live by is real and will not go away. Failing that, we pay experts to look after the problem and are reassured by the sound of their technical jargon. In either case, understanding is unnecessary. It appears that we are not ready for a vision of society as the infinite flux of our own highly subjective encounters, instead preferring to see money as a stable foundation in a transient world of constantly shifting relativities. That is why inflation is so upsetting: When the value of money refuses to stand still, what else is there to rely on? Fear of the unknown leads us into a crippling search for certainty in monetary affairs; and this is as much of an obstacle to effective understanding as was the old-time religion it so closely resembles.

Presumably the sentiment that "money is the root of all evil" is not widely shared by economists nor indeed by those who have a lot of it. I know many academic intellectuals who resent bitterly the fact that money has more power to influence this world than their ideas have; and this may have something to do with the low level of salaries in the universities. But, in demonizing money, they come close to endowing the institution with a power all its own, making it the cause of whatever is unsatisfactory in our lives. In a section of the first chapter of *Capital* called "The fetishism of commodities and the secret thereof,"[59] Marx shows us his dialectical side. The word *fetiche* is a Portuguese import from West Africa. It refers to the local custom of dedicating a shrine to a spirit thought to inhabit a particular place. So, if you need to swim across a dangerous river, a sacrifice to the spirit of the river will help you succeed. Marx considered this to be an example of religious alienation. In his view the spirit was an invention of the human mind; but the Africans experienced their own creation as an external agency capable of granting life or death. Something similar, he believed, was at work in our common attitudes to markets and money.

Commodities are things made by people, and money is the means we have created of facilitating their exchange. Yet we often experience markets as a force independent of our will and that force is usually manifested in the money form. Prices go up and down—more often up—in a way that seems to undermine our ability to manage our own lives. The cost of filling the car with gasoline is exorbitant and we feel oppressed. Only rarely do we blame the oil companies, government taxation or "the Arabs" for our plight. More often we experience the impersonal world of commodities and money as animated objects exercising a power over us that is devoid of human content. Marx argued that there is some hope of our overcoming this modern form of alienation since, unlike the spirits produced by our religious imagination, we know that human labor is the source of the commodities we exchange for money. His book was designed to show the way toward such an emancipation.[60]

Even if we do not feel ourselves to be victimized by money as a demonic force, most of us want to believe that the money we live by has a secure objective foundation. This issue was addressed most interestingly by the German sociologist Georg Simmel in *The Philosophy of Money,* published at the beginning of this century.[61] Simmel was a liberal who felt that we would have to get used to a society consisting of an endlessly proliferating network of exchanges (in other words, a market). He rejected the British attempt to base money on the objective certainty of a gold standard, since this lent support to the idea that money is something outside our individual or collective control. Rather, he saw it as a symbol of our interdependence in civil society; and he located its value in the trust that comes from membership of such a society. Like Marx, he identified a parallel between the abstraction of money prices in commodity exchange and the abstraction of thought (scientific analysis) that represents the highest level of our cognitive interaction with the world.

Simmel was a relativist. There is no objective truth out there, no absolute on which we can hang our faith in existence. All we have is our subjective experience and everything is relative to that experience. Relativism is the only theory, he claims, that can explain itself: Its truth is relative to the situation in which it is applied. (Remember that this was the time when Einstein was putting forward his general theory of relativity.) In a similar manner, the value of commodities is not based on some objective standard, but is simply the outcome of what people are willing to pay in relation to all the other goods and services they want and the resources they have at their disposal. Money is the means of making these complex calculations. This is roughly the position of the new marginalist economics of the day.[62]

So what marks out money, according to Simmel, is that, in this shifting world of relativities, it is the common measure of value uniting all the independent acts of exchange. It thus stabilizes the volatile world of commodity exchange in much the same way that Durkheim, following Plato, Kant and other idealist philosophers, thought the central ideas of society (God, the family and similar sacred notions) lend stability to the fluctuations of everyday life. Money, of course, is itself relative and, as we know all too well today, its value changes also; but Simmel held that it represents an element of coherence in a world of constantly shifting prices. In other words, we are not yet ready to face the complex relativity of the real world and take comfort from money's symbolic steadiness. Most people prefer to believe that there is something out there that we can rely on. If God is dead and Society has been killed off by the economists, then let Money be something real and enduring.

The meaning of money is thus what each of us makes of it. It is a symbol of our relationship, as an individual person, to the community (hitherto more often singular than plural) to which we belong. This relationship may be conceived of as a durable ground on which to stand, anchoring identity in a collective memory whose concrete symbol is money. Or it may be viewed as the outcome of a more creative process in which we each generate the personal credit linking us to society. This latter outlook, however, requires us to abandon the notion that society rests on anything more solid than the transient exchanges we participate in. And that is a step few people at present are prepared to take, preferring to receive the money they live by, rather than make it. This preference is also revealed in popular ideas concerning the history of money. Perhaps, if we can loosen the grip of these ideas, we may prepare the way somewhat for practical progress.

Money: Whence it came and whither it went[63]

The most elementary conceptions of history rest on notions like now and then, here and there. It is one of the features of our world that such simple paired contrasts are no longer as sustainable as they once were. Accordingly, questions concerning the origins of money and its spread between societies at different levels of market economy evoke the ideological premises of contemporary economic practices. Although any attempt to answer the question "Where did money come from?" is inevitably based on historical speculation, it does require us also to look at non-market exchange in the contemporary world, at exchange from which the medium of money is absent. And the impact of modern money and markets on societies that were until recently without them extends this inquiry into how to conceptualize the distinctive properties of exchanges based on money.

Barter is the exchange of commodities without recourse to the medium of money.[64] In this case, the two parties are equally buyer and seller; each must have what the other wants at the same time; and the price is the proportion of each good or service expressed directly in terms of the other. In some respects, as we shall see, barter is close enough to exchanges involving money to be regarded as a form of market transaction. Certainly exchange without money payment is quite common in the commercial world of modern businesses. But many have chosen to see in barter the primitive antecedent of the market, separated from it by the historical invention of money.

Adam Smith's *The Wealth of Nations*[65] is rightly considered to be the foundation of modern economic thought. His general aim was to prove that the economy was better left in the hands of a mass of individual buyers and sellers than controlled by a powerful few who thought they knew best. The book starts famously with his observation that "the propensity to truck, barter and exchange one thing for another" is part of human nature. He gives, as a speculative example of this primitive tendency, the case of North American Indians exchanging deer skins for beaver pelts at the ratio of two to one. Barter thus consists of me handing you what you want in return for whatever of yours I want. Smith considers this method of exchanging commodities to be cumbersome and restrictive; and he goes on to suggest that eventually some items will become more generally acceptable. Out of this process of economic evolution, a particular commodity will take on the function of being a specialized medium of exchange—money, in other words. Markets facilitated by general-purpose money are thus a more effective way of carrying out a universal human function, namely the exchange of specialist products generated by division of labor.

Karl Marx's book, *Capital,* is about money conceived of as a social force organized to exploit ordinary working people. The opening chapter lays out what he thinks money is and where it comes from.[66] The story is the same as Smith's, but more formally expressed. In the beginning was the commodity, something useful that also had a value in exchange. Commodities could be and probably were initially exchanged without the medium of money. Then some commodities—salt, oxhides, eventually gold and silver—would take on the function of a medium of exchange. Finally, money emerged as a commodity whose only use was to facilitate the exchange of other commodities. It did so by making it no longer necessary for the buyer to have specific commodities wanted by the seller; the latter could hold money instead, until using it to buy from someone else on another occasion. Markets superseded barter because of the greater flexibility introduced by monetized exchange. Finally, money evolves from being just a medium of exchange to taking the form of organized capital; and as such it injects into the circuit of commodities (markets, see Figure 3.1) a dynamic of accumulation that lends to ordinary alienation a wholly new impetus.

This origin myth is plausible, but closer inspection reveals that it assumes what any rigorous history of exchange would have to demonstrate. Note especially that primitive barter is here represented as an exchange between individuals each having private property in whatever they seek to dispose of. Yet we have seen in Chapter 5 that this is a highly implausible assumption to make about original economic conditions. It is more likely that small groups would exercise political influence over the participants in exchange, since the kind of security offered traders by an invisible state apparatus is an exceptional and historically evolved context for commerce. Smith and Marx appear to be trying to represent certain key elements of modern economy as natural by making them aboriginal and therefore eternal. (Although in Marx's case it has to be said that money is subsequently given a contradictory social history of its own.)

Polanyi, among others, has argued that a more plausible scenario would be to derive market trade from political evolution.[67] First of all, rulers opened up diplomatic exchanges between communities that might later offer an umbrella for their followers to indulge in commerce. Individual barter between strangers was only likely to take place under such circumstances of political protection. Eventually, and only if state power were omnipresent, markets based on private property might emerge. This is consistent with the account given of the Trobriand *kula* previously. Which, then, are we to suppose came first, heads or tails, states or markets? The origin myth is thus far from innocent, committing us to one side or other of the ideological struggle that has defined our own period.

It is remarkable how deeply inserted into the popular consciousness of Western societies is this idea that markets evolved from primitive barter. Yet there are strong grounds for thinking that barter or exchange without money is a phenomenon linked to the cutting edge of modern commercial development. Even Adam Smith's original example of natives bartering animal skins takes on a different aspect when seen in the light of the North American fur trade of the eighteenth century that gave him the concrete example in the first place. Far from being the product of intermittent and isolated encounters between savages, this was a lucrative trade driven by a global mercantilism originating in England and France. Money was scarce on the frontier, but the exchange ratio of hides was calculated on the basis of known world prices back home. Deerskin was sometimes used as a unit of account, which is why the U.S. dollar is still referred to as a "buck." None of this would have been possible without the previous historical expansion of markets and money.

Barter flourishes in the interstices of political authority, especially when conventional money is in short supply. Thus Caroline Humphrey has linked the prevalence of barter on the Nepalese–Tibetan border to economic dis-integration, a result of poverty and weak sovereignty.[68] Barter has long been the mainstay of trade between what were until recently the Eastern and Western blocs; and today Third World countries that lack the dollars to par-ticipate in normal trade reach barter agreements among themselves, such as Nigerian oil exchanged for Brazilian manufactures over a number of years. Much of the international trade in arms is conducted through barter. And multinational corporations increasingly resort to swapping bulk quantities of unsold commodities: Thus, for example, a chemicals company offloads 100,000 gallons of surplus paint in exchange for an out-of-season lease of an airline's half-empty hotels in the Caribbean.[69]

There are two notable aspects of the modern phenomenon of barter. First, shortage of cash is not in itself a limitation on trade, especially when the parallel existence of markets makes it relatively easy to calculate what the trade items are worth. Second, barter disrupts the ability of states to regulate markets and levy taxes from them. Money is an unambiguous means of payment and standard of value; but how can the Internal Revenue Service assess the value of paint and hotel rooms that otherwise would not have found a buyer? Seen in this light, barter is increasing in response to re-strictions imposed on exchange both by markets requiring payment in cash and by political authorities seeking to capture taxes from cash transactions. Which of them, then, is "primitive"?

Clearly there is more to heads and tails than the Cold War idea that states and markets are opposed principles, each with their separate myth of money's origins. Seen from the perspective of barter, the two sides of the coin are symbiotic and equally restrictive of the possibilities for exchange. In the twentieth century the dialectical unity of states and markets has been embraced by Germany and Japan with some success, as well as being en-dorsed by Maynard Keynes. It matters whether markets based on money is-sued by states are seen as the end-point of economic evolution or just as a transient phase of world history. And it matters whether barter is thought to be a quaint, outdated and inefficient form of exchange or a growth point in a new era of greater economic freedom.

Throughout *Argonauts of the Western Pacific,* Malinowski emphasizes the con-trast between ceremonial gift-exchange and ordinary barter in Trobriand economy.[70] The two differ in the degree of formality, the timing of the return (delayed or immediate) and avoidance or acceptance of conflict in the exchange mechanism. Ceremony reflects high social distance and weak political order, whereas haggling depends on low social distance and strong political order. The question is whether people belonging to different groups feel free to risk the conflict inherent in barter without invoking all the danger, magic, prestige and hierarchy that go with ceremonial exchange. Thus one form is a temporary social framework erected in the relative absence of society; the other is an atomized interaction predicated on the strong presence of society. Both are different means of securing the same ends, the circulation of commodities between communities. Variable conditions over time, a breakdown of the peace or fluctuations of supply will affect the choice of trading method.

So, in the Trobriand Islands economy, there are both political authorities of a sort (big men) and markets of a sort (barter). The exchange of valuables erects a temporary framework for trade that, under conditions of peace, gives way to individuated transactions with greater affinity to competitive markets. This example furnishes an interesting point of comparison with twentieth-century political economy, as Malinowski intended, but in a way that lends support to Mauss's insistence that individuals and society (read markets and states, if you like) are each indispensable to exchange.

I have been struck by the tenacity with which ordinary people in the modern world cling to the barter origin myth of money. Can this merely be an example of Keynes's famous claim that our ideas are nothing more than the echoes of some old economic theory?[71] In a conversation I had not long ago with someone raised in Sudan, he began by asserting that barter between villages was the original economic system of his country; and then, when pushed, he admitted that these villages had belonged to regions involved with mercantile networks and money for thousands of years. Given the obvious similarity between individual barter and markets, it would be more plausible to locate the origins of exchange in the gift, as Mauss, following Malinowski, argued. But to do so would be to insist on a personalized approach to money, to see markets as a form of symbolic human activity rather than as the circulation of dissociated objects between isolated individuals. The general appeal of the barter origin myth is that it leaves the alienating assumptions of the private property complex undisturbed.

Consistent with this vision, the "monetization" of traditional cultures has usually been treated as a process of subversion, undermining the integrity of ways of life that were hitherto resistant to insidious commerce.[72] Anthropologists, like most academics, are not very happy in the marketplace, and this gives many of them a jaundiced perspective on money. The American sociologist Thorstein Veblen once wrote a book in answer to the question of how capitalist societies could permit the pursuit of truth in their universities.[73] He concluded that the solution was to persuade academics that they belonged to the elite, while paying them the wages of artisans (who earned a lot less then than they do now). They consequently compromised themselves pursuing whatever sources of additional income might help them to maintain a lifestyle they could not afford. Academics are obsessed with money and loathe it, because they never have enough of it.

This "obsolete anti-market mentality" flourishes among the disciples of Polanyi and of these the doyen has undoubtedly been Paul Bohannan.[74] He wrote an article that remains to this day the main point of reference for anthropological discussion of money economy and its presumed antithesis. The Tiv are a numerous people without rulers who, before being colonized by the British at the turn of the century, maintained a mixed farming economy on the fringe of trade routes linking the Islamic civilization of the north with the rapidly Westernizing society of the coast. Bohannan did fieldwork among them after the Second World War, shortly before Nigerian independence. He argues that the Tiv pre-colonial economy was organized through "spheres of exchange." There were three levels of value, arranged in a hierarchy; and like could normally only be exchanged with like within each level or sphere. At the bottom were subsistence items like foodstuffs and household goods, which were often traded in small amounts at local markets. Then came a limited range of prestige goods, which were linked to long-distance trade and largely controlled by Tiv elders (not unlike Trobriand big men). These included cloth, cattle, slaves and copper bars, the last sometimes serving as a "special-purpose currency," that is, as a standard of value and means of exchange within its sphere. Lastly, the highest category was rights in persons,

MONEY AND THE MARKET

specifically women exchanged in marriage between male-dominated kin groups; and ideally, through sister exchange, an institution of mutual betrothal that allowed polygamous elders to keep most young men from marrying until well into their thirties.

The norm of exchanging within each sphere was sometimes breached. Conversion upward was an ideal and its opposite a source of disgrace. The absence of a general-purpose money made this difficult to achieve. Subsistence goods are high in bulk and low in value; they do not transport easily and their storage is problematic (food rots). Prestige goods are the opposite on all counts. How many peas would it take to buy a slave? One exception is livestock. Young men could raise chickens and, with luck, convert these into sheep and goats whose increase might lead to the acquisition of cattle. Moreover, by the onset of colonial rule, the content of the spheres had changed: Sister exchange had been largely replaced with bridewealth (payment of prestige goods for a wife); slavery was abolished and the supply of metal rods had dried up. Bohannan makes light of all this and insists that, in the absence of a general medium of exchange, Tiv culture was maintained as a series of separate compartments of value.

The introduction of modern money in the twentieth century was a disaster, according to him. Anyone could sell anything in small amounts, accumulate the money, buy prestige goods and enter the marriage circuit on their own terms, regardless of the elders. This amounted in Bohannan's view (and no doubt in the elders' view too) to the destruction of traditional culture. It is as if the technical properties of modern money alone were sufficient to undermine a way of life. Now, this argument has come under sustained criticism—for example, that it is idealist, with not enough attention paid to the organization of production.[75] Others have suggested that money is just a symbol of a whole complex of economic relations that might be summarized as capitalism.[76] But even these critics rely on a logic of commercial development that downplays the political dimension of historical transformations in the periphery. The Nupe case, cited above, makes the political dimensions of colonial economy brutally clear.

The contributors to the volume edited by Parry and Bloch largely share the view that indigenous societies around the world take Western money in their stride, turning it to their own social purposes rather than bending themselves to its supposedly impersonal logic. Thus one of them shows how Malays transform money earned in the wider economy by handing it over to the women, whose domestic rituals incorporate it into the long-run processes of social reproduction of which they are custodians.[77] The underlying theory is familiar; it is essentially Durkheim's. There are two circuits of social life: One, the everyday, is short-term, individuated and materialistic; the other, the social, is long-term, collective and idealized, even spiritual. The expediency of market transactions falls into the first category, and all societies seek to subordinate them to the logic of social reproduction in the long run. For some reason, which they do not investigate, money has acquired in Western economies a social force all of its own, whereas the rest of the world retains the ability to keep it in its place.

Parry and Bloch's argument, for all the distance they seek to put between themselves and Bohannan, is similar to his in that they postulate a hierarchy of value in which modern money comes second to the general ideas that secure society's continuity. The whole picture becomes clearer if we apply the spheres-of-exchange concept to Western societies. As Marshall indicated,[78] it is not uncommon for modern consumers to rank commodities according to a scale of value. Other things being equal, we would prefer not to have to trade in lifestyle goods (expensive consumer durables) in order to pay the rent and the grocery bills. And we would normally like to acquire the symbols or means of elite status, such as a first-rate education. If you asked how many toilet rolls a BMW is worth or how many oranges buys an Eton education, most people would think you were crazy. This despite the fact that all can be bought for money and have been for longer than we can remember. So the technical capacity for universal exchange introduced by modern money is not incompatible with the maintenance of cultural values denying that all goods are commensurate. Nor is this just a matter of ideas; there are real social barriers involved. It does not matter how many oranges an East End trader sells, for he will not get his son accepted for Eton. And the gatekeepers of the ancient universities insist that access to what they portray as an aristocracy of intelligence cannot be bought.

This provides us with a clue from nearer home to the logic of spheres of exchange. The aristocracy everywhere claim that "you cannot buy class." Money wealth and secular power are supposed to be subordinate to inherited position and spiritual leadership. Nowhere is this ideology set out more co-herently than by Hindu Brahmins. In practice, we know that money and power have long purchased entry into the ruling elite. De Tocqueville praised the flexibility of the English aristocracy in readily admitting success-ful merchants and soldiers to their ranks.[79] One class above all others still resists this knowledge, the academic intellectuals, for reasons touched on above. We cannot bear to admit that others, through control of resources that we have so little of, have marginalized our ability to influence society through our ideas. And so we line up with the Tiv elders in bemoaning the corrosive power of modern money and vainly insist that traditional culture should remain in the driving seat.

When time and space are injected into stories about money, often through the crude dichotomies of now and then, here and there, the result is to bring out, by affirmation or negation, the core beliefs associated with economic ideology. There is an interesting study to be carried out of the forms of gift-exchange and barter in the contemporary world; and these should inform the search for alternative approaches to money and markets in the age of the Internet. But before making such a study, it is necessary to expose the ideological character of much that has been written so far about the origins and spread of money.

Money in the age of the Internet

The transformation of money by electronic communications begins with plastic credit and debit cards. The post-war economic boom led to an explo-sion in the turnover generated by personal checking accounts in the USA.[80] The banks adopted ERMA (Electronic Recording Machine—Accounting) in the sixties to handle the growing volume of checks, which doubled in the decade 1943–52 before the boom had properly begun; and in doing so they reduced the labor needed for this task by over 80%. Ever since then, the banks have led the way in mechanizing money, encouraging their customers to write fewer checks, for example, by paying for utilities through monthly direct debits. Credit cards came out of America; they were adopted in Britain in the sixties and rather more slowly elsewhere. Checks themselves have come to be largely replaced by debit cards. The relationship between credit and debit cards is one to which we will return below. Automatic teller machines (ATMS) have spread rapidly, replacing the need to line up for cash inside the banks themselves and of late providing a viable alternative to travellers' checks for tourists. Direct banking by telephone is a more recent development.

Banknotes remain a staple of everyday life for all but the very rich. But one consequence of all the above is that electronic media have been substantially replacing paper money. Personal checks have largely given way to plastic. The current standing of our bank account is more quickly ascertained by ATM or phone than by written statements issued once a month. In the process, as fewer persons are employed to handle a vastly expanded service, negotiation with the banks over credit has become more mechanical and remote. Tales of mismanagement, bureaucratic error and indifference multiply. But the rise of digital money is inexorable. Many people in the rich countries now have several lines of credit, including an array of cards entitling them to run up bills at department stores, bookshops and gas stations. In this way, the old system of personal credit lines to suppliers has been digitalized. New forms of special-purpose money have arisen in recent years: Airmiles, reward points and the like encouraging people to favor particular companies in return for various entitlements and bonuses in kind.

By the time Keynes wrote in the 1930s, the main determinant of the money supply had shifted from whatever governments produced from their mints to the purchasing power of working people, as measured by the ratio of their income to savings and the national currency's exchange rate. The developments listed above go a long way toward making the money supply depend on ordinary people's capacity to manage debt, as well as to earn an income. In America today the credit card companies will often offer $5,000 free credit to new customers whom they know only remotely as names on machines. They have discovered that their losses from bad debts are exceeded by the profits to be made from the new business. In one celebrated case, a dog called Zabau Shepard was offered the benefits of plastic.[81] Of course, as the participants know, there is a "bottom line" in all this, defined by credit card owners' ability to pay off their debts using the cash they have deposited in their current accounts. And the penalties for failing to keep up necessary payments are dire indeed, involving a permanent blemish on one's public credit rating that might cause someone to fall out of the credit bonanza altogether. At the other extreme, people who manage their credit reasonably well are inundated with offers of further loans and cards. The system is not equal, by a long way, but a large number of reliably employed individuals have been introduced to a style of personal money management in the last three decades that was unheard of when Keynes wrote about purchasing power.

When credit cards were first introduced, many commentators assumed that they would precipitate large numbers of people into insolvency, simply because they would not be able to resist spending instant credit beyond their means. The average credit card debt of American households today is around $5,000, which hardly suggests uncontrolled spending. Moreover, consumers expand and contract their level of indebtedness in rhythms that are not understood by the economists, but clearly reflect their own collective determination of when they feel comfortable with debt and when they don't. In countries like France, people have not yet been given the chance to explore the possibilities of plastic credit already enjoyed by their anglophone cousins. There banks in effect offer the facility of debit cards, where funds are drawn directly from checking accounts. In Britain and the USA the same facility of drawing against deposited funds or an overdraft is offered by the banks, but credit cards proper offer the chance to spend up to an agreed maximum credit limit with minimum monthly payments required. Typically these limits are increased as the customer demonstrates creditworthiness.

In the light of this, it is of some interest to revisit the twin concepts of credit and debt. A credit theory of money emphasizes the trustworthiness of a person expecting something for nothing in the short run: I promise to pay in future for what I take from you now. An Englishman's word is his bond. Failing that, a bank or credit card company can vouch for a check or a payment by plastic. The seller has instant confirmation that payment will be made and the guarantor has to deal with the buyer's ability to pay up in future. Clearly there is a difference between drawing on funds already lodged with the bank (debit cards) and the expectation that eventually the debt will be repaid (credit cards). It seems to me that the Anglo-Saxons can be more daring with the expansion of new money forms and the decentralization of credit because they have long subscribed to a market ideology that emphasizes in principle the personal responsibility of ordinary citizens.

A recent book, *La Monnaie Souveraine,*[82] rests on the contrasting French idea that money is debt. The context for this book is the coming of the euro, the new European standard that opened as a money-of-account in January 1999 and is scheduled by the year 2002 to replace the franc as French currency (money-proper, in Keynes's terms). The sovereignty of money, in the authors' understanding, lies in its being a symbol of the *debt* tying each French citizen to the state. This in turn has its roots in the payments made by fief-holders to the king of the Franks when the state itself was being formed. Individuals owe their means of existence, the very money they spend, to the sovereign state; and they pay for the privilege. It is of interest that the German word for money is *Geld,* meaning a payment of debt.[83] And we have already encountered Adam Müller's romantic theory of money as the trust generated by a people working the land together. Clearly, then, the way that the communications revolution affects money in different societies is going to be conditional on such differences of emphasis in the relations between individuals and the collective. We could say, in the relative emphasis given to heads or tails within national cultures.

In all this talk of plastic, cash has certainly not gone away. Carrying cash involves greater risks and costs: the risk of its being lost or stolen, of its being counterfeit; the costs of foreign exchange, for similar considerations of risk, and of handling rather than machine-processing. Many people find it more convenient or are just too lazy to change their habits. The most enthusiastic users of cash are the criminal classes, since they do not want their transactions to be traced to actual persons. As we saw above, in Jamaica in the 1980s movements in the illegal marijuana economy (whose value was then estimated to be greater than the three biggest legal industries—bauxite, tourism and garments) were monitored through variations in the levels of cash withdrawals from the banks. This leads us to the curious speculation that the state's legal tender will end up appealing mainly to the criminal elements of society, John Locke's nightmare of a world dominated by an informal alliance between corrupt politicians and economic criminals.[84] But by then the respectable majority will have moved on somewhere else.

The shift toward electronic cash has already started. So-called smart cards have a chip in them that gives the bearer a fixed amount of money to carry on his person without having to bother with banknotes. These smart cards can be anonymous or stamped with the bearer's personal identity, making them harder to lose. Certainly, the use of plastic for small transactions, like buying a newspaper or a cup of coffee, has some way to go. A trial scheme carried out in Swindon, England by the smart-card company Mondex showed that it was feasible for people to use cards for everyday purposes normally reserved for cash, as long as the sellers were geared up to swipe the cards through vending machines linked directly to the sponsoring banks.[85] In principle, this does away with shopkeepers having to count cash, carry it to the bank and run the risk of being mugged for their pains. On another level altogether, some European authorities have argued against the issue of smart cards with values up to £10,000 on the grounds that it would be easier for drug gangs to smuggle large amounts of money across borders, as opposed, presumably, to having to stow sacks of paper money in the back of their cars. This seems to go against the dismantling of border controls in Europe and the increasing ease of moving money internationally by electronic means. But all these developments of money, from paper to bits as it were, stir up dangerous emotions, such as fear of the unknown and loss of control.

The great potential of the Internet is not restricted to the money form in a narrow sense, but lies rather in the expansion of electronic markets, in borderless trade at the speed of light. For electronic money will develop to the extent that it is needed for such trade. This is new to the 1990s, since the Internet went public, and it is more of an American phenomenon than anything else. For this reason, it is of interest to note what the U.S. Department of Commerce has to say in a bullish report on "the emerging digital economy" published in 1998.[86] It points out that the market capitalization of five companies linked to the Internet (Microsoft, Intel, Compaq, Dell and Cisco) grew from $12 billion to $588 billion between 1987 and 1997. There has been significant growth in both the sale of physical goods and digital delivery of services via the Internet. Sales of air tickets and securities are already big on the Internet (airlines can offer cheaper tickets by cutting out the travel agencies); while computers, software, cars, books and flowers are increasingly sold by this means. Other areas of business with a growing presence on the Internet are consulting, entertainment, banking, insurance, education and healthcare. It is already possible to have a virtual check-up, but for obvious reasons this has limited appeal at the present time.

American businesses use the Internet to cut purchasing costs; to manage their supplier relationships; to streamline logistics and inventory; to plan production and reduce cycle times; to reach customers more effectively; to lower marketing costs; and to find new sales opportunities. By 2002 it is expected that there will be Internet trade between American businesses worth $300 billion, in addition to consumer sales. The Internet operates around the clock and around the world, allowing production processes begun in San Francisco to be carried on in Singapore, while the Californian engineers are asleep. Not surprisingly, there is considerable enthusiasm in America for these developments, which, taken together, constitute one of the main reasons for the strength of that country's economy at this time.

Businessmen report that their main worries with the Internet are fourfold: unpredictable law; uncertain performance of the net; the insecurity of the net; and the potential for being overtaxed by the government. They therefore want, and the government claims to back them in this:

1.   a predictable, market-driven, legal framework for electronic commerce;

2.   non-bureaucratic means of making the Internet safe;

3.   human resource policies to develop the skills needed.

For commerce to expand, the greatest need is for parties to a contract to be sure of the identity of the person on the other end and that the contract is binding. In response to this need, verification procedures are being developed and recently there has been a rise in the use of more secure "extranets," or virtual private networks.[87] The issue, to which we will return, is the lack of overall supervision of the Internet. Businesses and individuals would not mind if the public authorities were able to increase their security of transaction; but equally they do not want to submit to economic coercion by governments.

The idea is slowly taking root that society is less an oppressive structure out there and more a subjective capacity that allows each of us to learn how to manage our relations with others. Money is a good symbol of this shift. It first took the form of objects outside ourselves (coins) of which we usually had a greater need than the available supply; but of late it has increasingly been manifested as personal credit, in the form of digitalized transfers mediated by plastic cards and telephone wires, thereby altering the notions of economic agency that we bring to participation in markets. If modern society has always been supposed to be individualistic, only now perhaps is the individual emerging as a social force to be reckoned with. This claim rests on a single overwhelming fact, that large amounts of information can now be processed cheaply concerning the individuals involved in economic transactions at any distance, thereby making possible the repersonalization of complex economic life. In the process the assumptions that supported mass society for a century are being undermined.

The Internet may confirm a trend that liberals have often asserted and socialists once denied, that economic power is being transferred from producers to consumers, from centralized bureaucracy to flexibly specialized markets in which individual consumers carry more weight than we ever did in the days when shopping involved picking undifferentiated products off a shelf.[88] One consequence of the developments reported above is that banking services are becoming much more specialized, less paternalistic and more consumer-driven. Many firms are turning to the new information technologies to tackle a long-standing problem that was intransigent in the days of mass consumption. It is often the case that up to 80% of sales are generated by the top 20% of customers. In the future, these customers will be targeted for special attention (it is called CRM, or Customer Relations Management) and treated in ways reminiscent of the customized shopping enjoyed by a privileged few before the bureaucratic revolution of a century ago. At the same time, others may find their business rejected because they do not spend enough to make it worth while to serve them. In general, it will be possible to take identification of customers' needs well beyond the hit-or-miss level of much current junk-mail.

In principle, the Internet overcomes one of the chief arguments made by the classical economists for barter's inefficiency as a form of exchange. This was that, in order for an exchange to take place, one seller has to find a buyer who also has what the seller wants for himself, in the required quantities. The use of traditional money allows this interdependence to be broken, with the seller holding cash against future purchases of his own. Under previous conditions, the constraints of market size and timing restricted the scope for barter. But, with the Internet, one can imagine swaps taking place within networks of infinite size and global scope. *Wanted:* In exchange for the collected works of Milton Friedman, a night in a Bangkok massage parlor. There must be somebody out there . . . Of course, problems of timing, trust and delivery will not disappear overnight. But we have scarcely tapped the potential for direct exchange as yet. As for Internet sales involving cash payments, a whole new industry has grown up concerned with developing forms of electronic money (*e-money*). It seems likely that a high proportion of these will be special-purpose currencies operating within closed circuits of exchange rather than general-purpose money capable of crossing the boundary between the Internet and the rest of the economy.

The Internet thus opens up the possibility for people to form closed circuits of labor exchange with their own nominal currency. Local Exchange Trading Systems, or LETS schemes[89] (the precise wording is less important than the acronym's call for us to be proactive), were invented in British Columbia in the early 1980s as a way of generating local employment during a recession. There are perhaps a thousand of these organizations in the world today, with membership ranging from a few dozen to two thousand. In France, SEL (*Systèmes d'Echange Local,* where the acronym carries the connotation of salt as a barter currency) have attracted favorable publicity in newspapers like *Le Monde* as a possible source for the democratic socialist revival. Some schemes operate with paper chits, and so LETS is not necessarily a digitalized form of exchange, but the system is obviously more effective when transactions are registered on a central computer. It works like this.

People living in what they feel to be a local community agree to exchange labor services and, less often, products using a money-of-account designated by themselves. This usually has a name related to local history and culture, like "tales" in Canterbury. It may or may not be linked to the standard currency of the country. Thus the original British Columbia scheme used "green dollars" with the same nominal value as the Canadian dollar; but elsewhere any straightforward link between the two may be denied. Members usually pay a small signing-on fee to cover administrative costs and list the services they want to offer and receive in a central directory. They contact each other by phone or personal introduction. It is not necessary for the seller and buyer to exchange in both directions, so that transactions are not strictly barter, but market sales using a special-purpose currency that restricts exchange to a closed and usually quite local circuit. Prices are negotiated for each transaction and, because there is no particular emphasis on balancing one's account, it is quite common for buyers to be generous in setting the price level. The logic of getting something for nothing or of buying cheap and selling dear is largely absent. The transaction is recorded centrally. In most cases, the accounts of individuals are transparent, so that it is possible for anyone to inspect someone else's transaction record, at least the length of time they have been trading, the volume of business and the balance of credit or debt. As in a normal market economy, the health of the system is measured by turnover. It is just as anti-social for someone to hoard credits by never buying as it is to incur debt through buying without ever selling.

Apart from communitarian goals, LETS schemes often explicitly stress an ecological theme (organic vegetables, not the ordinary kind) and the embedded character of transactions (getting to know you, not just buying and selling). In many cases they are geared to the needs of the unemployed and the poor, offering an alternative income when the mainstream economy refuses to make one available. But they are just as likely to bring a small middle-class network together. The main problems they face are: start-up costs (someone usually has to put in a lot of free labor); transaction costs (a lot of effort is taken up with setting up a deal); variable quality of service (how do you tell whether the person you have hired really knows the job?); the network is too small and intermittent to be relied on; plumbers are in higher demand than amateur artists; and quite a few more. These add up to recognizing that it is labor-intensive to set up a new market that works effectively. For enthusiasts this handicap can be overcome. But this perhaps explains why most LETS schemes so far are rather small and not particularly durable.

The most interesting feature of the political economy of LETS is the relationship between these exchange circuits and the system of public finance in the wider economy (taxation, unemployment benefits, etc.). At times officials have taken the hard line that all LETS transactions constitute normal income, to be deducted from eligibility for benefits and added to income tax liabilities. They have insisted that all transactions should incur indirect taxes such as those levied on sales in the normal economy. Given the dependence of modern government on revenues levied from market transactions, one can easily understand why they would want to close a tax loophole that could, in the long run, become substantial. But LETS activists have resisted this ruling and have made their own accountancy more opaque in some cases, by delinking their money-of-account from the national currency. They have argued, often successfully, that their currency is not really money, but a way of recording non-market exchanges between friends, not unlike domestic services within the family. And this battle seems largely to have been won. The authorities have settled on what I think of as a "mice in the basement" formula. As long as LETS participants are not conducting what they, the authorities, consider to be a normal business, but are only part-time employed to no significant commercial effect, they will not be taxed.

So far, computerized exchange systems such as LETS have tended to be small local schemes driven by communitarian, welfarist and eco-socialist ideologies. The largest British LETS scheme, which is in Manchester, however, has made an effort to extend the purchasing power of individuals rather than to promote any idea of local community. It doesn't make sense, in a large conurbation, to pretend that a small exchange network constitutes a community in any localized sense. Here a number of businesses have been persuaded to take "bobbins" (the LETS currency named nostalgically for Manchester's long-gone textile industry) in full or part payment for their goods and services. This scheme also insists on integrating its transactions fully into the normal economy, with participants paying income and sales taxes, as if they were conducting a normal business. The emphasis here is just on adding to the range of economic activities that individuals can participate in, if the wider market economy does not yield them the money they need.

This experiment, consistent with the old Manchester liberal emphasis on free trade, has enraged many LETS activists elsewhere who see it as a betrayal of the spirit of William Morris underlying their own communitarian efforts.[90] Rather than integrate LETS into the wider economy, they see it as a way of sealing off a more wholesome kind of circuit from the contaminations of capitalism. It is interesting that the originator of the first LETS scheme near Vancouver, Michael Linton, is closely associated with the Manchester initiative.[91] He envisages a day not so far ahead when many of us will carry one smart card with several currencies, to match the credit and debit cards we already have in growing profusion, recording our participation in any number of labor service exchange circuits (involving our profession, neighborhood, sporting interests, church or whatever). These additional ways of working for others will not replace impersonal means of payment for goods and services, employing dollars, euros and the like; but they would extend considerably our capacities to buy and sell without relying on some exogenous source of employment (a job) to finance our purchases.

In America there is a growing number of similar attempts to establish exchange circuits relying on what people have (spare time) rather than on what they don't have (spare dollars). A recent book by David Boyle, *Funny Money*,[92] offers a personal guide to some of them. Edgar Cahn's initiative in setting up an exchange system using *time dollars* puts the emphasis back squarely on the labor theory of value. People are encouraged to accept service credits for their labor, to be exchanged in the future against services they need. Here the focus has initially been on reaching disadvantaged groups such as old people, the poor and minorities. But, as in most of these alternative economic initiatives, the aim is to reform society itself, from small beginnings but with big ideas. A similar scheme, with more of an emphasis on community self-sufficiency, is in Ithaca, New York, home of Cornell University. Here the currency for a local exchange circuit is known as *Ithaca hours* (motto: "In Ithaca we trust") and the scheme is strongly associated with a leading activist, Paul Glover, who built up this one after an earlier LETS scheme had failed.

Ithaca, like much of upstate New York, has suffered economic decline in recent decades. For some of its inhabitants it seems as if the money has simply gone elsewhere. The idea of Ithaca hours is to keep more of it within the community by tying transactions to a closed circuit motivated by local interests. The unit-of-account is a time standard, but it is linked to the wider economy, so that businesses that operate in both circuits can easily make the conversion. The hour is valued at $10, rather more than the minimum wage, and participants are encouraged to value their services equally. But it is recognized that some professionals, like lawyers and dentists, can earn so much more in the open market that they are allowed to charge multiples of hours for an hour's work. An individual or company might offer a couple of hours at the Ithaca minimum rate, a few more at less than market rate and some more at the full rate, but still within the Ithaca-hour circuit, leaving the rest of his time to be charged as dollars in the normal way. The results are already substantial and, whether it advertises itself as such or not, Ithaca has become a leading example of the LETS movement.

The principle of these alternative economies is not new. During the Great Depression of the 1930s, numerous local currencies sprang up to help generate exchange in the absence of liquid cash. One of the most imaginative of these was strips of deerskin known as the "buck." Before that, in the nineteenth century, America hosted numerous self-help schemes and communitarian utopias, some of which survive in modified form today. I have already mentioned the communitarian socialism of William Morris and his followers in Britain. What makes LETS and similar initiatives potentially different is their link to the communications revolution. Cheap information—cheap in the sense of both the processing machines and their running costs—changes the scope of these activities. At present we have only seen some very limited small-scale experiments drawing on some pretty conventional ideas designed for another age. Similarly, we have yet to see the pay-off in terms of direct democracy that interactive closed-circuit television networks allow for in principle. But the potential for development is clearly there. When it comes to the world of money itself, there are also some remarkable instances and future possibilities to report. I will limit myself here to two examples.

JAK Members Bank[93] is a Swedish interest-free savings and loan association that was registered as a bank in 1997 but has been operating since 1965. JAK stands for land, labor and capital in Swedish. The association is a telephone bank with 20,000 members and twenty-five local branches. These branches are for information and study-groups. JAK's members have deposited $60 million in addition to equity of $8 million and this has been allocated as loans to 5,000 members. The insistence on loans being interest-free is linked to a crusading ideology that stresses the avoidance of exploitation of people and nature. Subscribers accumulate "savings points" rather than interest, and these are used to determine eligibility for loans. The bank is a non-profit organization, but recipients of loans are charged an administration fee to cover wages and related costs. The main point of JAK Members' Bank, however, is to promote dialogue about how to achieve a fair and sustainable economy, as much as it is about financing loans through savings. Average deposits of $3,000 and loans of $12,000 suggest that the bank appeals to people of middle income. The scale of operations is significantly larger than any LETS scheme.

Private owners of capital in the forms of savings, life insurance, pension funds and the like have the chance not just to be more involved in the management of their own portfolios but to band together as collective institutions exercising a growing influence on financial markets. Robin Blackburn (personal communication) is preparing a paper on what he calls "grey capitalism," reflecting both the average age of the constituency he is interested in and the murky character of the property law involved. Over half the value of equities in the USA and Britain at this time are owned by pension funds and life insurance companies. What would be the result if contributors banded together under various identities to exert more concerted pressure on the managers? At present, the latter are protected by laws that ask of them only that they demonstrate reasonable caution in their investments. This accounts for the herd mentality of these people, since, as long as they do what everyone else does, they cannot be accused of professional mismanagement.

The scope for increased intervention by investors, acting alone or in groups, but with the benefit of electronic information, is great. Already investment clubs formed on the Internet are playing a significant role in the behavior of stock markets. Institutional investors often follow computerized programs that, acting together, can precipitate a market meltdown under conditions such as those triggered in Wall Street by the 1998 Far-Eastern financial crisis; whereas these small investors, pooling ideas, information and resources, have the capacity to act independently in such crises. By some estimates their actions were critical in generating a recovery from that same crisis. If capitalism, far from being on its last legs, as socialists have been wont to imagine, is entering a strong phase of restructuring as a global phenomenon, then the democratic currents beginning to stir on the Internet suggest that, in the heartlands of virtual capitalism itself, the large corporations may not have things entirely their own way.

Finally, we return to the recurrent theme of this chapter, the issue of heads or tails, symbolizing the relationship between states and markets that has dominated twentieth-century political economy. The U.S. government has a very interesting position on taxation of the Internet. It is currently promoting an international treaty that will effectively keep the hands of governments off the Internet. This treaty would seek to be consistent with existing international conventions, to be simple to administer and easy to understand. It would avoid double taxation and ban discriminatory taxes and customs duties on electronic transmissions. The report of the U.S. Department of Commerce cited earlier[94] makes it clear that at least some parts of the American government are worried that their country's apparent lead in the communications revolution could quickly be dissipated if Congress got round to thinking of the Internet as a milch cow for its spending habit, thereby driving electronic commerce abroad to places with a less predatory attitude. They worry that the potential for electronic commerce will be held back by the conventional dispositions of most adult Americans; and they place their hopes for the future partly in a massive educational campaign, but mainly in the children who are growing up with the explosion in information technology that has characterized the 1990s.

In Finland, which by some measures is the world leader in use of both the Internet and mobile phones, the local presence of a major supplier has stimulated rapid innovation in the use of mobile telephones as a means of Internet connection, with widely ramifying consequences for markets and money. It is even said there that they expect soon to dispense altogether with money in its traditional forms of coins and banknotes. I have limited this account of money in the age of the Internet to developments that have already occurred. Some of them may sound quite futuristic, but they are actual, if perhaps still minor phenomena. The economic forms that will dominate the twenty-first century are probably already visible in embryo. But to prepare ourselves for what lies ahead and to influence things in the direction we want, we must also think about what is possible and relate the possible to the actual that we already know. This is the task of the next chapter, in which the future of money and the market becomes the subject of an even more speculative approach.

Guide to further reading

Ah, money! While I was writing this book, friends kept telling me of all the new titles coming out on the topic. I took it as confirmation that I was on the right track. I suggest starting with literary approaches. James Buchan's *Frozen Desire* (note 28) is a brilliant, humane book; he knows more about money than I do and he writes better, but I think I have the edge when it comes to historical vision and social theory. Kevin Jackson's bedtime companion, *The Oxford Book of Money,* and Granta's special edition on money[95] are both diverting in different ways. Slightly more serious is the maverick economist, J.K. Galbraith, *Money:Whence It Came,Whither It Went* (note 58). The career of the artist Boggs is a wonderful contemporary parable (note 5).

When it comes to the history of economic ideas, I rely on Schumpeter's *History of Economic Analysis* as a work of reference (note 4). But the key theorists, in my opinion, are Locke, Marx, Simmel and Keynes. Caffentzis (note 6) is much more interesting than anything Locke wrote himself on money (an exception to my normal rule of going to the source). Unfortunately, Marx wrote a three-volume work, *Capital,* on the subject (see the guide to Chapter 3). Simmel's *The Philosophy of Money* was translated into English quite recently and is highly original, if rather dense (note 22). But Maynard Keynes is still the main source for thinking about money at the millennium. His *Essays in Persuasion* are a model of clear writing (note 10); *The General Theory* is simply the most important economics text written in the twentieth century (note 9); and *A Treatise on Money,* although written for economists, is largely accessible to the general reader (note 18). It is worth finding out about Keynes's life as the context for all this; and Harrod's biography does the job, even if it is rather long and stodgy.[96] Bagehot's study of *Lombard Street* (note 29) gives an account of the formation of the Victorian financial system whose demise stimulated Keynes's work.

Anthropologists have paid more attention to nonmarket exchange and money in non-Western cultures than to the operations of money in the capitalist heartlands. The collection on barter edited by Humphrey and Hugh-Jones is authoritative (note 64), while the Parry and Bloch collection on money in exotic cultures has the strengths and weaknesses of the genre (note 76). But now Chris Gregory has produced *Savage Money,* the first serious attempt to combine exotic ethnography with a feeling for modern world history.[97] Thomas Crump's *The Phenomenon of Money* is a speculative work by an anthropologist with a great interest in quantification.[98] Mary Douglas has written about money as originally as any anthropologist.[99] Jane Guyer's edited collection *Money Matters* is both valuable and recent.[100]

David Boyle's entertaining romp through today's alternative currencies, *Funny Money,* has the merit of being up to date (note 81). There is no full-length treatment in English of LETS, the most significant of the new systems of exchange, but Servet's book on the French equivalent, SEL, is serious and provocative (note 89). The same can be said of *La Monnaie Souveraine,* by Aglietta and his associates, which has an anthropological cast to it (note 82). I found several recent works on "the digital economy" disappointing and turned instead to the solid report published on this topic by the U.S. Department of Commerce (note 86).

On the meaning of money, a rather different take from mine can be found in Viviana Zelizer's *The Social Meaning of Money.*[101] Finally, what to read on money as memory? I can't say; but I do know that Giambattista Vico's *The New Science* (note 46) probably contains the key. Vico deserves more prominent billing in this work than he gets. See Berlin (note 47) for an introduction to this fascinating thinker.

Notes

1. *American Heritage Dictionary* (third edition, 1993).
2. B. Malinowski, "Primitive Currency," *Economic Journal,* 1923; see note 47.
3. M. Mauss, *The Gift* (Norton, New York, 1990), pp. 100–102n.
4. The great historian of economic ideas, Joseph Schumpeter, once said, "There is no denying that views on money are as difficult to describe as shifting clouds." J. Schumpeter, *History of Economic Analysis* (Oxford University Press, New York, 1954), p. 289.
5. L. Weschler, *Boggs: A Comedy of Values* (University of Chicago Press, Chicago, 1999).
6. G. Caffentzis, *Clipped Coins, Abused Words and Civil Government in John Locke's Philosophy of Money* (Autonomedia, New York, 1989).
7. G. Bannock, R. Baxter and E. Davies, *The Penguin Dictionary of Economics* (third edition, Penguin, Harmondsworth, 1984); D. Foley, "Money in Economic Activity" in J. Eatwell, M. Milgate and P. Newman, eds, *New Palgrave Dictionary of Economic Theory and Doctrine. Volume 3* (3 vols., Macmillan, London, 1987), pp. 519–25.
8. J.M. Keynes, *A Treatise on Money, Volume 1* (Macmillan, London, 1930).

9. J.M. Keynes, *The General Theory of Employment, Interest and Money* (Macmillan, London, 1936).

10. J.M. Keynes, "Social Consequences of Changes in the Value of Money" (1923) in *Essays in Persuasion* (Norton, New York, 1963; first pub. 1931), pp. 80–104.

11. As I have said, I came to Locke late, when writing this book, and mainly through the work of Caffentzis (see note 6).

12. Notably, *Some Considerations of the Consequences of Lowering the Interest and Raising the Value of Money* and *Further Considerations Concerning Raising the Value of Money.*

13. See note 6, op. cit., pp. 182–3.

14. Ibid., p. 21.

15. Soros has since become a poacher-turned-gamekeeper, having launched numerous cultural and educational initiatives, especially in Eastern Europe, and written a book in which he claims that the contemporary version of capitalism cannot last. He ought to know! G. Soros, *The Crisis of Global Capitalism: Open Society Endangered* (Little, Brown, London, 1998).

16. A. Hamilton, *The Financial Revolution* (Penguin, London, 1976), p. 8.

17. K. Hart, "Heads or Tails? Two Sides of the Coin," *Man,* December 1986.

18. As someone who plays around with acronyms myself, I am intrigued that Keynes chose ATOM as his title at a time when atomic physics led the way towards a relativistic worldview, of which this book is a rare example in the social sciences. J.M. Keynes, *A Treatise on Money. Volume 1: The Pure Theory of Money. Volume 2: The Applied Theory of Money* (Macmillan, London, 1930).

19. See note 16, op. cit., *Volume I,* p. 12 (Keynes's emphasis).

20. Ibid., p. 4 (Keynes's emphasis).

21. Figure 6.1 draws on two diagrams in the original, ibid., pp. 9–11.

22. G. Simmel, *The Philosophy of Money* (Routledge & Kegan Paul, London, 1978; first pub. as *Die Philosophie des Geldes,* 1900).

23. Ibid., p. 13.

24. Here Keynes borrowed from G.F. Knapp (1924) the contrast between *metallism* (money's value being based on precious metal, such as gold or silver) and *chartalism* (its value being declared by a legal decree of the state). See note 33.

25. *Fiat* is Latin for "let it be," a species of wilful subjectivity we associate with the likes of Lewis Carroll's Humpty Dumpty or the Queen of Hearts, but one that is not inappropriate to the mindset of modern governments, at least before the fall.

26. See note 23, p. 8.

27. ". . . the glittering economies of *not* holding metal being as characteristically attractive to north Britain as the glittering certainties of holding it to Nearer Asia." See note 23, p. 16n (original emphasis).

28. J. Buchan, *Frozen Desire: An Inquiry into the Meaning of Money* (Picador, London, 1997), "Mississippi Dreaming: On the Fame of John Law," pp. 127–51.

29. W. Bagehot, *Lombard Street: A Description of the Money Market* (John Wiley, New York, 1999; first pub. 1873).

30. Republics may use a depersonalized image, such as a heraldic design, to symbolize the political authority. It is interesting, therefore, that many republics, not to be outdone by constitutional monarchies, use the heads of presidents for this side of the coin.

31. J. Schumpeter, *History of Economic Analysis* (Oxford University Press, New York, 1954, pp. 647–8).

32. Ibid., pp. 421–2.

33. G.F. Knapp, *A State Theory of Money* (Macmillan, London, 1924; first pub. 1905).

34. K. Hart, contribution to *History of Political Economy* Symposium, 2000.

35. See note 26.

36. This is the basic message of Mauss's *The Gift* (1925) and of Simmel's *The Philosophy of Money* (1900) too. It is the humanist side of a liberal tradition that has taken its anti-humanist path principally through mainstream economics. In fact, humanist liberalism and social democracy overlap considerably. Mauss thought of himself as a co-operative socialist, for example. M. Mauss, *Ecrits Politiques* (M. Fournier, ed., Fayard, Paris, 1997).

37. The World Bank, *World Development Report* (Oxford University Press, New York, 1996), pp. 210–11.

38. We are all familiar with the game *Monopoly,* but few know that it originated as a propaganda vehicle for Henry George's social credit party (which had as its principal policy a tax on all landed property). The aim was to demonstrate how unfair the property system is. The game was subsequently marketed by Parker Bros. as an enjoyable pastime celebrating the American way of capitalism. George and his followers lost the legal suit to regain control of their artifact.

39. K. Polanyi, *The Great Transformation* (Beacon Books, Boston, Mass., 1944), pp. 240–1.

40. See note 14, op. cit., pp. 30–49.

41. I. Hacking, *The Taming of Chance* (Cambridge University Press, Cambridge, 1990).

42. It is interesting that David Boyle's recent book, *Funny Money* (1999), which explores lines similar to this one, refers to money in its subtitle as "cash." My sense of the demotic resonance of this word in modern English leads me to guess that the etymology from French *caisse* or Latin *capsa* may be spurious and that the Asian coin points to an earlier, pre-Indo-European source. D. Boyle, *Funny Money: In Search of Alternative Cash* (HarperCollins, London, 1999).

43. C. Lewis and C. Short, *A Latin Dictionary* (Oxford University Press, London, 1933).

44. Buchan is a Scot, a matter of some significance for his narrative. There may be an implicit reference to his fellow Scot, Adam Smith, *An Inquiry into the Nature and Causes of the Wealth of Nations* (1776). See note 27.

45. Note 28, pp. 269, 19.

46. G. Vico, *The New Science of Giambattista Vico* (T. Bergin and M. Frisch, eds, Cornell University Press, Ithaca, NY, 1984; first pub. 1744).

47. I. Berlin, *Vico and Herder: Two Studies in the History of Ideas* (Hogarth Press, London, 1976).

48. See note 41, op. cit., para. 699, p. 264.

49. Once again much in this passage is drawn from Caffentzis's analysis, especially pp. 53ff. See note 6.

50. J. Locke, *Two Treatises of Government* (Cambridge University Press, Cambridge, 1960), Book 2, 44.

51. J. Locke, *An Essay on Human Understanding*, Book 2, Chapter 27, § 11, cited by Caffentzis (note 6), p. 53.

52. See note 6, op.cit., pp. 53–4.

53. See note 5, pp. 65–6.

54. *American Heritage Dictionary* (third edition, 1993).

55. I avoid entering into debates concerning the meanings of the word "culture," which are, as is well known, legion. K. Hart, "German Idealism and Jamaican National Culture," *Caribbean Quarterly*, July 1990.

56. B. Malinowski, *Crime and Custom in Savage Societies* (Routledge & Kegan Paul, London, 1966).

57. See note 34.

58. J.K. Galbraith, *Money: Whence It Came, Whither It Went* (Penguin, Harmondsworth, 1995; first pub. 1975).

59. K. Marx, *Capital: A Critique of Political Economy. Volume. 1* (Lawrence & Wishart, London, 1970), pp. 71–83.

60. M. Taussig, *The Devil and Commodity Fetishism in South America* (University of North Carolina Press, Chapel Hill, 1980).

61. G. Simmel, *The Philosophy of Money* (Routledge & Kegan Paul, London, 1978; first pub. as *Die Philosophie des Geldes*, 1900).

62. The marginalist revolution is attributed to Jevons (England), Menger (Austria) and Walras (Switzerland) in the 1870s; but Alfred Marshall's *Principles of Economics* (1890) was the main instrument of its diffusion. A. Marshall, *Principles of Economics* (Macmillan, London, 1979; first pub. 1890).

63. See note 58.

64. K. Hart, "Barter" in J. Eatwell, M. Milgate and P. Newman, eds, *New Palgrave Dictionary of Economic Theory and Doctrine. Volume 1* (Macmillan, London, 1987); C. Humphrey and S. Hugh-Jones, eds, *Barter, Exchange and Value* (Cambridge University Press, Cambridge, 1992).

65. A. Smith, *An Inquiry into the Nature and Causes of the Wealth of Nations* (Methuen, London, 1961; first pub. 1776), p. 17.

66. See note 59, op. cit., Chapter 1, "Commodities."

67. See note 39, op. cit., Chapter 5, "Evolution of the Market Pattern."

68. C. Humphrey, "Barter and Economic Disintegration," *Man,* 1985; "Fair Dealing, Just Rewards: The Ethics of Barter in North-east Nepal" in C. Humphrey and S. Hugh-Jones, eds, *Barter, Exchange and Value: An Anthropological Approach* (Cambridge University Press, Cambridge, 1992).

69. D. Marin, *The Economic Institution of International Barter* (Center for Economic Policy Research, London, No. 1658, 1997).

70. B. Malinowski, *Argonauts of the Western Pacific* (Dutton, New York, 1961; first pub. 1922); K. Hart, "Heads or Tails? Two Sides of the Coin," *Man,* December 1986.

71. ". . . the ideas of economists and political philosophers, both when they are right and when they are wrong, are more powerful than is commonly understood. Indeed the world is ruled by little else. Practical men, who believe themselves to be quite exempt from any intellectual influences, are usually the slaves of some defunct economist. Madmen in authority, who hear voices in the air, are distilling their frenzy from some academic scribbler of a few years back. I am sure that the power of vested interests is vastly exaggerated, compared with the gradual encroachment of ideas." Not bad for the closing pages of the most influential economics text this century. The issue of leaders and followers in the human conversation may perhaps not be quite as he envisaged it, but it clearly worked for him. J.M. Keynes, *The General Theory of Employment, Interest and Money* (Macmillan, London, 1936), p. 383.

72. P. Bohannan, "The Impact of Money on an African Subsistence Economy," *Journal of Economic History,* vol. 19, 1959.

73. T. Veblen, *The Higher Learning in America: A Memorandum on the Conduct of Universities* (New York, Sagamore Press, 1957; first pub. 1918).

74. S. Cook, "The Obsolete "Anti-market" Mentality: A Critique of the Substantive Approach to Economic Anthropology," *American Anthropologist,* vol. 8, 1966; P. Bohannan, "Some Principles of Exchange and Investment among the Tiv of Central Nigeria," *American Anthropologist,* 1955.

75. G. Dupré and P.-P. Rey, "Reflections on the Relevance of a Theory of the History of Exchange" in D. Seddon, ed., *Relations of Production: Marxist Approaches to Economic Anthropology* (Frank Cass, London, 1978; first pub. 1973).

76. J. Parry and M. Bloch, "Introduction," *Money and the Morality of Exchange* (Cambridge University Press, Cambridge, 1990).

77. J. Carsten, in ibid., "Cooking Money: Gender and the Symbolic Transformation of Means of Exchange in a Malay Fishing Village."

78. See note 56, cited by S.F. Nadel in *A Black Byzantium* (Oxford University Press, London, 1942).

79. A. de Tocqueville, *The Old Regime and the French Revolution* (Doubleday, New York, 1955; first pub. 1856).

80. See note 86.

81. D. Boyle, *Funny Money: In Search of Alternative Cash* (HarperCollins, London, 1999), p. xi.

82. M. Aglietta and A. Orléan, eds, *La Monnaie Souveraine* (Odile Jacob, Paris, 1998).

83. C.S. Buck, *A Dictionary of Selected Synonyms in the Principal Indo-European Languages* (University of Chicago Press, Chicago, 1949), p. 773.

84. See note 6.

85. I learned about this scheme and some other facts enlisted in this section while appearing on a television program, "The Future of Money," put out by Sky News on 11 August 1997. A lot more of the material referred to here comes from newspapers, especially the *Financial Times.*

86. U.S. Department of Commerce, *The Emerging Digital Economy* (Washington DC, 1998, published on www.commerce.gov).

87. Thus, for example, American Express has recently introduced a micro-chipped security card for use on the Internet that is supposed to eliminate fraud.

88. D. Miller, *Capitalism: An Ethnographic Approach* (Berg, Oxford, 1997).

89. See note 76; J.-M. Servet, ed., *Une économie sans argent: les systèmes d'échange local* (Seuil, Paris, 1999); F. Bowring, "LETS: An Eco-Socialist Alternative?", *New Left Review,* December 1998; J. Croall, *LETS Act Locally: The Growth of Local Exchange Trading Systems* (Calouste Gulbenkian Foundation, London, 1997); G. Seyfang, "The Local Exchange Trading System: Political Economy and Social Audit" (G. Seyfang, dissertation, 1994).

90. F. MacCarthy, *William Morris: A Life for Our Time* (Faber & Faber, London, 1995).

91. I took an interest in the LETS systems of my home town and once met Michael Linton there, through Angus Soutar, his colleague and one of Manchester's innovative LETS activists. Their Web page is very informative: www.gmlets.u-net.com.

92. See note 81.

93. I am grateful to Oscar Kjellberg for the information in this paragraph.

94. See note 80.

95. K. Jackson, *The Oxford Book of Money* (Oxford University Press, Oxford, 1995); *Granta,* "Money" (Penguin, Harmondsworth, winter 1994, no. 49), especially articles by Jackson and Buchan.

96. R. Harrod, *The Life of John Maynard Keynes* (Norton, New York, 1951).

97. C. Gregory, *Savage Money: The Anthropology and Politics of Commodity Exchange* (Harwood, Amsterdam, 1997).

98. T. Crump, *The Phenomenon of Money* (Routledge & Kegan Paul, London, 1981).

99. M. Douglas, *In the Active Voice* (Routledge & Kegan Paul, London, 1982).

100. J. Guyer, ed., *Money Matters* (Heinemann, London, 1995).

101. V. Zelizer, *The Social Meaning of Money* (Basic Books, New York, 1994).

Chapter 7
The Future of Money and
the Market

Making money, making scenarios

The latest phase of the machine revolution sharpens our awareness of an impending break in human history of a sort that bears comparison with Childe's two revolutions, the inventions of agriculture and cities, ten and five millennia ago respectively.[1] For some time now writers about late-twentieth-century society have used labels suggesting that we have passed beyond whatever stage we were in before. This "afterology"[2] takes various forms, of which the most common are: *post-modernism,* implying a break with whatever made us modern, presumably the institutions of state capitalism; *post-industrialism,* reflecting the shift from manufacturing to services; and *post-colonialism,* suggesting that the world has moved beyond the phase of Western empire. Echoing all this, the academic fashion of the day is *post-structuralism,* with Michel Foucault having replaced Marx as the most frequently cited icon of the left intelligentsia. What they are saying is that it seems we have come to the end of something; and I can hardly dissent from that. But I have also argued in this book that the world is not yet even *post-agricultural,* in that half of humanity still work in the fields with their hands and the rest remain in the grip of institutions whose origin and logic lie in five thousand years of agrarian civilization.

So, while there are undoubtedly tremendous changes afoot, it would be unwise to write off the forces of modernity, industry and empire. The world is still ruled by nation-states pursuing an economic agenda of Victorian vintage. The rise of countries like China is underpinned by the industrial techniques that once fuelled Western expansion. The collapse of Europe's empires has merely paved the way for an American version that operates through puppet dictators, military strikes and multilateral institutions. And world society bears a striking resemblance to the old regime of eighteenth-century France. Let us assume, therefore, that we are not yet past anything, much as we would sometimes like to be. There is no guarantee that a new age, better than the last, is already born, or even that we have entered a limbo phase between two contrasting stages of social development. Everything remains to be fought for; and the evidence of the last century is that the forces of counter-revolution, the drive of states and corporations to control society from the top and exclude most people from meaningful power, will only be displaced by a mighty social movement or, to employ a much abused expression, a world revolution.

How do we go about exchanging the squalor of contemporary society for one in which economic justice is taken seriously? A prerequisite is to learn to think creatively in terms that both reflect reality and reach out for imagined possibilities. This in turn depends on capturing what is essential about the world we live in, its movement and direction, not just its stable forms. I have argued that the stage of capitalism we have reached is at the same time global and virtual, each term reflecting the phase of mechanization I have called the communications revolution. The idea of *virtual reality* goes to the heart of the questions I have raised here. It contains the movement that links the book's form to its content, *extension from the actual to the possible*. "Virtual" means existing in the mind, but not in fact. When combined with "reality," it means a product of the imagination that is "as good as real," almost but not quite real. In technical terms, "virtual reality" is a computer simulation that enables the effects of operations to be shown in real time. The word "real" connotes something genuine, authentic, serious. In philosophy it means existing objectively in the world; in economics it is actual purchasing power; in law it is fixed, landed property; in physics it is an image formed by the convergence of light rays in space; and in mathematics real numbers are, of course, not imaginary ones.[3] "Reality" is present, in terms of both time and space ("seeing is believing"), and its opposite is imagined connection at distance, something as old as story-telling and books, but now given a new impetus by the convergence of telephones, television and computers.

Already the experience of near synchrony at distance, the compression of time and space, is altering our conceptions of social relationships, of place and movement. When Hegel set out to show how thought could move from the known to the unknown by means of dialectical reason, constructing imagined futures on the basis of knowledge of the real past, he was hardly aware of the machine revolution's first steam-driven stirrings.[4] Yet he understood that analytical reason was too far from normal human thought processes to be able to grasp the movement of history. For that we need narrative in some form. There are many words for made-up stories and the one I choose for this chapter is *scenario*. This is in origin the plot outline for a dramatic or literary work, but for us it is usually a screenplay, the story-line of a movie. It can also be used as "a model for an expected or supposed sequence of events"; and, in this sense, scenarios are often plural, a range of possibilities in a planning exercise.[5] Here, it is time to extend the retrospective analysis of money in history to the task of making it in future; and that depends on making scenarios with many facets and possible outcomes, all addressing a single question that defines our plot: Will we or won't we—humanity that is—be able to make a more just society (as the market) than the one in which money (as capitalism) currently confines us? And, as a step towards that end, how may we learn to make our own money rather than just take it as it comes?

In the previous chapter, I made much of the symbolism of coins, that form of objective money that (*pace* Keynes) so clearly represents the economy of agrarian civilization from which we would emancipate ourselves. It is worth recalling that states and markets of the kind with which we are most familiar developed as institutions designed to meet the needs of small urban elites living off the coerced production of the rural masses. We have seen that the dialectical interplay of heads and tails, of public hierarchy and private exchange conceived of alike as impersonal institutions, has dogged twentieth-century society, finding nightmarish expression in the nuclear stand-off of the Cold War. It should not have been difficult to see the interdependence of the two sides; and some nations like Germany and Japan recognized this, although their example was not inspiring from a humanist point of view. And this is the point: Humanity stands in dire need of an alternative to this unholy pair, a third way that is more conducive to self-expression through the money form and hence to economic democracy.

Coins gave way to paper currency in the modern period and recently money has taken the predominant form of electronic digits (or *bits*) transmitted through telephone wires. If paper marked a move toward the assertion of state authority over money, the cheap information contained in bits allows exchange to admit a higher degree of personal agency than before. So that, instead of debating whether money resides objectively in precious metals or is made by political authorities, we can revive the tradition of banking that emphasized money as personal credit or acknowledgement of debt. Seen in this light, money is an expression of trust between individuals in society, an act of remembering that allows us to bring calculation to some of our interactions and relationships. This trust is two-sided also, residing in both personal responsibility and the shared memory of communities, in personality and culture, to echo an American school of anthropology.[6] But we can no longer afford the oversimplified assumption that nation-states monopolize, in their relations with individual citizens, either the source of money or the only meaningful locus of community. Most of us now live, thanks to cheap transport and telecommunications, in a plural set of associations of potentially infinite scope, the most inclusive of which is the world market. Money must evolve to reflect that plurality, and this, I have argued, is precisely what has been happening already.

It seems likely that, for the foreseeable future, any moves towards more personalized forms of money will co-exist with those that are already dominant. A large number of transactions, involving people and institutions around the world, will have the need of a money or moneys that have wide acceptability both as money-of-account and as money-proper, to use Keynes's terms. At present the dollar and, to a lesser extent, some other national currencies play such a role; and this has been enhanced by the financial turbulence in East Asia, Russia and elsewhere during the late 1990s. There are moves to strengthen the dollar zone of currencies tied to the USA economy. This comes at the same time that Western Europe has explicitly set out to establish a rival currency, the euro. The timing of this initiative was not ideal, since the American economy has been enjoying remarkable buoyancy when Europe is still struggling with high unemployment and low growth. In the aftermath of Japan's economic difficulties, the Chinese have let it be known that they may seek to establish the yuan as an international currency; but that may have unacceptable political consequences. In any case, the regional power blocs are shaping up to offer currencies that aspire to general use in the world economy.

One obvious victim of this development is the independence of national currencies. Many of these have been more or less useless for international transactions for a long time, being "soft" or non-convertible rather than "hard" currencies. And those few that are still actively traded in international money markets experience wide and destabilizing fluctuations in their exchange rate, as a result of the growing size of the free-floating funds that shape these markets. Keynes called these state-made currencies "managed money," accepting, within an established range, the logic of markets and banking. It seems probable that these will persist as an expression of feelings of national sovereignty, as a medium of public expenditure and taxation supporting the reduced pretensions of government in countries whose citizens have traditions they wish to cling to. But it is my prediction that this level of the economy will be squeezed between global and local interests, and the money associated with it marginalized as a result.

The majority of European Union countries, as a result of the Maastricht Treaty, opted to replace their national currencies with the euro in 2002. An independent central bank, modelled on the German Bundesbank, was set up to ensure that the euro would be "hard," i.e., managed to be as inflation-proof as possible. But France's tradition of state intervention and a currently high unemployment rate, as well as the difficulties arising from Germany's absorption of the former East, have led to a modification of that line in favor of a "softer" approach, one reflecting the need to accommodate domestic political pressures. This shift, as well as the region's inferior economic performance, may account for the dramatic deterioration in the euro's exchange rate with the dollar in the first two years after it was floated as a money-of-account in January 1999. Incidentally, the 1999–2002 timetable of Maastricht makes the euro the first wholly virtual currency in history during its transition period. The relationship of Britain to all this is of more than parochial interest, because of that country's role in the theory and history of money and its equivocating participation in Europe's monetary evolution.

Britain's Conservatives, who have become extremely sceptical of Europe, once proposed, instead of monetary union, the floating of what was called at the time the "hard ecu," a bank-managed sound money that would exist in parallel with national currencies, leaving businesses and individuals free to choose between them in their various transactions. But their partners wanted monetary reform to point the way to political union and envisaged the euro as a bridge towards a United States of Europe, capable of matching America in the world economy. After being forcibly ejected from European monetary union by the financial turmoil of "Black September" in 1993, a Britain now governed by the center-left (Labor) is still half in, half out of Europe's leap towards greater integration. As a result, it looks as if, for a time at least, sterling and the euro will exist side by side in a relationship not unlike the one proposed for the hard ecu. Of course, the euro may turn out to be softer than was once envisaged; and Labor, having returned management of interest rates to the Bank of England and espoused anti-inflation policies, may succeed in maintaining confidence in sterling, even as a reserve currency of sorts. At the same time, the integrity of the United Kingdom itself has been thrown into the balance by devolution in Scotland and Wales, as well as Ireland's protracted post-colonial struggle. The situation could develop in any of a number of directions. The main point is that money will remain a potent symbol and a practical means of political change.

Once we move down from scenarios of history on a grand scale to money management by ordinary people, the question shifts to the relative use of the money instruments available. In Britain, for example, right up to the nineteenth century, there were normally several currencies in circulation in addition to sterling; and this situation, having been temporarily banished by state capitalism, is likely to be restored. A growing number of people spend time occasionally or regularly outside their own country, and this requires them to hold different currencies, paying conversion costs when necessary. For them the advantage of a currency like the dollar or the euro would be its acceptance in many places. The money could be held as banknotes, travellers' checks or plastic cards drawing on bank deposits anywhere. In terms of everyday economic life, it seems probable that most people will want to make purchases at short notice using a money-of-account that is locally acceptable and paying on a cash or credit basis. They will continue to be paid in this kind of money for most of the jobs they perform. So what scope is there for using special electronic forms of money such as those described briefly in the last chapter?

The great advantage of setting up or joining closed circuits of exchange with their own money-of-account is that they offer some respite from the exigencies of the markets for normal money. They can give communities or networks of individuals a means of organizing some of their activities independently, without fear that the value of their transactions will somehow be sucked off to an anonymous center of accumulation. We have already seen that they suffer from high transaction costs, variable quality of service, small scale and inadequate division of labor, as well as unresolved costs of starting-up and managing such schemes. But these are early days and the participants are handicapped as often as not by antiquated ideologies. Developments affecting electronic money on the Internet may bring commercial sophistication to these alternative economic practices. At the very least an area has been opened up where people can explore different methods of livelihood and co-operation. Having absorbed plastic cards faster than some pundits predicted, they can now discover ways of integrating a wide variety of money forms into their lives—as many kinds of money, in fact, as the associations in which they are regularly involved.

We have to take society as it comes a good deal of the time; and no one could pretend that a time when we routinely make our own money is just round the corner. It is a question of degree. What matters is to escape from the sense that we are trapped in an iron cage not of our own making, Max Weber's gloomy prediction of the fate of modern societies.[7] Weber would have been astonished by the peaceful and rapid collapse of the Soviet empire, one of the most awesome bureaucracies known to history. This is because he underrated the human resilience of ordinary people. No doubt the ability of people to become self-conscious economic agents, manipulating the social possibilities for personal credit, will long be unevenly distributed among humanity. But intellectuals, who prefer to live in the closed world of their own rationalizations, may be as astonished as Weber would have been, had he lived, by the speed with which people take up the chance now being offered for increasing their degree of economic self-reliance.

The old regime and the middle-class revolution

In this book I have tried to present a vision of history that might offer readers a means of engaging with the situation confronting humanity at this time. It is widely believed that we now live in a world that has made a decisive break with the past. Society today claims to rest on science and democracy, the twin foundations of modernity and the lasting legacy of the eighteenth-century revolutions. This modern religion is similar in many ways to older claims made on behalf of God: If society is omniscient and good, how can there be so much suffering in the world? The obvious answer to this question is that world society is not run by and for the people as a whole, and, whatever its principles, they are not based on effective knowledge. Perhaps we are less emancipated from the past than we imagine and are further from a desirable future than we hope.

I have argued that human history may be conceived of as having four phases:

1. the state of nature, before agriculture and property;

2. agrarian civilization, landed property and the naturalization of unequal society;[8]

3. the age of money or capitalism, where power goes to the owners of capital in a market economy;

4. universal community founded on just reward for human creativity and the need to reconcile market economy and nature.

These phases overlap. We live in an age of money where the institutions of agrarian civilization still predominate, but the machine revolution is propelling us towards at least the possibility of forming a democratic human community. The forces of technology are amplified by a massive social contradiction: The world is growing closer together and more unequal at the same time. The same process that has spawned the Internet, virtual capitalism, is also generating a wide gap between haves and have-nots. It follows that we must seek ways of using the means of improved social connection to combat economic inequality. This is similar to Marx and Engels's proposal that centralization of machine industry in the factory system should be used to develop more effective resistance by workers to capitalist exploitation. To say this is not to belittle the power of world capitalism, nor to suggest that a revolutionary alternative can easily be found. It is to base a radical politics on the same social forces that constitute economic oppression.

In truth, world society today is at base as rotten as the aristocratic regimes that preceded the modern age.[9] Power has been concentrated into forms held against the people, first in the hands of owners of big money and then in a revived and strengthened state apparatus. In the course of the last century the rule of elites has been restored: State bureaucracy is absolute; and world society is divided into national fragments. There is no popular government anywhere; and most people have forgotten when they last took an active interest in such a possibility. The confusing part lies in the widespread use of a rhetoric derived from the democratic revolutions to cloak the purposes of those who reserve effective power to themselves. Western states are no more liberal than the Soviet Union was Marxist. At least the old regime of agrarian civilization called itself what it was. The vast majority of intellectuals are complicit in the lies needed to sustain this latter-day revival of the state. Behind a smokescreen of democratic slogans, the bureaucracy relies on impersonal institutions to maintain grotesquely unfair levels of inequality.

The breakout from agrarian civilization was led by urban middle-class elements in a few places, beginning with the Italian Renaissance. This was not the first time: For a thousand years class coalitions based on property in land and money respectively slugged it out for control of ancient Mediterranean society, before the Romans made the world safe for landed aristocracy.[10] In the modern period it did seem as if what its detractors call the bourgeois revolution was home and dry when mechanization was married to capital accumulation. But this was precisely the moment when, fearful of the proletarian monster they had made, the middle classes shrank back and embraced an alliance with the military landowning class. Society was reconceived as nations whose origins were shrouded in a rural past;[11] and the counter-revolution took off with a vengeance. Marx was right to rely on a feudal metaphor for the new wage-labor system, since everywhere old forms of property and power were harnessed to the task of holding the workers down.

Even so, as the nineteenth century drew to a close, the issue was in the balance. The world was drawn together by a revolution in transport and communications (steamships, railways, the telegraph). The workers were concentrated in smokestack industries. Could they seize power from the owners and their allies? The issue was settled by the First World War, when governments discovered that they now possessed unprecedented powers of social mobilization and control. Society was centralized at the top and twentieth-century state capitalism was inaugurated. Since then, until recently, when another revolution in transport and communications has begun to undermine territorial states, the question was not whether the people or their rulers would win out but to which form of state people all over the world would be made subordinate. The middle classes abandoned their previous commitment to commerce in order to sup copiously at the trough of national bureaucracy, relying on their university diplomas for a lifetime of privilege as experts in social reproduction.

The result is that the middle-class revolution with which the modern age began has stalled, even regressed, first allying itself with landed power and then assuming the form of rule traditional for agrarian civilization. No serious mid-nineteenth-century social thinker imagined that the restless energies of industrial/commercial society could be controlled from the top by a remote centralized mechanism. Yet a century later most of us are conditioned to think that no other form of society is imaginable. The institutions of agrarian civilization, developed over five millennia with a passive rural workforce in mind, are our institutions today. And our taxes since the Second World War have been largely spent on subsidizing food supplies and armaments, which is more or less what the elites of any agrarian civilization would have done. No, we have never been modern (as Bruno Latour says).[12] We are like the first digging stick operators of the neolithic revolution, primitives who cannot yet think what do with our new machines, beyond repeating the inhumanity of a society built unequally on agriculture.

Human society is caught between mechanization and agrarian institutions, and the combination is potentially lethal. Its most striking pathology is the polarization of rich and poor at every level of society. It should not be necessary to explain why economic inequality is a problem for world society; but, after two decades of "loadsamoney" economics, it is.

I. Inequality undermines democracy. Broadly equal access to the world's resources is a condition for free co-operation in society.

2. Inequality makes us feel bad. Human compassion struggles with indifference, the desire for connection with that for distance.

3. Inequality is a threat to world peace. Resentment of historical wrongs fuels terrorism and ultimately war.

4. Inequality obstructs joint stewardship of the planet's ecology. The rich cannot pursue the goal of conservation mainly through restricting the development of the poor.

5. Inequality reduces market demand. Economic growth in the modern world comes from increasing the purchasing power of the masses. Everyone benefits from redistribution.

Nothing less than a world revolution is adequate to redressing the inequality of our times; and it will not succeed without an appropriate explanation for the phenomenon in question. Mine is roughly as follows.

First, we are living with the consequences of five thousand years of agrarian civilization (Childe's urban revolution),[13] which cannot be discarded overnight. When 3 billion peasants work in the fields with their hands and archaic institutions like the territorial state rule the world, we must not attribute all wrongs to capitalism. Even so, it is not hard to see that a system of making money with money favors those who have a lot of it at the expense of those who don't.[14] Without some corrective, the rich will get richer and the poor stay poor. The money system has now reached a social scale and technical form that make it impossible for states to control it. This may be good news for democrats and anarchists in the long run; but in the meantime Hegel's recipe for state moderation of capitalism[15] has been subverted, with inevitable results: rampant inequality at all levels and appalling human distress without any apparent remedy. Moreover, capitalism has flourished when linked to machine production. Mechanization too, in order to take root, requires cultural and social institutions (science, education, work discipline, finance, property law) that are unevenly spread between and within societies. Every stage of the machine revolution has been initially concentrated in a narrow enclave of world society, and ours is no different. Many poorer regions now appear to be stuck in phases of production that have been marginalized by this latest round of uneven development.

A major corollary of the above is the tendency for labor markets to take on a dualistic character: two streams of workers, one highly paid in jobs using sophisticated machinery, the other performing tasks of little skill for low wages and in poor working conditions, often no better than those prevailing in traditional agriculture. Institutions have been developed at every level of world society to justify inequality and to keep the poor in their place by controlling any movement that might undermine the separation of rich and poor. In a word, this is *apartheid.* The territorial state and nationalism effectively reinforce indifference to others, leaving the world stage to be ruled by the most powerful, while undermining whatever sense of our common humanity might lead us to want to alleviate the horrors of poverty. That the world economy in based on inhuman principles is a commonplace. Compassion and similar human qualities are unlikely to be influential in economic life when power is concentrated in remote, faceless centers. When confronted with the consequences of their own actions, people shrug their shoulders: It is nothing to do with us. Society will only be democratic when people can assume meaningful responsibility for themselves and for others.

Contemporary world society thus has more in common with the old regime of agrarian civilization than it does with the modernist rhetoric inaugurated by the democratic revolutions. This is not just because of the sheer gap in lifestyle and prospects between rich and poor, but because the ideology justifying global inequality is still identifiably racist, explaining difference as the expression of innate superiority and inferiority. The European empires have collapsed, but the people have not yet inherited the earth. What, then, is to be done?

In his trilogy on the information age, Manuel Castells[16] makes a convincing link between the core network form of contemporary society and the current phase of capitalist development. His is a functionalist conception that says that membership of a network lasts only as long as someone is useful to its central purposes. This rather brutal sense of a world devoid of trust, solidarity or reciprocity captures quite well at least one side of our experience. But Castells turns to identity politics on the margins of capitalism for a forlorn hope of resistance. This would be like Marx and Engels looking for a revolutionary alternative to capitalism, not from the sociology of machine industry itself, but from the tribal identities of the migrant workers who formed the first industrial proletariat.[17] Our intellectual task is surely to show that what is intrinsic to modern networks points to a way forward other than capitalism.

A common intellectual error is to overstate the dominance of ideal types in social relations.[18] Thus economically rational behavior becomes something else when we place markets in real time and space. Weber's iron cage of bureaucracy cannot explain how Stalinism could be overthrown. Marx's concept of a proletariat with only its labor power to sell omits the self-generated resources of the informal economy. A vision of state capitalism as resting on impersonal institutions misses how we have all been trying to make them personal. Reliance on these one-sided abstractions leads us to imagine change as a leap from one idea to its negation; whereas a more nuanced interpretation allows us to build on what has already been going on, if only in the cracks of the old system. What all these rationalizations omit is the people who live in them. Castells's networks may be dehumanized, but the people who constitute them can do nothing other than to try to make them human.

We need powerful abstractions as a way of cutting through the empirical confusion. But these are always dialectical constructs whose movement in real time and space is the outcome of what people do in their everyday lives. Chapter 5 on the market from a humanist perspective perhaps best illustrates this approach. If we allow an overdetermined idea of state capitalism to sway our minds, we are likely to imagine that the historical movement of which we are part consists in a digital shift from impersonal to personal society. This would be misleading on several grounds. First, impersonal society was always constituted by people trying to make it personal in some way; second, as a plural social phenomenon it has been moving for some time; and, third, the changes we envisage are less a leap in the dark, more an extension of developments already in train. From this I conclude that social improvement requires a new emphasis in impersonal and personal relations, as opposed to an idealized switch from one to the other; and that this must be grounded in what people do and want.

Having said this, what general grounds might we have for trying to deploy the Internet against economic inequality rather than for it? Many users of the Internet express a commitment to building a better society drawing on principles made more feasible by the new medium. These are often self-consciously opposed to traditional attitudes to money and the market. They include an ethos of helping out without pay; interest-free loans; community barter schemes; and so on. At the same time electronic commerce is growing rapidly, both as exchanges between firms and, as we have seen, in consumer markets like books, flowers and airline tickets. Some see these developments as being inevitably opposed; others seek to reconcile them, for example in ecological investment consultancies or customized marketing. It is one thing, however, to demonstrate how the Internet might help some of its users to achieve a higher level of personal agency in economic life, quite another to show how it might be used to address the causes of poverty. Even so, a fragment of the middle classes, stirred by the possibilities unleashed by the Internet, may come to see the way towards general social reform as a more permanent solution to their private dilemmas. We might, for example, focus on a campaign to alter the world's economic institutions along lines pioneered by Keynes.

The main reason agrarian society was economically stagnant for millennia was that it was not in the interests of the ruling class to improve the conditions of most ordinary working people. Modern economic growth has been sustained by bringing these working masses into a market mechanism driven in large part by the need to supply what their money buys. In the 1930s, when economic depression gripped Europe and America, the spectre of mass unemployment, poverty and political disaffection at home stimulated national governments to find ways of reviving consumer demand, largely by printing money and putting it in citizens' pockets. Today escalating inequality stands in the way of world economic growth and threatens to swamp the rich with the social pathologies of the poor. It is only the constitution of world society as an old regime that prevents this obvious truth from being more widely understood. A Keynesian remedy, consisting of redistribution and a new approach to global credit, is hardly unthinkable.[19] It is unlikely, however, that such a revolutionary approach to money at the global level will emerge before the scale of the economic and ecological disaster we face has become even more apparent than at present.

There exists a precedent for this in the international campaigns to abolish slavery, colonialism and apartheid, when representatives of oppressed groups found willing allies in the middle classes of Europe and America. I often wonder what Thomas Clarkson might have achieved if he had had access to the Internet.[20] Clarkson could be said to have pioneered the techniques of modern single-issue politics while campaigning for the abolition of slavery. In seven years he travelled 35,000 miles on horseback around Britain, relying for support on a network of Quakers in many cases. He undertook what we would call fieldwork trips, insisting on going to Liverpool and Bristol to see for himself. This is the hallmark of modern social anthropology, and Clarkson knew it instinctively. He wanted evidence; he wanted first-hand knowledge. But he also wanted to show it to people, so he bought thumbscrews, whips and all kinds of things; and he made a personal portable museum, a chest that he used to carry around with him to demonstrate both the evils of the slave trade and the benefits of legitimate trade with Africa, artifacts and crops like coffee.[21] He hoped that this collection of visual things would shock his audiences into recognizing the truth of what he had to say.

Clarkson may not have invented petitions, but he played a very major role in developing and articulating them as an instrument of mass politics. He was involved in boycotts, of West Indian sugar in particular. He was a tremendous pamphleteer. He and others in his network perfected the art of lobbying parliament, threatening their representatives with deselection if they didn't toe the line on abolition. Above all, Clarkson recognized that there was a need for someone to personify the movement, to take personal responsibility for its organization. He knew that, in this kind of network-based movement, somebody has to take on his shoulders the responsibility for originating, developing and managing the process of getting things done. That was what everyone recognized as his tremendous contribution. So the method of campaigning that Clarkson developed, a method based on fact-finding, public display, petitions, lobbying, pamphleteering and the rest, is the best early example of single-issue politics we have; and there is a great deal to be gained from examining it today.

I have not concealed the two main problems that seem to stand in the way of realizing any such program as that outlined in this section. First, the Internet is dominated by the big players, the governments and corporations of this world, whose power could be said to overshadow whatever the rest of us may be capable of. We will address that question in the next section. Second, the vast majority of human beings are excluded from participating in the Internet, which may well be seen as reinforcing global divisions instead of removing them. This last point has always seemed to me to be a cop-out. Just because only a few people have access to the Internet, this need not prevent some of them from engaging with world problems by this means. Who else will stand against the social forces that would reduce this enormous advance for humanity to a way of consolidating the old regime? There is a revolution to be made and it has to start now. The people, after all, is each one of us.

People's money: beyond economic coercion

Inequality has been used in this book as a shorthand expression for the social contradiction that a future democratic society would have to redress. "The people," whose will is universally declared to be sovereign today, have had to content themselves with a lot of propaganda and little of the reality of power in the twentieth century. Rather, a bureaucratic elite, distinguished by its uniform ("the men in suits") and divided in principle between government and commerce, has supervised one of the most unequal systems of rule seen in history, state capitalism. For all the rhetoric of freedom that abounds in our societies, state capitalism is based on legal and economic coercion, on the ancient principle of territorial monopoly and on the newer one of having to sell oneself in order to live. State power looks as if it is on the wane; and, while the world's money system totters from one crisis to the next, the concentration of economic power in the hands of a few large corporations seems inexorable. This is our chance to find new forms of political association, more appropriate to popular needs, and perhaps even to subvert the dominance of a capitalism enjoying the fruits of globalization. The one strategic asset we have is the fast-breaking medium of the Internet and, at a time when society increasingly takes the form of a world market, our efforts at self-emancipation must be focused on the money instruments themselves.

For, too often in modern times, the goal of political democracy has been undermined by the absence of any realistic economic counterpart. After the heads and tails of state-money and commodity-money, it is time to make people's money.

The word "socialism" has fallen out of fashion. I prefer the expression "economic democracy," which Marx and Engels acknowledged as an acceptable substitute. Socialism emphasizes the collective above all else, whereas democracy can refer to both collective and individual agency. In a late essay, "Socialism: Utopian and Scientific,"[22] Engels explained why his version of socialism was scientific, and social experiments such as those of William Morris were the former. Utopian socialists looked back to a pre-industrial age of communities and craftsmanship; whereas scientific socialists looked ahead, with the benefit of the best knowledge available, to the reshaping of the modern world by contemporary social and material forces. He, along with all the leading social scientists of the day, correctly saw the world moving along a path of centralization fuelled by machine industry. He was concerned, however, that this centralization was proceeding faster and more effectively at the top of society than at the bottom; and he was right to be, as it soon turned out.

I have tried in this book to lay the groundwork for a similar exercise a century later. Now the nostalgic left is likely to dream of rebuilding the states that once seemed to carry the aspirations of the masses everywhere. This is a utopian exercise, since it fails to come to grips with the forces changing our world. What are these? Virtual capitalism, a corollary of the communications revolution; weakening state management of capitalism; and the apparent dominance of markets driven by "wild" money.[23] Global integration is linked to a decentralizing technology that favors increased mobility at the expense of national political controls. The result is that whatever safeguards had been built up to protect the poor in some countries have been undermined. It sometimes seems that only a capitalist crash on the scale of the Great Depression could restore the political will to intervene in markets as strongly as governments did in mid-century. But the political framework for such intervention is much less obvious now.

This is why I have been keen to place my work within the traditions of liberal and social democracy, since the thinkers on whose work I have drawn heavily belong to both. Locke, Simmel and Keynes have done more than most to advance our understanding of money, and they did so in the belief that it was indispensable to prospects for greater human freedom.[24] Yet I have obviously also been much influenced by the romantic/socialist critique of money developed by Rousseau and Marx. The first of these is impossible to classify in terms of subsequent polarities of right and left, straddling as he does the divide between liberal and social democracy. When social structures are highly mobile and unreliable, it pays to emphasize the education of individuals to be responsible members of whatever forms of society they attach themselves to. But, as we know, liberalism as a theory has been compromised by the inequality and coercion it masks; and there has grown up an urgent popular agenda claiming that the "bourgeois" revolution has fallen short of the need for a genuinely democratic solution to society's ills.

I have argued, nevertheless, that it is time to go beyond the established positions of right and left. If money is the problem, it is also an indispensable part of the solution. We are living in a rapidly urbanizing world of great complexity and increasing social connection whose affairs cannot be managed by means of handouts, either on a bureaucratic or on a customary basis. Apart from the obvious issue of hierarchy entailed in this method, people will expect to use any economic freedom they win for themselves to calculate the costs and benefits of many contracts they enter in the course of normal daily life. We cannot afford to oppose collective and individual solutions to our common human dilemmas. If I have turned to markets and money as a focus for social reform, it is because, by emphasizing the means of extending social credit to responsible persons, we may be able to address more effectively the causes and remedies of what makes contemporary society so unequal.

The immediate and long-run causes of economic inequality, therefore, are an unfair and unstable system of money-making; the lack of legal guarantees ameliorating poverty; arbitrary power, whether political or economic; cultural barriers to entry, in the form of state rules and informal prejudice; and the uneven development of machine technology. Virtual capitalism has exacerbated this by marginalizing whole sectors of the world economy where agriculture and mining are predominant, as well as by unleashing savage swings in the money system that can impoverish national economies at a single blow. The Americans, who started off in the present monetary crisis worrying that the pensions of Midwesterners could be wiped out by the bursting of the Far-Eastern equities bubble, seem now to be sustaining global stock markets through confidence in their own technological innovation and financial strength. A world dominated by American capital to the degree that we are now witnessing would be even more unequal than that country's internal economy. There would then be no end to an age of money dominated by the rich.

I have gone out of my way to insist on the archaic institutional make-up of our societies, claiming that the world today is in some ways more the offspring of agrarian civilization than of modern machines and democratic government. The obstacles to progressive change are thus twofold: the need to democratize the age of money, to bring capitalism under control; and the need to break down "natural" structures based on territorial monopoly, to foster mobility at the expense of being tied to the land. The aim should be to improve the scope for human beings to see themselves as free economic agents; to make it more possible for people to express their personalities in social life; and to build up the stable infrastructures of money, law, education and technology capable of providing impersonal guarantees of such activity. Even then, reducing inequality may require wider social mobilization and a reform program with many dimensions. At the very least, the emergence of a single interactive social network at the global level makes it possible to address questions that are in fact universal.

Just as the classical political economists focused their energies on denouncing the mechanisms of distribution that they saw as hindering capitalist development, we too might benefit from examining the forms of revenue that sustain governments and companies in our day. It bears repeating that the bureaucratic power of states and corporate capital rests on coercion. Tax and rent both depend on the authorities being able to force people to pay through the threat of punishment; and territorial monopoly is indispensable to both. This, for all their conflicts of interest, underlies the continuing alliance between large firms and particular nation-states. The issue is whether borderless trade at the speed of light will permit governments still to extract revenue from markets and whether every Internet user in the world will pay rent to Bill Gates, or his equivalent, whenever they switch on their computers.

Recent improvements in the mobility of people, goods, money and information have systematically undermined the ability of governments to exact payment on threat of punishment. Sir James Mirlees, Professor of Political Economy at Cambridge University, recently received a Nobel Prize and a knighthood for proving that you cannot tax the rich any more than they want to pay. When asked by his university's alumni magazine to explain his theory, he told them that it was far too technical for lay people to understand.[25] Alfred Marshall and Maynard Keynes, two of his Cambridge predecessors who both favored income redistribution and found it possible to communicate with the public, would no doubt have been interested in his answer. Of course, the rich and the corporations have enjoyed relative freedom from taxation for some time. The poor dropped underneath the tax net long ago. And criminals of all classes have succeeded in avoiding regulation with growing impunity. This leaves mainly the middle classes to pay for the tax burden; and they have now been given the technical means of effective resistance, as well as the incentive of being more financially insecure than ever before. Instead of working out how to clobber the rich, the rest of us might benefit from learning how to emulate them.

In France, as I write, the left pins its hopes on two measures: a "Tobin tax"[26] on financial transactions (the money flows of virtual capitalism) and a statutory 35-hour working week (to share the jobs more equally). This comes at a time when the borders between European countries are increasingly open and French capital has joined vigorously in the global movement of markets that I take to be undermining the power of states. It constitutes the kind of utopian socialism that inhibits the left from coming up with genuinely radical solutions to the inequalities of our day. Even so, I have been impressed enough by the solidarity and militancy of French people at all levels of society to recognize that I have written this book from a perspective that finds more support among the "Anglo-Saxons." If the state is to be put to constructive purposes in the present crisis, then it is likely to be in the country that celebrates its republic as heir to the first democratic revolution of the modern age.

Future generations may well conclude that we are passing through a cumulative tax revolt of proportions not seen since the end of the Roman empire. It is salutary to reflect on Max Weber's magisterial essay on that topic.[27] He argued that the Roman empire was at its peak in AD 150, when territorial expansion reached its limits. The imperial system rested on converting Italian peasants into soldiers and resettling them in conquered lands as *coloni*. The wars generated a ready supply of captives who could be put to work as slaves on large estates carved by the Roman aristocracy out of the former holdings of the peasantry. The slaves were kept in single-sex barracks and no attempt was made to breed with them, since their replacement price in the market was cheap. A wide social gulf existed between free and unfree labor.[28]

The end of expansion meant that the supply of new slaves gradually dried up, prices rose and owners were obliged to allow the ones they had to reproduce, introducing a form of family life that was eventually reinforced by Christianity. The slaves began to take on some of the features of a peasantry. At the same time the state bore down more heavily on the settlers, reducing their legal freedoms in various ways and exacting a heavy tax burden. The empire's need for money was exigent, since the army and a large bureaucracy would only work for cash[29] and cash came from taxes on earnings from trade. Demands made on the towns became so onerous that rich individuals took to escaping into the countryside, where they established their own armed camps (or *villas*) and resisted the authority of the state. This reduced the latter's revenues even more and led to further crackdowns on those sectors of the "free" population who were not able to escape. Eventually the system broke down and the different forms of labor merged into a single semi-free type that we associate with feudalism. The emperor, Weber concludes, became a rural illiterate, forcing his company onto a sequence of dependent warlords; and the air of his travelling court was permeated with the smell of dung. It took Europe a thousand years to recover.

This cautionary tale may be more or less relevant to us, depending on how society responds to the weakening of the nation-state. I do not intend here to explore how people might further evade paying taxes. It is ironic enough that the state's paper money is the anonymous medium of exchange preferred by criminals; and, for those who choose to risk being identified through electronic transactions, the sheer volume, speed and spatial dispersion of these transactions will ultimately defeat revenue-collecting bureaucracies. At present, the system of taxation depends on citizens' belief in its inevitabilty. We have not yet reached the stage of extra-terrestrial banking by satellite, the ultimate offshore facility; but imagine the legal arguments over political jurisdiction when we do. It is not long ago—the middle of the past century, in fact—that governments seriously doubted whether they could make people pay tax on more than a nominal proportion of their income.[30]

If governments, with all their powers of surveillance and punishment, will find it increasingly difficult to enforce their claims, how much more will this apply to corporations seeking to secure rental income from their "property." The Internet has opened up a revolution in intellectual property rights by making the reproduction and diffusion of print publications almost costless. The backlog of copyright cases waiting for legal processing mounts up daily. When computer software is one of the growth industries and a company specializing in its development is the richest in the world, the Internet is bound to become a site in which the battle for control of information and the wealth to be derived from it is fought out. Already there are web pages and mailing lists devoted to disseminating free the software to which Microsoft claims copyright. This is one of the main arenas in which the relative power of governments, corporations and ordinary people will be tested. The conflict of values and interests has already been joined.

This discussion has obvious relevance to the forms of political association that are likely to develop. The centralized state depended on convincing its citizens that they had no alternative means of joining world society than through its auspices. This is no longer so. Let me give a hypothetical example. In 1945 Britain's new Labor government was committed to nationalizing the means of finance as well as education, among many similar projects. It backed off from both of these in the face of entrenched establishment interests. To take only the latter, if the government had announced then that the public schools (that is, the fee-paying elite schools) were to be abolished, it was technically feasible for them to do so. Today, if any British government made a similar proposal, Eton would simply relocate to Jersey or Switzerland, and the children of the rich would jump on a plane three times a year. If this is true for a privileged elite, it is becoming increasingly true for the rest of us; and that means that people are now freer than ever to decide which forms of government to submit to. In consequence, decentralization or devolution of powers to regional or local government bodies will grow in significance, since people are more likely to fund public projects nearer to home. At the same time, they will become aware of national governments' inability to address global problems and will seek out more inclusive institutions (federations, international networks and single-issue pressure groups) better suited to addressing them.

It seems likely, therefore, that the territorial dimension of society will devolve to more local units. These will retain a modified ability to coerce taxes and rents from their members, at a level limited by the sanction of personal mobility. If I want to live in Paris, I will have to agree to pay the dues that support that city's excellent public services. If I find them unaffordable, I can join in the fight to get them reduced or go and live somewhere cheaper. What I would not wish to support is France's nuclear arsenal or the expenses incurred in maintaining far-flung outposts of empire. As a European, I would naturally be interested in joining schemes to promote fast and reliable public transport throughout the region. To some extent, supporting bodies and projects beyond the local level will be voluntary because of the scope for evading unwanted taxes. There will no doubt be a large class of nomads who put down their roots in no one place for long enough to be made to pay any taxes, beyond those assessed on commercial services and at controllable points in the transport system. The U.S. government is, now and for similar reasons, seeking to persuade others to keep their hands off the Internet.

Under these circumstances we have to ask what would have been an unthinkable question for most of the twentieth century: How might public economies be financed without effective means of coercing payment? The Swiss government has recently admitted that, in the face of delocalization, it can no longer make good its threat to punish financial offenders using the national stock exchange.[31] It has therefore encouraged the latter to draw up its own self-policed rules with the principal sanction of excluding transgressors. Britain's Serious Fraud Office, set up explicitly to control financial crime, has largely failed to bring successful prosecutions. It may be that we need to face up to the notion that in the future people will be free to participate in the system of money and markets only on their own terms. It may seem far-fetched now to suggest that public economies will have to be largely financed on a voluntary basis. But there are many precedents for this in history, as well as relevant examples in contemporary world society; and, if the above argument has a grain of truth in it, we have good reason to suppose that the underlying social and technological trends of our day point in that direction too.

If people cannot be forced to pay, they must be motivated to support public ends. At its peak, state capitalism enjoyed considerable legitimacy, and it is more than the threat of punishment that keeps the law-abiding majority paying taxes today. But, as Weber insisted, when society makes its demands in the name of an impersonal norm of rational government, the moral basis for individual conformity is weakened.[32] As the saying goes, morality tells you what you ought to do, the law what you can get away with. Modern bureaucracy, as embodied in law, markets and science, has undermined the meaningful attachment of persons to the social order of which they are a part. It follows that, when bureaucracy fails, the means of personal connection will have to be reinvented. There are many antecedents for building communities on the basis of individual members' moral and religious commitment. The history of the Protestant international movement that launched the modern democratic revolution is just the most obvious source of comparison.[33] Modern Islam, in its many variants, is another. The growth of NGOs financed by charitable donations could likewise be enrolled in expanding this point. Marcel Mauss was far-sighted when he sought to trace the foundations of the modern economy to its origin in the gift, rather than in barter as the conventional myth holds.

The idea of money as personal credit, linked less to the history of state coinage than to the acknowledgement of private debts, is consistent both with Mauss's emphasis and with the scenario outlined here. I have suggested that we should look for the meaning of money in the myriad acts of remembering that link individuals to their communities. In this interpretation, the need to keep track of proliferating connections with others is mediated by money in its many forms as the principal instrument of collective memory. To an increasing extent, it will be possible for people to enter circuits of exchange based on voluntary association and defined by special currencies of the sort pioneered in LETS schemes. At the other extreme, we will be able to participate as individuals in global markets of infinite scope, using international moneys-of-account, such as the dollar, electronic payment systems of various sorts or even direct barter via the Internet. In many ways, it will be a world whose plurality of association, even fragmentation, will resemble feudalism more than the Roman empire. This is quite a frightening prospect; for who would want to be prey to personal rule by gangsters unrestrained by impersonal law? And that is why we urgently need to harness the potential of current trends to the development of more effective institutions at the level of world society.

Building economic infrastructure for the coming century

If the emphasis in this book has been on making money, on how the market economy may be remade as a means of self-expression for each of us, this is because twentieth-century society has been based on impersonal economic institutions that made most people feel largely powerless. I have argued that a shift towards repersonalization of the economy has been made possible in part by cheap information. But society and the individual, the impersonal and the personal, are equally necessary to human existence; and working out specific ways of combining them is durably problematic. We have to take society as it comes, but we can also try to make it. The communications revolution has been so sudden and far-reaching that it is the most each of us can do to work out a way of adjusting to it. Every little advance in mastery of technique is celebrated as a personal victory, each setback is experienced as a crushing defeat. It is wonderful to learn how to send an e-mail message. We have little time or inclination to ask how these messages reach their destination, who supervises the standards we all rely on, what happens if the system fails? How did it get there in the first place and who takes responsibility for the next stage in the process?

The Internet represents a colossal human achievement, yet its origins and future are shrouded in anonymity;[34] rather like money, as a matter of fact. Like the successors to the Roman empire, we are living on the infrastructures built up by earlier phases of the middle-class revolution, but we have largely lost the taste or the ability for renewing them. I have in mind the political and intellectual inheritance of the eighteenth century, the engineering achievements of the nineteenth century, even the attempt to build a new world order after the linked disasters of the period 1914–45. In Britain, which pioneered so much of what makes the modern world distinctive, the water now drains away because no one can find the money to repair the leaks, the railways are falling apart, and the local authorities compete for Asian and American investment. Need I go on? The world is so conditioned by the mean outlook of our century that we can only imagine ethnic identity as xenophobia and individuality as something hostile to the public good. World society, after a century of wars, is unthinkable at present. Yet somehow humanity is propelling itself to a new stage of global integration through the development of new communications systems, through markets and money as much as through the exchange of words and images.

That is why I take inspiration from John Locke's example. He addressed squarely the infrastructure needs of a new and better society. He was concerned with placing knowledge and the words we use on a foundation of truth, government on a stable basis of property and money on a metallic standard. He understood that a new civil religion and morality would have to take root if liberal democracy was to work. This is to say that people have to be able to rely on stable objective conditions that anchor their volatile subjectivities. Such universals must be, to a degree, made up; but their operation depends on people being able eventually to assume them as given. The most important of these is the rule of law (especially the law of contract); but money is not far behind in significance. Other standards include time, or perhaps "universal timespace" would be better, an enabling feature of world society now that deserves more recognition than it gets;[35] and we are fast approaching the stage when universal language (computing codes, numbers, the use of English) enters the frame. If you have children and want to prepare them for the twenty-first century world they will live in, what aptitudes would you want them to cultivate and what infrastructures would you hope they could benefit from? What do you imagine society as a whole will need so that we can live together and prosper?

Mention of Locke recalls the issue of money and language.[36] Communities share meanings by means of markets and conversation, through objective and subjective exchange. Locke was concerned that state regulation of money could be imposed by threat of punishment, but people were relatively free to say what they liked, without much fear of public sanction. Isaac Newton could string up counterfeiters from Tyburn in an attempt to purify money; but who would restore confidence in public discourse by controlling the semantic criminals, the politicians who never said what they meant? In the following century the dictionary movement and other educational initiatives set about the task of stabilizing language, a process that was ultimately centralized by modern nation-states. But if money in our time is escaping from its bounds of state-made law, so too is language, as an increasingly mobile world population develops cosmopolitan cultural skills that often include English as a lingua franca with many regional variations. It may be that money is about to follow the example of language, just as language followed the example of money in the era of state capitalism.

What this means is that, once the threat of state sanction is weakened, people have to turn to their own forms of association and to more informal means of regulation. The example given earlier of the Swiss stock exchange, released from state supervision and left to its own internal devices as a self-regulating body, is likely to become much more widespread with the erosion of territorial power. The direction of economic change will be that of linguistic development. Each of us will participate in several, even many, forms of money and the corresponding circuits of exchange they allow us to enter, just as we enter many conversational circles in the course of a lifetime. Under these circumstances, money, like language, becomes a subjective capacity of the individual, personal credit the counterpart of the private idiolect that each of us speaks.

For me there is something exciting about these possibilities. But I understand why many people would view them with dread as the collapse of a familiar order into potential chaos. Repersonalization, if it means the decline of state powers with which we are familiar, opens the way perhaps to feudalism, to a Tower of Babel in which nobody understands anyone else. That is why it is not so fruitful to imagine the present transition as a shift from the impersonal to the personal, but rather as a change in emphasis affecting the relationship between the two. If economy has in the twentieth century become more impersonal, responding in part to the increased scale and complexity of exchange, this does not mean that the personal basis of economic relations has been entirely displaced; nor indeed that the dialectic of individual and collective agency was ever absent from societies in which money and the market as we know them were traditionally marginal. The recent phase of modern history has been dominated by bureaucratic management of the economy. The process is dialectical, however. Most people are quite anxious

about being economically dependent on impersonal and anonymous institutions. This is an immense force for reversing the historical pattern of alienation on which the modern economy has been built. Consequently, any
renewed emphasis on human personality and concrete social relations in
economic life must go hand in hand with the search for forms of impersonal
society appropriate to such a goal.

I have sketched a scenario that leads from state-made money to greater
reliance on personal credit. This does entail a repersonalization of economic
life, as exchange absorbs more and more information about persons. Plastic
credit cards are just the first step in this process. But humanism, as outlined
here, also recognizes our increased dependence on impersonal abstraction
of the sort associated with the operations of digital computers, as well as the
need for impersonal standards and guarantees for contractual exchange. If
persons are to make a comeback in the post-modern economy, it will not be
on a face-to-face basis, but as bits on a screen who sometimes materialize as
living people in the present. In the process we may become less weighed
down by the concept of money as an objective force, more open to the idea
that it is simply a way of keeping track of complex social networks that we
each generate as active individual subjects. There is every reason why money
should take a wide variety of forms compatible with both personal agency
and human interdependence at every level from the local to the global.

How such a future might be achieved is something I have merely indicated. This is not a practical manual, but a contribution to the ongoing
human conversation about making a better world. Our overwhelming need
at this time is to rebuild meaningful connection between self and world society. I have pushed beyond the limits of normal scholarship to draw as fully
as I can on my own reserves of knowledge and experience to this end. I do
so less in the belief that what I have written is certain, but more in the hope
that readers will be stimulated to enter into a similar exercise for themselves. As a researcher I have usually practiced whatever I wanted to study.
As Vico pointed out, you can only truly know what you have made yourself.[37] In my pursuit of the principles underlying modern economy, I have
been a gambler, a gangster, a consultant, a desktop publisher and many other
things. Above all, I have conceived of anthropology, my professional discipline, as a way of learning to live in the world, to feel more at home in it if

you like. We need to learn how to make economic relations that work for us, for each one and for all of us. One path toward that is to learn how to make money and not just in the senses we have come to give to that phrase.

Guide to further reading

The work of V. Gordon Childe in identifying the neolithic and urban revolutions, particularly *Man Makes Himself* (note 1), is indispensable to the long-run view of history presented in this book. Ernest Gellner's *Plough, Sword and Book* and Jack Goody's *The East in the West* are more recent attempts at anthropological generalization relevant to this grand evolutionary theme.[38]

The issue of democracy takes us to Alexis de Tocqueville, whose *Democracy in America* and *The Old Regime and the French Revolution* still have much to teach us.[39] I have learned a lot from Martin Thom's remarkable study of the shift from republicanism to nationalism (note 11). Engels's inspiring essay on socialism is about democracy by another name (note 22). Otherwise, I would have preferred to spend more time exploring the Ancient Mediterranean for parallels to our own times; and I recommend that course to readers. Start with two Victorian classics: Fustel de Coulanges's *The Ancient City* and Engels's *Origins of the Family*, etc. (note 10). Then take in Weber's *Agrarian Sociology of Ancient Civilizations* (with Perry Anderson's derivative *Passages from Antiquity to Feudalism*) (note 27) and Moses Finley's *The Ancient Economy* (note 28).

As for our times, the following trio capture something of what I have aimed for in this book: Castells's *The Rise of the Network Society* (note 16), Latour's *We Have Never Been Modern* (note 12) and Gregory's *Savage Money* (note 23). If some readers have discovered a latent taste for dialectic from this book, James's *Notes on Dialectics* (note 4) is worth chasing up, with Avineri's *Hegel's Theory of the Modern State* (note 15) to provide the background to the method. No one exemplifies the creative mixture of factual and fictional approaches explored in the chapter more effectively than Jean-Jacques Rousseau. I recommend his *Emile, Confessions* and *Reveries of the Solitary Walker*, in addition to the main political texts, the *Discourse on Inequality* and *The Social Contract*.[40] In fact, read anything by Rousseau and ask what it takes to make this stinking world a better place for humanity.

Notes

1. V. Gordon Childe has been the writer most responsible for establishing a materialist conception of human history in which the two most important events before our machine revolution were the inventions of agriculture and then of cities, ten and five millennia ago respectively. I like to think that the spirit of this book reflects that of Childe's work half a century ago or more. V.G. Childe, *Man Makes Himself* (Moonraker Press, London, 1981).

2. I get the term from Marshall Sahlins (*Waiting for Foucault,* Prickly Pear, pamphlet no. 12), who credits Jacqueline Mraz with the expression "afterological studies." M. Sahlins, *Waiting for Foucault* (Prickly Pear Press, Charlottesville, Va., pamphlet no. 12, 1999).

3. *American Heritage Dictionary* (third edition, 1993).

4. G.W.F. Hegel, *The Science of Logic* (Allen & Unwin, London, 1966; first pub. 1812–16); C.L.R. James, *Notes on Dialectics: Hegel, Marx, Lenin* (Allison & Busby, London, 1980; first pub. 1948).

5. See note 3.

6. The "culture and personality" school of Boas's students, especially Margaret Mead and Ruth Benedict.

7. A. Giddens, *Capitalism and Modern Social Theory* (Cambridge University Press, Cambridge, 1971), p. 235.

8. Writers on social evolution are divided over whether to count a phase of agriculture before the city as distinctive from the agrarian civilizations that followed. I have chosen to treat agrarian civilization as entailed in the invention of agriculture (see Chapter 2); but all such typologies are relative to specific intellectual purposes.

9. K. Hart, "World Society as an Old Regime" in S. Nugent and C. Shore, eds, *Elites: Anthropological Perspectives* (Routledge, London, 2001).

10. After spending my teenage years as a classicist, it has taken me some time to acquire a vision of the first millennium BC as a whole. I now consider the finest general account to be Fustel de Coulanges's *La Cité Antique* (1863), closely followed by Engels's *The Origins of the Family, Private Property and the State* (1884). Both put most present-day academic scholarship on the period to shame. N.D. Fustel de Coulanges, *The Ancient City: A Study on the Religion, Laws and Institutions of Greece and Rome* (Doubleday, New York; first pub. as *La Cité antique,* 1864); F. Engels, *The Origin of the Family, Private Property and the State* in Marx–Engels, *Selected Works* (Lawrence & Wishart, London, 1968; first pub. 1884).

11. M. Thom, *Republics, Nations and Tribes* (Verso, London, 1995).

12. B. Latour, *We Have Never Been Modern* (Harvester Wheatsheaf, London, 1993).

13. See note 1.

14. Not an entirely original idea. "For to him who has will more be given, and he will have abundance; but from him who has not, even what he has will be taken away." (Matthew 13:12).

15. Because of misrepresentations of Hegel by Marxists (not least by Marx himself), it is not widely understood that the former developed his theory of the modern state as an explicit antidote to the excesses of capitalism (which he called *bürgerlich Gesellschaft,* or civil society). His *The Philosophy of Right* (1821) could be said to have anticipated the main work of all three founders of modern social theory, Marx, Weber and Durkheim. S. Avineri, *Hegel's Theory of the Modern State* (Cambridge University Press, Cambridge, 1972); G.W.F. Hegel, *The Philosophy of Right* (Oxford University Press, London, 1952; first pub. 1821).

16. Manuel Castells has every right to be considered the Max Weber of the late twentieth century for his monumental work on the sociology of the Information Age. If I express a difference from him here, it should not detract from his achievement. I do believe, however, that, like Weber, Castells's reliance on an impersonal social science leads him to underestimate the sources of human resilience in the face of his rationalist constructions. M. Castells, *The Information Age: Economy, Society and Culture* (3 vols, Blackwell, Oxford, 1996), especially *Volume 1: The Rise of the Network Society.*

17. Just to confuse matters, I happen to think that they seriously mistook the source of the buoyant solidarity they found among the Lancashire working class in the 1840s and after. This came not from the experience of industrial work *per se,* but from their non-feudalized Celtic homes of origin. They were, in other words, an early instance of what Sahlins calls a "translocal community," which I explored among the Frafra migrants of Ghana in the 1960s. Identity politics on the margin has never been revolutionary (*pace* Castells). Marx and Engels's strategy was the right one, but they did not understand what they saw.

18. An "ideal type" is an intellectual construct based on selective exaggeration of the features rationally associated with a phenomenon.

19. Indeed, Keynes himself saw such a scheme as indispensable to the long-term success of Bretton-Woods, but he was overruled by the Americans. R. Harrod, *The Life of John Maynard Keynes* (Norton, New York, 1951).

20. This speculation occurred to me in 1996 when I gave an improvised public lecture at St John's College, Cambridge, on the occasion of the 150th anniversary of Clarkson's death. I would like to thank Ray Jobling and the Master, Peter Goddard, for the invitation to give this lecture. E.G. Wilson, *Thomas Clarkson: A Biography* (Macmillan, London, 1989).

21. Clarkson's chest is on display in the Wisbech Museum, Cambridgeshire. I am grateful to the Bishop of Ely, Stephen Sykes, for having encouraged me to join the campaign for Clarkson's rehabilitation, which had its roots in his home town. Clarkson was, as a result, commemorated by a plaque in Westminster Abbey.

22. F. Engels, "Socialism: Utopian and Scientific" in Marx–Engels, *Selected Works* (Lawrence & Wishart, London, 1968).

23. C. Gregory, *Savage Money: The Anthropology and Politics of Commodity Exchange* (Harwood, Amsterdam, 1997).

24. Keynes answered his own question "Am I a liberal?" in a positive but rather facetious manner by suggesting that he could hardly sign up for a party that promoted the interests of a class (workers) that was not his own. Yet if anyone made economics a tool of social democracy, it was he. J.M. Keynes, "Am I a liberal?" (1925) in *Essays in Persuasion* (Norton, New York, 1963; first pub. 1931).

25. I tried to find a readily accessible example of Sir James's work, but I couldn't.

26. After the American Nobel laureate economist, James Tobin, who kept the flag flying for Keynesian remedies to Reaganomics in the dark years of the 1980s.

27. M. Weber, "The Social Causes of the Decline of Ancient Civilization" in *The Agrarian Sociology of Ancient Civilizations* (New Left Books, London, 1976; first pub. 1904). See also P. Anderson, *Passages from Antiquity to Feudalism* (New Left Books, London, 1974).

28. M. Finley, *The Ancient Economy* (University of California Press, Berkeley, 1973).

29. The word "soldier" is itself derived from the Latin word, *solidus,* meaning pay and originally a gold coin.

30. The anecdotal evidence for this comes from many literary sources. For example, Abraham Lincoln's government was under severe financial pressure in the American Civil War, but levying an income tax was rejected as being impracticable at the time. (Gore Vidal, *Lincoln*). The tax authorities, like writers of fiction, require a great deal of co-operation from their target populations.

31. Derived from a conversation with Alain Hirsch, who is not responsible for this version.

32. That is why Weber considered modern rational-legal government to be a form of non-legitimate domination. This point was consistently misrepresented by the American sociologist Talcott Parsons and his followers, who were keen to claim for the rational division of labor a measure of traditional legitimacy. The difference can be seen in the

translation by Parsons and Henderson of Weber's mammoth work, *Wirtschaft und Gesellschaft,* and that of Roth and Wittich, which in my view is more faithful to the original. T. Parsons, *The Structure of Social Action* (Free Press, Glencoe, Ill., 1937).

33. There is a wall in Geneva celebrating the history of the political struggle to win the freedom of religious worship. Here are Protestant heroes such as Jean Calvin, of course, but also Henry IV signing the Edict of Nantes, Oliver Cromwell addressing parliament and the organizer of the Mayflower expedition. The message is obvious: the democratic and republican movements were largely fuelled by an international network of Protestants seeking independence from an oppressive Church and no less oppressive states.

34. This history is rather less anonymous since the publication of John Naughton's fascinating *A Brief History of the Future: The Origins of the Internet* (1999). J. Naughton *A Brief History of the Future: The Origins of the Internet* (Weidenfeld and Nicolson, London, 1999).

35. It is only recently that the whole world became organized by a single framework of time; and already some corporations are making use of this to co-ordinate global production schedules, employing workers from complementary regions. What I have in mind, however, is the development of new attitudes to time compatible with the potential of the world civilization I have pointed towards in this book.

36. G. Caffentzis, *Clipped Coins, Abused Words and Civil Government in John Locke's Philosophy of Money* (Autonomedia, New York, 1989).

37. G. Vico, *The New Science of Giambattista Vico* (T. Bergin and M. Frisch, eds, Cornell University Press, Ithaca, NY, 1984; first pub. 1744), p. xliv.

38. E. Gellner, *Plough, Sword and Book: The Structure of Human History* (Collins Harvill, London, 1988); J. Goody, *The East in the West* (Cambridge University Press, Cambridge, 1996).

39. A. de Tocqueville, *Democracy in America* (2 vols, Vintage, New York, 1945; first pub. 1840); *The Old Regime and the French Revolution* (Doubleday, New York, 1955; first pub. 1856).

40. J.-J. Rousseau, *Emile: or, On Education* (Basic Books, New York, 1979; first pub. 1862); *The Confessions* (Penguin, Harmondsworth, 1953; first pub. 1781); *Reveries of the Solitary Walker* (Penguin, Harmondsworth, 1979; first pub. 1776); *Discourse of the Origins and Foundations of Inequality among Men* (Penguin, Harmondsworth, 1984; first pub. 1762); *The Social Contract and Other Later Political Writings* (V. Gourevitch, ed., Cambridge University Press, Cambridge, 1997).

Acknowledgments

Many people have helped me in the course of writing this book, especially all those who constituted my network of e-mail correspondents. As I wrote from the traditional isolation of a Paris flat, I was conscious that I was one of the first generation of writers to be involved in continuous electronic dialogue with readers all over the world. This tension between stability and movement seems to have worked for me. I hoped to keep a record of those exchanges over two to three years, but my laptop computer was stolen not long ago. I would like to express my gratitude here to all those who kept me going with their comments when transhumance made their disembodied conversation the mainstay of my social life. These stalwarts of e-mail dialogue, all of whom stimulated fresh thinking and nourished me with their friendship, included: Bob Dewar, Meraud Grant Ferguson, Tom Hall, Heonik Kwon, Ted Leggett, Joanna Lewis, William Mazzarella, Alexandra Ouroussoff, Ato Quayson, Alison Richard, Don Robotham, Alison Tierney, Carol Upadhya, Huon Wardle and Eric Worby.

Jack Goody would not claim responsibility for me, but I know how much he formed me. Anna Grimshaw helped me recover from the dark years. Peter Clarke showed the way from scholarship to the general public. Vishnu Padayachee, intellectual companion, was the benign face of macroeconomics. Marilyn Strathern gave me encouragement at the right time. John Thompson commissioned the first, aborted version of this book. Jean-Michel Kerr, software developer and green politician, made our brief encounters count. Don Billingsley, an American in Paris, had faith in me. Simon Schaffer, Renaissance man, put me onto the key to John Locke and gave me glimpses of his own vision. Jim Murray, founder of the C.L.R. James Institute, reminds me that America is the world. Big Brother and the Blue Sisters, (Frances Pine, Helen Watson, and me), was and is a class act.

Paula Uimonen, ethnographer of cyberspace, shared with me her knowledge and belief. Tobias Hecht, writer and student of humanity, offered advice on how to bridge genres. Caspian Richards knows how intensive and rewarding our exchanges have been in this period. Matthew

Engelke, publisher of Prickly Pear Press, has shown his friendship in more ways than I can say. Philip Fergusson, NGO pioneer, has offered me theoretical and practical guidance where I most needed it. My most recent Ph.D. students, Brian Alleyne and Knut Nustad, have given me the invaluable support of their enthusiasm and criticism.

Ruth Van Velsen has been a constantly reliable ally in these years of upheaval. John Bryden, my old friend and laird of the Highlands and Islands, helped me to escape from Cambridge. Patrick Verdon is my inspiration and source of whatever IT competence I have acquired. Gabriel Gbadamosi, for whom these years have not been easy, was always there. Louise Hart kept my spirits up with her shining progress. Sophie Chevalier was my anchorage.

In the preparation of the book, I would like to thank Sunil Khilnani for his example and for making the publishing connection. John Tresch found the title. Ruth Van Velsen proofread the manuscript. Catherine Alexander was typically generous at the end, giving my tables "the Coopers look" and much more. Terry Roopnaraine lent his home, technology and unstinting support to help me finish the job. My association with Peter Carson and the crew at Profile Books has been short-lived and happy. I never dreamed that, after such a long gestation, the process of realizing this book in print could have turned out to be so streamlined. Thanks too to Donna Poppy for an excellent job of copyediting. Thanks to Joe Spieler for negotiating the Texere contract and to the Texere production team for turning this edition round so quickly.

I lost my sister and a close friend while I was writing this book, both of them, it seemed to me, well before their time. I had hoped to share my old age with Janice, who meant more to me than I ever told her. Skip Rappaport gave me the example of his own great book, which I helped to bring to print; but again the loss of his presence in the world has at times been unbearable.

Paris
January 2001

The river of time carries its own banks along with it.
ROBERT MUSIL

INDEX OF NAMES

GENERAL INDEX

Note: page numbers in italic indicate tables or figures.

A

abortion laws 216
absolute surplus value 88
Accra 99, 151
afterology 295
Age of Extremes: The Short Twentieth Century 124
age of money 76–82
agrarian civilization 67, 121, 207, 220, 302
   and the machine revolution 62–68, 301–303
   stagnation of 308
agricultural revolution 49–50
agriculture 45, 49, 63
alienation 13, 211, 263, 270, 322
   and money 213, 261
Amoro (Frafra) 102, 105
Anaba (Frafra) 100, 108, 111
analog computation 51
Ananga (Frafra) 100
Annie Hall (film) 135
anthropology 13, 46, 322
   social 12, 263
Anthropology and the Modern Economy (Hart) 17
apartheid 137, 138, 139, 306
Argonauts of the Western Pacific (Malinowski) 190, 267
armaments industry 154–155
Atia (Frafra) 106–108, 111
Atibila (Frafra) 100, 102
Atinga's bar 151–154
automatic teller machines (ATMs) 272–273

B

bank
   notes 273
   rate 249
bankruptcy 254
banks 14, 244, 253
   memory 14–15
   mismanagement by 163
   offshore 244–245
   services of 279–280

bargaining 200
barter 80–81, 190, 264–269, 280, 318
betting 157–159
Boggs' money pictures 235–237
Bretton Woods agreement 242–243
bridewealth 219–220, 270
bureaucracy 166, 208, 318
bureaucratic revolution 39–40, 125, 204–205, 215
businessmen and the Internet 277

C

capital 83
   industrial 85
   and labor 91
Capital: A Critique of Political Economy (Marx) 80, 81, 86, 87, 124, 261, 265
capitalism 3, 4, 9, 33, *34* 59
   definition of 10, 270
   familistic 97
   grey 284
   and markets 206, 222
   ongoing origins of 91–96
   state *see* state, capitalism
   theory of 82–91
   virtual *see* virtual, capitalism
centralization 40, 127, 205–206
change, rates of 58–59 *see also* time, perspectives
chartalism 251
cities, growth of *41*
City, The (Weber) 208
class alliances 94–95
classes 120–121, *167*, 195, 271–272
   and resources 167
cocoa industry 93–95
   futures 158, 159–160
coinage 53, 237, 239, 242, 297
   crisis 53, 185, 188
Cold War 32, 57, 74, 75, 96, 127, 145
commodity
   circuits 85, *85,* 199, 249
   theory of money 233, 237, 249